**Indigenous Legalities, Pipeline Viscosities**

# Indigenous Legalities, Pipeline Viscosities

*Colonial Extractivism and Wet'suwet'en Resistance*

Tyler McCreary

UNIVERSITY *of* ALBERTA PRESS

Published by

University of Alberta Press
1-16 Rutherford Library South
11204 89 Avenue NW
Edmonton, Alberta, Canada  T6G 2J4
amiskwacîwâskahikan | Treaty 6 |
Métis Territory
ualbertapress.ca | uapress@ualberta.ca

Copyright © 2024 Tyler McCreary

LIBRARY AND ARCHIVES CANADA
CATALOGUING IN PUBLICATION

Title: Indigenous legalities, pipeline viscosities :
   colonial extractivism and Wet'suwet'en
   resistance / Tyler McCreary.
Names: McCreary, Tyler, author.
Description: Includes bibliographical
   references and index.
Identifiers: Canadiana (print) 20230528872 |
   Canadiana (ebook) 20230529216 |
   ISBN 9781772127041 (softcover) |
   ISBN 9781772127263 (EPUB) |
   ISBN 9781772127270 (PDF)
Subjects: LCSH: Pipelines—British
   Columbia. | CSH: Wet'suwet'en—British
   Columbia—Government relations | CSH:
   Wet'suwet'en—Political activity—British
   Columbia
Classification: LCC E99.W56 M325 2024 |
   DDC 971.1004/972—dc23

First edition, first printing, 2024.
First printed and bound in Canada by
Houghton Boston Printers, Saskatoon,
Saskatchewan.
Copyediting and proofreading by Kay Rollans.
Maps 1 and 2 by Caitlin Jones, map 3 by Caitlin
Jones and Adam Rose.
Indexing by Stephen Ullstrom.

All rights reserved. No part of this publication
may be reproduced, stored in a retrieval
system, or transmitted in any form or by any
means (electronic, mechanical, photocopying,
recording, generative artificial intelligence [AI]
training, or otherwise) without prior written
consent. Contact University of Alberta Press
for further details.

University of Alberta Press supports copyright.
Copyright fuels creativity, encourages diverse
voices, promotes free speech, and creates
a vibrant culture. Thank you for buying
an authorized edition of this book and for
complying with the copyright laws by not
reproducing, scanning, or distributing any part
of it in any form without permission. You are
supporting writers and allowing University of
Alberta Press to continue to publish books for
every reader.

This book has been published with the help of
a grant from the Federation for the Humanities
and Social Sciences, through the Awards to
Scholarly Publications Program, using funds
provided by the Social Sciences and Humanities
Research Council of Canada.

University of Alberta Press gratefully
acknowledges the support received for its
publishing program from the Government of
Canada, the Canada Council for the Arts, and
the Government of Alberta through the Alberta
Media Fund.

This work is published with the assistance
of the Western Canadiana Publications
Endowment.

# Contents

*Acknowledgements* VII
*A Note on Terminology and Orthography* XI
*Introduction* XV
*Indigenous Peoples and the Infrastructure of Colonialism*

## I The Historical Context of the Wet'suwet'en Encounter with Colonialism

1 The First Century  3
   *Early Wet'suwet'en-Settler Relations*
2 From Renunciation to Reconciliation  45
   *Colonialism Goes to Court*

## II Pipeline Governance and the Arts of Reconciling Indigenous Peoples with Development

3 Indigeneity on the Page  89
   *Land Use and Occupancy Studies*
4 Indigenizing Infrastructure  133
   *New Industrial Partnerships*

## III Indigenous Resurgence and Enduring Conflicts over Territorial Sovereignty

5 Sovereignty's Returns  175
6 The Ongoing Cycle of Struggle  213

*Appendix 1*  251
*The Five Wet'suwet'en Dïdikh and Their Yikh, Chiefs, and Other Hereditary Titles*
*Appendix 2*  253
*Wet'suwet'en Bands*
*Glossary*  255
*Wet'suwet'en Place Names, Witsuwit'en Terms, and Gitxsanimaax Terms*
*Notes*  257
*Bibliography*  285
*Index*  315

# Acknowledgements

THIS BOOK PROJECT BEGAN over a decade ago and has involved a long process of coming to know a place that I called home, the Bulkley Valley, again—as part of Wet'suwet'en territories. This endeavour has consistently and deeply entangled personal and research connections. It would be impossible to thank everyone to whom I owe an intellectual and emotional debt. To everyone who has aided me in this process, please know that I appreciate you deeply.

Throughout this work I have been inspired by the dedication of the Wet'suwet'en hereditary chiefs and the Wet'suwet'en community to building new relationships with the newcomers to their lands, including my family. My understanding of the meaning of Indigenous relations is a product of the hours that so many Wet'suwet'en community members spent with me. I especially want to acknowledge the friendship and guidance of the late Henry Alfred, who held the Laksilyu hereditary title Wah Tah K'eght, and whom I dearly miss. I also greatly benefited from my interactions with individuals from other nations in the region, including Dakelh, Gitxsan, Haisla, Haida, Nedut'en, Tse'khene, and Tsimshian. I have relied upon the guidance of settlers, too, who have taught me how to take responsibility for the colonial legacies we inherit. The late Bill Goodacre, in particular, spent countless hours with me explaining how to act respectfully with relation to the gift of living alongside the Wet'suwet'en on their territories.

This book began as my dissertation research in the Department of Geography at York University, and I need to express my deepest appreciation to the people who supported me in its development. Patricia Monture and Kristina Fagan, thank you for convincing me to begin and continue with graduate school. In my doctoral studies, my supervisor, Patricia Wood, and committee members, Ranu Basu and Deb McGregor, were sources of patient guidance and constant encouragement. I also benefited immensely from the careful reading and suggestions of the other members of my dissertation examination committee: Celia Haig-Brown, Kent McNeil, and Scott Prudham. On Wet'suwet'en territories, I am indebted to Birdy Markert, Aboriginal Principal of the Bulkley Valley School District, who arranged for me to share my dissertation research with the Wet'suwet'en hereditary chiefs and Witset leadership in 2014. John Ridsdale and Violet Gellenbeck, who respectively hold the hereditary titles Na'Moks and Kiliset, carefully read early drafts and provided feedback on the manuscript.

Since beginning this work, I have been fortunate to be part of the tremendous intellectual communities in the Department of Geography and the Department of First Nations Studies at the University of Northern British Columbia, the Department of Geography at the University of British Columbia, and the Department of Geography at Florida State University. In Prince George, my gratitude goes out to Paul Bowles, Ross Hoffman, Zoë Meletis, Antonia Mills, Catherine Nolin, and Daniel Sims. For the guidance and support that they provided in Vancouver, I specifically want to thank Trevor Barnes, Marwan Hassan, Phillipe Le Billon, and Jamie Peck. In Tallahassee, I am indebted to Mary Lawhon and Joseph Pierce, who originally brought me to the South. I also want to acknowledge how much I have benefited from the tremendous colleagues that I have had in Florida, including Adam Bledsoe, Shantel Buggs, Mabel Gergan, Tisha Holmes, April Jackson, Sarah Lester, Aaron Mallory, John Mathias, Dan Okamoto, Stephanie Pau, Sage Ponder, Chris Uejio, Sandy Wong, and Willie Wright. Thanks, too, to my amazing students who have helped my thinking. Caitlin Jones and Adam Rose contributed maps for this book. Helena Safron helped copy edit the final draft.

Over the years, my ideas have been fortified by many intellectual collaborators and I want to acknowledge those who have allowed me to think with them. Rick Budhwa, Miltonette Craig, Heather Dorries, Anne Godlewska, Robert Henry, Maya Henderson, David Hugill, Dawn Hoogeeven, Na'taki Osborne Jelks, Vanessa Lamb, Richard Milligan, Suzanne Mills, Ann Marie Murnaghan, Usha Natarajan, Julie Tomiak, Jerome Turner, and Shauna Wouters, I appreciate all of you.

There are also a few additional friends I need to recognize for the roles they played in challenging, refining, and expanding my thinking. For both their feedback and encouragement, I remain indebted to Josh Barkan, Warren Bernauer, Amar Bhatia, Kai Bosworth, Julia Dehm, Nick Estes, Brenda Gunn, Sharmeen Khan, Ruth Green, Robert Knox, Sergio Latorre, Anthony Levenda, Kyle Loewen, Sheelah McLean, David Mitchell, Lori Mishibinijima, Val Napoleon, Bram Noble, Reecia Orzeck, Richard Overstall, Tom Özden-Schilling, Shiri Pasternak, Evelyn Peters, Jen Preston, Corvin Russell, Dayna Scott, Jimena Sierra, Melanie Sommerville, Verna St. Denis, and Trevor Wideman.

This work was also supported by funding from the Social Sciences and Humanities Research Council of Canada and the Faculty of Graduate Studies at York University. I am also grateful for the support of the staff at University of Alberta Press, particularly Douglas Hildebrand, Mat Buntin, and Duncan Turner. Special thanks, too, to Kay Rollans, my patient and careful copy editor.

My deepest gratitude is reserved for my family. My parents and siblings have always been there for me. I benefited from the support of Barbara Barker, my former spouse, while I was conducting much of my research in the North. Since 2015, my partner, Rebecca Hall, has been my enduring source of support and encouragement through the often-difficult writing process as well as the broader arduous journey of life. Thank you for bearing with my absent presence as I wrote, listening as I obsessively worked through ideas, and patiently supporting me through all my struggles. I simply would not have made it to this point without you.

# A Note on Terminology and Orthography

I WANT TO BRIEFLY RECOGNIZE that linguistic, terminological, and stylistic complexities abound when writing about Indigenous histories. I have made choices throughout this book that I hope recognize and honour these complexities while also providing a thorough and accurate historical record. I note some of these choices here.

Throughout the text, I use the term *Aboriginal* to refer to the rights of Indigenous peoples recognized by the Canadian state. While state recognition undoubtedly effects the expression of Indigenous politics, I semantically differentiate the state category *Aboriginal* from expressions of Indigeneity, which are grounded in practices of Indigenous self-governance that do not simply or easily accord with the categories of colonial statecraft. I also refer to Wet'suwet'en and Gitxsan peoples and community members using the spellings that community-led organizations and community members used to enter their names into the records of Canadian legal and regulatory proceedings. In many instances, the spellings or terminology people used in these records does not match the spellings or terminology that people and communities, including the Wet'suwet'en, Gitxsan, and others, use today. I also use Canadian legal terms, such as *Status Indians* and *bands*, where these are the defined terms of operant legislation, aware that these settler-colonial state categories regularly do not match Indigenous communities' self-definitions. I have included contextual notes where explanations are warranted.

Recording terms and phrases in the Witsuwit'en language is another challenge. The orthography of the Witsuwit'en-Nedut'en language has shifted over the years and remains in flux. In an unpublished work from 1974, Hank Hildebrandt and Gillian Story first codified the language. This work created the foundation for orthography used to spell many Wet'suwet'en names in the 1980s, including in documentation of land claims and legal proceedings. James Kari was the linguist employed to create the orthography for these court proceedings.

Wet'suwet'en hereditary chiefs, who continue to advance land claims originating in that period, still regularly use these original transliterations of their names. Linguist Sharon Hargus has, however, been developing a new orthographic system since the 1980s, which better represents the phonemes of the Witsuwit'en-Nedut'en language. I have updated the spelling of general Witsuwit'en terms and place names in accordance with Hargus's more recent linguistic research. For names of Wet'suwet'en *didikh* and *yikh*, and for hereditary titles, I have used older orthography in text. Where an old and new spelling differ, I have included the Hargus spelling in a footnote following the name's first appearance.

This orthographic approach follows the direction of the Wet'suwet'en hereditary chiefs. As court proceedings institutionalized recognition of the hereditary system, they maintain this spelling in legal processes. However, language revitalization work has centered the Hargus orthography for general Witsuwit'en language use. I do, however, update the spelling of a chiefs' name when they have indicated to me a preferred alternative spelling.

I have also included two appendices at the back of the book that may help some readers better follow the structure of traditional Wet'suwet'en governance and the shifting history of Wet'suwet'en bands. Finally, I have included a short glossary that lists the handful Wisuwit'en and Gitxsanimaax words and place names I use in the book, alongside their definitions or corresponding names in English.

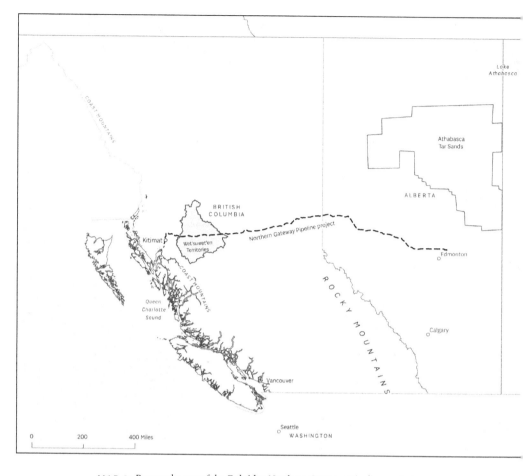

MAP 1: *Proposed route of the Enbridge Northern Gateway Pipeline project.*

# Introduction

*Indigenous Peoples and the Infrastructure of Colonialism*

IN JULY 2006, Stephen Harper, the newly elected Conservative prime minister of Canada, used his debut international speech to tout the nation's "emergence as a global energy powerhouse." Speaking at a Canada-UK Chamber of Commerce event in London, he boasted that Canada was "the only non-OPEC country with growing oil deliverability," capable of ensuring global energy security as "a stable, reliable producer in a volatile, unpredictable world." He bragged that "Canadian oil production is forecast to reach almost 4 million barrels a day."[1] At the time, this was a conservative estimate. The Canadian Association of Petroleum Producers (CAPP) had projected that oil production would grow from 2.5 million barrels per day in 2005 to 4.6 million by 2015.[2] By 2020, they anticipated production would almost double, reaching 4.9 million barrels per day. The vast majority of this projected expansion was to come from bitumen in Alberta's Athabasca tar sands, which represented 45 percent of Canadian oil production in 2005. CAPP anticipated tar sands production would grow by over 80 percent by 2020. In London, Harper described the Athabasca tar sands, the third largest recoverable hydrocarbon reserve in the world, as "an ocean of oil-soaked sand" that "lies under the muskeg of northern Alberta." Exploiting this reserve would be "a monumental challenge" and an "enterprise of epic proportions." Exploiting this reserve, he stated, would require vast sums of capital and "an army of skilled workers" aided by what he called "Brobdingnagian technology," invoking the mythic land of giants encountered in *Gulliver's Travels*. But Canada, Harper proclaimed, was equal to the task. Trumpeting the muscularity of Canada's developing extractive might, Harper declared that Canada had "the most attractive combination of circumstances for energy investment of any place in the world."[3]

At the heart of this claim was a particular imagination of Canada as a liberal democracy with a commitment to inclusive free-market development. Presenting this national narrative, Harper told the Canada-UK Chamber of Commerce that Canadians "believe in the free exchange of energy products based on competitive market principles, not self-serving monopolistic political strategies." Although unstated, his implicit contrast was the imagined autocracy of oil sheiks in the Middle East, riven by strife and enduring tribal conflicts. Instead, he suggested that Canada's "origins as a colony of the British Empire" had endowed it with a political tradition both "patient and peaceful." Acknowledging that "it's unfashionable to refer to colonialism in anything other than negative terms," Harper nonetheless argued that "in the Canadian context, the actions of the British Empire were largely benign and occasionally brilliant." Specifically, he applauded the relations that colonial officials had built with Indigenous peoples, suggesting that "the treaties negotiated with the Aboriginal inhabitants of our country, while far from perfect, were some of the fairest and most generous of the period." Built upon purported traditions of inclusive development, Harper pitched the Athabasca tar sands as the paragon of Canadian ethical oil production.

The ideal of inclusive development that Harper evoked was illusive if not illusory in practice. While there are vast bitumen reserves under the boreal forests in the heart of the continent, developing these reserves required the transportation infrastructure to link production to global markets.[4] And building pipelines has provoked resistance from Indigenous peoples along the Canadian West Coast who have never signed treaties or ceded title to their lands. In June 2008, less than two years after Harper's speech, Indigenous peoples from across Western Canada assembled for an Energy Summit in the heart of Wet'suwet'en territories in Northern British Columbia. Gathered in the community of Witset (Moricetown), along the shores of the lower Widzin Kwah (Bulkley River) where Wet'suwet'en hereditary chiefs have conducted community governance feasts since time immemorial, Indigenous leaders discussed how to respond to the expansion of the tar sands and its related pipeline infrastructure. With an on-reserve population of 590 in 2006, Witset was a small community that had long played an outsized role in Indigenous struggles.[5] On the basis of Wet'suwet'en governance traditions, the hereditary chiefs launched the first Aboriginal title case in Canadian history in the 1984.[6] A quarter-century later, they again took a leadership role in challenging colonialism in Canada.

The 2008 Energy Summit on Wet'suwet'en territories represented the opening salvo in a battle against the expansion of tar sands pipelines to the West Coast. The gathering included over two hundred people from Indigenous communities stretching over a thousand kilometres, from the boreal forests of Northern Alberta to the islands of the Northwest Coast. The intensification of tar sands development and the expansion of the network of pipelines and tankers transporting diluted bitumen around the globe threatened the lands and waters of the nations assembled in Witset. Wet'suwet'en hereditary chief Kloumkhun, Alphonse Gagnon, stressed that the environmental burdens of tar sands expansion were being disproportionately imposed on Indigenous peoples. "This Energy Summit was a reminder that the tar sands affects us all," he said. "We can only protect our lands and waters if we stand together."[7] Other attendees echoed his message, giving voice to their environmental concerns and standing in opposition to a recently proposed Enbridge tar sands pipeline. If Harper's first international gathering signalled his commitment to continuing Canada's colonial relationships to Indigenous peoples, the convergence of Indigenous nations in Witset presented its counterpoint: an enduring decolonial commitment to defending the land.

*Indigenous Legalities, Pipeline Viscosities* examines how Wet'suwet'en territorial claims intersected with the development agendas of the Canadian state and the energy transportation company Enbridge in the governance of the Northern Gateway project. In order to facilitate tar sands development, Enbridge proposed to develop a set of twin 1,177-kilometre pipelines connecting extractive operations in Alberta to the West Coast for global distribution. The project, which was officially proposed in 2005, faced staunch Indigenous resistance and was ultimately cancelled in 2016. This book unpacks how the fate of this pipeline become entangled with Indigenous mobilizations. Specifically, it examines how state and corporate actors tried to incorporate Wet'suwet'en concerns into formal governance processes and how Wet'suwet'en resistance exceeded these frames, ultimately becoming part of the constellation of forces that blocked the proposed project. The development of the Northern Gateway project would have expanded market access for Canadian bitumen, impacting the course of world energy development and the associated climate crisis. This is, therefore, a story with global resonance. *Indigenous Legalities, Pipeline Viscosities* highlights the role that Indigenous movements play in shaping global futures, demonstrating the friction that Indigenous claims have created for the flow of hydrocarbon exports.

But this story is about more than a pipeline. It is a story about how Indigenous territorial claims intersect with settler-colonial resource governance processes. The Wet'suwet'en have governed their territory since time immemorial, developing "a complex system of ownership and jurisdiction...where the [hereditary] chiefs continually validate their rights and responsibilities to their people, their lands, and the resources contained within them."[8] Following the arrival of newcomers to their territories, Wet'suwet'en leaders have been in prolonged negotiations over how the practice of their Indigenous legal order interfaces with settler authorities who purport to act in the name of colonial sovereignty. Often, this has been a story of a conflict of laws, with settler authorities forcibly preventing Indigenous authorities from upholding Indigenous laws. However, it has also involved various connections and concatenations across legal orders. Wet'suwet'en authorities have adopted a variety of strategies to ensure their survival as a people and their ongoing access to means of maintaining livelihoods. Thus, beyond any specific industrial development proposal, it is necessary to examine how Indigenous peoples continue to protect and construct lifeways in the path of development.

## New Relationships on the Northwestern Frontier

The conflicts between the Wet'suwet'en and pipeline developments sit within a long history of Indigenous struggles in Canada to maintain territorial self-determination and stop the introduction of extractive infrastructure on their lands without their consent. As Glen Coulthard describes, settler colonialism "has been structured into a relatively secure or sedimented set of hierarchical social relations that continue to facilitate the *dispossession* of Indigenous peoples of their lands and self-determining authority."[9] Dispossession, Coulthard reminds us, is neither historically inevitable nor complete. Ongoing processes of dispossession provide the territorial basis for unfolding regimes of fossil fuel extraction on colonized lands. Indigenous struggles for land continue to call into question the territorial foundation of settler society and create spaces to recognize the existence of other ways of being in the world. In these struggles, as Leanne Betasamosake Simpson stresses, Indigenous modes of life remain central to the production of critical consciousness and articulation of challenges to the logic of resource extraction on the basis of other-than-capitalist lifeways.[10] Coulthard demonstrates how settler institutions control Indigenous challenges, routing communities into complex but ultimately circumscribed negotiations over the recognition and accommodation of Indigenous interests. However, Indigenous life always exceeds efforts to discipline and contain it. The ongoing resurgence of Indigenous frameworks for being in the world, as Simpson reminds us, continues to assert forms of Indigenous presence that exceed the constraints of state recognition.

Studying Wet'suwet'en interactions with pipeline governance thus provides a lens through which to examine fundamental questions about relationships between Indigenous peoples and resource governance in Canada. On the one hand, it provides an opportunity to investigate how government and corporate entities are addressing Indigenous interests. On the other hand, it highlights how Indigenous mobilizations introduce new considerations into the formulae of resource governance, challenging, modifying, and even blocking programs of extractive resource development. Wet'suwet'en struggles showcase the capacity of Indigenous mobilizations to reshape resource politics in Canada and indeed globally.

The question of Indigenous relationships to resource-extractive development, particularly fossil fuel pipelines, is long-standing. In 1974, the Government of Canada commissioned Justice Thomas Berger to investigate the environmental and socio-economic impact of a proposed pipeline through the Yukon and down the Mackenzie River Valley in the Northwest Territories. In *Northern Frontier, Northern Homeland*, the 1977 report of the Mackenzie Valley Pipeline Inquiry, Berger depicted the conflict as revolving around two distinct visions on the North: "one as frontier, the other as homeland." According to Berger's report, southern metropolitan visions of the North rationalized "subduing the land and extracting its resources" as simply "the next advance in a series of frontier advances that have been intimately bound up with Canadian history." In contrast, Indigenous peoples claimed that "the North is their homeland" and that "they have a right to say what its future ought to be."[11] Sympathetic to the Indigenous position, Berger denounced "the rapid expansion of the industrial system" and "its intrusion into every part of the native people's lives."[12] The commission report recommended delaying the pipeline project until political solutions addressed the conflict between Indigenous peoples and industrial development. The project was subsequently and repeatedly delayed as it sought to deal with various political, legal, and financial concerns, eventually being cancelled in 2017.

Arguing that resource governance processes on the northern frontier needed to be interpreted in the context of Indigenous counterclaims, Berger's analysis was prescient, prefiguring scholarship that would develop on the contested frontier politics of settler colonialism. In the decades that followed Berger's report, scholars such as Patricia Limerick, Jean Barman, Elizabeth Furniss, Adele Perry, and Penelope Edmonds reconceptualized the frontier as an interactional space constituted through encounters between Indigenous peoples and settlers.[13] The original frontier thesis, articulated by Frederick Jackson Turner in 1893, held that "free land and an abundance of natural resources open to a fit people" forged the foundation of American democracy.[14] Thus, American politics for Turner emerged from the process of conquering the forest and domesticating the wild, bringing the territory under the aegis of an emerging settler society. Combating the entrenched racism of established narratives of North American history, critical scholars insisted that the frontier, while made through the violent and forcible reoccupation of lands that Indigenous peoples already lived on and owned, was not closed. Although the displacement of Indigenous peoples accompanied the development of the frontier, these settler-colonial dispossessions were never complete. The frontier established interactional spaces governed by continuous negotiations—convergences and conflicts—between settlers and Indigenous peoples.[15] Colonialism is not a completed historic event or closed historic process that simply transferred territorial control to the settler state; rather it is an ongoing process, continually contested by Indigenous peoples who remain and continue to enact claims to territory that unsettle colonial sureties.[16]

Placing the development of resource frontiers in the context of Indigenous relationships to the land, Berger radically reoriented Canadian resource governance. More than simply highlighting the disjuncture between Indigenous and industrial visions, Berger modelled an approach to resource governance that took seriously the impacts of resource development on Indigenous peoples. Berger found that existing pipeline governance processes in Northern Yukon and Mackenzie Valley had failed to attend to the impacts of development on traditional Indigenous ways of life and fundamentally disrespected Indigenous aspirations to exercise jurisdiction over development on their lands. Rather than subjugating Indigenous peoples to national development agendas, Berger argued that the Canadian government must recognize a space for Indigenous self-determination in the nation, constructing opportunities for Indigenous peoples to thrive in "a new partnership of interests."[17] Building a pipeline necessitated reconciling Indigenous peoples and development. In the fifty years since the Mackenzie Valley Pipeline Inquiry, relationships have evolved substantially. The politics of resource governance now regularly involves complex negotiations between Indigenous and colonial structures of territoriality and jurisdiction; however, the tensions over territorial jurisdiction and land ownership endure.

Questions of land title and political authority remain particularly salient concerns in British Columbia, where the majority of the territory remains unceded by Indigenous peoples.[18] Through the last half-century, Indigenous political resurgence has wedged open questions of territorial and jurisdictional authority on the West Coast. Legal mobilizations, particularly in the wake of the 1982 constitutionalization of Aboriginal rights in Canada, have been strategically important within Indigenous efforts to contest colonial power. The Wet'suwet'en hereditary chiefs and their Gitxsan neighbours went to court in the 1980s and 1990s, intent on winning legal recognition of their traditional territorial ownership and jurisdiction.[19] This case is known by lawyers as *Delgamuukw v. British Columbia*, referencing the lead Gitxsan plaintiff in the litigation. I follow community practice and refer to the case as *Delgamuukw, Gisdaywa v. British Columbia*, or simply *Delgamuukw, Gisdaywa*, recognizing both the Gitxsan and Wet'suwet'en lead plaintiffs.[20] The case ultimately went to the Supreme Court of Canada. *Delgamuukw, Gisdaywa* did not resolve the status of Gitxsan or Wet'suwet'en lands within Canadian law; however, it did initiate a proliferating series of negotiations. On the basis that "we are all here to stay," the court directed Indigenous and state authorities to find "negotiated settlements, with good faith and give and take on all sides."[21] The decision added substance to earlier jurisprudence that recognized Aboriginal rights to traditional land use practices, such as hunting and fishing, by extending state obligations to reconcile colonial settlement and development with enduring Indigenous relations to the land itself. Identifying the need to reconcile competing Indigenous and colonial relationships to the land, *Delgamuukw, Gisdaywa* incited discussion over contemporary land claims in British Columbia.[22] However, at the insistence of the provincial government, the framework of British Columbia treaty process focused on the resolution of Indigenous claims through negotiating the modification and release of Aboriginal rights to provide certainty of unfettered settler-state territorial jurisdiction.[23] As many Indigenous nations, including the Wet'suwet'en, remain committed to maintaining an enduring relationship to their territories, there has been limited progress at the vast majority of treaty tables.[24] Thus, it remains pertinent to examine how relations between Indigenous peoples and colonial authorities continue to be negotiated in resource governance in the absence of modern treaties.

Following the track of unsettled negotiations, this book examines how the governance of resource extraction is continually entangled with, modified in relation to, and offset by Indigenous life projects. It documents how corporate capital and settler-state authorities have sought to effect constrained recognition of Aboriginal rights. The Canadian government increasingly relies upon environmental assessment and project review processes to fulfill its court-recognized duties to Aboriginal peoples.[25] Through these regulatory processes, corporations and project review panels address Indigenous interests through Aboriginal traditional knowledge studies and the construction of programs for Indigenous industrial employment, subcontracting, and investment. These forms of recognition, while delimited, serve to modify development plans. However, the extent to which these regulatory processes meaningfully address the legal duties of the government to Indigenous peoples remains an open and highly contentious question, and one that will significantly shape the future trajectory of resource development in Canada.

Parallel to recognition of Aboriginal rights in the Canadian courts, Indigenous peoples have been actively asserting the vitality of their distinct frameworks of governance.[26] As organized societies that predate the introduction of the British common law, Indigenous communities maintain distinct legal traditions and approaches to governance, and do not find the only legal articulation of their rights in the settler courts. Ethnographies prepared for the *Delgamuukw, Gisdaywa* litigation highlight the reciprocal modes of gifting that underpin Wet'suwet'en law and organize the practice of territorial jurisdiction in the *balhats* (referred to as the potlatch in classical anthropology).[27] These cycles of reciprocity within the *balhats* echoed the continual renewal of territorial connections through the seasonal movements of Wet'suwet'en family groups. As Leslie Main Johnson has emphasized, Wet'suwet'en relationships to place are shaped by their experiences as people "who use a variety of resource sites located in different places throughout the cycle of the year, who hunt, encountering animals which sustain them in different places and at distinct times."[28] Theorizing these types of Indigenous knowledge that are constructed beneath the foot, Coulthard uses the term *grounded normativity* to describe the "place-based foundation of Indigenous decolonial thought and practice." He suggests that "Indigenous land-connected practices and longstanding experiential knowledge…inform and structure our ethical engagements with the world and our relationships with human and nonhuman others over time."[29]

In cases where state-led governance processes have failed to protect Indigenous peoples' relationships to the land or uphold Indigenous peoples' stewardship responsibilities for the land, community members have mobilized on the basis of Indigenous law.[30] By reoccupying traditional lands that are in the way of development and mobilizing against geographies of state and corporate power, Indigenous peoples materialize forms of sovereignty that contest the settler authorization of regimes of resource extraction.[31] Self-recognition, as Simpson theorizes, creates the grounds for Indigenous resurgence "while naming very clearly the processes of domination and extermination that they have so fiercely resisted in the past century."[32] Thus, it is necessary to take seriously not only Indigenous claims within the Canadian court system, but also assertions based on Indigenous law and the ability of Indigenous peoples to stretch concepts of responsibility from Indigenous legal orders to encompass state and corporate actors.

**Indigenous Mobilizations in the Context of Global Energy Dilemmas**
Examining the Wet'suwet'en relationship to the Northern Gateway Pipelines showcases how Indigenous politics intersect with contested energy developments in Canada and the broader

world. The world is currently faced with fundamental energy dilemmas related to simultaneous demands to address climate change and secure reliable energy supplies.[33] There are growing concerns about the climatic implications of ongoing fossil fuel production and consumption, as well as the security of global energy supplies. The Canadian government has consistently elevated resource-extractive economic agendas over global climatic concerns, making it a national priority to secure access to markets for diluted bitumen from the Athabasca tar sands. Under Harper, reforms to natural resource legislation and policy in Canada removed many legal levers for environmental opposition to extractive development.[34] However, pipelines crossing unceded Indigenous territory in British Columbia still face significant legal hurdles. In this context, Indigenous movements, and the political and legal pressure they are capable of exerting, have played a key role in shaping development trajectories. Wet'suwet'en struggles thus showcase the capacity of Indigenous mobilizations to reshape global dynamics of climate change, energy development, and capitalist accumulation.

The climatic effects of carbon dioxide emissions from fossil fuel consumption have forced the issue of climate change into energy policy debates. The evidence for climate change is now unequivocal. The *Fifth Assessment Report* of the Intergovernmental Panel on Climate Change found that "each of the last three decades has been successively warmer...than any preceding decade since 1850."[35] The policy implications of climate science appear to be clear: as anthropogenic emissions of carbon dioxide are the leading cause of climate change, and as burning fossil fuels is the largest source of carbon dioxide emissions, it follows that addressing climate change requires a reduction in the consumption of fossil fuels for energy. As the International Energy Agency (IEA) emphasizes, "effective action in the energy sector is essential to tackling the climate change problem."[36]

However, capping atmospheric carbon dioxide levels below 450 parts per million—an international target with the goal of limiting the rise in long-term average global temperature to 2 degrees Celcius—requires a massive reduction in the use of fossil fuels for energy. In 2014, the IEA projected that meeting the carbon dioxide target of 450 parts per million would require a 23 percent reduction in the annual quantity of oil consumed globally by 2040.[37] With each passing year without substantive emissions reductions, the situation grows more dire, and these projections may drastically understate the degree of transformation needed. James Hansen, one of the world's leading climatologists, has argued that substantially greater emissions cuts will be necessary. "If humanity wishes to preserve a planet similar to that on which civilization developed and to which life on Earth is adapted, paleoclimate evidence and ongoing climate change suggest that $CO_2$ will need to be reduced...to at most 350 ppm [parts per million], but likely less than that."[38] The need to reduce carbon dioxide emissions has increased scrutiny of the Athabasca tar sands by environmental activists and researchers, in particular because high energy costs of mining and refining bitumen make it a far more carbon-intensive fuel than conventional crude oil.[39]

The global economy's dependence on fossil fuels has made energy policy change exceedingly difficult. Through the last century, the accessibility of oil as a dense, fluid, and easily extracted energy source has shaped the global organization of political and economic life.[40] To borrow a phrase from Matthew Huber, oil is the lifeblood of the capitalist political economy.[41] The concerted policy action that would be required to decarbonize the global economy has been continually thwarted by national governments, such as Canada, who fear that emissions reductions targets may retard their economic growth.[42] Discussions of energy security continue to centre upon the need to ensure hydrocarbon supply.[43] "The global energy system is in danger of falling short of the hopes and expectations placed upon it," writes the IEA. "Turmoil in parts of the Middle East—which remains the only large source of low-cost oil—has rarely been greater since the oil shocks in the 1970s."[44] Ongoing political unrest in Libya, Syria, Iraq, and Yemen is destabilizing oil production regimes, creating substantial security concerns for developed capitalist economies dependent upon access to oil from these states. The broader energy landscape also remains uncertain. The Russian invasion of Ukraine, which began in 2022, has further disrupted gas supplies, and questions about nuclear power linger in the wake of the 2011 Fukushima Daiichi disaster. The tumult of recent years lends credence to the claims of Ezra Levant that "Alberta's political and economic stability make it the most important alternative to the Organization of the Petroleum Exporting Countries (OPEC)."[45]

Because of the large amount of bitumen in the tar sands, Canada remains one of the countries with the greatest potential to expand hydrocarbon production over the next quarter-century. In the early 2010s, the oil and gas industry held considerable optimism about the prospects for growth in tar sands production. In 2015, the Alberta Energy Regulator estimated that the province's established bitumen reserves constituted 166 billion barrels, representing approximately 10 percent of proven reserves globally.[46] Because of the Alberta tar sands, Canada is an increasingly important producer within uncertain future global oil production scenarios. A 2014 report from the Canadian Energy Research Institute, for instance, forecast an increase in tar sands production "from the current level of 1.98 million barrels per day to 3.7 million barrels per day by 2020 and 5.2 million barrels per day by 2030."[47] The scarcity of access to oil investment opportunities globally, due to that fact that most reserves of oil are nationalized in postcolonial states, further elevates the importance of the Athabasca tar sands' production potential for capital. Following Third World decolonization, oil industry nationalizations radically transformed the structure of global reserve ownership. In the mid-twentieth century, international oil companies dominated production and controlled most of the world's reserves; resource nationalization broke the hegemony of international oil companies associated with developed nations.[48] A 2013 IEA report estimated that "nearly 80% of the world's proven-plus-probable reserves of conventional and unconventional oil are controlled by national oil companies (NOCs) or their host governments."[49] With limited access to conventional reserves to exploit, investors have looked to unconventional resource developments such as the tar sands.[50]

Exploiting the Athabasca tar sands requires transportation infrastructure to gain access to the markets that would allow extractive companies to realize their production potential. As David Harvey elucidated in his classic study *The Limits of Capital*, processes of capital accumulation are closely tied to the transportation networks that facilitate flows of commodities. As Harvey explains, "the drive to accumulate must also be manifest as a drive to reduce these costs of circulation...The removal or reduction of these barriers is as much a part of the historical mission of the bourgeoisie as is accumulation for accumulation's sake."[51] In the Canadian context, industry backers have expressed considerable consternation about pipeline bottlenecks "inflicting economic and financial losses not only on petroleum companies and their shareholders, but also on governments of oil-producing provinces and territories."[52] Bitumen production in Alberta is effectively networked to refineries in the American Midwest, but not to heavy crude refineries on the Gulf Coast or to tidewaters that would allow global export. In the mid-2010s, Canadian producers were particularly intent on reaching Asian markets, the projected major growth markets in energy futures. With developed economies increasingly implementing measures to address climate change, there was concern that US climate policy could impair tar sands development. In 2014, the IEA predicted that 97 percent of the growth in demand would come from developing nations, with "the developing Asian countries—led by China—account[ing] for 65%."[53] In 2009, China overtook the United States as the biggest consumer of energy in the world. Building infrastructure to link hydrocarbon exports to China would have diversified the markets that Canadian bitumen can access and reduced the vulnerability of Canadian producers to changes in US climate policy.

To support the expansion of the Athabasca tar sands, Conservative governments in Canada actively sought to remove regulatory barriers to tar sands pipeline development. In the province of Alberta, the long-ruling Progressive Conservative Party established itself as a champion of tar sands development from the beginning of its reign in the 1970s through to the early twenty-first century.[54] Under the rule of the federal Liberal Party, the Canadian government made token gestures to climate action, such as signing the Kyoto Accord in 1997, but made no meaningful policy movement to address the emerging global crisis before they were unseated in 2006.[55] That year, Harper, newly elected prime minister of a minority Conservative government, eschewed even token gestures to environmental protection, moving tar sands development to the centre of national economic policy and abandoning any pretense of upholding Kyoto commitments.[56] Winning a majority in 2011, Harper's Conservative government made sweeping changes to Canadian environmental laws. In 2012, omnibus Bills C-38 and C-45—the Jobs, Growth and Long-Term Prosperity Act and the Jobs and Growth Act, respectively—radically altered project review processes for energy infrastructure. They sharply curtailed consideration of environmental concerns and concentrated decision-making authority in the executive branch of the Canadian government.[57] The reforms repealed and replaced the legislation governing both the Canadian Environmental Assessment Agency and the National Energy Board, narrowing the scope of review processes and restricting the authority of these agencies to control development. Oriented toward expanding the export of tar sands bitumen, the reforms fit within a national economic growth strategy focused on exploitation of the country's natural resource endowment.[58]

However, despite the early pollyannaish projections for tar sands development, the reliance of global commodity flows on infrastructural networks constituted new points of weakness. In 2014, the IEA flagged that the main uncertainty in projecting the potential course of bitumen development in Canada "is not related to the resource base, but rather to the transport capacity required to get the oil to market."[59] Environmentalists strategically targeted pipeline infrastructure in order to suffocate the development of the tar sands, particularly linking with local resistance movements in regions where pipelines present the greatest environmental risk and least economic benefits.[60] As Canadian resource governance reforms had limited the opportunities available for environmentalists to challenge pipeline development directly, environmental movements were pushed to seek greater alliances with Indigenous movements. As Tony Weis et al. describe, "while the implications of the tar sands extend up to the scale of the whole planet, the movement to stop them fundamentally demands solidarity with the Indigenous communities struggling to defend their land, water, and sovereignty."[61] In addition to greater moral authority, Indigenous peoples possessed constitutional rights that they could effectively leverage in the struggle over climatic and fossil fuel futures.

This strategy has been tremendously effective. Despite government and industry efforts, no major new tar sands pipeline has been built and put in service between 2010 and 2023. Without additional infrastructure, land-locked Canadian tar sands production has been plagued by regional overproduction crises and unable to realize resource value.[62] The limits of regionally networked transportation and storage capacity is highlighted by discounted prices for Western Canadian Select—a blended heavy crude oil containing a mix of diluted bitumen and conventional heavy crude oil—as well as periodic collapses in its value.[63] While there continues to be substantial financial investment in the oil sector globally, the infrastructural landlocking of the tar sands has led major international investors to withdraw from Canadian production in recent years. In 2017, total capital spending in the Canadian oil and gas sector was $45 billion—"a 44 per cent decline compared to $81 billion in 2014."[64] To better understand the forces shaping pipeline development, and thus global dilemmas around climate change and energy security, it is necessary to pay closer attention to Indigenous struggles against settler colonialism.

**Home on Native Land**

Indigenous contestation of colonial regimes of resource extraction are vital forces remaking the world. To understand these Indigenous movements, it is necessary for those analyzing them—such as myself—to embed their analysis in the local politics and traditions of Indigenous communities and these communities' encounters with colonial regimes. In *Indigenous Legalities, Pipeline Viscosities*, I examine relations between settler-colonial and Wet'suwet'en authorities, employing a methodology of reading pipeline politics in parallax. A concept borrowed from classical astronomy, parallax—from the Ancient Greek term παράλλαξις, meaning alternation—refers to how the positions of objects differ when viewed along different lines of sight. Methodologically, I trace the distinct conceptions of Indigenous relations to the land constructed through the governance practices of corporate capital and the settler state as well as those of Wet'suwet'en authorities. From these different perspectives, different relationships come into view. These visions frame different ways for not only understanding the world, but also enacting trajectories of development and making future worlds. Crucially, the undetermined interplay of these different worldings shapes the way that development unfolds and guides the future we make.

While this research has national and global resonances, for me it also begins from a personal engagement with the question of how to understand the history, present, and future of my home. It asks what it means to live responsibly on colonized lands. I am the descendant of white settlers, newcomers to Wet'suwet'en territories. I grew up in a small northern town, Smithers, originally built as a railway town to facilitate the export of resources from Wet'suwet'en lands and the broader Canadian Northwest.[65] Set in a wide, fertile valley, between majestic mountains and imposing coniferous forests, the regional economy around Smithers relied upon the exploitation of its abundant mineral riches and forest resources. The broader resource frontier that I called home, the Northwest Interior of British Columbia, remains now, as it has been for a hundred years, a site of contact and also contestation.[66]

Growing up in a community struggling with the legacies of colonialism, such disputes were a backdrop to my development, although often overshadowed by my own teenage angst and personal dramas. In 1984, when the Gitxsan and Wet'suwet'en hereditary chiefs first went to court and filed their claim to ownership and jurisdiction over the land, I was four years old. The case slowly advanced through the courts from my early childhood to late teens. While I would like to brag of my early awareness of these issues, I was not particularly conscious of the political and legal battles that enveloped my community. I did not understand the brutality that settler society has inflicted upon Indigenous peoples. While I had Indigenous friends, our bonds centred more on shared desires to escape the banality of our lives through drugs and alcohol than any broader shared understanding or political commitment.

Learning to see my home critically, in relation to the ongoing history of colonial violence on those lands, was a product of sustained reflection and dialogue. When I left home to attend university, I was introduced to the concept of settler colonialism and to scholarship on Indigenous governance traditions. Through my classes, I began to learn about the enduring structures of colonial power in settler society, as well as the significance of Indigenous traditions to mobilizations that confront contemporary colonialism in Canada. Outside of class, I became involved in community organizing around renewing the spirit and intent of treaties between Indigenous peoples and settlers on the Prairies.[67] As I deepened my understanding of Indigenous-settler relations, I became increasingly interested in revisiting my origins in Northwest British Columbia.

Returning to Wet'suwet'en territories, I began to build new relationships and understanding. The research in this book is informed by more than a decade of study on Indigenous-settler relationships in Northwest British Columbia. It most explicitly focuses on negotiations that occurred during the eighteen months between 2010 and 2012. However, my engagements in regional environmental politics date to 2006, when I first returned to the region to take a teaching position at what was then Northwest Community College (now Coast Mountain College). After two years at the college, I left again to pursue a doctorate and further think through the intersection of Indigenous politics with resource governance issues. I moved back to Northwest British Columbia in the summer of 2010 and stayed until the end of 2012 conducting my doctoral fieldwork. I have continued to spend extended periods in the summer in Northwest British Columbia, with a three-year interlude during the coronavirus pandemic from 2020 to 2022 when life moved online.

Through my research, my relationship to the place where I grew up changed. Learning from Wet'suwet'en community members, I began to understand distinct Indigenous relationships to the place. I listened to elders share their memories of childhood and how their grandparents taught them the names of the territories. I sat with youth as they learned to make their first drum. I camped on the territories and spent time cleaning fish, washing dishes, and hiking through the bush. I visited blockades, attended rallies, and participated in traditional governance feasts. I also followed corporate and state regimes for engaging Indigenous peoples. I attended corporate open houses, sat through project review hearings, talked to consultants and intervenors, and read a voluminous evidentiary record. Through it all, I gained a greater appreciation for the different forms of knowledge and conduct that shape the politics of development in the North.

While the place I write about is my home, I do not claim insider knowledge of Wet'suwet'en society. Nor do I seek to capture or expose the secret internal strategies through which community members escape or subvert structures of colonial dominance.[68] Such subaltern strategies of survivance are effective because they are unseen by the state and are thus best left unexposed. Instead, I focus on the public processes of resistance and reconciliation that occur within resource governance processes. I particularly focus on the relations between Indigenous peoples, settler authorities, and transnational companies. Doing so reveals emergent relationships between Indigenous peoples, the settler state, and extractive capital, which enable me to see my home community, province, nation, and world in new ways.

My research has fostered new roles for me within the community. This is in keeping with the thinking of Margaret Elizabeth Kovach, who writes that responsible scholarship on Indigenous peoples involves situating yourself and your understanding of the world, and of Shawn Wilson, who describes how respectful scholarship requires that researchers recognize Indigenous practices of reciprocity and give back to the communities with which we engage.[69] Through my research, I have sought to foster greater recognition of Wet'suwet'en history and struggles. I have collaborated in developing local public educational resources to support people learning about Wet'suwet'en culture and history.[70] I also published a book detailing how the subdivision in which I grew up was formed through the historic displacement of Indiantown, a small Wet'suwet'en community at the edge of the Smithers townsite.[71] Beyond my local engagement, my involvement with the academy has provided me with avenues to share Wet'suwet'en stories with a broader audience and reflect upon what the world can learn from their struggles.

While conventional narratives juxtapose local traditions with global development processes, my research highlights how processes of globalization become entangled with contemporary forces of Indigenous place-based mobilizations. An oppositional and binary framing of the local and global emphasizes the fraught relation between local desires for self-determination among Indigenous peoples and global designs for resource extraction. However, it also understates the imbrication of the global with the local, and the way that Indigenous resistances are reshaping the ostensibly global development of colonialism and capitalism. Indigenous peoples are not simply mounting desperate, tragic, localized resistance to the inevitability of globalizing forces. Global processes necessitate the organization and coordination of activities in particular local places. Doreen Massey argues that local place-based struggles are not simply isolated or bounded political events. Rather they engage and remake global relationships through negotiations of "a particular constellation of social relations, meeting and weaving together at a particular locus."[72] This means that what we conventionally consider local politics has global purchase. As Anna Lowenhaupt Tsing describes, global processes are necessarily articulated through local contexts, shaped by the "grip of the worldly encounter."[73] Tsing argues that the embodied worldliness of global flows involves a form of a friction—which provides the footing to mobilize global connections but also necessarily modifies global processes through their encounter with local politics. As they are actively reshaping global processes, it is inaccurate to simply depict Indigenous peoples as local or traditional; they are not historic remnants frozen in a place out-of-time. Indigenous struggles are altering the ways that global processes are operationalized, and the ways that global processes unfold. They are contemporary forces changing the world and its future.[74]

Studying how the Wet'suwet'en interact with resource governance is vital to understanding the unfolding of questions around the colonial present and climatic future. As Indigenous movements shape global processes, understanding Indigenous politics cannot be bracketed to simply examining local development dynamics or even national economic strategies. Critical inquiry must ask how Indigenous political and legal mobilizations modified the conduct of settler-state institutions and transnational corporate capital. How do histories of Indigenous relations to corporate capital and colonial authorities continue to shape the present? What strategies have Indigenous peoples used to contest colonial dispossession? In this book, I examine the history of the Wet'suwet'en encounter with colonialism to take up these questions. In particular, I explore how the Wet'suwet'en leveraged settler courts to press colonial authorities to uphold historical commitments to Indigenous communities, and the potentials and pitfalls that have accompanied legal recognition of Aboriginal rights. Conversely, I also ask after the strategies that corporations and government authorities use to address Indigenous interests, and what delimitations attend these modes of recognizing Aboriginal rights. Locating my inquiry with regard to hydrocarbon pipeline development, I question what possibilities these projects present for Indigenous livelihoods and relations to the land. Conversely, I ask how Indigenous authorities challenge dominant frameworks of organizing and administering relations between people and the world, and to what effect. How can Indigenous traditions offer a framework to rethink issues of resource use and ownership? How are Indigenous mobilizations reshaping pipeline development and thus national economic and global environmental futures?

### The Enbridge Encounter with Wet'suwet'en Authority

This book examines the friction that Wet'suwet'en territorial and jurisdictional claims have presented to extractive capital and settler political authorities. Canadian political and economic life relies upon the continual dispossession of Indigenous peoples, on which the nation was founded. These relations are mystified through settler legal discourses that cover colonialism with a patina of consensuality and inevitability. Nevertheless, Indigenous peoples continue to mobilize against the colonial order, challenging the contradictions of settler law and posing alternative modes of governing based on Indigenous legal orders. These Indigenous mobilizations disrupt the legal foundations of the political economy of resource extraction in Canada, throwing into question the territorial and jurisdictional basis of the settler-colonial rule. To resecure the territorial grounds for development, settler authorities seek to renew the mythological just foundations of Canadian law in "the honour of the Crown." Canadian authorities selectively incorporate consideration of Indigenous concerns into resource governance processes, constructing a veneer of justice through measures to mitigate project impacts and distribute a share of development benefits to Indigenous peoples. However, the politics of colonial recognition are always partial, screening from view the full extent to which Indigenous peoples challenge colonial sovereignty. Thus, the contested relationship between colonialism and Indigeneity endures, with reiterative cycles of Indigenous struggle continually opening new spaces of negotiation. Throughout *Indigenous Legalities, Pipeline Viscosities*, I use the case of the Wet'suwet'en in the Northwest Interior of British Columbia to argue that Canadian resource governance processes need to be understood in the context of the unfolding relationship between Indigenous peoples and colonialism.

The book is organized into three major parts. The first part situates the problem of Wet'suwet'en relationships to settler colonialism historically. Chapters 1 and 2 address the historical context of Wet'suwet'en relations with colonialism that presage present political and economic engagements around pipelines. Chapter 1 discusses the historical settlement and development of resource-extractive infrastructures in Wet'suwet'en territories. It highlights not only the impacts of colonialism, but also the ways that Wet'suwet'en authorities negotiated colonialism's impositions, and how this history conditioned the rise of contemporary Indigenous struggles. Chapter 2 turns specifically to the *Delgamuukw, Gisdaywa* case, in which Gitxsan and Wet'suwet'en hereditary chiefs challenged the legal basis of the settler-colonial political economy in the dispossession of Indigenous peoples. It details how the Gitxsan and Wet'suwet'en hereditary chiefs challenged the evidentiary doctrines and procedural norms of settler law. In its decision on the case in 1997, the Supreme Court of Canada introduced a doctrine of reconciliation that impacted how resource governance is conducted. By recognizing the validity of Indigenous oral histories as evidence of relationships to the land, the Supreme Court decision transformed the forms of knowledge considered in governance proceedings and introduced new requirements for settler authorities to balance their goals for economic development with recognition of the continued existence of Indigenous peoples and traditions.

The second part of the book turns to how pipeline regulatory review processes seek to effect the reconciliation of Indigeneity with development. Chapter 3 examines the use of Aboriginal traditional knowledge studies within the federally appointed review of the Northern Gateway project. These studies aim to protect vital Indigenous traditions from extractive development by establishing and bounding particular sites of import to Indigenous traditions and recommending that pipeline development be routed around them. Chapter 4 explores how Enbridge and state authorities sought to incorporate Indigenous interests within the development and operations of the proposed Northern Gateway project, establishing opportunities for Indigenous people through project procurement, contracting, training, and employment. In other words, they attempted to use corporate offers and regulatory conditions as avenues to secure Indigenous well-being through pipeline development. These strategies of inclusion aim to foster the continuation of Indigenous life projects alongside and through development, and thereby suspend the conflict between them. Indigenous peoples are not universally opposed to industrial developments, and some Indigenous communities have been enticed by such offers to participate in and benefit from development. Exceedingly few, however, publicly endorsed the Enbridge Northern Gateway project. The vast majority of Indigenous peoples in British Columbia, including the Wet'suwet'en, were adamant in their opposition. Wet'suwet'en regulatory submissions argued that the issue was the question of territorial self-determination, not the distribution of impacts and benefits.

The third part of the book considers the enduring conflict over territorial sovereignty—the conflict over the right to decide the course of development. Chapter 5 addresses how grassroots mobilizations and Wet'suwet'en oral evidence before the federal Joint Review Panel for the Enbridge Northern Gateway Project exceeded the terms of regulatory integration. These challenges to the calculus of inclusion problematized the grounds of colonial government and resource extraction, unsettling the trajectory of development. Ultimately, these mobilizations, in combination with those of neighbouring Indigenous peoples and the broader political effects of their claims, blocked the Northern Gateway project. The final chapter carries the analysis from the end of Northern Gateway to the conflicts over the Coastal GasLink Pipeline, reiterating the cyclical and ongoing movements between resistance and reconciliation. I ultimately argue that the actually existing form of development that results from these cycles must be understood not simply as a colonial will, but as an emergent effect of contested relations between Indigenous peoples, settler authorities, and extractive capital.

# I

**The Historical Context of the Wet'suwet'en Encounter with Colonialism**

# 1

# The First Century

*Early Wet'suwet'en-Settler Relations*

THE HISTORIES WE TELL inform how we understand who we are. Thus, questions over belonging and identity, duties and rights, are mediated by our understanding of our collective history. Critically, it is necessary to historicize the social formations we encounter today in order to denaturalize them. Where classic colonial narratives present a story of settlers heroically conquering the frontier and the inevitable tragic decline of Indigenous peoples, they masked the violence of colonialism in an air of triumphalism.[1] However, even critical accounts of settler violence can circumscribe and silence Indigenous histories by overstating the dominance of colonial regimes.[2] In 1990, Thomas King critiqued the propensity of critical discourse on colonialism to reduce Indigenous peoples to its victims, conceptually cutting Indigenous peoples off "from our traditions, traditions that were in place before colonialism ever became a question, traditions which have come down to through our cultures in spite of colonization."[3] A critical account that preserves space for Indigenous agency, as Daniel Paul has argued, must not only document colonial violence but also recognize how Indigenous peoples continue to enact an "indomitable will to survive in spite of the incredible odds against them."[4] Beyond simply recounting colonial history, it is necessary to emphasize the multiple flows of history, its ruptures and repeated patterns.

Thinking about the unfolding of time differently also requires more seriously engaging with Wet'suwet'en approaches to history. In this regard, scholars have sought to understand Wet'suwet'en historical consciousness with relation to the concept of *cin k'ikh*, most often translated as oral history, although more directly transliterated as "trail of song."[5] Within Wet'suwet'en society, as Hugh Brody argues, modes of conveying history through song "are central expressions of a people's rights to, and their management of, territory."[6] The performance of a *cin k'ikh* provides an enduring track of the connection of particular family groups to their distinct territories.

The concept of *cin k'ikh* helps unpack central components of Wet'suwet'en historical consciousness. Leslie Main Johnson emphasizes the importance of the trail metaphor for Wet'suwet'en families, who followed rhythmic seasonal movements through their territories.[7] Like a trail, historical consciousness is deeply geographical and marked by regular rhythms and patterns of return. Herb George, Wet'suwet'en hereditary chief Satsan, argues that *cin k'ikh* consists of "memories tied to a specific time and place and purpose."[8] George stresses, the *cin k'ikh* are "songs about laws; the laws that govern our relationships and the way we use the lands and resources."[9] As Neil Sterritt notes, the Wet'suwet'en approach "history in cycles rather than a straight line through time."[10] This reflects what Kyle Whyte has elsewhere described as Indigenous forms of "spiraling time," where the past, present, and future interpenetrate one another and notions of cyclicality connect ancestors and future generations.[11] "Incidents from the past and from the future inform decisions made today," says Sterritt.[12]

This broad cyclic movement frames Wet'suwet'en historical knowledge, incorporating the historical experiences of not only Indigenous sovereignty, but also territorial displacements and reclamations. As a dynamic form of historical knowledge, Indigenous oral histories provide a record not only of traditional land use and governance but also the history of colonial disrespect to these systems of Indigenous territoriality. Following John Borrows, Indigenous histories remain vital to recount as they include "memories of their unconscionable mistreatment at the hands of the British and Canadian legal systems."[13] Echoing this point, George tells how the *cin k'ikh* includes "songs of despair" that lament the legacy of colonial dispossession and how Wet'suwet'en families "miss being on the lands together."[14] However, the story does not end with displacement. The Wet'suwet'en song cycle also charts the trail of return to a renewal of territorial jurisdiction. As George recounts, hereditary leaders have resisted colonialism and continue to assert that they "have the right to use the resources in the territory and have responsibilities for their protection."[15] Thus, thinking with this sense of cyclic movements helps elucidate not only Wet'suwet'en ancestral connections to place but also their historical relationship with colonialism. This chapter begins to trace this cyclic movement of the Wet'suwet'en historical encounter with colonialism.

## The Fur Trade and the Foundations for Transcultural Exchange

On the northwestern edge of the continent, the Wet'suwet'en were peripheral to much of the early colonial history. The North American fur trade had operated for a century and a half prior to the first record of a trader visiting Witset in 1823. This earlier fur trade history presaged the encounter with the Wet'suwet'en in important ways. It established norms for the conduct of trade and set standards for the treatment of Indigenous peoples that would constitute the foundations for the subsequent development of the Canadian legal order.[16] Thus, to understand the colonial systems that Wet'suwet'en authorities encountered, it is necessary to begin with a broader account of Indigenous-colonial relations in British North America.

The invention of colonialism fundamentally transformed the ways in which British authorities conducted political and economic relationships. In feudal Europe, as Shaunnagh Dorsett and Shaun McVeigh describe, "sovereignty was a personal political denomination, at its highest in the form of the monarch, and based on personal protection and obligation, but without the modern connection to a territorial state unit."[17] Extending the reach of imperial power relations to the antipodes required the constitution of new forms of authority and modes of conduct that would enable ruling at a distance. To extend their imperial reach, European monarchs chartered early modern corporations, granting new collective entities "powers to manage, direct, and channel the conduct of the corporate body, its individual members, and the lives of whole populations."[18]

Archetypical of the early British corporation was the Hudson's Bay Company (HBC), incorporated under a royal charter in 1670. The charter granted the mercantile venture a trading monopoly over the vast region draining into Hudson Bay.[19] The new corporate form within the British Empire was, as Philip Stern characterizes, "a typically early modern fusion of private capacities of property ownership and legal personality mixed with the responsibilities and rights to govern over a particular form of public and its well-being."[20] These early corporations were contradictory entities; holding liberties beyond the effective control of the state in order to extend the domain of sovereign rule, they existed at the "boundary between the apogee of a totalizing sovereign power and beginnings of a new form of semi-autonomous corporate authority."[21]

Although the British sovereign granted the HBC authority over trading within a grand drainage, in practice the company had little effective control of the region beyond the shoreline. Its operations centred on a series of forts at relatively convenient shipping locations that Indigenous peoples could access through local waterways. The HBC relied on a trade network mediated by Indigenous interlocutors. As John Roberts describes, "aboriginal tribes, whose homelands were located away from Hudson Bay, traded with ones nearer the forts, who then traded with the HBC."[22]

The exigencies of the fur trade required colonial agents to integrate into the networks of Indigenous kinship that oriented relations at the edge of empire. To garner status and authority within Indigenous kinship systems, traders intermarried with Indigenous women.[23] The forts and traders remained dependent on the protection of men of rank and authority within Indigenous societies.[24] As Harold Innis argues, borrowing "Indian cultural traits was important…to the success of the Company."[25]

Expanding the trade into the interior of the continent evolved slowly, reliant on Indigenous peoples. Conversely, there was an expansion of the authority of the principal men of Indigenous groups located in close proximity with the forts, who had privileged access to European goods and the ability to extract favourable terms of exchange as mediators of the trade inland.[26]

British efforts to secure peaceful relations with Indigenous peoples in North America, following its victory over the French in the Seven Years War, further transformed relationships. To reaffirm the British commitment to respect Indigenous nations and mediate their relationships to an emergent population of settlers, King George III issued the Royal Proclamation of 1763.[27] Through it, the king sought to stabilize relations with the Indigenous nations of the continent, a considerable number of whom had been allied to the French. The proclamation asserted that Indigenous peoples under the protection of the British Crown had an exclusive right to any territories they possessed. Prior to settlement, representatives of the Crown had to call an assembly of the Indigenous nation concerned and negotiate a land surrender agreement. In the absence of such a treaty, the Royal Proclamation forbade colonial authorities from granting Indigenous lands to settlers and required the removal of settlers who implanted themselves on unceded Indigenous lands. Representatives of the British Crown subsequently communicated this commitment to Indigenous nations through the 1764 Treaty of Niagara.[28] These representatives met with more than two thousand Indigenous leaders, reassuring them that settlement would only proceed with Indigenous consent. Following the practices of the fur trade, this gathering employed established language and rituals to renew the kinship between the British sovereign and Indigenous peoples. It communicated a shared understanding of treaties as the foundation of peaceful coexistence between Indigenous peoples and settlers.[29]

The integration of the settler-colonial population of New France into British North America coincided with a transformation in relations between mercantilists and the state. Montréal-based traders, previously operating under the name of a competing French imperial sovereign, were now brought under the aegis of the British. Rather than operating in the name of competing imperial sovereignties, traders mounted private ventures, competing with one another within a common market. Although the HBC had a monopoly by royal charter, Montréal-based traders adopted new techniques, organizing the trade to operate beyond the limits of HBC influence.[30] The Montréal traders consolidated into a competing firm, the North West Company (NWC), and pushed trade inland. The NWC emerged from not a royal charter but "a series of co-partnerships between small groups of men who were promoters, merchants or fur traders."[31] It thus represented a newly emergent form of private corporation independent of the sovereign. Indeed, the NWC was founded on an explicit disregard of the sovereign grant of the HBC monopoly.

Moving inland, Nor'Westers, as the NWC traders were called, produced new geographies of trade. While the London-based HBC had centralized decision-making in the distant metropole and relied on Indigenous intermediaries bringing the trade to them, the NWC adopted a much more open corporate structure, granting greater autonomy to traders and allowing them to more directly engage Indigenous people in their own territories.[32] Although the HBC's financing was superior to the NWC, Indigenous middlemen had acted as a brake on HBC fur trade development. These Indigenous intermediaries lacked access to the financial capital necessary to manage the long temporal delays and uncertainties involved in extending the trade across the continent. The entrepreneurial Nor'Westers extended the geographic reach of financing and transportation.[33] This served to establish a new geography of profitable trade nodes and corridors, "mapped and shaped by specific imperial forms of knowledge and administration."[34] The emergent geography of the fur trade became the prototypical Canadian national imaginary, in which the colonial entitlement to space was naturalized through voyages by canoe across the continent.[35] Through these enterprises, explorer-cum-traders transformed foreign lands into imperial peripheries. The Nor'Wester Alexander Mackenzie crossed the Rocky Mountains in 1793.[36] Following Mackenzie's explorations, the NWC established trading posts on Tsek'ehne and Dakelh territories southeast of the Wet'suwet'en, including Fort McLeod in 1805, Fort St. James and Fort Fraser in 1806, and Fort George in 1807.[37] When the HBC merged with the NWC in 1821, it adopted the Nor'Westers' mode of conducting trade and took over the posts on Tsek'ehne and Dakelh territories. It further expanded operations to open Fort Kilmaurs on Babine Lake among the Nedut'en in 1822, improving Wet'suwet'en hereditary chiefs' access to trade.[38] The first recorded visit to Witset by a fur trader occurred in 1823.[39]

As the trade was pushed across the continent, it deepened engagement with Indigenous geographies. While Indigenous peoples had always been instrumental to the trade, the early forts on Hudson Bay had distorting effects on Indigenous geographies. The trade expanded the influence of the peoples adjacent to the fort, privileging them relative to inland communities who remained both economically and culturally distant from European influences.[40] However, as the fur trade moved further inland, eventually stretching to reach the Western Cordillera, it increasingly integrated with existing forms of Indigenous authority. As Robin Fisher has argued, Indigenous peoples retained agency in the trade and often benefited from these early exchanges with newcomers to their regions.[41]

**Wet'suwet'en Territorial Governance**

When fur traders first visited the Wet'suwet'en, they encountered an organized society with established customs for negotiating relations to outsiders. Prior to contact in the Northwest Interior and Northwest Coast, Indigenous peoples primarily related to each other on the basis of complex webs of kinship.[42] In Wet'suwet'en society, the most important kinship networks were those of the *yikh* and *dïdikh*, terms often translated as "house" and "clan," respectively. The *yikh* was the intimate matrilineal kinship group that held distinct hunting territories where they spent most of the year. In the summer, the Wet'suwet'en gathered along the canyon at Witset to catch salmon, with each *yikh* occupying a different longhouse in the village. Closely affiliated *yikh* formed *dïdikh* that would collectively host *balhats*, where they would reaffirm their territorial and kinship relations before the larger community.

These *balhats*, or feasts, were the principal governance institution of Wet'suwet'en society. These webs of kinship still organize Wet'suwet'en society today.

Political authority within a *yikh* is associated with a network of hereditary titles, particularly centring on the figure of a hereditary chief. The authority of a hereditary chief is limited to representing their matrilineal kin group. Wet'suwet'en society has no supreme leader. Within a *yikh*, there are elaborate hierarchies in which particular family members possess hereditary names of varying rank.[43] The authority associated with particular hereditary titles within a *yikh* is defined by a vital, ongoing lineage. Wet'suwet'en hereditary names and territorial authority are constantly revitalized as subsequent generations take on the titles of their predecessors. The entire system is dynamic. When a *yikh* lacks a member capable of taking on the chiefly title, for example, they induct someone from a related *yikh* within their *dïdikh* into the role of hereditary chief. The number of *yikh* and size of their membership can vary. Historically, when a *yikh* had too few members to fulfill its kinship obligations, it would either adopt new members or amalgamate with a related *yikh*. Conversely, excessively large *yikh* would subdivide. There are currently five Wet'suwet'en *dïdikh* with thirteen Wet'suwet'en *yikh* divided among them. The five *dïdikh* are the Gitdumden, Gilserhyu, Laksilyu, Laksamshu, and Tsayu.[44]

A connection to the land underpins the authority of a *yikh* and its capacity to demonstrate its "claim to territory through the proper ceremonies."[45] The Witsuwit'en term for territory, *yin tah*, emphasizes this connection, modifying the root *yin*, which means earth, to highlight its connection to a particular people. The hosts of the *balhats* wear ceremonial regalia adorned with crests symbolizing their distinct *yikh* and *dïdikh* identity. These crests also symbolize *yikh* connection to their *yin tah*. As Richard Daly describes, "crests themselves are considered gifts of power from the life forces in the land to the human beings living on that land."[46] Through feasting, *yikh* publicly reaffirm their identity, signalling their possession of their titles.

*Yikh* also affirm their broader kinship relations at the *balhats*. In Wet'suwet'en society, marriages were traditionally exogamous, with people marrying outside of their dïdikh. The father's yikh has responsibility to support the well-being of his descendants. While one's primary identity was matrilineal, territorial usage rights were extended based on broader kinship connections.⁴⁷ The children of male members of a yikh were regularly permitted to access the yin tah associated with their father's yikh while their father was alive. Similarly, the spouses of yikh members typically could access land use rights. Other people could seek permission to use specific yin tah, typically offering the hereditary chief responsible for those lands a form of payment. These payments and other land use rights were announced to the broader community in the balhats, where yikh demonstrated the fulfillment of their obligations to their kin and the management of the yin tah.

The distribution of gifts by the hosts of the balhats is central to reaffirming these relationships before the broader community. The guests, by witnessing the proceedings and accepting the gifts, validate the authority of the hosts and verify the maintenance of 'anuc niwh'it'en, the proper conduct of lawful relations. These gift exchanges, as described by Daly, enable yikh to "requite the gift of land, history, and legitimacy they inherited at birth."⁴⁸ Thus, the practices of gifting renew the lineage of a yikh and its territorial connections. Other yikh reciprocate these gifts, holding feasts with their dïdikh that reaffirm their own bonds of kinship and territorial responsibilities.

The authority of Wet'suwet'en yikh over the land was materialized through the active management of the landscape. For instance, ethnoecologist Scott Trusler estimates that Gitxsan and Wet'suwet'en and communities historically harvested between 57,700 and 370,000 gallons of huckleberries for winter use, which would require a harvesting area between 264 and 1,693 hectares.⁴⁹ Adding the berries that were consumed or traded fresh, he argues that "the total area under management for huckleberry production would comprise several thousand hectares." To maintain a harvesting area of this size, Wet'suwet'en yikh and other neighbouring Indigenous peoples, would use fires to burn forest vegetation, maintaining the berry patches and maximizing their productivity.⁵⁰

The conduct of lawful relations in Wet'suwet'en society was guided by open-ended ethics focused on maintaining ongoing relationships—extended through cyclic movements of reciprocal gifting.[51] When the first trader visited Witset, he noted that "a meal was speedily prepared, and set before me."[52] In return, the trader reciprocated, sharing his tobacco. "So it was, that eating and smoking...prepared the way for a good understanding with the chief, to whom I communicated...the precise object which led me to visit his lands."[53] Reaffirming this connection, "presents of furs were made...by 'Sniggletrum,' and several of his principal men."[54]

Prior to regular visits by fur traders, Wet'suwet'en participation in the fur trade was mediated through relationships to neighbouring Indigenous peoples. The first fur trader to visit the Wet'suwet'en in 1823 noted, despite being "perfect strangers to the sight of Europeans," they already possessed an abundance of "articles indicative of a commercial intercourse."[55] Wet'suwet'en *yikh* and *dïdikh* maintained extensive relationships throughout the region based on ties of both kinship and trade.[56] The structure of matrilineal clan relations governed through the feast extended links across the region. Wet'suwet'en *yikh* and *dïdikh* intermarried with the houses and clans of neighbouring nations, building a dense weave of connections between families in the broader region. "Feasts were a way to maintain peaceful relations and resolve conflicts that occurred periodically," as Mélanie Morin describes, facilitating "opportunities for trade, cultural exchanges and marriage connections."[57] Commerce was long established between Indigenous peoples in Interior British Columbia and villages on the Pacific Coast, with trade along rivers as well as a network of trails used to transport oolichan grease and other goods across watersheds in the region.[58] As competing Russian, British, American, and Spanish merchant ships developed a maritime fur trade along the Northwest Coast in the eighteenth century, newcomers and their trade goods became linked to dynamic relationships within and between Indigenous communities.[59]

While distinct, Wet'suwet'en language and culture interwove with that of neighbouring nations, demonstrating the depth of regional linguistic exchange and transculturation. The Witsuwit'en language is a dialect of a language shared with the Nedut'en to the east, belonging to the same linguistic family as the Dakelh spoken to the south.[60] Gitxsan families, who occupy the lands immediately north of the Wet'suwet'en, speak two dialects of Gitxsanimaax, a language closely related to that of their coastal Tsimshian and Nisga'a neighbours. To the west of the Wet'suwet'en, the Haisla belong to a third distinct language family. Despite these linguistic boundaries, the majority of Wet'suwet'en names and crests originate among the Gitxsan, with a lesser number coming from the Haisla and Nisga'a.[61] Wet'suwet'en *yikh* and *didikh* also acquired names as gifts from the Dakelh communities of the Cheslatta and Ulkatcho to the south.[62]

When fur traders first encountered the Wet'suwet'en, they had recently established a new summer fishing village. A rockfall in the early 1820s had partially blocked the Widzin Kwah downstream of Witset in a canyon east of where the Widzin Kwah joins the Skeena River. To maintain access to the vital salmon fishery, the Wet'suwet'en negotiated with the Gitxsan chief Spookwx to establish another fishing village in the canyon on his territories.[63] It would become the major Wet'suwet'en summer village for the next sixty-five years. The Wet'suwet'en called the village Tsë Kyah, while the Gitxsan would refer to the community as Hagwilget. Located on Gitxsan territories, it was most often called Hagwilget. Not until 1887, when missionary Father A.G. Morice relocated Catholic Wet'suwet'en converts away from the Gitxsan to the area of their abandoned village, which he rechristened as Moricetown, did a substantial population again reside in the Witset area.[64]

As the HBC attained dominance in the regional fur trade, its agents further embedded themselves in connections to established systems of authority within Wet'suwet'en communities. Drawing on his examination of the journals of William Brown, the trader who established Fort Kilmaurs, Arthur Ray has stressed how Nedut'en and Wet'suwet'en systems of territorial authority shaped the fur trade.[65] Brown was particularly attentive to how the Indigenous land tenure system governed trapping activity. He described the Wet'suwet'en and Nedut'en hereditary chiefs as "men of property" who possessed lands and regulated access to their territories through a kinship structure.[66] Brown complained about the impact of territorial restrictions on pelt yields. For instance, he estimated there were seventy capable hunters among the Nedut'en people in 1826, but only half this number had territorial access to trapping opportunities. Hereditary chiefs closely regulated trapping on their *yin tah*, limiting hunting and trapping rights. Furthermore, according to Ray, fur trade records reveal that the majority of trade in beaver pelts was conducted by hereditary chiefs themselves, despite the fact that they often were not the ones who collected the furs. This evidences the chiefs' jurisdiction over trapping within their *yikh*. Fur trade records also show how chiefs balanced participation in the fur trade with obligations to maintain relationships through the feast system. For instance, the clerk at Fort St. James in 1824 reported that the Nak'azdli, a Dakelh community adjacent to Stuart Lake, withheld beaver from the trading company to use in exchange with the Nedut'en.[67]

Therefore, when colonial agents arrived, there were elaborate systems ordering Wet'suwet'en life. Wet'suwet'en *yikh* exercised authority over their lands. They reaffirmed their authority over their *yin tah* through the *balhats*. Kinship relations were also affirmed through the *balhats*, conditioning the rights and responsibilities of each Wet'suwet'en person based on webs of relationships through not only *yikh* membership but also marriage and patrilineal descent. Although these systems included aspects of sovereign decision-making, they did not strictly parallel the technologies of power prevalent within European society at the time. Rather, they presented distinct modalities of power that colonial agents needed to negotiate, creating part of the structure of relations that would shape the colonial encounter.

**The Inscription of a Settler-Colonial Design**
The nineteenth-century arrival of newcomers to Wet'suwet'en territories produced new relationships. Early traders had relied heavily on Indigenous guides and translators to negotiate the structures of Indigenous authority and territory.[68] However, the

fur trade and early missionary activity catalogued knowledge of the biophysical and social landscape that contributed to the expansion of colonial regimes. The knowledge produced through the fur trade supported Britain's mid-century claim to imperial sovereignty over the space, which it subsequently incorporated as a province within the emergent Canadian dominion. While these changes in systems of imperial and settler-colonial administration generally had limited immediate impact on Wet'suwet'en territories, they did introduce a new structure of settler territorial government. Previously the territorial authority of Indigenous legal orders had been uncontested, and fur traders focused on regulating and protecting trade. The arrival of settler society introduced new modes of exploiting and governing the land and its resources. Regulating individual rights to claim and exchange the land itself, settler-colonial authorities constructed a new legal imaginary of the earth as a commodity that could be owned and traded.[69]

In the early decades of the nineteenth century, Russian, Spanish, American, and British traders pursued commercial endeavours in the Pacific Northwest and their governments leveraged competing claims to jurisdiction over this trade.[70] In 1846, the *Oregon Treaty* set the territorial boundary between American and British domains at the 49th parallel. However, colonial influence was largely limited to private trading ventures, and neither American nor British political authorities had effectively operationalized territorial jurisdiction in the region. Nevertheless, the agreement began to reorder relationships. The HBC had previously headquartered its Pacific operations at the mouth of the Columbia River, which was now south of the border. In 1848, US Congress established the Oregon Territory south of the boundary. A year later, the British created the Colony of Vancouver Island and leased it to the HBC, who relocated their operations to Victoria. Beyond the HBC there were still no functional British authorities in the region; Indigenous societies continued to maintain their territorial authority.

The transformation in the colonial regime, from corporate authority acting in the name of the sovereign to imposition of a new regime of colonial sovereignty, occurred in 1858 with the formal establishment of the Colony of British Columbia, encompassing the mainland west of the Rockies. This change occurred in response to the Fraser Canyon Gold Rush, when thousands of prospectors entered the area in pursuit of the dream of individual riches.[71] The colonial population surged from 150 fur traders to 20,000 prospectors, speculators, and merchants. To assert British authority, James Douglas was appointed governor of the newly created colony. A former employee of the Northwest Company who rose to chief factor of the HBC, Douglas represented the evolving forms of colonial authority in the British Pacific Northwest.[72] With the formation of the colony, Britain terminated the HBC monopoly and inaugurated a new system of political rule over the thousands of independent wealth seekers. Operationalizing this authority, Douglas installed a new set of mining regulations and mineral staking regimes.[73]

British authorities did not consult Indigenous landholders, such as the Wet'suwet'en hereditary chiefs, in the formation of British Columbia. Counter the dictates of the Royal Proclamation of 1763, the mainland Colony of British Columbia had not entered treaties with Indigenous peoples.[74] Rather than negotiate treaties, Governor Douglas sought to instill order to the process of settlement already underway, appointing a magistrate in 1859 to set aside Indigenous villages and cultivated lands as Indian reserves. Formalizing early land policy, Douglas issued Proclamation No. 15 in 1860, which enabled settlers to pre-empt and settle "unoccupied" lands in British Columbia while protecting lands that were already a site of Indigenous settlement. These edicts were issued without consulting Indigenous communities about the disposition of the land. The subsequent entry of British Columbia into the Canadian Confederation in 1871 also occurred without the consent of Wet'suwet'en or other Indigenous peoples. Despite constituting the majority of the regional population in the period, Indigenous people were denied the right to vote or otherwise participate in the colonial and early provincial political system.

The declaration of a new colonial regime of territorial governance initially had limited direct effect over Wet'suwet'en territories. Early development initiatives approached Wet'suwet'en territories as an area to be traversed rather than as land to appropriate. The peripherality of the region protected Wet'suwet'en interests and limited the early impacts of development. The Western Union Company began building the Collins Overland Telegraph Line in 1865, seeking to connect San Francisco to Moscow.[75] In 1866, surveyors for the telegraph charted a path through Wet'suwet'en territories; however, the completion that same year of a transAtlantic underwater cable from Ireland to Newfoundland rendered the project obsolete, and the Collins Overland Telegraph was abandoned just north of the Gitxsan community of Kispiox. The cartographic trace of the failed endeavour appeared on new maps, where the lower Widzin Kwah was renamed after the project's chief engineer, Colonel Bulkley. Despite its abandonment, the telegraph improved regional communications and transportation infrastructure, both enabling colonial officials to send instructions north and constructing a new travel route to the North.

In a subsequent gold rush in the early 1870s, prospectors began heading to the Omineca Mountains on Tse'khene territories, northeast of the Wet'suwet'en territories. The principal route, laid by surveyor and road builder Edgar Dewdney, followed the telegraph trail through Dakelh territories, then along Stuart and Takla lakes to the Omineca area.[76] A secondary route for prospectors followed the Skeena River up to its junction with the Widzin Kwah, or Bulkley River, where the community of Hazelton was established as a provisioning point adjacent to the Gitxsan village of Gitanmaax.[77] From Hazelton, prospectors would hire packers, often using Indigenous labour, to carry supplies along trails across Wet'suwet'en, Nedut'en, and Dakelh territories to the Omineca on Tse'khene lands.[78]

While Indigenous hereditary chiefs continued to govern their lands through their legal orders, settler authorities in Victoria and Ottawa increasingly claimed jurisdiction over Indigenous activities in the Northwest Interior of British Columbia. First, the government began to assert the paramountcy of Canadian criminal law jurisdiction over Indigenous people.[79] In 1884, Gitxsan hereditary chief Haatq was jailed for murdering Amos Youmans, a white trader who failed to compensate Haatq's family after his son Billy died in Youmans's employ.[80] Then, in 1888, settler authorities intervened in an internal Gitxsan conflict, seeking to apprehend Gitxsan hereditary chief Kamalmuk after he murdered a Gitxsan shaman suspected of cursing his son and thereby causing his death. Police killed Kamalmuk in a botched attempt at his arrest, heightening tensions between Indigenous peoples and settlers in Hazelton.[81] In 1889, responding to fears of a potential Skeena uprising, government officials temporarily mobilized a military force to assert the dominance of settler law. They then created the Babine Indian Agency to orchestrate enduring administrative control over the local Indigenous communities.[82] This brought the Gitxsan, Wet'suwet'en, and Nedut'en under the Indian Act, which the Canadian government had originally enacted in 1876, racializing diverse Indigenous communities as subjects of a common regime of state management.[83]

The Indian Act imposed a new system of band organization on Indigenous communities. For administrative purposes, different communities were agglomerated together into larger, combined bands that ignored both pre-existent Indigenous systems of social organization and linguistic boundaries. The Wet'suwet'en community of Hagwilget was combined with the nearby Gitxsan community at Gitanmaax, while the community in Witset was administratively joined with Nedut'en living around Nin (Babine Lake area).[84] Moreover, the band system defined Indian status on the basis of patrilineal connections to a particular band. A woman's identity was determined by who she married: she was assigned to her husband's band. Indigenous women who married white men lost Indian status entirely.[85] This created tensions with Indigenous systems of identification based on matrilineal kinship relations that were at play in Wet'suwet'en, Gitxsan, and Nedut'en communities.

Through the Babine Indian Agency, the government also imposed a new system of band governance under the aegis of the federal Department of Indian Affairs. In 1884, the government amended the Indian Act, banning traditional Indigenous potlatch governance systems such as the *balhats*.[86] R.E. Loring, the newly appointed Indian agent for the Babine Indian Agency, initially instituted a system of village elections, but quickly suspended them after the Gitxsan community of Kispiox elected a council that sought "to drive [out] white settlers."[87] For decades, Indian agents simply appointed Indigenous band leadership amenable to settlement.[88] Community elections of band leadership in Witset were not recognized by the federal Indian agent until 1941.[89] Moreover, the Canadian government reserved the right to suspend Indian band governments that it deemed politically or financially irresponsible (a capacity that it still maintains).[90]

Land policy in British Columbia explicitly served to open the province to white settlement, offering settlers access to agricultural lands through a number of mechanisms.[91] First, through a process known as pre-emption, a settler could claim legal title of up to 320 acres of "unoccupied" land upon payment of a small settlement fee, provided that the possessor made permanent improvements, clearing and cultivating a portion of the land, building a dwelling, and demonstrating continuous residency. Second, people could directly purchase land from the government, without the requirement to occupy and work it. Third, the government provided veterans of the Boer War with script to 160 acres of land. Through the settlement and development of agricultural lands, the government aimed to establish the basis of a new society of free landholders. In 1891, the province sent N.B. Gauvreau to evaluate the potential of the Widzin Kwah Valley for agricultural settlement.[92] Based on his positive assessment, provincial surveyor A.L. Poudrier laid out townships in the valley in 1892. This created the legal grid that would enable settlers to claim ownership to distinct tracts of the land in the region.[93]

During this time, Indigenous geography was reimagined as synonymous with the spatiality of parsimoniously allocated reserves.[94] Although each matrilineal *yikh* possessed its own distinct territories, bureaucrats in the provincial capital ignored Wet'suwet'en territorial systems. The government sought to ignore and silence Indigenous land tenure by narrowing discussions to focus only on the issue of reserve allocations.[95] On top of this, provincial land policy restricted Indigenous people from participating in the settlement of land through the pre-emption process. In claiming reserve lands, Indigenous peoples sought to protect the geography of established Indigenous food fisheries and village sites, ensuring that elements of pre-existing Indigenous geographies were inscribed in government registers.[96] In September 1891, the Indian Reserve Commissioner, Peter O'Reilly, first arrived in Wet'suwet'en territories and began laying out early reserves. O'Reilly set aside 1,690 acres of reserve lands at Moricetown (Witset).[97] Ten days later, he outlined reserve lands for the Wet'suwet'en village of Hagwilget, which he labelled Tsitsk No. 3 and allocated 455 acres.[98] In contrast to the 320 acres allocated to pre-empting settlers and 160 acres for veterans of imperial wars, these Wet'suwet'en communities had been allocated, respectively, 24.9 and 14.4 acres per person.[99]

Despite the introduction of the band system and establishment of reserves, Wet'suwet'en families continued to maintain *yikh* relationships and use their traditional lands. Indeed, to even construct the territorial knowledge necessary to administer Indian reserves, settler authorities needed to reckon with Indigenous regimes of land use and community governance. To minimize resistance to the surveying of reserves, O'Reilly told the Wet'suwet'en that the reserve system only "protects the land from trespass from others, but the Indian still has the right to hunt, fish or gather berries outside."[100] The Canadian government was only able to advance the system of band and reserve governance through allowing *balhats* to continue unmolested, in spite of official legislative potlatch bans, and promising Indigenous peoples continued use of their territories.[101] Moreover, although Loring, the Indian agent, formally administered Gitanmaax and Hagwilget as a single Hazelton Band with common reserve lands, he maintained discretion and avoided disclosing this fact, ensuring "no one of either band has ever had a glimpse at the tracing containing Tsitsk [Tsë Kyah]—for fear to precipitate a conflict."[102] Eventually, the Hazelton Band was administratively separated into the Gitxsan community of Gitanmaax and the Wet'suwet'en village of Hagwilget, while the Wet'suwet'en community of Witset was split from the Nedut'en around Nin (Babine Lake area) to form the Moricetown Band. The outline of a new colonial order had thus been inscribed on paper, creating the legal infrastructure and territorial knowledge for the settlement of Wet'suwet'en territories. In its actual effect at the time, however, settler jurisdiction remained limited.

Early conflicts over Indigenous fisheries and lands foreshadowed the tensions to come.[103] Beginning in 1877, commercial fish canneries began to operate on Tsimshian territories at the mouth of the Skeena River during salmon runs. Government authorities saw Indigenous fisheries as a threat to the commercial fishing industry developing on the British Columbia Coast, and thus sought to control them.[104] Initially, the influence of these operations on inland Indigenous communities was primarily economic, with the canneries recruiting low-wage Indigenous labour.[105] Government policy further channelled Indigenous workers into cannery work by limiting their ability to participate in commercial fisheries. In 1881, government officials began to close Indigenous fisheries that were selling fish commercially.[106] A federal fishing permit system introduced in 1888 institutionalized a licensing requirement for any Indigenous commercial fisheries.[107]

At the turn of the century, as overfishing on the coast caused a crisis, fisheries officials began to look inland to relieve pressure on salmon stocks. While the government recognized an Indigenous right to sustenance food fisheries, officials demanded that Indigenous fishermen abandon traditional fishing technologies, particularly weirs, or barricades, which they deemed to be limiting the movement of spawning salmon.[108] A.W. Vowel, the superintendent of Indian Affairs for British Columbia, argued that "the barricades and other obstructions can hardly fail to have deleterious effect on the propagation of the salmon."[109] This led to pronounced conflict with the Nedut'en, who operated weirs across the U'in Ts'ah C'ikwah (Babine River). The government arrested eight Nedut'en men for operating illegal weirs.[110] The conflict was eventually resolved with the 1906 Barricade Treaty, in which the government promised to provide nets, farm equipment, and a school in exchange for the Nedut'en discontinuing use of the weirs. Subsequently, fisheries expanded the policy, banning the use of weirs by neighbouring Indigenous communities, such as the Wet'suwet'en. These conflicts over access to fish would prefigure subsequent conflicts over land. However, the settlement and development of an extractive economy in the Northwest Interior required, as travel writer F.A. Talbot described after visiting the region in 1911, "the advent of the railway, as the cost of transport is so high."[111]

**Imposing a Regime of Resource Extraction**
The effective integration of the Northwest Interior into the province, as well as its broader linkage to the global economy, would require creating the physical infrastructure to traverse space in new ways. "Improvements in transportation and communication enabled the world economy to use British Columbia's space not through Native intermediaries, as during the fur trade, but by distributing Western technologies, labour, and settlers across the land," Cole Harris explains. "The systems of transportation and communication that spread into British Columbia were the capillaries of colonial appropriation."[112] Without transportation infrastructure, development was hindered by the lack of access to markets.

Pursuing new markets and development opportunities, investors financed new infrastructure development, reshaping economic geographies. British capital invested in the Grand Trunk Pacific (GTP), a northern railway route that would reduce shipping time across the continent and on to Asia.[113] The railroad was completed in April 1914 and radically changed local geography, creating a division point within Wet'suwet'en territories. GTP named the new town after the company's chairman, Sir Alfred Waldron Smithers.[114] A 1914 GTP promotional brochure for Smithers described how railroad infrastructure transformed remote locations into "collecting points for business for the railway—places where...wagon roads come, serving as feeders to the railway, and where natural conditions form centres for distribution as well as for collection."[115] The town, the first site of concentrated white settlement on Wet'suwet'en territories, would become the centre for a new economy in the area.[116]

As colonial land policies sought to reterritorialize space, other resource conservation policies expanded oversight of traditional forms of Wet'suwet'en land use. In 1917, amendments to fishery regulations sought to restrict Indigenous fishers' capacity to sell salmon, re-enforcing that Indigenous rights were limited to subsistence, not commercial activity.[117] In 1933, the provincial wildlife officials required Indigenous hunters get permits, even when they were hunting in season for food.[118] Also in the 1930s, forest rangers engaged in a concerted campaign to end Indigenous traditional burns. A 1932 Prince Rupert Forest District report described how "Indian-caused fires have decreased during the past two years. As early as possible in the spring all Indian settlements were visited and our policy explained in plain words. Notices were written out and posted at Indian trading posts which seemed to get results."[119] The regulations, as well as fines and arrests for violations of the rules, restricted the terms on which Indigenous people could maintain their traditional subsistence economies.

The government introduced Indian residential schools to facilitate the cultural transformation of Indigenous communities to fit white settler norms. At their most basic conception, the church-run schools constituted a direct attack on the capacity of Indigenous families to transfer knowledge to future generations.[120] The residential model of education explicitly aimed to sever the link between children and their families, taking youth from their homes to live under the superintendence of church officials. An amendment to the Indian Act in 1920 made schooling compulsory for Status Indian children. For the next two decades, Wet'suwet'en children were taken from their families and sent to schools such as the Catholic Lejac Indian Residential School on the shore of Fraser Lake in Dakelh territories.[121] The schools displaced Wet'suwet'en children from the kinship relations of their *yikh* and the rhythms of life on the territories, aiming to transform them into agricultural labourers.

As an educational enterprise, the Indian residential schools were an abysmal failure, submitting students to significant trauma and providing remarkably little education. Government parsimony created a network of badly constructed and undersupplied institutes operated without accountability. The schools operated under the presumption that child labour at school-run farms would make the institutions self-sustaining. They were not, and the results were horrific. Malnutrition was common, communicable disease outbreaks regular, overcrowding the norm. Educational materials were lacking, and children were over-worked and under-educated.[122]

Without adequate government oversight, children at the schools faced physical and sexual abuse.[123] At Lejac, where large numbers of Wet'suwet'en youth were students in the 1920s and 1930s, the spectre of communicable disease haunted the institution, and according to Mary-Ellen Kelm, "some kind of infection passed through the school almost every year."[124] Large numbers of children died from illness and abuse, eventually leading Moricetown Band to establish a day school in Witset so that Chief Jack Joseph could withdraw the majority of Wet'suwet'en children from Lejac in the late 1930s.[125] For those who had attended, the schools were an intensely damaging experience that followed them throughout their lives. Psychically wounded school survivors often spiralled into patterns of violence and addiction.[126] The government slowly began phasing out the Indian residential school system in the postwar period, but it would take decades for the system to be completely shut down.

Despite the traumatic history of Indian residential schooling and colonial conservation laws, Wet'suwet'en people did not abandon their connections to their lands. Instead, Wet'suwet'en families used a mix of livelihood strategies, including subsistence farming, harvesting food from the territories, working for wages, and selling furs and homemade goods, such as baskets and clothing.[127] While agricultural and resource-extractive developments impacted some parts of Wet'suwet'en territories, large parts of *yikh* lands remained intact. Indigenous workers in early twentieth-century British Columbia used paid work to supplement the subsistence livelihoods that they had already established on their territories.[128] Moreover, the capacity of Wet'suwet'en families to shift between livelihood strategies enabled them to effectively adjust to seasonal layoffs and economic downturns by increasing the proportion of time they spent in subsistence activities. Indigenous workers had greater adaptability to economic fluctuations, as John Lutz emphasizes, because "they had a subsistence economy that persisted well past those of other Canadians, and this supplied them with food when other work did not."[129] Where they previously balanced late-summer fishing in the canyons at Witset or Hagwilget with winter months spent on the *yin tah*,

Wet'suwet'en families increasingly integrated paid work in their seasonal movements. For instance, "fishing might be interspersed with sawmill work or with a variety of subsistence tasks."[130] Since the creation of salmon canneries in the late nineteenth century, there had been Wet'suwet'en workers seasonally travelling to work on the coast during the salmon run. Others had begun to mix farming into their seasonal rounds.

For Wet'suwet'en who took up farming, holding their farms would often prove difficult. Early land conflicts preceded the railway as land speculators began purchasing properties in the region and settlers began to move to Wet'suwet'en territories. Although the provincial government ignored broader questions of Indigenous title, its land policy still stipulated that Indigenous cultivated lands should be set aside as reserves and excluded from settler pre-emption or purchase. Regardless, the process of formalizing reserve allocation was exceedingly slow, taking decades to formalize the registration of reserve lands. The Indian agent surveyed many Wet'suwet'en farms in 1906 but had to wait for the Royal Commission on Indian Affairs to formally register these areas as reserves. The Royal Commission held hearings throughout the province from 1913 to 1916, eventually adopting amended reserve allocations in the 1924 British Columbia Indian Lands Settlement Act.[131]

Several Wet'suwet'en families had farmland registered as reserve land in the relatively remote southern portion of Wet'suwet'en territories, where competition for land was less intense. Skin Tyee established reserve land for his family in close proximity to the Cheslatta along Netanlï Bin (Skins Lake).[132] Maxan Tom and his brothers had land set aside on Tasdlegh (Maxan Lake).[133] Sam Willie established reserve land at T'aco (Decker Lake); Willie's daughter and her husband Antoine created another farm to be reserved at Tselh K'iz (Tsichgass Lake).[134] Other families had lands set aside in the areas of Honcagh Bin (Uncha Lake) and C'iggiz (Broman Lake).

With the long lapse between surveying and recognizing reserves, however, conflicts often arose over the allocation of lands close to the railway route. Settlers regularly pre-empted lands that had been surveyed for Indian reserves. When the members of the Royal Commission on Indian Affairs were faced with competing claims between white settlers and Wet'suwet'en farmers, they regularly favoured the settlers. Along the shores of Tselh K'iz Bin (Burns Lake), an Indian agent named David Tibbetts sought to secure reserve lands for a group of Wet'suwet'en families, which he designated the Burns Lake Band. Tibbetts submitted surveys of these lands in 1906. After the Royal Commission reviewed these claims in 1915, it determined that the majority of the lots to be set aside for the Burns Lake Band had been pre-empted and could no longer be reserved.[135] In 1916, the commission removed additional acreage from the Burns Lake Reserve to make way for the railway, a road, and the creation of the settler village site of Burns Lake. A similar overlap occurred at Nïntah Bin (Francois Lake), with settlers pre-empting Indigenous farmlands that had been surveyed by the Indian agent but not formalized as reserves. Again, by the time the Royal Commission was established, a substantial portion of the proposed Wet'suwet'en reserve lands along Nïntah Bin had been pre-empted.[136] Felix George, a Wet'suwet'en man who, along with his brothers, had tried to establish himself on Nïntah Bin, grew so frustrated that he moved and set up another farm at Bïwinï (Owen Lake), which would eventually become the Felix George Reserve.[137]

Other Wet'suwet'en families had their farms simply stolen without compensation or were forced to purchase lands on their own territories. For instance, Round Lake Tommy, who held the hereditary title Wah Tah Kwets, had a farm on his *yin tah*.[138] Although Round Lake Tommy had cleared six acres, put up a barn, and built two houses, a settler named John Bekkie would subsequently claim the land, displacing Round Lake Tommy and his family.[139] Similarly, Wet'suwet'en families who established farms in the C'inu'iy Ïkwah (Canyon Creek) area struggled to maintain their homes, which the government failed to set aside as reserve lands.[140] They were displaced by J.W. (Happy) Turner, who claimed the land as a war veteran.[141] Some Wet'suwet'en, such as Tyee Lake David, simply purchased private lands to establish farms.[142] David's brother, Jean Baptiste, uniquely resisted eviction in a prolonged conflict that included threats of armed resistance. Although Baptiste had established a farm near Tacot (Tyee Lake), land speculators had invested in the land, which eventually came under the control of the Toronto-based

National Trust Company. Faced with Baptiste's staunch resistance, the federal government purchased the land to ameliorate the dispute, eventually deciding to set it aside as a reserve.[143] Other Wet'suwet'en chose to avoid this type of conflict and instead secured special permission to pre-empt land that white settlers had not otherwise claimed. Jack Joseph, Round Lake Tommy, August Pete, Johnny David, Mathew Sam, Thomas George, and Bill Alec would all eventually secure special land pre-emptions.[144] For most Wet'suwet'en families, however, these avenues to securing even limited recognition of their land rights off reserve remained inaccessible, and they instead established residence on the allotted reserve lands at the summer fishing villages of Witset and Hagwilget.

In 1927, the federal government suspended discussion of Indigenous land rights, amending the Indian Act to ban Indigenous peoples from pursuing legal remedies for their unrecognized land rights.[145] Summarizing the situation in 1932, Diamond Jenness described the Wet'suwet'en (whom he referred to as part of the Carrier tribe) as "confined to reserves within its [the tribe's] old territory, which is now traversed by a transcontinental railway," and elaborated on their struggles with white settlers who "begrudge them even the narrow lands the government has set aside for them."[146] As provincial laws privileged settler interests over those of Indigenous people, most Wet'suwet'en families were dispossessed of their lands and pushed into seasonal labour.

Wet'suwet'en were able to negotiate a position in the emerging economy as labourers. Commercial farming in the early twentieth century remained labour intensive. Despite local boosters advertising investment and immigration to the Northwest Interior, the anticipated rush of migrants did not arrive. Instead, World War I, which began shortly after the completion of the railroad, restricted northern development. The employment of Indigenous workers was necessary to address labour shortages in Northwest British Columbia.[147] Displaced from the land, Indigenous workers in the agricultural sector, as Lutz describes, "provided waged or piecerate labour for other farmers."[148] Agriculture provided a major source of income for Wet'suwet'en families. Between 1910 and 1926, the agricultural sector "supplied more income to BC Indians than any other."[149] This income supplemented the capacity of Wet'suwet'en families to provide for themselves and uphold their kinship responsibilities in the *balhats*.

Complementing summer fishing or farming, commercial forestry provided a source of winter employment. Like agriculture, the forest sector did not develop in earnest until the arrival of the railway. The provincial government enacted forest regulations in 1910 that, in practice, involved substantial racial discrimination in the allocation of provincial harvesting permits.[150] This restricted the ability of Indigenous people to run timber operations, pushing them into subcontracting and working for settlers. In the early twentieth century, the local industry was oriented to supplying ties to the railway. Half of the forestry contracts in the region were held by local settler and politician Olaf Hanson, who ran a system of subcontracts to fill his orders, getting wood from both settlers who were clearing pre-empted lands and Wet'suwet'en timber camps.[151]

In the late 1930s, as lumber demand and timber prices increased, the forestry industry diversified with an increase in the number of independent operations.[152] In northern forestry, there was a spatial division of labour between sawmill and planer operations.[153] A large amount of work occurred in the bush, where small portable sawmills produced roughhewn lumber. This was subsequently sold to large planer mills situated on the rail lines, which smoothed and dried the lumber for global distribution.[154] While the planer mills often relied on distant investor capital, the small portable bush mills were almost always locally owned and operated, and thus were inclined to hire local labour. The small bush mills relied upon seasonal employment and required workers to live for extended periods in remote bush camps. Bush mill operators in the Bulkley Valley employed substantial numbers of Wet'suwet'en workers, who were accustomed to seasonal work and spending extensive periods on the land.[155]

Wet'suwet'en families continued to trap on their territories through the first half of the twentieth century. While the government sought to ignore and silence Indigenous land tenure by narrowly focusing discussion on the issue of reserve allocations,

Wet'suwet'en *yikh* continued to use their *yin tah* both to support themselves and to fight for their territorial rights. In the absence of any governmental recognition of territorial title, Wet'suwet'en *yikh* sought to protect their territorial interests through registering their *yin tah* in the provincial trapline registry.[156] By registering their *yin tah* as traplines, Wet'suwet'en *yikh* did not abandon their own systems of understanding their lands. Rather, they layered their knowledge of territorial rights and responsibilities onto the colonial system of trapline registration.[157] However, the trapline registry complicated processes of maintaining *yikh* identity and territorial control. Trapline boundaries often deviated from those of Wet'suwet'en *yin tah*, and many traplines were registered to the patriarch of the family and passed down patrilineally in accordance with Canadian law, countering the matrilineal norms of Wet'suwet'en *yikh*.[158]

Through all these changes, Wet'suwet'en *yikh* and *dïdikh* continued to host *balhats*, maintaining their kinship and territorial relations.[159] As Richard Daly describes, Wet'suwet'en *yikh* and *dïdikh* adapted monetary exchanges "from the market economy to the social needs of the gift economy."[160] Thus, wealth accumulated through Indigenous labour and business ventures was reintegrated into the *balhats*, serving as another medium for reciprocal exchanges that renew kinship responsibilities and uphold the status of a lineage.

However, the resource-extractive economy also created and intensified territorial conflicts.[161] Provincial modes of governing the resource economy, for instance through forestry regulations, disregarded the territorial jurisdiction of Indigenous peoples.[162] Some members of Wet'suwet'en *yikh* tried to find work on their own *yin tah*; however, many worked on territories to which they lacked rights under Wet'suwet'en law. Early on, when forestry operated on a relatively small scale, Wet'suwet'en resource labourers could make efforts to compensate *yikh* for work done on their *yin tah* through exchanges in the *balhats*.[163] Over time, however, conflicts between settler resource exploitation and Wet'suwet'en land use intensified, particularly as the scale of industry increased after World War II.

### Keynesian Colonialism in the Northwest Interior

The conditions of the Great Depression and its repercussions in World War II transformed dominant political and economic imaginaries in the Western world. In the wake of this economic catastrophe wrought by unregulated capitalism, and amidst its fallout in the form of extremist doctrines of fascism and communism, a new liberal political and economic order emerged. The doctrine of John Maynard Keynes ascended: the government needed to regulate the economy to maintain market stability and ensure sustainable patterns of economic growth.[164] Thus, in the decades after World War II, there was a massive reorganization in the apparatuses of state. Western governments adopted social security systems to protect public welfare through programs such as health insurance, unemployment insurance, and social assistance. There was also a new focus on formal equality and universal rights. However, alongside the expansion of human rights doctrine and the social safety net, the government guided processes of economic change that significantly intensified the dispossession of Indigenous peoples in Northwest British Columbia.

Seeking to rationalize the governance of Indian bands, the federal government introduced new administrative structures in the Department of Indian Affairs. It constructed a new Burns Lake Agency, which placed the Indian reserves in the southern portion of Wet'suwet'en territories—those at C'iggiz (Broman Lake), Honcagh Bin (Uncha Lake), Netanlï Bin (Skins Lake), Nïntah Bin (Francois Lake), Tasdlegh (Maxan Lake), Tselh K'iz Bin (Burns Lake), and T'aco (Decker Lake)—into a new administrative jurisdiction. This split the small southern reserves established by Wet'suwet'en farming families from the larger, historic communities of Witset and Hagwilget on the Widzin Kwah, where the Wet'suwet'en *dïdikh* would fish and feast. The Wet'suwet'en bands of Moricetown and Hagwilget in the north belonged to one agency, while the southern reserves belonged to another. Indian Affairs officials also agglomerated the majority of the small southern Wet'suwet'en reserves, each of which consisted of a few families, into the Omineca Band in 1959.[165] The only Wet'suwet'en band in the area to remain independent was Burns Lake Band.

In contrast to the remoteness of the other small southern Wet'suwet'en reserves, the Burns Lake Reserve, at the centre of the frontier town of Burns Lake, was not peripheral to the emerging geography of settlement and development. The Burns Lake reserve lands had been steadily eroded, appropriated by settler authorities who prioritized road, rail, and municipal development over the protection of reserves.[166] Moreover, the already small Burns Lake Reserve was growing increasingly overcrowded, as members of other bands, particularly the Nedut'en from the Lake Babine Band, "lived on the Burns Lake reserve because it was closer to town than their own more remote Indian reserves."[167] Economic marginalization and housing market discrimination made it difficult for Status Indians to buy or rent homes in the settler municipality; thus, they congregated on the reserve lands of the Burns Lake Band. To create separate space for the Nedut'en and encourage them to build permanent homes rather than makeshift camps, the Indian agent in Burns Lake arranged the sale of a portion of the Burns Lake Reserve to the Lake Babine Band in 1959. This subsequently became the Woyenne Reserve. The majority of the Nedut'en relocated to Woyenne from their remote reserves around Nin (Babine Lake area), on their traditional territories. This was alienating for many Nedut'en, as they could not "afford to routinely visit their clan [*dïdikh*] lands and, thus, [were] unable to harvest foods traditionally served at the *balhats*."[168]

Also in the 1950s, hydro developments displaced the Dakelh members of the Cheslatta Band onto a series of new reserves scattered in the south of Wet'suwet'en territories.[169] In particular, the Kemano Project, a massive hydroelectric project on the Nechako River, would radically transform the lands and waters of the Dakelh and Wet'suwet'en. Designed by the aluminum manufacturer Alcan to exploit the potential of water stored in the interior of the province to power a new smelter on the coast, Kemano re-engineered the region's hydrology. It blocked the upper Nechako River, reversing the flow of the river and forcing it through a 16-kilometre tunnel in the coastal mountains, where it dropped 790 vertical metres to a generating station.[170] In 1956, a feature in *National Geographic* extolled how the project made a chain of lakes into "an inland sea" that flowed backwards through a mountain where it descended through a manufactured "water fall 16 times higher than Niagara."[171] The provincial government legalized the damming of the Nechako in 1949, making an agreement with Alcan the following year that allowed the company to build the Kenney Dam and nine saddle dams to control the flow of water. Indigenous communities were not, however, consulted about the project and were only notified of it as the reservoir began to fill.[172] The installation of the dams was particularly devastating for the Cheslatta people whose communities would be flooded by the rising waters. "They had to move quick because the water was already coming up, so they didn't take too many things, just a few belongings," Cheslatta elder Ann Troy explained to geographer Soren Larsen.[173] The Cheslatta were initially forced into refugee camps, where they had to reorganize their displaced lives. Eventually, they reestablished themselves across a disparate patchwork of reserves on Wet'suwet'en territories.

Kemano disrupted the movements of fish, wildlife, and people around the Nechako River. Prior to the development, the federal Department of Fisheries and Oceans and the International Pacific Salmon Fisheries Commission had recommended design changes to protect spawning salmon; however, these recommendations were ignored.[174] The initial water licence issued by the province to Alcan did not include clauses to protect either migrating salmon or perennial fish stocks. Between 1952 and 1957, while the reservoir was initially filling with water, levels were so low that "the salmon... virtually disappeared."[175] After 1957, the company would release some water to the Nechako, but the river never regained its historic flow. In 1987, only an estimated 20 percent of the original flow remained, increasing river temperatures and impairing fish stocks.[176]

The Kemano Project would transform the rhythms of life in the watershed and across Northwest British Columbia. The giant reservoir disrupted the seasonal movements of salmon and caribou.[177] Among the Wet'suwet'en, this was particularly disruptive for the families associated with the Omineca Band whose reserves lay within the Nechako watershed. More than disrupting Indigenous lifeways, the project facilitated the transformation of a remote wilderness into the exemplar of a planned industrial development.[178] Industry magazines celebrated the Kemano Project as "the largest integrated engineering feat in history," enabling the company to build "the largest aluminum manufacturing center in the world, run by the largest power plant ever built."[179] Creating a place where a workingman could have "a year-round job" with "a three-bedroom house for the wife and children," the project exemplified Canadian aspirations for both industrial might and secure modern livelihoods.[180] In addition to producing a new industrial form of life at the smelter, the Kemano Project contributed to the electrification of households across the province through the sale of excess power to the public utility BC Hydro.[181] Harnessing the energetic capacity of the river, the project ruptured prior relations between Indigenous peoples and their waterways in order to create new possibilities for a modern life governed by industrial rhythms rather than natural seasons.[182]

The 1950s also saw government fisheries management in the Widzin Kwah watershed eroding vital access to sockeye salmon fisheries in Witset and Hagwilget. The historic sockeye salmon returns to the Widzin Kwah watershed ranged between fifty thousand and seventy thousand fish, but sockeye populations collapsed in the mid-1950s; from 1955 to 1975, Allen S. Gottesfeld and Ken A. Rabnett document that "an annual average of 4,000 sockeye returned to the watershed."[183] Overexploitation of resources was to blame: the viability of salmon stocks had been endangered by a combination of commercial overfishing on the coasts and logging of forest cover that sheltered the inland streams where salmon spawned.

The federal government imposed stricter regulations on fishing and hunting to address fish and wildlife conservation concerns.[184] They also made changes to the riverscape to aid fish movement and limit Indigenous fishing. Specifically, the government sought to remedy declining fish stocks first by building fish ladders in the canyon at Witset in 1951, then by blasting rocks from the Hagwilget Canyon in 1958.[185] Changing the geophysical structure of the canyon deprived several *yikh* of their traditional access to the fishery, as each *yikh* had specific fishing sites. In Hagwilget, the blasting effectively eliminated the entire fishery in the canyon.[186] These actions facilitated the colonization of the Widzin Kwah by pink salmon, but did not help sockeye numbers.[187] By the 1980s, annual sockeye returns had further declined to an average of 2,500 fish. The ultimate effect of Canadian fisheries management in the Widzin Kwah was to undermine the autonomy and self-sufficiency of Wet'suwet'en families.

Forestry had emerged as a prominent industry in the Bulkley Valley with the arrival of the railway, and the transformation of forestry in the postwar period radically remade the resource economy in Northwest British Columbia. Concerned with the unstable boom-and-bust patterns of resource development, the government appointed two successive Royal Commissions on Forestry, both headed by Chief Justice Gordon Sloan, which issued reports in 1945 and 1956. Sloan recommended changes in forest governance to maximize the value derived from provincial forests, emphasizing the importance of installing a system of sustained-yield management that ensured stable profit margins for resource companies.[188] Specifically, he proposed stabilizing forest economies by transforming the system of temporary forest tenures to a structure that provided secure access to particular companies through area-based or volume-based tenures. Providing firms with exclusive rights to appropriate forest resources, he argued, would guarantee a stable timber supply that would encourage large investments and could help rationalize the provision of steady employment.

The new forest regulations privileged large companies and led to centralizing production in resource towns. Mechanization further transformed logging, increasing productivity while reducing labour requirements.[189] A shift from horse teams to truck hauling enabled loggers to work shifts and return to town rather than spending weeks in isolated camps.[190] In town, standardizing production at modern mills further reorganized labour processes, establishing new forms of expertise as the territorial knowledge required of bush mill operators was replaced with new, engineered milling processes.[191] The impacts on the Bulkley Valley forest industry were dramatic. In the local forest management area, the number of operations holding timber tenure went from thirty to three between 1960 and 1969.[192] With modernization, the nature of milling was transformed. Small seasonal bush mills were replaced by huge mill operations concentrated in central resource towns and operated year-round.[193]

To better connect the region, the government made massive investments in road and airport infrastructure. In 1941, the federal Department of Transportation built the Smithers airport, easing access to the Bulkley Valley.[194] After the war, the provincial government made massive investments in roads and highways to expand development to the North. Between 1952 and 1958, "more money was spent building highways than in the entire history of the province."[195] In peripheral resource-dependent regions, the transformation of transportation systems "enabled immigrants to settle, knowing that they would be in touch with home and with many familiar ways."[196] In 1941, there were 4,862 people in the regional Skeena-Bulkley census subdivision, with Indigenous people composing 38 percent of the population. Over the next twenty years, the population would more than double, reaching 10,121, with European immigrants composing the bulk of the increase.[197]

With employer discrimination providing white newcomers advantages over Indigenous workers, the rise in the settler population resulted in escalating rates of Wet'suwet'en unemployment. Previously, regional labour shortages had ensured that Wet'suwet'en workers were able to find work. Increased immigration transformed these dynamics, excluding Wet'suwet'en families from the benefits of postwar economic growth.[198] In the midst of growing prosperity, Indigenous peoples faced increased relative poverty.[199] Describing conditions for Indigenous workers in 1967, J.N. McFarlane, the superintendent of the Babine Indian Agency, expressed that there "was not enough work in the area to employ all of the employables."[200] Alongside the decline in Wet'suwet'en employment opportunities, there was a significant erosion of sustenance livelihood opportunities.

The intensification of resource-extractive regimes simultaneously undermined the capacity of Wet'suwet'en *yikh* to use their territories. For instance, to maximize the exploitation of timber, the government promoted clearcutting practices that damaged forest ecosystems.[201] Expanded resource extraction, Harris explains, had far more harmful impacts to Indigenous territories than the earlier reserve allocation process.

> *As long as Natives had been able to hunt, fish, and gather in their former territories, the small reserves the reserve commissioners laid out for them had little meaning; however, the implications of reserves, and the exclusions they entailed, became ever more apparent as non-Natives occupied and used the surrounding land. A logging operation in a mountain valley previously used for seasonal hunting marked a huge transformation of land use and power. For those experiencing it, colonialism was enacted locally, on the ground.*[202]

As the network of roads and cutblocks extended into the resource hinterland, Indigenous territories were continuously opened for development and Indigenous hunters were forced to travel further and further to find game.

Denied access to work and subsistence activities, a growing number of Wet'suwet'en families were pushed into reliance on emerging welfare programs. At the beginning of the twentieth century, Indigenous dependence on the colonial state was virtually unknown. By 1966, Lutz documents that "25.4 percent of the on-reserve Indian population in British Columbia received financial assistance, more than eight times the provincial average." Indigenous dependency continued to intensify as corporate regimes of resource extraction expanded. By 1972–1973, 47 percent of Indigenous people in British Columbia had become dependent on social assistance. [203]

In the 1960s, there was also an explosion in the rate of Indigenous child apprehensions, as provincial social workers began to surveil Indigenous families. The federal government had until then long relied upon Indian residential schools to act as orphanages and child welfare facilities. In an effort to reorient policy to integrate Indigenous people into provincial governance structures, the federal government negotiated with the province to extend British Columbia's child and family services jurisdiction over Indigenous children.

In 1960, the provincial Department of Social Welfare reported that "60 per cent of the almost 500 children in foster-home care are of Native Indian extraction."[204] This issue was particularly acute in the Smithers-Hazelton area—on Wet'suwet'en and Gitxsan territories—where the local Department of Social Welfare supervisor had assessed that 23.5 percent of the regional population of Status Indian children was in a condition of neglect.[205] He deemed 112 cases—representing ten percent of the population—to be in need of immediate intervention, observing the highest rates of neglect in the Moricetown, Hagwilget, and Gitanmaax bands.

The high rate of assessed child neglect had a number of interconnected causes. Social workers, typically from middle-class suburban areas in the Lower Mainland, focused on evaluating nuclear family units and did not appreciate the broad networks of kinship that supported children in Wet'suwet'en and Gitxsan society.[206] Moreover, the economic marginalization of many Indigenous families, displaced from both the job market and subsistence opportunities, made them "vulnerable to especially negative appraisal by middle-class reformers."[207] Indigenous families had also been burdened with the damaging legacy of the Indian residential schools. The abuse and neglect that former students experienced at residential schools had lasting effects. Among the Wet'suwet'en, "alcoholism increased dramatically as a result of children being removed and families being torn apart, which also increased family violence."[208] These conditions, combined with provincial policies criminalizing Indigenous drinking, led to high rates of arrests and significantly contributed to child apprehensions.[209]

Child apprehensions decimated Wet'suwet'en families and tore apart kinship networks, already weakened by the Indian residential school system. As Molly Wickham describes,

> *children and youth are often disconnected from their families and communities, which necessarily disrupts cultural transmission and a sense of belonging. Children grow up learning that white people must care for Indigenous children because native families either cannot or do not want to care for their own children...*

*Consequently, confusion, hate, internalized racism, and anger are often emotions and feelings with which young displaced Indigenous people must contend.*[210]

Like Indian residential schools, the foster care system was underfunded and lacked adequate oversight, contributing to alarming rates of neglect and abuse in foster homes. Unlike residential schools, where children would continue to periodically return to the community and spend summers with their families, in many cases child apprehensions completely severed community and kin connections. Many apprehended Indigenous children either remained permanently in the foster care system or were adopted out.

Thus, while the postwar period yielded sustained economic security and improved material conditions for many white settlers, it was a period of sustained, violent attack on Wet'suwet'en territorial and kinship relations. The colonial subtext of the expansion of the corporate extractive economy was obscured by an emergent public discourse of colour-blindness and multicultural acceptance. While explicitly racist legislation in the early twentieth century had sought to systemically privilege white workers, northern labour shortages ensured that opportunities remained for Wet'suwet'en workers. Moreover, the relatively limited scale of development in Northwest British Columbia ensured that opportunities for traditional subsistence practices endured. The intensified rate of development, aided by provincial policies favouring the corporatization of extractive industries, greatly eroded conditions for many Wet'suwet'en families.

**The Reassertion of Indigenous Rights**

Indigenous peoples did not simply acquiesce to the intensification of processes of colonial dispossession. Indigenous mobilizations expanded in response to postwar political and economic changes. For almost a century, the government of British Columbia had made Indigenous people subject to racially discriminatory laws without giving them the opportunity to participate in the political system making those laws. However, after World War II, the governments of British Columbia and Canada began to expand recognition of Indigenous political freedoms. In 1949, the government of British Columbia extended the franchise to Indigenous people, allowing them to vote in provincial elections.[211] In 1951, the Canadian government repealed the bans on the potlatch and the pursuit of Indigenous land claims, which went into effect, respectively, in 1886 and 1927. Then, in 1960, the Canadian government recognized the ability of Indigenous people to vote in federal elections.[212] As government policy in the second half of the twentieth century shifted towards the integration of Indigenous people as rights-bearing subjects in Canadian society, Indigenous peoples leveraged these rights to challenge colonial relations.

Initially, settler authorities treated the postwar political integration of Indigenous citizens as the culmination of the colonial project of assimilating Indigenous people into Canadian society. These aspirations were made explicit in the 1969 White Paper, a policy proposal to eliminate the legal distinction between Indian peoples and other Canadians.[213] The document, officially titled "Statement of the Government of Canada on Indian Policy," specifically proposed the repeal of the Indian Act, the elimination of legal recognition of Indian status, the dissolution of the Department of Indian Affairs, the transfer of responsibility for Indigenous peoples to provincial governments, and the termination of Indigenous treaty rights. The assimilationist White Paper sought to instill a common citizenship based on a historical amnesia that foreclosed consideration of how Canadian sovereignty was founded upon the suppression of Indigenous polities. Prime Minister Pierre Elliott Trudeau argued that to progress, a nation must forget many things and "not try to undo...the past."[214] Attempting to completely efface Indigenous polities and project Canada as a singular and unified people, Trudeau rejected the historical and contemporary relevance of treaties with Indigenous peoples. "It's inconceivable," Trudeau stated, "that in a given society one section of the society have a treaty with the other section of the society."[215]

The White Paper was undergirded by an impulse to reduce the financial costs of administering the Indian Affairs system, which the government increasingly recognized as failing to improve Indigenous life conditions.[216] In particular, the policy proposal aimed to address increasing Indigenous dependency on the state and encourage a renewal of Indigenous self-sufficiency. The language of the White Paper was explicit: "To be an Indian is to lack power—the power to act as owner of your lands, the power to spend your own money and, too often, the power to change your own condition."[217] The policy proposal specifically targeted the Indian band and reserve system that the government had created a century earlier, recognizing that reserves had not protected Indigenous interests. They had concentrated Indigenous populations in a state of deprivation, excluding them from the extractive economy that was developing on their broader territories. As a solution, the government sought to simply assimilate Indigenous people into the Canadian body politic, removing reserve protections and extending Indigenous access to private property rights.

Indigenous leaders denounced the proposal as a form of cultural genocide that abandoned government responsibilities to Indigenous peoples in a callous campaign to cut costs.[218] They refused to accept that a settler government possessed the authority to define the terms of contemporary Indigenous political life without meaningful engagement with Indigenous communities. Indigenous peoples became increasingly politicized in the process of fighting the White Paper, and their challenge to the federal government was effective.[219] The White Paper was shelved, and the contemporary Indigenous movement was born of a shared struggle against colonial authority. Indigenous peoples demanded the devolution of control over disciplinary institutions governing Indigenous life, such as schools and community economic development programs, to Indigenous authorities.[220] Recognizing that Indigenous people possessed rights to self-government, the federal government devolved control of services and programming to Indian band governments.[221] This resulted in increasing administrative authority for band governments over the operation of institutions and services on reserve, creating opportunities to integrate Indigenous projects of subjectification within disciplinary institutions, like schools, that were originally established as colonial enterprises.

Indigenous peoples also used their expanding access to the courts to press rights claims, asserting the continued salience of foundational relationships established between Indigenous peoples and the Crown during the fur trade. For Indigenous peoples, access to justice provided a pathway not to integration and formal equality with white settler subjects but to recognition of their distinct position as Indigenous peoples. After the removal of the federal ban on Indian land claims activity, the Nishga Tribal Council was established to advance Nisga'a title claims.[222] In this, they extended the legacy of the Nishga Land Committee, which had sought to advance Nisga'a title claims in the early twentieth century.[223] Frank Calder led the Nishga Tribal Council from its founding in 1955 until 1974. When the Nisga'a took their title claim to court in 1967, Calder's name was on the case. In *Calder et al. v. Attorney-General of British Columbia*, the Nishga Tribal Council sought a declaration that their Aboriginal title to the lands they historically occupied on the Northwest Coast of British Columbia had never been extinguished. Conversely, the British Columbia government argued that, although it never enacted legislation to explicitly extinguish Indigenous land claims, the fact that it had enacted laws regarding land use implied government intent to extinguish any Indigenous land rights that interfered with the general application of provincial laws.

In its 1973 decision, the Supreme Court of Canada provided partial recognition of Nisga'a title.[224] A majority of the court's seven justices recognized the validity of the concept of Aboriginal title in common law. The six justices that rendered substantive decisions in *Calder* agreed that the Nisga'a possessed the rights they claimed in court prior to contact. However, the court was split on the question of whether colonial legislation had extinguished Nisga'a title. Three justices ruled that Nisga'a title had not been extinguished by statute or treaty, three justices ruled that it had. The deciding justice ruled against the Nisga'a on a procedural technicality, thereby avoiding the question of title.

Though the Nisga'a technically lost their case, the Supreme Court's ruling in *Calder* created legal uncertainty regarding the status of Aboriginal title, and thus troubled settler-colonial claims to unfettered sovereign authority over the land. Subsequently, the federal government released the 1973 "Statement on Claims of

Indian and Inuit People," indicating its willingness to negotiate comprehensive land claims with Indigenous peoples in Canada.[225] However, in British Columbia, the provincial government remained steadfast in opposing Indigenous land claims and resolute in their conviction that no precedent had been established by the split decision in *Calder*. It maintained that British Columbian legislation of general application had demonstrated a clear and plain intent to extinguish Indigenous land claims and provide an unfettered land title to settlers. Despite the provincial government's obstinance, Indigenous peoples in British Columbia continued to organize around the land question.

Following the model of the Nisga'a, Gitxsan and Wet'suwet'en community members also created a new organization to advance their rights. In 1968, they formed the Gitksan-Carrier Tribal Council (named according to the convention at the time to refer to the Wet'suwet'en as a Carrier people). Its mandate included preserving Gitxsan and Wet'suwet'en heritage and identity, improving their social and economic conditions, and achieving a just resolution to their legal claims to land and self-government rights. The organization claimed to represent "all people of Gitksan and Carrier ancestry, regardless of [Indian] status, if they belong to or descend from one of the following villages: Kitwangak, Kitseguecla, Gitanmaax, Sikadoak, Kispiox, Hagwilget and Moricetown."[226] This constituted all the Gitxsan bands at the time except Kitwancool, and all the Wet'suwet'en bands at the time except Omineca and Burns Lake.[227]

The Gitksan-Carrier Tribal Council, and its exclusions, reflected the divisions that the Department of Indian Affairs' mid-century reorganization of agency boundaries had created. To the south, the Lakes District Tribal Council was incorporated in 1979 to represent the interests of bands in the Central Interior of British Columbia in land claims negotiations. Soon renamed the Carrier Sekani Tribal Council, the council included not only the Dakelh and Tse'khene peoples to the south and east of Wet'suwet'en territories, but also the Wet'suwet'en members of the Omineca and Burns Lake bands, as well as the Nedut'en and Dakelh members of the Lake Babine and Cheslatta bands who had been displaced to reserves on Wet'suwet'en territories.

Political resistance to the White Paper and legal challenges in the *Calder* case represent two poles of Indigenous political resurgence that emerged through the late 1960s and early 1970s. Resistance to the White Paper reconfigured the workings of Indian politics. Bands, and lobby groups representing their interests, fought for and won control over reserve communities. Instead of terminating the Indian Act, bands demanded an end to settler government paternalism and the transfer of administrative authority over programming and services for band members. Rather than simply erasing the colonially imposed structures of reserve lands and band governance, chiefs operating under the Indian Act demanded that authority over band members on reserve be devolved to community-elected band councils. The *Calder* case, in contrast, focused on forwarding the distinct claim of the Nisga'a. This case raised the spectre of Indigenous legal claims based on relationships to territories beyond the reserve, unsettling not only the presumption of colonial authority over the lives of Status Indians but the claim of settler sovereignty over unceded Indigenous lands. These two challenges fettered the exercise of colonial power. The uncertainty created by Indigenous mobilizations made room for new spaces of negotiation and contestation that would be expanded in subsequent decades, particularly as Wet'suwet'en authorities asserted further claims to self-government and territorial jurisdiction.

# 2

# From Renunciation to Reconciliation

*Colonialism Goes to Court*

ON MAY 11, 1987, the historic *Delgamuukw, Gisdaywa v. British Columbia* trial began in the Smithers courthouse. In the case, the Gitxsan and Wet'suwet'en hereditary chiefs presented to the British Columbia Supreme Court a claim to ownership of and jurisdiction over their traditional territories. The case would fundamentally call into question settler-colonial presumptions about territory and sovereignty in the Northwest Interior. Through the case, the Gitxsan and Wet'suwet'en hereditary chiefs provided evidence on their distinct system of laws and sought to force the provincial government to recognize Indigenous forms of authority and territorial governance. The case has become one of the most monumental not only in Canadian history, but also in the global history of anti-colonial legal struggles. The *Delgamuukw, Gisdaywa* case required 318 days to introduce the evidence and 56 days to argue. The trial record includes 23,503 pages of transcribed trial evidence, 5,898 pages of transcribed oral argument, 3,039 pages of commission evidence, 2,553 pages of cross-examination on affidavits, and approximately 9,200 exhibits comprising 50,000 pages, making the case one of the most extensive ever tried in Canada.[1] From the filing of writ in 1984 through to trial and subsequent appeals, legal proceedings lasted over a decade. The Supreme Court of Canada issued its decision in 1997.

In *Delgamuukw, Gisdaywa*, the Gitxsan and Wet'suwet'en plaintiffs grounded their case in the expertise of hereditary chiefs in their own legal traditions. Two hereditary chiefs—Delgamuukw on behalf of the Gitxsan and Gisdaywa on behalf of the Wet'suwet'en, titles then respectively held by Ken Muldoe and Alfred Joseph—collaborated to make the opening statement. Delgamuukw explained, "For us, the ownership of the territory is a marriage of the Chief and the land. Each Chief has an ancestor who encountered and acknowledged the life of the land. From such encounters come power...This is the basis of our law."[2] Gisdaywa elaborated:

*The Chief is responsible for ensuring that all the people in his House [yikh] respect the spirit in the land and in all living things. When a Chief directs his House [yikh] properly and the laws are followed, then that original power can be recreated. That is the source of the Chief's authority...That authority is what makes the Chiefs the real experts in this case.*[3]

Placing Gitxsan and Wet'suwet'en forms of authority and territory before the judge, the hereditary chiefs sought to pluralize the legal traditions operant within the Canadian courts. The hereditary chiefs strategically forced the Canadian judiciary to reckon with Indigenous law, articulating an Indigenous alterity that exceeded colonial frames.

The litigation strategy sought to reorder relationships between settler and Indigenous authorities, but also subjected Gitxsan and Wet'suwet'en claims to the potential violence of a disavowal by the colonial judiciary. On March 8, 1991, Justice Allan McEachern, who presided over *Delgamuukw, Gisdaywa*, issued a decision that can aptly be described as violent. McEachern's decision was replete with racist calumny depicting the Gitxsan and Wet'suwet'en as uncivilized and, quoting Thomas Hobbes, going so far as to describe how pre-contact "aboriginal life in the territory was, at best, 'nasty, brutish and short.'"[4] Ultimately, he found that Gitxsan and Wet'suwet'en ownership and jurisdiction were displaced by the superiority of settler society.

McEachern's decision would be overturned on appeal. A decade after the trial began, on December 11, 1997, the Supreme Court of Canada issued its decision on the *Delgamuukw, Gisdaywa* case. The majority of the court overturned the lower court's decision and ordered a retrial on the basis of mishandled evidence at trial.[5] Although the Supreme Court of Canada justices retained and entrenched substantial elements of colonial thought in their reasoning, they nonetheless established an important precedent that requires the Crown, both federally and provincially, to consider Indigenous knowledge and negotiate with Indigenous peoples. The decision explicitly urged the Canadian and provincial governments to negotiate with Indigenous peoples around the unresolved question of land title in British Columbia. While the Supreme Court of Canada's decision on *Delgamuukw, Gisdaywa* offered the Gitxsan and Wet'suwet'en hereditary chiefs no immediate remedy, it significantly contributed to the emergence of new regimes of engagement and new devices to reconcile the exercise of colonial power with Indigenous peoples and their interests.

*Delgamuukw, Gisdaywa* challenged the disciplinary processes governing conduct in the courtroom, the normalized assumptions of colonial territorial authority, and ultimately the way in which the land is governed in British Columbia. Focusing on what legal geographies scholar Nicholas Blomley refers to as "the law-space nexus,"[6] my analysis aims to elucidate the productive effects of courtroom interactions between colonial law and Indigenous peoples. From one angle, I explore how settler law shapes the spatialities of courtroom conduct and the juridical determinations of territorial jurisdiction; from another angle, I examine how performances of Indigenous alterity in the courtroom challenge dominant conceptions of space and reorder Canadian law by introducing different relations of territorial jurisdiction. Rather than simply critiquing colonial presumptions or celebrating Indigenous traditions, I pursue questions of knowledge, authority, and reconciliation raised by the case and bring attention to how this instance of Indigenous legal contestation has produced new relationships with the settler state. My argument can be distilled to the following: although settler norms within the courts constrained and enframed Gitxsan and Wet'suwet'en claims by setting the terms of what could and could not be said, the hereditary chiefs' litigation in *Delgamuukw, Gisdaywa* nonetheless served to work at the fractures of colonial law. The *Delgamuukw, Gisdaywa* case highlighted the incredible disjuncture between historical recognition of Indigenous peoples in the fur trade and contemporary British Columbian practice of colonial disregard. Into this gap, the hereditary chiefs sought to press recognition of Indigenous legal orders, thus disrupting and reforming the dominant Canadian legal paradigm.

The following pages lay out debates over courtroom proceedings, unpack how the court approached the standing and authority of Gitxsan and Wet'suwet'en hereditary chiefs, and ultimately ask political questions of how settlement and development should be reconciled with Aboriginal rights. This analysis highlights the productive as well as oppressive character of relations established between Indigeneity and colonialism in the courts. Throughout *Delgamuukw, Gisdaywa*, settler authority and the colonial conduct of lawful relations were consistently entangled with Indigenous systems of knowledge and authority. While I am sympathetic to critiques of the colonizing logic of Canadian juridical authority, this entanglement suggests that settler sovereignty should not be understood as monolithic or overarching, nor as the simple and unfettered possession of settler authorities. Ultimately, I argue the effect of the *Delgamuukw, Gisdaywa* decision was not to settle the issue of competing colonial and Indigenous claims but instead to midwife the emergence of new techniques for reconciling competing claims to territory and authority.

### Of Knowledge and Reason

The tactical decision of the plaintiffs in *Delgamuukw, Gisdaywa* to lead not with the expertise of Western-trained academics but rather with that of the Gitxsan and Wet'suwet'en authorities on their legal traditions raised significant questions regarding evidentiary norms. As previously mentioned, the incredible evidentiary complexity involved in the case made *Delgamuukw, Gisdaywa* one of the longest cases in Canadian history. Eighteen hereditary chiefs testified in the trial, and an additional ten Gitxsan and Wet'suwet'en community members, elders, and other experts gave evidence. A further fifteen witnesses provided evidence on commission, and fifty-three Gitxsan and Wet'suwet'en community members provided territorial affidavits, thirty of which were subject to cross-examination. I was in elementary school when the case originally went to trial and had limited direct knowledge of its proceedings. However, the 369 volumes of trial transcripts, voir dire decisions related to the admissibility of evidence, and decisions on *Delgamuukw, Gisdaywa* produced through the trial, appellate court, and Supreme Court of Canada, have provided me a rich record for inquiry.

These texts bear the trace of both colonial discipline and an Indigenous alterity that disrupted colonial disciplinary regimes. In making their claims in the court, the hereditary chiefs both submitted themselves to the forms of power-knowledge that organized courtroom practice and challenged the norms governing these processes through systematically breaching their conventions. Herb George, who holds the Wet'suwet'en title Satsan, describes how the Gitxsan and Wet'suwet'en entered what they recognized as a rigged game with the intent of changing the rules. About the hereditary chiefs' decision to go to court, he writes, "We chose...to challenge the whole bloody game, to say that this game is wrong...This is a fixed game. We want to see a change."[7] In going to court, the Gitxsan and Wet'suwet'en hereditary chiefs exposed their traditions to the trial judge, McEachern, challenging him to recognize the depth of their knowledge.

This had mixed but ultimately transformative effects. McEachern allowed Gitxsan and Wet'suwet'en hereditary chiefs considerable latitude with regard to the types of evidence they submitted at trial; in weighing their evidence, however, he dismissed its value on the basis of Gitxsan and Wet'suwet'en witnesses' failure to accord with the Canadian judicial conventions of evidentiary behaviour.[8] McEachern's decision was largely upheld at the appellate court. The justices of the Supreme Court of Canada, however, declared McEachern's decision critically flawed based on his treatment of evidence, necessitating a retrial. This judgment established precedence for considering Indigenous knowledge and giving it weight in decision-making, redefining the evidentiary frameworks governing legal procedure in Canada.[9] Thus, although the initial reception of Gitxsan and Wet'suwet'en performances highlighted how juridical norms discipline subaltern speech in the courts, Gitxsan and Wet'suwet'en manifestations were not simply controlled by court discipline. These witnesses presented challenges that ultimately reordered courtroom practice and expanded space for performing Indigenous difference within legal proceedings.

At trial, Gitxsan and Wet'suwet'en witnesses testified to the complexity of their social order and the elaborate practices involved in maintaining and reaffirming the connection between a house—the common English translation of the Wet'suwet'en *yikh* and Gitxsan *wilp*—and its territories. Rather than casting their existence within the bureaucratic frames of colonial legislation, the Gitxsan and Wet'suwet'en witnesses focused on the enduring matrilineal system organizing their society. As Wet'suwet'en witnesses described, children are born into a *yikh* and *dïdikh* by virtue of conventions of matrilineal descent. Similarly, Gitxsan children are born into a *wilp* and *p'teex*. Each *wilp* or *yikh*, led by a hereditary chief, possesses distinct territories.[10] A *yikh* or *wilp* publicly exhibits their claim to a particular territory in the feast hall by demonstrating their possession of particular histories, displaying specific crests, and enacting unique performances. The account of Gitxsan and Wet'suwet'en culture accrued through an accumulation of evidence from a range of witnesses who, following the conventions of Gitxsan and Wet'suwet'en law, only spoke about the conduct of their own *yikh* or *wilp* and *dïdikh* or *p'teex* at the trial. The evidence these witnesses presented posed a number of difficult questions to the court. For instance, how would the court approach knowledge emplaced within Indigenous epistemologies and ontologies? And how could knowledge of Indigenous systems of territoriality be transliterated to fit within conventions familiar to settler authorities?

The performances of the Gitxsan and Wet'suwet'en witnesses in the court were enframed by the spatiality of the state. Critically interrogating the power relations immanent to the organization of the court through the *Delgamuukw, Gisdaywa* trial, Matthew

Sparke argues that "radically resistant courtroom performances were simply policed and cordoned off with bold disrespect."[11] Despite conjuring a supposedly neutral space of colonial statecraft, as Timothy Mitchell argues with regard to the colonial exhibitionary order in Egypt, a set of disciplinary regimes coordinated discursive possibilities and normalized particular power relations.[12]

The dislocating effects of placing Gitxsan and Wet'suwet'en performances within the court system were made abundantly clear when, six weeks into the trial, Justice McEachern, faced with the unsettling issues raised by the plaintiffs' evidence, decided to move the trial from Wet'suwet'en territories in Smithers to Vancouver, 1,200 kilometres to the south, to ease conditions for the court. The move increased the cost of the trial for the Indigenous plaintiffs, as Gitxsan and Wet'suwet'en witnesses now had to travel a great distance from their community to testify. More importantly, the move, which the hereditary chiefs lacked the authority within the court to prevent, placed a terrible strain on the Gitxsan and Wet'suwet'en communities. Motivated by what Sparke describes as "a modern western concept of justice applying equally, everywhere within the abstract space of the state," McEachern privileged his own convenience over the hardship that dislocating the trial hundreds of kilometres would have on the impoverished northern Indigenous communities.[13] Beyond the financial burden, the move isolated the court from the local networks of community support that had surrounded Gitxsan and Wet'suwet'en witnesses in the North. As Sparke again ably articulates, the geographies orienting the courtroom evidenced a "geometry of power" that demonstrated how "the spatial order of the legal system tends to be mapped out in abstract state-space."[14] Thus, the desires and intentions of administrators of state law, such as McEachern, coordinated the operations of the legal system with little regard for the concerns of the Gitxsan and Wet'suwet'en people seeking justice through that legal system.

The disciplinary workings of the power within the courtroom extended beyond questions of the trial location to micro-geographies of court architecture and performance. The court worked to individualize witnesses on the stand, closing them off from the contexts of their lives and separating them from the interwoven community connections that defined their communal identities. Sparke critiques this individualized geography as constructing "a very difficult space for the Gitxsan and Wet'suwet'en people to enter into as collective nations."[15] The spatial compartmentalization of the court's disciplinary apparatus isolated each witness. Further, the practices of antagonistic courtroom exchange did not accord well with the traditional forms of exposition and debate within Gitxsan and Wet'suwet'en legal practice in the feast hall. The court was conducted in a foreign language for many of the eldest Gitxsan and Wet'suwet'en witnesses; even for those familiar with the English, courtroom discourse relied upon a technical jargon that was often incomprehensible to those untrained in the traditions of British and Canadian common law. The court presented a difficult space for Gitxsan and Wet'suwet'en witnesses because the structures of Gitxsan and Wet'suwet'en law that underpinned the authority of the hereditary chiefs was fragmented and reordered within the disciplinary system of the courtroom.

Similarly, the disciplinary apparatus governing courtroom procedure limited the extent to which Gitxsan and Wet'suwet'en traditions could be introduced into the court. The Gitxsan evidence centred on the *adaawk*, the oral histories that contain the stories of a *wilp*, which define the *wilp* members' relationship to their territories. To an extent, this parallels the Wet'suwet'en concept of *cin k'ikh*, the trail of song that tracks the connection of particular *yikh* to its land. Leslie Hall Pinder, one of the plaintiffs' lawyers, put it plainly: the *adaawk* and *cin k'ikh* are "their evidence, their proof, their case."[16] When counsel for the plaintiffs directed Mary Johnson, who then held the Gitxsan hereditary title Antgulilibix, to perform a *limx'ooy*, or dirge song, associated with her *adaawk*, McEachern complained.

> MR. GRANT *(Plaintiffs' Counsel): The song is part of the history, and I am asking the witness to sing the song as part of the history, because I think in the song itself, invokes the*

> *history of the—of the particular* adaawk *to which she is referring.*
>
> JUSTICE MCEACHERN: *How long is it?*
>
> GRANT: *It's not very long, it's very short.*
>
> MCEACHERN: *Could it not be written out and asked if this is the wording? Really, we are on the verge of getting way off track here, Mr. Grant. Again, I don't want to be skeptical, but to have witnesses singing songs in court is in my respectful view not the proper way to approach this problem.*
>
> GRANT: *My Lord, Mr. Jackson [another member of the Plaintiffs' Counsel] will make a submission to you with respect—*
>
> MCEACHERN: *No, no, that isn't necessary. If this has to be done, if you say as counsel this has to be done, I'm going to listen to it. I just say, with respect, I've never heard it happen before, I never thought it necessary, and I don't think it necessary now. But I'll be glad to hear what the witness says if you say that this is what she has to do. It doesn't seem to me she has to sing it.*
>
> GRANT: *Well, My Lord, with respect, the song is—is what one may refer to as a death song. It's a song which itself invokes the history and the depth of the history of what she is telling. And as counsel, it is—it is my submission that it is necessary for you to appreciate—*
>
> MCEACHERN: *I have a tin ear, Mr. Grant, so it's not going to do any good to sing it to me.*[17]

Antgulilibix sang her *limx'ooy* to the court. McEachern instructed that it would be unnecessary to have the translator conduct a line-by-line translation of the song, so Antgulilibix roughly translated it. The song related a story about two sisters who caught a grouse, subsequently remembered their deceased brother, and cried and sang a dirge for the grouse who "gave himself up to die for them to help them save their lives."[18]

While the plaintiffs' counsel argued that the song, as part of Antgulilibix's *adaawk*, served as a vital part of her history and claim to the territory, the judge disagreed.

*FIGURE 3.1 Mary Johnson, Gitxsan hereditary chief Antgulilibix, singing a song associated with her adaawk to Justice McEachern. (Used with permission from Don Monet.)*

> *It seems to me the fact of expressing their ownership or their claim to ownership through songs is a fact to be proven in the ordinary way. It is not necessary, in my view, and in a matter of this kind for that song to have been sung, and I think that I must say now that I—I think I ought not to have been exposed to it. I don't think it should happen again. If it is sought to be—to have that sort of evidence adduced in future, I will expect further and more detailed submissions, because I think I'm being imposed upon and I don't think that should happen in a trial like this.*[19]

Although McEachern permitted a significant amount of oral history, including the recounting of various stories of seemingly fantastical creatures and events, his comments constructed an unwelcoming climate that discouraged the hereditary chiefs from presenting particular forms of evidence. Indeed, Antgulilibix's *limx'ooy* is notable as a variation from the norms of courtroom behaviour but also as a particularly bold performance of Indigenous alterity before the court.

As trial proceeded, counsel for the plaintiffs worked to construct alternative processes to enable a more efficacious method of collecting evidence. Four weeks into the trial, McEachern complained to the plaintiffs' counsel that evidence was being adduced at "less than a snail's pace," and he was having "terrible problems" with the nature of the evidence involved in the case.[20] To speed the collection of evidence and reduce the necessary court time, the plaintiffs made a series of proposals to amend the process of adducing evidence. First, rather than trying to comprehensively prove the territorial and jurisdictional claims of every *wilp* and *yikh* in the action, the plaintiffs focused on a representative subset of them whose evidence would stand for the broader collective. Second, witnesses gave evidence on commission. Prior to trial, evidence was collected by commission, in the presence of counsel for both the plaintiffs and the defence, from eight witnesses who were deemed potentially unable to attend trial due to physical disability or illness. This process was expanded to reduce the amount of court time used in the case and particularly to expedite the lengthy delays associated with translating evidence from Indigenous languages to English. Third, the plaintiffs provided territorial evidence in a series of territorial affidavits, which the defence had the opportunity to cross-examine. The commission evidence and territorial affidavits served to abridge the lengthy process of taking direct evidence on the territorial holdings on the stand.

Accepting evidence collected on commission enabled the judge to both abbreviate the trial time and bracket unsettling performances, such as evidence adduced through song, to the pages of commission evidence. Thus, although Wet'suwet'en hereditary chiefs Lilloos (Emma Michell) and Maxlaxlex (Johnny David), and Gitxsan hereditary chiefs Xhliimlaxha (Martha Brown), Lelt (Fred Johnson), and 'Niik'aap (David Gunanoot) included songs as part of the commission evidence they provided, their songs were effectively excluded from court.[21] Their evidence was only included in the *Delgamuukw, Gisdaywa* proceedings in the form of written transcripts, and these transcripts only recorded Indigenous language proceedings in English "translations" that left much to be desired. Even when a song was sung in court, then, it was largely quieted from the record. For instance, when Lilloos sang the beaver song, the record reports "WITNESS SINGS SONG." When Peter Grant, counsel for the plaintiffs, asked for a full translation of the song, the translator, George Holland, offered, "Courses are repeating. Watch him slap his tail as he swims and watch the bark flow from him. Basically what the song is about."[22] The cadence and effect of the song thus dissolve into the summary of a few repeated lines. The court process, as Pinder describes in her memoir, amounted to a "sophisticated technology" through which lawyers "destroyed the stories" by requiring witnesses to "cut the words, even our written words, away from the environment, and hold them up as pieces of meaning, hacked up pieces of meaning."[23]

Signalling his leanings on the inclusion of Gitxsan and Wet'suwet'en oral evidence in the courtroom, McEachern issued a preliminary declaration on the admissibility of historical evidence after six weeks of trial.[24] Conventionally, the hearsay rule in Canadian courts delimits the extent to which witnesses can report the words and experiences of others. Indigenous oral history, which relies upon the knowledge of previous generations who are not available for cross-examination, presented a challenge to the court. Counsel for the Gitxsan and Wet'suwet'en argued for a wider interpretation of evidentiary rules, emphasizing that a narrow interpretation of admissible evidence would prevent the hereditary chiefs from demonstrating the origins of their crests and connections to their territories—the foundation of their legal claim. McEachern allowed Gitxsan and Wet'suwet'en witnesses to share elements of their *adaawk* and *cin k'ikh*, deferring final judgment on the weight of Indigenous oral evidence. However, he expressed concern regarding what he referred to as the "anecdotal" character of much Indigenous oral history: "Historical facts sought to be adduced must be truly historical and not anecdotal."[25] The issue of evidence remained contentious at trial. In March 1989, after listening to Gitxsan and Wet'suwet'en expert testimony for nearly two years, McEachern reiterated that while he was willing to allow the submission of Indigenous oral history, he intended to disregard it "if it is contradicted, or if its value as evidence is destroyed or lessened either internally or by other admissible evidence, or by common sense."[26]

Eliding the salience of Indigenous testimony to understanding jurisdiction within Gitxsan and Wet'suwet'en legal orders, McEachern gave very little weight to the *adaawk* and *cin k'ikh* in his final reasons for judgment. "Except in a very few cases, the totality of the evidence raises serious doubts about the reliability of the *adaawk* and *kungax* [*cin k'ikh*] as evidence of detailed history, or land ownership, use or occupation"[27] McEachern dismissed the reliability of Indigenous processes of witnessing oral histories, criticizing the plaintiffs for espousing "a romantic view of their history, which leads them to believe their remote ancestors were always in specific parts of the territory, in perfect harmony with natural forces, actually doing what the plaintiffs remember."[28] Distinguishing between what he considered fact and belief, McEachern consistently disregarded evidence that he considered an article of myth or faith. He criticized Antgulilibix, in particular, not simply for singing, but for failing to provide any territorial knowledge recognizable to the court through her songs. In his final decision, McEachern suggested Antgulilibix's evidence demonstrated comprehensive knowledge of "legends" about the connection of her *wilp* to the land, but lacked "a clear understanding of the boundaries."[29] As McEachern categorized legends as mythology rather than fact, he dismissed Antgulilibix's evidence as presenting no value. Moreover, McEachern expressed distrust in the *adaawk* and *cin k'ikh* as forms of knowledge confined to the Gitxsan and Wet'suwet'en communities and deemed them difficult to cross-validate. With a notable distrust for any histories that "exist only in the memory of the plaintiffs," McEachern's approach to oral history was to discard it in all instances except those in which it either reflected an individual's personal experiences or could be substantiated by written records or scientific research.[30]

There have been a number of exemplary critiques of McEachern's treatment of Gitxsan and Wet'suwet'en evidence. Julie Cruikshank, in an appropriately scathing indictment of the rationality of the judge, argues that his decision to "evaluate oral tradition as positivistic, literal evidence for 'history' is both ethnocentric and reductionist."[31] Cruikshank argues that in failing to address Indigenous oral history on its own terms, the judge undermines the complex nature of the oral evidence the Gitxsan and Wet'suwet'en witnesses brought before the court. Dara Culhane expands this critique exposing the racist logic the judge veiled beneath the language of cultural difference. She argues that McEachern could not recognize Indigenous histories as subject to Indigenous processes of validation because he fundamentally believed in the cultural inferiority of Indigenous peoples.[32] In his worldview, McEachern had already determined that Indigenous systems were emotional, subjective, and irrational, and thus not worthy of equal weight in crafting his judgment. He complained, "I have heard much at this trial about beliefs, feelings, and justice. I must again say, as I endeavored to say during the trial, that Courts of law are frequently unable to respond to these subjective considerations."[33] But, as Culhane argues, McEachern's decision was coloured by his own subjective ideological commitments and emotional responses.

A particularly central bias was an undergirding assumption that the capacity to claim territory depends on cartographic knowledge, which the hereditary chiefs lacked. Employing cartography to claim territory was foundational to colonialism, as competing imperial powers employed maps to demonstrate their knowledge of the land.[34] However, while these techniques of mapping enabled rule at a distance, their foundations lay in relationships to Indigenous guides, which provided the territorial knowledge necessary for colonial explorers to negotiate foreign geographies.[35] Eliding this history, government lawyers argued that the territorial knowledge underpinning the Gitxsan and Wet'suwet'en claim was created by those who drew the maps. Thus, they attributed the fur trade records of Wet'suwet'en territorial knowledge not as documentation of Indigenous systems of land tenure but rather evidence of how fur traders helped Indigenous peoples organize their hunting activities.[36] Similarly, they presented the registration of Indigenous traplines as evidence that provincial officials created territorial knowledge and granted land rights. Recycling these arguments in his final decision, McEachern argued that the Gitxsan and Wet'suwet'en hereditary chiefs lacked the technological sophistication to possess territorial holdings. Specifically addressing the overlap between registered traplines and the hereditary chiefs' claimed territories, McEachern opined that *wilp* and *yikh* territorial tenure likely derived from "the arrival of European influences" rather than "indefinite, long use prior to European influences."[37] Assuming that territorial knowledge could not pre-exist maps, pre-contact Indigenous peoples were presented as living in a state of nature where they were incapable of systematic knowledge of the land prior to its colonial inscription.[38]

Rationalizing these racist assumptions, government lawyers at trial and McEachern in his judgment emphasized the discord between maps and the territorial knowledge encoded in the *adaawk* and *cin k'ikh*. Indeed, beginning with pretrial arguments, government lawyers sought to establish that the idea of Gitxsan and Wet'suwet'en territoriality originated not with the hereditary chiefs but instead with Gitxsan activist and researcher Neil Sterritt.[39] While the Gitxsan and Wet'suwet'en sought to centre the voices and expertise of the hereditary chiefs, provincial government lawyers obsessed about the role that cartographic research played in their claim. Sterritt was held on the stand for thirty-two days— significantly longer than any other witness. As Tom Özden-Schilling has documented, provincial government lawyers sought to establish that Sterritt had not simply mapped *wilp* and *yikh* land claims, but had in fact invented the idea that these lands were bounded territories.[40] In rendering his decision, McEachern stressed the unreliability of the hereditary chiefs' knowledge of territorial boundaries. As Sparke has brilliantly elucidated, efforts to map a counter-cartography of Wet'suwet'en and Gitxsan territorial claims subjected their claims to evaluation in accordance with the territorial logic of the state.[41] Mapping Indigenous territories rendered them vulnerable to evaluation within the standards of

Western cartographic fixity.[42] When the lines between territories presented a degree of liminality that did not meet Cartesian expectations of a territory, the territorial claims of the Gitxsan and Wet'suwet'en were impugned. McEachern thus dismissed Gitxsan and Wet'suwet'en territorial claims on the basis of the gap between the calculated cartographic gaze of colonial authority and traditional Indigenous methods of demonstrating territorial claims: using story and song as markers of connection to the land. Of course, McEachern's reasoning did not hold; the Supreme Court of Canada overturned his decision on appeal.

The contrapuntal voice of Indigenous tradition with established court procedure resonated in the higher court, ultimately transforming judicial and government frameworks for understanding Indigenous relationships to the land. In the Supreme Court of Canada, the *adaawk* and *cin k'ikh* presented a productive challenge to extant evidentiary conventions. Indeed, the Supreme Court of Canada decision ultimately reformulated evidentiary doctrine to explicitly include space for the performance of Indigenous traditions.[43] Most of the Supreme Court justices found that McEachern was correct to admit the *adaawk* and *cin k'ikh* as exceptions to the hearsay rule, but that he erred in giving "these oral histories no independent weight at all."[44] The justices determined that many of the features that McEachern used to dismiss Gitxsan and Wet'suwet'en oral histories—especially their lack of historical detail and the court's difficulty validating them against written records outside the community—were generic features of Indigenous oral histories. The court ruled that the implication of McEachern's ruling was "that oral histories should never be given any independent weight and are only useful as confirmatory evidence in aboriginal rights litigation."[45] To ensure that Indigenous oral histories were not systematically undervalued in the legal system, the court overturned McEachern's decision.

The Supreme Court's decision set important new precedents, recognizing the admissibility of Indigenous oral histories in the court and, moreover, the necessity of giving these histories weight in decisions. The court dismantled the reasoning that McEachern used to dismiss the evidence tendered by the Gitxsan and Wet'suwet'en community members. Thus, much as Hereditary Chief Satsan suggested, the Gitxsan and Wet'suwet'en had succeeded in playing the game to change it. Through systematically breaching and challenging the rules of courtroom evidence, the hereditary chiefs were able to redefine them. Thus, it is not sufficient to critique the colonial court as a rigged game controlled by colonial procedural apparatuses. Relations of power are not fixed, and resistance can restructure the rationalities of power. However, if Indigenous interventions within the courts can challenge the system in certain ways, it must be noted that court processes also work to consolidate colonial power in other ways.

### Of the Authority to Speak the Law

In bringing their case for ownership and jurisdiction before the Canadian judiciary, the Gitxsan and Wet'suwet'en hereditary chiefs raised not only issues relating to evidentiary procedure but also fundamental questions regarding who constituted the competent authority to make decisions with respect to their traditional territories. The Gitxsan and Wet'suwet'en hereditary chiefs strategically entered the Canadian courts to assert Indigenous jurisdiction, initiating a complex play between Indigenous and colonial forms of authority. Through this action, the Gitxsan and Wet'suwet'en asked the court to recognize forms of Indigenous authority that, at least in part, offset the colonial sovereign authority in whose name the court itself acted. The hereditary chiefs hoped that, in bringing their legal orders to the Canadian courts, they could achieve at least partial recognition of forms of Indigenous territorial sovereignty nested within the settler state.[46] Government lawyers, however, argued that the Gitxsan and Wet'suwet'en appeal to the authority of the Canadian courts itself was a demonstration of their submission to the sovereignty of the settler state. McEachern accepted this argument. Although the Supreme Court of Canada overturned McEachern's decision, it maintained the presumption of the settler state's allodial possession of its sovereign territory.[47] It placed limits, however, on the exercise of settler sovereignty vis-à-vis Indigenous peoples, and determined that the province did not have jurisdictional authority to annul Indigenous territorial claims. Moreover, the court found that government authorities had the responsibility to reconcile the conduct of their authority with Aboriginal rights and title. The Gitxsan and Wet'suwet'en intervention in the Canadian courts, then, problematized questions of jurisdiction—what it is and who has it over whom. It also productively shifted the courts' understanding of the sources of governing authority and how those sources shape lawful relations.

The Gitxsan and Wet'suwet'en entered the courts making a jurisdictional claim to authority over decisions regarding the disposition of the land. In doing so, they invited the court to consider that forms of settler and Indigenous authority exist in parallel, and asked after the principles that should direct the lawful exercise of these parallel forms of authority and their relationship to one another. As Stuart Rush, counsel for the Gitxsan and Wet'suwet'en, explained, the hereditary chiefs were "seeking recognition of their societies as equals and contemporaries."[48] Thus, they specifically invited consideration of how settler authorities lawfully conduct themselves in relation to the Gitxsan and Wet'suwet'en authorities: their hereditary chiefs. The purpose of the case, as Delgamuukw told the court, "is to find a process to place Gitksan and Wet'suwet'en ownership and jurisdiction within the context of Canada. We do not seek a decision as to whether our system might continue or not. It will continue."[49] Thus, the litigation initiated a process of mutual reckoning as settler authorities encountered competing claims to Indigenous jurisdiction in the courtroom.

These questions of jurisdiction draw attention to the ways in which competing legal orders encounter one another. As Shaunnagh Dorsett and Shaun McVeigh argue, the "relation between jurisdiction and authority need not run through European forms of sovereign territorial jurisdiction."[50] Jurisdiction can be understood as "the exercise by sometimes vaguely defined legal authorities of the power to regulate and administer sanctions over particular actions or people, including groups defined by personal status, territorial boundaries, and corporate membership."[51] Thinking through encounters between Indigenous and settler legal orders, Shiri Pasternak has particularly emphasized the utility of jurisdictional analysis that examines how people constitute the authority to proclaim the law and what principles guide its application.[52] As she notes, the meaning of jurisdiction is embedded within its etymology. The Oxford English Dictionary traces the term through French back to its Latin roots in *dicere* and *jūs*, respectively "to say, declare" and "law."[53] Thus, jurisdictional practice in effect "declares the existence of law and the authority to speak in the name of the law."[54] Applying jurisdictional analysis in the context of Indigenous-settler territorial relations, we need to analyze how law is enunciated and what modes of conduct shape the exercise of lawful authority.

In bringing their claims before the Canadian courts, the hereditary chiefs sought to force settler authorities to reckon with Gitxsan and Wet'suwet'en forms of authority and territoriality. Their legal strategy hinged on a historic argument.[55] They sought to demonstrate, first, that prior to contact with Europeans, the Gitxsan and Wet'suwet'en people possessed their territories and exercised jurisdiction over them in accordance with the conduct of lawful authority in their societies; second, that the Gitxsan and Wet'suwet'en hereditary chiefs had never ceded their territories or authority; and third, that both international and British legal traditions framed obligations between colonial sovereigns and Indigenous peoples, requiring the reconciliation of the exercise of colonial authority on Gitxsan and Wet'suwet'en territories with the continuation of Gitxsan and Wet'suwet'en legal orders.

In the case, the Gitxsan and Wet'suwet'en hereditary chiefs asserted their authority to speak for their communities and nations. While there has been sustained commentary on the Gitxsan and Wet'suwet'en witnesses in the courtroom, there has been more limited discussion of the question of the hereditary chiefs' authority or standing as plaintiffs before the court. This was a matter of some contention at trial and remains a significant issue in ongoing land conflicts.[56] As noted in the introduction to this chapter, the Gitxsan and Wet'suwet'en grounded their authority in the original encounter and marriage between a hereditary lineage and the spirit of the land. This connection between land and lineage is well documented as the grounds for authority in Wet'suwet'en law. In 1923–1924, an unnamed Wet'suwet'en informant explained to anthropologist Diamond Jenness that the foundation of *yikh* authority lay in its marriage to the more-than-human world.

> *We know what the animals do, what are the needs of the beaver, the bear, the salmon, and other creatures, because long ago men married them and acquired this knowledge from their animal wives...The white man has been only a short time in this country and knows very little about animals; we have lived here thousands of years and were taught long ago by the animals themselves. The white man writes everything down in a book so that it will not be forgotten; but our ancestors married the animals, learned their ways, and passed on the knowledge from one generation to another.*[57]

These are the connections that are emblematized in the *cin k'ikh* and symbolically renewed in the *balhats*, as members of a *yikh* take on the hereditary titles of their ancestors. When younger generations take on the names of their ancestors, they also renew their responsibility for their more-than-human relations. Because the authority of a *yikh* depends on the connection of its lineage to the land, the exercise of that authority must be in concordance with the principles of that relationship.

In the *Delgamuukw, Gisdaywa* trial, counsel for the province took issue with the authority of Gitxsan and Wet'suwet'en chiefs, and their capacity to represent the membership of their *wilp* and *yikh* and their territorial interests. Challenging the standing of the chiefs, Geoff Plant, counsel for the province in the case, raised a number of issues, highlighting what he perceived as inconsistencies in the Gitxsan and Wet'suwet'en evidence and pleadings at trial.[58] First, he argued that individual hereditary chiefs could not represent all the people with interests in their territories because the evidence in the case demonstrated that territorial authority and rights within Gitxsan and Wet'suwet'en legal orders were structured by complex kinship relations that extended beyond a single *wilp* or *yikh*. Since people could access the territories of their spouse and father, exogamous marriages and patrilines provided rights that were external to the matrilineal kinship group of a *wilp* or *yikh*. Second, he stressed that the evidence demonstrated that hereditary chiefs within Gitxsan and Wet'suwet'en legal orders were not absolute sovereigns with unfettered authority to decide the fate of their *wilp* or *yikh* territories but part of a network of authorities bound by kinship obligations. Third, he emphasized that the plaintiff group was not synonymous with or inclusive of the entire community of Gitxsan and Wet'suwet'en hereditary chiefs. Specifically, Plant noted the absence of the Gitxsan hereditary chiefs of Kitwancool, who lived along the western edge of Gitxsan territories abutting the Nisga'a, from the plaintiff group.[59] He argued that the exclusion of some hereditary chiefs from the court action invalidated the ability of the plaintiffs to represent the interests of the Gitxsan and Wet'suwet'en community. Plant suggested the absence of part of the Gitxsan Nation from the litigation crucially impaired the plaintiffs' claim, as the argument for collective Gitxsan and Wet'suwet'en jurisdiction hinged on consolidating the individual authority of distinct hereditary chiefs into a collective national claim. The fact that the plaintiff group did not fully represent the two nations was further demonstrated, Plant argued, by the repeated amendments to the Gitxsan and Wet'suwet'en statement of claim, originally filed at the beginning of the lawsuit, which recorded shifting numbers of plaintiff chiefs and of the *wilp* and *yikh* that they claimed to represent.

The fluidity in the organization of *wilp* and *yikh* was evident at trial. In the 1984 writ of summons, by which the *Delgamuukw, Gisdaywa* action was commenced, there were forty-eight plaintiffs, each of whom was said to be the hereditary chief of a named *wilp* or *yikh*. By the beginning of trial in 1987, the number of plaintiffs had increased to fifty-four, of which thirty-nine represented their *wilp* or *yikh* alone, and fifteen represented their *wilp* or *yikh* as well as another related *wilp* or *yikh*.[60] The judgment at the conclusion of the trial lists fifty-one plaintiffs, including forty-one who represent their *wilp* or *yikh* alone, and ten who represent their *wilp* or *yikh* alongside a second, related *wilp* or *yikh*.[61] However, if only to further underline the ambiguity and fluidity of *wilp* or *yikh* numbers,

McEachern refers to "35 Gitxsan and 13 Wet'suwet'en hereditary chiefs," the original 48 plaintiffs, in the text of his final decision.[62]

For a variety of reasons, such as the illness or death of a chief or a protracted conflict over the succession of a name, the leadership of a *wilp* or *yikh* could be either incapacitated or vacant. These circumstances necessitated alternative representation, either by a subchief in the *wilp* or *yikh* or an outside hereditary chief from the same *p'teex* or *dïdikh*. For instance, Wigetimschol, a name then held by Dan Michell, represented his *yikh* when the Tsayu title of Na'Moks, the highest chiefly title in that *yikh*, was vacant.[63] Similarly, the Gilserhyu hereditary chief Goohlaht, a title then held by Lucy Namox, temporarily represented the *yikh* of Samooh, which belonged to the same *dïdikh* as Goohlaht.[64] Furthermore, *wilp* and *yikh* occasionally amalgamate or separate as issues related to resource access, population, and political differences require. The amalgamation or division of a *wilp* or *yikh* typically relates to its ability to maintain its responsibilities in the feast hall, repaying debts through cycles of feasting.[65] Historically, this related to the size of a *wilp* or *yikh*, the productivity of its territories, or conflicts between members of a kinship group. As *wilp* or *yikh* often held multiple territories, division could be accomplished through the subdivision of its territories. Conversely, merging *wilp* or *yikh* could offer members access to additional lands. The fluidity of *wilp* and *yikh* has been vital to the capacity of the Gitxsan and Wet'suwet'en to adapt to colonial impacts, such as the destruction of territories, the population impacts of disease outbreaks, and the exacerbated conflicts within the Gitxsan and Wet'suwet'en communities.

While the province's lawyers raised various issues with the standing of the hereditary chiefs as representatives of their people, the trial judge accepted the standing of the hereditary chiefs in advancing the claim of their people. McEachern wrote in his judgment, "There is no reason why the named plaintiffs should not represent the Gitksan and Wet'suwet'en people on whose behalf this action has been brought."[66] Of course, recognizing the authority of the Gitxsan and Wet'suwet'en hereditary chiefs was hardly generous, given that McEachern then rejected their claims. But his decision nonetheless established the hereditary chiefs as the appropriate representatives of their community's land interest. The Supreme Court of Canada would later recognize that these land interests needed to be reconciled with the exercise of colonial sovereignty. Thus, McEachern's recognition of the hereditary chiefs' standing was generative, creating the foundation for eventual negotiations between colonial authorities and the hereditary chiefs.[67] To understand these negotiations, it is necessary to address the question of colonial jurisdiction and the duties that encumber its exercise with relation to Indigenous peoples.

At trial and in the judgments to follow, the question of how settler authorities lawfully conduct themselves with regard to Indigenous peoples has been the subject of substantial debate. It has also been the focus of a substantial body of critical scholarship. Scholars have criticized the colonial doctrines of extinguishment operant in the trial decision in *Delgamuukw, Gisdaywa*.[68] The higher court decisions overturned the trial decision on extinguishment. However, as John Borrows and Gordon Christie have adroitly demonstrated, the various courts have consistently maintained the colonial fiction that underlying title is the unique possession of the settler sovereign.[69] Borrows and Christie rightly lament the failure of the court to substantially reckon with the Gitxsan and Wet'suwet'en claims to ownership and jurisdiction originally at issue in the case. The court did, however, devote substantial energy to evaluating the workings of settler jurisdiction vis-à-vis Indigenous peoples. Returning to the question of settler jurisdiction highlights the central question of how colonial authorities must lawfully conduct relations with Indigenous peoples. Counter to the findings of the various courts, sovereignty is not pregiven and absolute, but structured by the codes that guide its administration. Attending to the technical issues of jurisdiction—those processes that guide the exercise of settler authority—highlights the productive and transformative effects of the Gitxsan and Wet'suwet'en hereditary chiefs' litigation.

In the trial, two historical questions framed how the court approached the relationship of settler jurisdiction to the Gitxsan and Wet'suwet'en hereditary chiefs. First, had the Gitxsan and Wet'suwet'en hereditary chiefs effectively acceded to the supremacy of the settler state by virtue of simply acting in accordance with its laws and making appeals to settler authorities? Second, was the colonial sovereign bound by any duties to reconcile the exercise of its authority with the jurisdiction of the Gitxsan and Wet'suwet'en hereditary chiefs? At trial, provincial lawyers argued that Gitxsan and Wet'suwet'en regard for laws of general application demonstrated the effective and absolute sovereignty of the settler state. McEachern would ultimately concur with this view, with his rationalization of this conclusion filling hundreds of pages.

Historical discussions in the case extended from sixteenth-century Spanish jurisprudence to the 1973 *Calder* decision; however, the most significant arguments hinged on the interpretation of the Royal Proclamation of 1763. This proclamation established that Indian nations living under the asserted protection of the Crown had an exclusive right to any territories they possessed that had not been ceded to the sovereign.[70] On the basis of this proclamation, representatives of the Crown were required to negotiate treaties with Indigenous peoples prior to expanding colonial settlements onto Indigenous lands. In the absence of such a treaty, the proclamation forbade colonial governments from granting Indigenous lands to settlers and, moreover, required the removal of settlers from unceded Indigenous lands. Legal counsel for the Gitxsan and Wet'suwet'en argued that this historic proclamation established a framework that necessitated negotiating territorial relations with Indigenous peoples in British Columbia.[71] The province countered that British Columbia was uncharted territory in 1763, and as colonial authorities did not know of the lands in question, they could not intend to include these Indigenous lands in the domain covered by the proclamation.

In the trial decision, Justice McEachern unequivocally voiced his commitment to the principle of the unencumbered title and jurisdiction of the colonial sovereign. McEachern dismissed the relevance of treaty making to relations between Canadian and Indigenous jurisdiction. Instead, he recycled a model of sovereignty inherited as the legacy of colonialism. Max Weber's classic definition of sovereignty captures this model perfectly: a sovereign state is imagined to be "a human community that (successfully) claims the monopoly of the legitimate use of physical force within a given territory."[72] This conception of sovereignty, built on a doctrine of mutual exclusion in which no sovereign rightly interferes within the domain of any other without invitation, served imperial powers as they sought to carve up the world—excluding the possibility that Indigenous populations could possess self-determination.[73] Historians and geographers have repeatedly emphasized that there have always been multiple forms of authority overlapping in colonial spaces.[74] However, for McEachern, the supremacy of colonial sovereignty simply erased antecedent and competing forms of authority.

McEachern invented rationales to dismiss most of the legal arguments that challenged his colonial logic. In his view, the law "never recognized that the settlement of new lands depended upon the consent of the Indians."[75] Obviating any sovereign obligation to Indigenous peoples, McEachern suggested the colonial sovereign's responsibility was to the progressive replacement of Indigenous territorialities with white settlement. He particularly employed the British Privy Council's opinion in the 1919 case *Re Southern Rhodesia* to rationalize this narrative of colonial progress. The case established that, while recognizing the law of the Native peoples in what was then Southern Rhodesia would necessitate getting permission prior to settlement, the fact that the sovereign's aim was settlement, and the fact settlement occurred, indicated that the law of the colonial sovereign had replaced the Native legal order.[76] McEachern argued that the history of development on Gitxsan and Wet'suwet'en territories was analogous: "The aboriginal system, to the extent it constituted aboriginal jurisdiction of sovereignty, or ownership apart from occupation for residence and use, gave way to a new colonial form of government which the law recognizes to the exclusion of all other systems."[77] He recognized that Indigenous peoples in British Columbia were never conquered and never signed treaties, but considered this point largely irrelevant. "The events of the last 200 years are far more significant than any military conquest or treaties would have been," McEachern declared.[78] Following the province's submissions, he found effective British sovereignty did not yet extend to British Columbia at the time of the Royal Proclamation of 1763. Justifying a narrow reading of the proclamation, he suggested it must be understood as a purposive instrument, directed at furthering mercantile policy in the period, not a general directive that extended beyond that time and place. For McEachern, it is the simple fact of the "actual dominion" of the colonial sovereign in the present that determines "ownership of the soil of all the lands of the province is not open to question."[79]

As the converse to the pronounced dominion of the colonial sovereign over its territory, McEachern denied that the Gitxsan and Wet'suwet'en possessed the attributes of a civilized people, and thus the capacity to exercise effective territorial jurisdiction. "The plaintiffs' ancestors had no written language, no horses or wheeled vehicles, slavery and starvation was not uncommon, wars with neighbouring peoples were common," he wrote.[80] Indigenous peoples must present, as Paul Nadasdy describes, "the entailments of sovereignty—a set of assumptions about the nature of space, time, knowledge, and sociality that is intimately bound up with the state form—or risk not being heard at all."[81] Judging the Gitxsan and Wet'suwet'en to be primitive societies, McEachern found that their land interest "at the time of British sovereignty, except for village sites, was nothing more than the right to live on and use the land for aboriginal purposes."[82] Post-contact, McEachern suggested the patterns of Indigenous life had been readily superseded by those of a white settler society. Thus, he read the "present life-style of the great majority of the Gitksan and Wet'suwet'en people," by which he meant living in villages with "minimal contact with individual territories," as a sign of their acquiescence to the arrival of a superior settler society.[83] Indeed, he interpreted the Gitxsan and Wet'suwet'en hereditary chiefs' appeal to the authority of the court itself as a sign of their submission to settler sovereignty. He further suggested that colonial sovereignty and jurisdiction prohibits "as a matter of law" the unilateral exercise of an "independent or separate status" for Indigenous peoples.[84]

Within this framework, Aboriginal rights, as well as the specific Gitxsan and Wet'suwet'en claim to ownership and jurisdiction, are not inherent to Indigenous peoples but a gift from the colonial sovereign. McEachern wrote that "aboriginal rights, arising by operation of law, are non-proprietary rights of occupation for residence and aboriginal user [sic] which are extinguishable at the pleasure of the Sovereign."[85] Thus, he suggested, Aboriginal rights "may be extinguished whenever the intention of the Crown to do so is clear and plain."[86] Because pre-Confederation colonial land policies intended to convey an unfettered title to settlers, McEachern argued, these enactments exhibited "a clear and plain intention to extinguish aboriginal interests."[87] In his view, Aboriginal interests only remained where the sovereign had explicitly made an exception to set them aside. For instance, he found that the Gitxsan and Wet'suwet'en had limited "non-exclusive aboriginal sustenance and ceremonial rights" to use specific sites, and the right to "continued residence in their villages."[88] Unsurprisingly, the hereditary chiefs appealed this decision. On appeal, the province moderated its arguments, recognizing residual Aboriginal rights to self-government. The British Columbia Court of Appeal amended the ruling with respect to the revised provincial position.[89]

After further appeal, the Supreme Court of Canada Justices overturned the lower court decisions and recognized a contemporary doctrine of Aboriginal title.[90] The Supreme Court did not, however, register a decision on the Gitxsan and Wet'suwet'en claims to Aboriginal title because of the already-mentioned mishandling of evidence, and because of defects in the format of the original pleadings. The reversal of the lower court decisions has been much celebrated as a win for Indigenous peoples as it opened much broader spaces of negotiation. But in spite of the many laudatory discussions of the case, the Supreme Court decision conserved the colonial foundation of the earlier judgments, presuming underlying title as the unique possession of the settler sovereign.[91] Like McEachern's decision, the Supreme Court's judgment, which is still used as precedent today, effaces Indigenous sovereignty. Discursively, it nullifies the extent to which Indigenous territorial claims present competing land claims to those of the state. Of course, Indigenous sovereignty, understood as a will to decide what occurs within a particular territory, has never been reliant on state recognition. As Audra Simpson and Leanne Betasamosake Simpson write, Indigenous peoples continue to enact their independence in the ways that they maintain relations to a world beyond the purview of state law.[92] What the Supreme Court of Canada conceptualized in its decision was the burden that obligations to Indigenous peoples place upon settler jurisdiction.

At the Supreme Court, the arguments in *Delgamuukw, Gisdaywa* principally dealt with five questions. The first was whether reorientations in Gitxsan and Wet'suwet'en pleadings, which shifted from the hereditary chiefs' language of ownership and jurisdiction at the trial court to the more delimited concepts of Aboriginal title and self-government at the appellate court (a decision made by the plaintiffs' legal team), unfairly prejudiced the defendants, who had constructed their defence in response to the original pleadings. Second, the court asked whether the factual findings of the trial judge were appropriate or had appropriately weighted the evidence. The third question concerned what the content of Aboriginal title was, and involved the related questions of what protection it was entitled to, and how a claim to Aboriginal title could be proven before the court. Fourth, the court interrogated whether the Gitxsan and Wet'suwet'en had effectively made out a claim to self-government. Finally, fifth, it asked whether British Columbia, which now agreed that no blanket extinguishment occurred prior to 1871, had the power to extinguish Aboriginal rights after 1871. In answering these questions, the court established that a case for contemporary Aboriginal title could be made, but it had not been made in the original *Delgamuukw, Gisdaywa* trial, which had too many defects.

Examining the first question, the Supreme Court of Canada decided that the shifting language was an idiosyncrasy of the original case, which it suggested had initially been argued at a period when the concepts of Aboriginal law were not well developed in Canadian jurisprudence. More problematic for the court was the way that the hereditary chiefs had consolidated their claims at appeal not as a collection of individual holdings but as the collective claim of two distinct peoples. In their original case, the claimed external boundaries of the Gitxsan and Wet'suwet'en people were a product of the agglomeration of the distinct *yikh* and *wilp* territories. Thus, in the original argument, they needed to prove the internal *yikh* and *wilp* boundaries to establish the national external boundaries. After McEachern found that the Gitxsan and Wet'suwet'en had failed to prove their internal boundaries, the plaintiffs' legal team decided that, at appeal, they would forward the Gitxsan and Wet'suwet'en collective claims as two unified wholes rather than contest the trial judge's interpretation of individual internal boundaries. The Supreme Court found this to be a substantive change in the pleadings that, alongside the evidentiary problems already discussed, necessitated retrial.

To establish a standard for subsequent trials, the court then elaborated a doctrine of Aboriginal title. With Chief Justice Antonio Lamer writing for the majority, the court specifically delineated the content of Aboriginal title as encompassing "the right to exclusive use and occupation of the land held pursuant to that title for a variety of purposes, which need not be aspects of those aboriginal practices, customs and traditions which are integral to distinctive aboriginal cultures."[93] The court depicted Aboriginal title generally as usufructuary, sui generis, and inalienable to third parties. Moreover, it found that the Royal Proclamation of 1763 recognized Aboriginal title but did not create it. In the view of the court, Aboriginal title, as a species of Aboriginal right, was recognized and affirmed in the Constitution Act of 1982, and thereby had constitutional protection. The origins of Aboriginal title lay, however, not in imperial decree or settler legislation but in Aboriginal peoples' prior occupation of the land. The sui generis nature of Aboriginal title demonstrated its status as a bridging concept, reflective of no right previously known within British common law or any Indigenous system of law, but rather flowing from the translation of rights across the gap between these legal systems.[94] Thus, Aboriginal title was a bridging concept of a communal right held by Indigenous peoples that codified elements of Indigenous legal orders within Canadian jurisprudence.

The court recognized Aboriginal title as the right to use lands for a variety of purposes, which could be dynamic, but not so dynamic as to undermine the fundamental asserted connection of an Indigenous people and their land. As the judgment states, "protected uses must not be irreconcilable with the nature of the group's attachment to that land."[95] Explicating this point, Chief

Justice Lamer describes how, "if occupation is established with reference to the use of the land as a hunting ground, then the group that successfully claims aboriginal title to that land may not use it in such a fashion as to destroy its value for such a use (e.g., by strip mining it)."[96] This finding reflected acknowledgement that the exercise of Indigenous jurisdiction was conditioned by the norms and procedures that governed the actions of Indigenous authorities. However, it problematically situated assessment of the conduct of Indigenous authorities within the domain of the settler court.

The Supreme Court thus reproduced elements of colonial paternalism, situating settler authorities as paramount. Through what Borrows refers to as "sovereignty's alchemy," the court constructed Aboriginal title as a burden on the underlying title of the colonial sovereign.[97] "Because it does not make sense to speak of a burden on the underlying title before that title existed," Chief Justice Lamer reasoned, "aboriginal title crystallized at the time [colonial] sovereignty was asserted"[98] As Borrows explains, through the magic of colonial sovereignty, Indigenous jurisdiction over their own lands "is ostensibly transformed, for use and occupation are found to be extinguished, infringed, or made subject to another's designs."[99] Conceptualizing Aboriginal title as a burden on the underlying title of the colonial sovereign, the Supreme Court justices render Indigenous territory and jurisdiction subject to the legal order of the colonial state. As Christie notes, "Aboriginal sovereignty is removed from the scene at the point of the assertion of Crown sovereignty (replaced with, at most, the notion of 'self-government'—another construct within domestic Canadian law)."[100]

In the *Delgamuukw, Gisdaywa* decision, the Supreme Court of Canada established a test for Aboriginal title, but no test to determine whether the authority of the colonial sovereign has been effected. The proof of an Aboriginal title claim relates to three criteria. First, "the land must have been occupied prior to [colonial] sovereignty."[101] Second, if present occupation is used as proof of occupation prior to the assertion of colonial sovereignty, "there must be a continuity between present and pre-sovereignty occupation."[102] Third, occupation of Aboriginal title lands at the moment that colonial sovereignty was asserted must have been exclusive. These tests founded the basis for judging a subsequent claim to Aboriginal title. But as Christie notes, the mere assertion of colonial sovereignty and title is deemed sufficient to establish it.[103]

While the court only provided delimited recognition of Gitxsan and Wet'suwet'en authority, its decision, which effectively constrained the jurisdiction of the provincial government, was productive of new relationships. In answering the question of whether the province of British Columbia had the jurisdiction to extinguish Aboriginal rights after it joined Confederation in 1871, the Supreme Court said no. The court determined that the province could not independently determine the status of Aboriginal peoples. Thus, the most important effect of the *Delgamuukw, Gisdaywa* case was not establishing Gitxsan and Wet'suwet'en jurisdiction, which in practice always remained beyond the purview of the court, but instead establishing limits on the conduct of settler authority vis-à-vis Indigenous peoples.

## Of the Kingdom of Reconciliation

The most significant effects of the *Delgamuukw, Gisdaywa* decision are seen in the emergence of new realms of governmental negotiation. Ultimately, despite all the discussion and valorization of the colonial sovereign's authority to extinguish Aboriginal rights, the courts suspended not Indigeneity but judgment. Deferring judgment, the Supreme Court of Canada did not simply declare the necessity of a retrial but strongly pressed the need to negotiate. Thus, the legacy of the trial rests most fundamentally with the construction of new processes of negotiation and consultation. The Gitxsan and Wet'suwet'en had originally gone to court with the intent of coercing the province to negotiate by using the system of settler law against it. While this was an incredibly fraught exercise, it also proved a productive one. Through their court battles, the Gitxsan and Wet'suwet'en opened new spaces of negotiation. Through the lower courts, negotiations were spurred less by the actual decisions of the courts and more by the political effects that knowledge of Indigenous claims had on the public and the economic disruption that direct-action campaigns caused.[104] The Supreme Court decision, however, contributed to a proliferation of governmental techniques to reconcile Indigenous claims with regimes for regulating development. The doctrine of Aboriginal title, while relying upon and reproducing colonial rationalities, nevertheless burdened government authority with counterclaims and undermined the security of resource sector investments in British Columbia. This problem of insecurity could not simply be solved by suspending Indigenous claims. Rather, through and consequent to *Delgamuukw, Gisdaywa*, techniques for negotiating Indigenous claims expanded. In subsequent chapters, I address the negotiations that have followed *Delgamuukw, Gisdaywa* within pipeline governance processes. Here, as context to situate those more recent negotiations, I trace the efforts and failures of negotiation that led to and coincided with the *Delgamuukw, Gisdaywa* court case before ultimately stalling despite court direction.

Although the hereditary chiefs have always carried on their practices of territorial governance, contemporary Gitxsan and Wet'suwet'en claims to land and jurisdiction were initially mobilized through the Gitksan-Carrier Tribal Council. This tribal council represented the members of the Gitxsan bands of Kitwangak, Kitseguecla, Gitanmaax, Sikadoak, and Kispiox, as well as the Wet'suwet'en bands of Hagwilget and Moricetown. The council was composed of representatives of each village, as well as two representatives for non-resident members.[105] The Gitksan-Carrier Tribal Council entered land claim negotiations in 1977 and began to document the extent of their territorial interests. Negotiations were stymied by the provincial refusal to consider Indigenous political claims that effectively extended beyond those of a municipality. Changing their name in 1982 to the Gitksan Wet'suwet'en Tribal Council, the group began to organize litigation to press their claim to ownership and jurisdiction based on the distinct Gitxsan and Wet'suwet'en systems of laws. This would become the *Delgamuukw, Gisdaywa* case. As Sterritt describes, their strategy was to build on the mapping work done for land claims negotiations, "transferring the chiefs' extensive knowledge of the land onto maps that would form a permanent Gitxsan aboriginal title record" and a similar Wet'suwet'en record.[106] The Gitksan Wet'suwet'en Tribal Council was dissolved during the *Delgamuukw, Gisdaywa* case, as the community decided to advance the claims of the hereditary chiefs. The individual bands, which were registered under the Indian Act, continued to exist and provide services to registered band members, but were not represented in the litigation.

As the *Delgamuukw, Gisdaywa* case advanced through the courts, the province was enmeshed in a debate about how to address unceded Aboriginal title and rights. While the trial-level decision in *Delgamuukw, Gisdaywa* obviously did not aid the Gitxsan and Wet'suwet'en efforts to achieve recognition of their land interests, it had significantly raised the profile of Indigenous issues in British Columbia. Further, the Gitxsan and Wet'suwet'en commitment to publicly assert their territorial jurisdiction using extra-legal means, such as blockades and informational pickets on the highway, created additional political and economic pressure to address their claims.[107]

The advocates of treaty negotiations made an economic argument for treaty settlements. As Christopher McKee describes, they argued that the costs of not settling with Indigenous peoples "would be higher in the long run, as the province would run the risk of losing potential investment capital and other economic development opportunities."[108] According to McKee, two economic studies strongly backed this position. First, in 1989, the accounting firm Price Waterhouse estimated that failing to settle Indigenous land claims would cost the province $1 billion in lost investment in mining and forestry alone. Second, the accounting firm KPMG, in a report commissioned by the provincial government, suggested one of the most significant benefits of treaty settlement would be greater certainty for provincial resource industries. As McKee summarizes, "clarification of Aboriginal rights to ownership of lands and natural resources would reduce the rationale for blockades, demonstrations, and other disruptions by Native groups."[109]

Concerns about economic security led government officials to establish a tripartite task force, including Indigenous, provincial, and federal representatives, to examine a process for contemporary treaty negotiations in 1990. In March 1991, McEachern released his judgment, suggesting Indigenous territorial claims were largely extinguished; in June, the British Columbia Claims Task Force released its report, recommending that Indigenous land claims negotiations continue.[110] The two documents presented clashing conclusions. Ultimately economic concerns about Indigenous resistance alongside political pressure to address colonial legacies led the provincial government to soften its stance, expressing a willingness to negotiate recognition of some limited Aboriginal rights.

The Gitxsan and Wet'suwet'en appealed the trial decision to enhance their bargaining position. At appeal, counsel for the province no longer argued for the blanket extinguishment of Indigenous territorial and jurisdictional claims. However, they continued to argue against Gitxsan and Wet'suwet'en ownership and jurisdiction, instead proposing more limited Aboriginal sustenance rights and self-government subject to the laws of the Canadian and British Columbian governments. In 1993, the Court of Appeal upheld McEachern's original rejection of Gitxsan and Wet'suwet'en claims to ownership and jurisdiction in a three-to-two decision, but recognized the existence of more delimited Aboriginal rights to use the land for sustenance, which it suggested needed to be addressed through political negotiations.[111] That same year, the provincial government established the British Columbia treaty process to resolve economic uncertainties in the resource sector.[112]

While these developments finally created an opportunity for Indigenous peoples with unceded lands in the province to enter into treaty negotiations, the framework for negotiations had the effect of pitting Indigenous communities against one another. Prior to the court case in 1986, the Wet'suwet'en hereditary chiefs had feasted with the Nedut'en, Cheslatta, and other Dakelh, and agreed to resolve boundary issues through Indigenous legal traditions.[113] However, with the creation of the new treaty process, overlapping claims emerged.[114] The Carrier Sekani Tribal Council (CSTC) issued a statement of intent to negotiate a treaty in January 1994.[115] Their claim area incorporated the territorial claims of some southern Wet'suwet'en bands outside the original Gitksan Wet'suwet'en Tribal Council. This landscape of overlapping claims was further complicated by the fragmentation of the historic Omineca Band and of the CSTC itself. In 1984, the Omineca Band, which had been associated with CSTC and governed the numerous small southern Wet'suwet'en reserves, dissolved.[116] The families associated with the Francois Lake, Uncha Lake, and Skin Tyee reserves became Nee-Tahi-Buhn, an independent band that left the CSTC. The families connected to the Broman Lake, Decker Lake, and Maxan Lake reserve lands became the Broman Lake Band, which, together with the Burns Lake Band, maintained an affiliation with the CSTC. Representing the territorial interests of the Wet'suwet'en members of the Broman Lake and Burns Lake bands, the CSTC asserted claims to lands overlapping with those claimed by the Wet'suwet'en hereditary chiefs. Lake Babine Nation and Cheslatta Carrier Nation (formerly Cheslatta Band), the Nedut'en and Dakelh bands that had been historically displaced onto Wet'suwet'en territories, also left the CSTC and filed independent land claims in 1994 and 1995.[117] Lake Babine Nation and Cheslatta Carrier Nation claims also overlapped those of the Wet'suwet'en hereditary chiefs, along the eastern and southern extent of Wet'suwet'en traditional territories, respectively.

The framework of the British Columbia treaty process aimed to ultimately resolve all the conflicting land claims by negotiating the erasure of Aboriginal title and rights from most of the provincial land base.[118] Echoing the frames of the original 1974 federal comprehensive claims policy, the British Columbia process was designed to remove the encumbrance of Indigenous claims from the majority of lands in the province and thereby resolve any uncertainty that might dissuade resource sector investments. The modern approach to treaty making centred on forging exhaustively long, technical documents that sought to resolve the final terms of Indigenous political and economic integration.[119] This differed from historic treaties, which were short, written agreements typically negotiated over a few days. However, in their basic intent and structure, the written text of modern land claims still mirrored that of the historic land cession agreements signed across the Prairies, which had provided monetary payments and a delimited set of defined treaty rights in exchange for Indigenous peoples' surrender of title to most of their lands. As Arthur Manuel describes, the new model of the contemporary land claims process effectively followed the shape of "the old ceding and releasing of our [Indigenous] rights...replaced by what amounted to, in the best case, slightly expanded reserves and the menu of municipal and non-profit organization powers that were defined in the policy."[120]

Nevertheless, the Gitxsan and Wet'suwet'en hereditary chiefs signed an accord of respect and recognition with the provincial government in 1994, adjourning the *Delgamuukw, Gisdaywa* action to enter tripartite negotiations with the provincial and federal governments.[121] The accord stipulated that the parties intended to agree on and sign a treaty within eighteen months, with the possibility of continuing the adjournment if negotiations were progressing well. At this point, the Gitxsan and Wet'suwet'en split into two distinct organizations.[122] Under pressure from provincial authorities, the Gitxsan and Wet'suwet'en hereditary chiefs created non-profit societies under the provincial Societies Act, respectively named the Gitxsan Treaty Office and the Wet'suwet'en Treaty Office. Representatives of the hereditary chiefs sat on the boards of these organizations, directing their activities. The individual Gitxsan *wilp* and Wet'suwet'en *yikh* land claims were also reorganized into the collective claim of two distinct peoples. The consolidation of the hereditary chiefs' claims into two national claims rather than an (indeterminate) number of *wilp* and *yikh* claims simplified the political geography of the Gitxsan and Wet'suwet'en for the sake of negotiations, enabling the creation of collective bodies with which the state could interface. This avoided the administrative issues associated with individually addressing the distinct claims of every *wilp* and *yikh* to its own territories.

The creation of the treaty offices consolidated new forms of Indigenous authority in land claim negotiations, with new central offices that were emboldened to act in the name of the hereditary chiefs but governed in accordance with provincial legislation guiding the conduct of non-profit societies. From the perspective of settler authorities, the creation of treaty offices resolved the complexity of negotiating directly with hereditary authorities, whose conduct continued to be guided by Indigenous legal orders that remained beyond colonial cognizance. The government could now negotiate with just two bodies, one representing the collective body of Wet'suwet'en hereditary chiefs on behalf of their *yikh*, another representing the collective body of Gitxsan hereditary chiefs on behalf of their *wilp*.

In the negotiations, the Gitxsan and Wet'suwet'en sought to establish a model of self-government based on the traditional governance system and create a territorial co-management process where they could collaborate with settler authorities in overseeing development. Thus, from the perspective of the Gitxsan and Wet'suwet'en hereditary chiefs, the mandate of the treaty offices was not to establish a final resolution that would end negotiations, but to establish a working relationship through which provincial ministries could interface with the hereditary chiefs. They sought to ensure the Gitxsan and Wet'suwet'en hereditary authorities were both integrated into development decision-making and able to benefit from development. "The over-riding aim was to channel revenue from resource extraction back into the region, in order to support self-government," P. Dawn Mills explains.[123] In contrast, the provincial government, in line with the Court of Appeal's decision, held that self-government rights should be constrained to reserves and site-specific use rights. The opposing positions created significant tensions, and negotiations eventually broke down. Rather than renew the accord of respect and recognition, the province appealed the *Delgamuukw, Gisdaywa* case to the Supreme Court of Canada to establish the definitive limits of Aboriginal title and rights.

As already discussed, while the Supreme Court decision did not provide a definitive decision regarding the status of Gitxsan and Wet'suwet'en title, it did establish a clear contemporary doctrine of Aboriginal title that would set the foundation for negotiations and new relationships between Indigenous peoples and settler authorities. The court's framing of Aboriginal title established that the government had a vital role in reconciling Indigenous peoples with the settlement and development of the land, as it was the duty of the colonial sovereign to negotiate land transfers with Indigenous peoples. As the court described, Aboriginal title lands could not be alienated in private transactions.

*What the inalienability of lands held pursuant to aboriginal title suggests is that those lands are more than just a fungible commodity.*

> *The relationship between an aboriginal community and the lands over which it has aboriginal title has an important non-economic component. The land has an inherent and unique value in itself, which is enjoyed by the community with aboriginal title to it.*[124]

In the eyes of the court, Indigenous peoples possessed an exclusive right to use and occupy the land, so long as they protected the inherent connection to those lands for future generations. If an Indigenous people were to use the land in ways that were irreconcilable with the nature of Aboriginal title, the court reasoned, the titleholders needed to negotiate a land surrender to the colonial sovereign. Conversely, settler authorities needed to be mindful of their duty to respect Indigenous interests in Aboriginal title lands. Recognizing that Indigenous peoples possessed economic interests in their traditional land use, the court outlined a specific government duty to respect the "inescapable economic component" of Aboriginal title, ensuring that Indigenous peoples were appropriately compensated when their economic interests were eroded.[125]

This was a significant victory for the Gitxsan and Wet'suwet'en in that it reinforced their negotiating position. As Brian Slattery describes, *Delgamuukw, Gisdaywa* established a contemporary doctrine of Aboriginal title, transforming the historical Aboriginal claims to land as their distinct possession into a latent form of title that could serve as the basis of negotiation.[126] However, the contemporary form of Aboriginal title, as Slattery explains, was still only partially articulated by the courts.

> *In effect, the courts have the power to recognize certain core elements of a generative right—sufficient to provide the foundation for negotiations and to ensure that the Indigenous party enjoys a significant portion of its rights pending final agreement. However, the courts are not in a position to give a detailed and exhaustive account of a generative right in all its facets. This result can be achieved only by negotiations between the parties.*[127]

Thus, the Supreme Court's deferral of judgment in *Delgamuukw, Gisdaywa* was productive of new spaces of negotiation between settler and Indigenous authorities.

The Supreme Court of Canada's *Delgamuukw, Gisdaywa* decision challenged settler authorities to adopt a stance that more substantively engaged Indigenous concerns. In the wake of the decision, the British Columbia Treaty Commission initiated a formal review of the treaty-making process. In its 1999 report, the review panel listed several measures that could serve to reconcile Indigenous interests with resource-extractive development. They recommended that

> *resources be devoted to community-based planning activities; traditional knowledge of land use and resource management be incorporated into the planning exercise; additional resources devoted to those First Nations requiring enhanced capacity to negotiate;...programs and services be developed to promote educational opportunities among Aboriginal peoples and to enhance their efforts at career mobility; and governments encourage the formation of commercial joint ventures between First Nations and the public and private sectors.*[128]

Thus, the government began to build the knowledge infrastructure necessary to more effectively calculate Indigenous land interests and more effectively integrate Indigenous people into the economy. In this period immediately following *Delgamuukw, Gisdaywa*, provincial and federal authorities focused on negotiating comprehensive agreements with Indigenous groups that would provide "certainty in land rights, lands and resources, and Aboriginal title."[129]

In 2000, the first modern treaty in British Columbia, the Nisga'a Final Agreement, was established. The treaty provided a model for the type of reconciliation that the government aimed to effect. Technically, the Nisga'a Final Agreement was made outside the British Columbia treaty process because negotiations began after the 1973 *Calder* decision, well before the process had been established. However, as the first modern land claim to be resolved in the province, it demonstrated the government's approach to reconciliation.[130] The agreement defined Nisga'a treaty rights to self-government and resource allocations, but also required the surrender 92 percent of claimed Nisga'a territories in exchange for monetary compensation and recognition of the aforementioned treaty rights. Under the treaty process, the provincial government insisted that Indigenous peoples relinquish title to the majority of their lands. Again, the justification was that this was necessary to provide certainty of title for resource development.

The government's focus on certainty of title created tensions in treaty negotiations, as Indigenous communities wanted long-term security as well as enduring relationships to their lands.[131] Treaty talks have been remarkably slow to resolve, particularly among Indigenous claimants distant from major urban areas. Many Indigenous communities simply balked at abandoning the majority of their territories and land use rights; approximately 40 percent of Indigenous communities in British Columbia never participated in the treaty process. To ameliorate Indigenous concerns with the process, the government shifted the language of treaties so that they "modified" rather than extinguished Aboriginal rights. However, this simply placed a semantic veil over the extinguishment, as the language of treaties still required an Indigenous people to agree to modify their rights so that they could only exercise the delimited rights defined in the treaty, which amounts to much the same thing. Once one decodes the government doublespeak, as Manuel describes, "it is impossible to conclude other than 'certainty' means 'extinguishment.'"[132] In the decades following the signing of the Nisga'a Final Agreement, treaty talks produced very little certainty and Indigenous politics were far from extinguished. As I write this, fifty years after the creation of the federal comprehensive claims policy and thirty years after the establishment of the British Columbia treaty process, most treaty negotiations in the province, including those with the Wet'suwet'en hereditary chiefs, have stalled. Nevertheless, negotiations continue to unfold in other venues.

This is another example of how the *Delgamuukw, Gisdaywa* case successfully initiated processes that have situated Gitxsan and Wet'suwet'en authority and territorial knowledge in new relationships with colonial regimes. In the absence of a final treaty agreement, interim agreements between the province and Indigenous communities have been increasingly used to resolve issues around specific developments or resource sectors.[133] At the same time, the need to reconcile Indigenous claims with the exercise of provincial and federal government jurisdiction has inflected resource governance processes. Moreover, because Gitxsan and Wet'suwet'en testimony in court challenged conventions of evidentiary procedure, their intervention has not only expanded the spaces of negotiation but also reformulated evidentiary procedures in settler resource governance processes.

These evolving processes have reshaped economic relations beyond the state. While discussions of Indigenous peoples often focus on the colonial relation between Indigenous peoples and the settler state, it is necessary to apprehend the way in which global corporate capital has become implicated in these negotiations. The uncertainty generated by potentially unmet government duties to Indigenous peoples has led corporations to develop strategies to resecure their investments in resource development. Although the legal particularities of the relationship between colonial state authority and Indigenous peoples do not require corporate engagement with Indigenous peoples, the corporate need to maximize the security of investments does. Thus, both government and corporate actors have sought to reconcile Indigeneity and development. In these processes, Indigenous peoples have been subjected to new structures of discipline that aim to fit their concerns in the interstices of development or meld their interests within the unfolding of capitalist extraction.

To understand these emergent new relationships, it is necessary to examine new modes of transnational settler-Indigenous governance. Scholars thus must move beyond an oversimplified discussion of the violent exclusions of settler sovereignty. As Alan Hunt and Gary Wickham argue, law needs to be evaluated not just in the finality of decision or resolution, but in the effects of regulations that define an acceptable range of solutions within which people can fit.[134] Rather than functioning in accordance with a binary logic that simply suspends one claim and warrants another, regulatory apparatuses of government aim to establish "an average considered as optimal on the one hand, and, on the other, a bandwidth of the acceptable that must not be exceeded."[135] Beyond the decisiveness or imagined certainty of a final agreement or court declaration, contemporary negotiations around Indigenous rights need to be understood in terms of proliferating apparatuses of consultation and engagement, and as devices for constructing new grids of intelligibility through which to evaluate Indigenous interests. As Michel Foucault says, describing the emergence of new modes of liberal governance, new rationalities provide the frames through which "a completely different distribution of things and mechanisms takes shape."[136] In the context of Indigenous mobilization, new government regulatory regimes and corporate initiatives work to establish a productive engagement between Indigenous peoples and industrial development. This regulative pressure represents a key way in which Indigenous political movements have reconfigured the politics of development.

# II

Pipeline Governance and the Arts of Reconciling Indigenous Peoples with Development

# 3

## Indigeneity on the Page

*Land Use and Occupancy Studies*

FOLLOWING THE *CALDER* CASE IN 1973, traditional use and occupancy mapping techniques emerged as a technique for documenting Indigenous territorial interests to colonial authorities. In the wake of the *Delgamuukw, Gisdaywa* decision, these studies took on additional importance. The case had established the requirement that settler authorities reconcile enduring Aboriginal title and rights with the settlement and development of the land.[1] It had also established that Indigenous traditional knowledge was a valid source of evidence to be considered in evaluating their relationship to the land. However, in conceptualizing Aboriginal title, the court emphasized it was a product of the interaction of Canadian and Indigenous legal orders, thus best understood as a translation of Indigenous territorial relationships to the settler legal order rather than relations emic to Indigenous law. While the Supreme Court recognized that Indigenous oral histories have evidentiary weight in evaluating Aboriginal title claims, it also indicated that Indigenous peoples could use their ongoing physical use and occupation of territory to demonstrate their interests to colonial authorities.

This chapter takes up the questions of how Indigenous struggles for Canadian state recognition of their territorial rights have established new fields of research to codify Indigenous interests within resource governance processes. Specifically, it looks at types of research that are variously called land use and occupancy work,

Aboriginal traditional knowledge research, traditional use studies, traditional ecological knowledge research, and traditional use and occupancy studies. Terry Tobias describes use studies as documenting "where activities like hunting, fishing and travelling occur."[2] Occupancy mapping is broader. Settler legal discourse constructs occupancy as a means of holding and thereby possessing land as property. Occupancy studies involve collecting information on habitation sites like cabins and burial grounds, Indigenous place names, spiritual geographies, traditional ecological knowledge, and stories and songs, and using this information to build upon geographies of land use.[3]

I argue that Indigenous traditional use and occupancy studies are technologies of power-knowledge that both integrate into and interrupt settler regulatory processes. For one, these studies are much more readily cognizable to colonial authorities than other forms of knowledge, such as the *adaawk* and *cin k'ikh* that McEachern struggled to interpret in the *Delgamuukw, Gisdaywa* trial. As founder and former President of the Indigenous Bar Association David C. Nahwegahbow writes, "the only way to prove occupancy is by having a map that sets out the evidence in terms the people across the negotiating table, or a judge, will understand and accept."[4] I begin this chapter by tracing the development and employment of traditional use and occupancy studies in efforts to win court and government recognition of the impacts of development on Indigenous people. Then, using as a case study the once-proposed Enbridge Northern Gateway Pipeline project and its collection of Aboriginal land use information as part of its environmental assessment, I focus on the different ways that traditional use and occupancy studies have not only translated Wet'suwet'en territorial relationships for the courts, but advanced recognition of Indigenous geographies within Canadian resource governance processes. These studies do not operate to a singular end, but can be strategically employed to a spectrum of effects, ranging from highlighting specific sites of Indigenous significance around which to route development to more powerfully challenging the limited frames of Canadian resource governance itself. In the context of environmental and energy governance, occupancy claims can not only modify development trajectories, but be used to challenge the logic of resource governance itself.

### The Counter-inscription of Indigeneity

Indigenous territorial claims have created new legal precedents that require colonial authorities to engage with Indigenous communities and reconcile their claims with settlement and resource development. The effect of this jurisprudence has been to create a new problematic for the exercise of colonial jurisdiction over natural resources. The Supreme Court of Canada's decision in *Delgamuukw, Gisdaywa* recognized the validity and importance of considering Indigenous evidence of their territorial connections and shifted how settler authorities had to conduct resource governance processes vis-à-vis Indigenous peoples. Settler resource governance authorities had to meaningfully consider Indigenous evidence of their territorial interests, and the potential impacts of development projects on them. This juridical development dovetailed with the emergence of a new field of Aboriginal traditional knowledge research, in which professional consultants—typically with academic degrees in anthropology, environmental studies, geography, natural resource management, or Indigenous studies—articulated methods of collecting information from Indigenous knowledge holders and compiling evidence of Indigenous territorial interests. These Aboriginal traditional knowledge studies and their methods served to render Indigenous traditional use and occupancy legible to colonial officials.

Indigenous peoples in Canada have been inscribing elements of their relationships to their territories on maps and on the written page for decades. In the early twentieth century, as Gitxsan and Wet'suwet'en hereditary chiefs struggled to resist colonial dispossession, they collaborated with allies to construct petitions and early counter-cartographies.[5] Indigenous peoples continue to develop increasingly sophisticated techniques to translate Indigenous territorial knowledge into a series of digital images.[6] In the 1960s and 1970s, the Nisga'a litigation in the *Calder* case incited contemporary research on land use and occupancy.[7] To establish evidence of the Nisga'a territorial claim in the *Calder* case, anthropologist Wilson Duff provided expert evidence supporting the Nisga'a claim, testifying that they had clear notions of land ownership prior to the assertion of colonial sovereignty over their territories.[8] Duff largely relied on the historical fieldnotes of Marius Barbeau, an early-twentieth-century ethnographer at the national museum who catalogued information on the Indigenous peoples of the Northwest Coast.[9] Barbeau would conduct extensive research in the region, involving not only the Nisga'a but also the Gitxsan and Tsimshian.[10] The overall patchy coverage of early ethnographic studies, however, left many Indigenous peoples without evidence to advance their claims.

In 1971, the Inuit formed the Inuit Tapirisat of Canada, a national organization to advance their territorial concerns.[11] Following the *Calder* decision in February 1973, the Inuit Tapirisat of Canada requested funding from the federal minister of Indian and Northern Affairs so research could be undertaken to create a comprehensive record of Inuit land use and occupancy in the Northwest Territories.[12] Conducting this research in the mid-1970s, Milton Freeman and Carol Brice-Bennett developed methodologies to document Indigenous connections to their traditional lands.[13] These research projects relied on a methodology referred to as *map biography*. Interviewers asked Indigenous informants to diagram their personal land use activities by tracing on map transparencies places that they used for hunting, fishing, gathering, travel, camping, burials, and spiritual practices.[14] Researchers then aggregated the information gathered from individual interviews by map categories to construct a community portrait of land use activities (often gradating the boundaries to indicate higher-intensity core land use areas). By the early 1990s, Peter Usher, Frank Tough, and Robert Galois argued that map biography had become the primary method used in Indigenous traditional use mapping due to the perceived objectivity of the community survey methods and the legibility of the maps to colonial authorities.[15] Today, over three decades later, the techniques used to construct the maps have been updated to better utilize modern cartographic software and hardware, but the basic methodology of map biographies remains entrenched.

In addition to documenting Indigenous use of the land, traditional use studies also serve to highlight the conflict between Indigenous use patterns and resource development projects. Ethnographic fieldnotes from the early twentieth century were used in the Nisga'a litigation to establish that Nisga'a title existed prior to colonial sovereignty. But the Nisga'a were not the only Indigenous people facing intensifying resource development pressures. These issues came to national attention in 1974 with the Mackenzie Valley Pipeline Inquiry, also called the Berger Inquiry after Thomas Berger, the inquiry's commissioner and the lawyer who had represented the Nisga'a in the Calder case.[16]

Studying the impact of pipeline development on Arctic Indigenous communities, the Berger Inquiry signalled the beginning of more concerted consideration of Indigenous peoples in resource management processes.[17] Modifying the methods of map biography, research on the impacts of resource development projects on Indigenous peoples focused analysis on the overlap of Indigenous land use patterns with the geography of proposed industrial activity.[18] This methodology effectively highlighted the spatial conflicts between industrial development and Indigenous subsistence regimes, and established a counter-discourse that challenged governing paradigms of resource management. Berger's report, for instance, recognized how "subduing the land and extracting its resources" advanced an industrial economy that displaced traditional Indigenous sustenance economy.[19] Berger recognized that industrial development provided job opportunities, yet suggested this failed to adequately compensate for development impacts on Indigenous economies that continued to rely on a mix of wage labour and subsistence activities: "To the extent that the development of the northern frontier undermines the possibilities of self-employment provided by hunting, fishing and trapping, employment and unemployment will go hand-in-hand."[20] Recognizing that the North was home to Indigenous peoples whose lives would be dramatically and irreversibly altered by the introduction of a gas pipeline, Berger recommended delaying pipeline construction to allow time to address Indigenous interests.

After the *Calder* decision and the Berger Inquiry, Indigenous peoples increasingly sought to advance claims based on their traditional use and occupancy. In May 1979, the Trial Division of the Federal Court of Canada heard the case *Baker Lake (Hamlet) v. Canada (Minister of Indian Affairs and Northern Development)*.[21] In the case, the Hamlet of Baker Lake, the Baker Lake Hunters and Trappers Association, the Inuit Tapirisat of Canada, and 113 local residents brought forward a claim to Aboriginal title over 78,000 square kilometres in the Northwest Territories. The defendants in the case were the federal minister of Indian Affairs and Northern Development, various branches of the federal government, and six mining and exploration companies who had been issued exploration and land use permits by the federal government. The case followed the prior issuance of an interlocutory injunction based on evidence that mineral exploration activities would adversely affect Inuit caribou hunting.[22] The Inuit sought declarations that, first, the Baker Lake area was subject to an Inuit Aboriginal title to hunt and fish, and, subsequently, that the mining regulations licensing exploration activities did not apply in the Baker Lake area. On this basis, they aimed to elicit orders halting mining exploration in the region. In a partial recognition of Inuit title, Justice Mahoney determined that the Inuit had Aboriginal title to the majority of the Baker Lake area, but that rights pursuant to this title could be abridged by legislation.[23]

Although it was only a trial-level decision, *Baker Lake* nonetheless both outlined requirements for a proof of Aboriginal title and pressed the need for the government to account for Indigenous land interests. In his decision, Mahoney articulated four elements of a proof of Aboriginal title. First, the claimants and their ancestors must be members of an organized society. Second, that organized society must occupy the specific territory over which they assert Aboriginal title. Third, the claimants' occupation of that territory must work to the exclusion of other organized societies. Finally, fourth, the particular Indigenous occupation in question must have been an established fact at the time of the assertion of colonial sovereignty. Thus, legal processes required that Indigenous peoples provide proof of their connection to their lands in a form cognizable to the courts.[24]

*Baker Lake* also resonated with colonial authorities' increasing acknowledgement of the need to recognize Indigenous territorial claims and incorporate Indigenous peoples into resource governance. The case prefigured subsequent developments in the Northwest Territories, in which colonial authorities responded to Indigenous demands for recognition. In the territorial North, the terms of new comprehensive land claims, beginning with the Inuvialuit Final Agreement in 1984, required that wildlife management include "the relevant knowledge and experience of both the Inuvialuit and the scientific communities...in order to achieve conservation."[25] In 1993, the Northwest Territories adopted its Traditional Knowledge Policy, which defined Aboriginal traditional knowledge as "a valid and essential source of information about the natural environment and its resources, the use of natural resources, and the relationship of people to the land and to each other." The policy also stated that the government would "incorporate traditional knowledge into Government decisions and actions where appropriate."[26] In 1995, the Northwest Territories put the policy into effect in the environmental assessment process for a mine, requiring BHP Diamonds Inc. to incorporate consideration of traditional knowledge and science in its project application.[27]

The Supreme Court of Canada decision in *Delgamuukw, Gisdaywa* in 1997 conveyed further meaning and import to studies of Indigenous land use and occupancy. Writing for the majority, Chief Justice Antonio Lamer delineated three criteria necessary to make out a claim to Aboriginal title: "(i) the land must have been occupied prior to sovereignty, (ii) if present occupation is relied on as proof of occupation pre-sovereignty, there must be a continuity between present and pre-sovereignty occupation, and (iii) at sovereignty, that occupation must have been exclusive."[28] As discussed in the previous chapter, Lamer situated Aboriginal title uniquely at the interface of colonial and Indigenous territorial visions, with sources in both Indigenous legal orders and colonial doctrine. Lamer advised that evidence based in both Indigenous traditions and colonial historical records "should be taken into account in establishing the proof of occupancy."[29] Thus, although Lamer recognized the import of the Gitxsan *adaawk* and Wet'suwet'en *cin k'ikh* as a form of evidence, he stressed the need to translate these forms of knowledge into proof of the occupation of territory in order to prove claims of Aboriginal title to colonial authorities.[30] Citing Kent McNeil, Lamer particularly emphasized that "physical occupation is proof of possession at law, which in turn will ground title to the land."[31] To provide proof of Aboriginal title, Lamer wrote in his decision that "an aboriginal community may provide evidence of present occupation as proof of pre-sovereignty occupation."[32] Lamer listed a variety of ways that a claim to physical occupation could be established, "ranging from the construction of dwellings through cultivation and enclosure of fields to regular use of definite tracts of land for hunting, fishing or otherwise exploiting its resources."[33]

The Supreme Court recognized the ways Indigenous relationships to the lands have changed post-contact, but expected "a continuity between present and pre-sovereignty occupation" on Aboriginal title land.[34] Framing the concept of Aboriginal title, the court relied upon a colonial temporal schema. As Lamer described, "the relevant time for the determination of aboriginal title is at the time before sovereignty."[35] However, the justices recognized a degree of dynamism in Indigenous land use practices. The court did not completely restrict Aboriginal occupancy to the exact ways that an Indigenous people historically used the land at the moment in which colonial sovereignty was asserted. For instance, it did not stop being traditional use of the territory when Indigenous hunters picked up guns. However, the court constrained Aboriginal title, requiring that the use of Aboriginal title lands remain congruent with how that Indigenous people used the land at the moment of the assertion of colonial sovereignty. If an Indigenous people traditionally had a sustainable relationship to their territory based on the careful stewardship and conservation of animal species, the court suggested that they could not exploit contemporary Aboriginal title lands as gold mines.

The Supreme Court further noted that the discontinuation of certain Aboriginal land uses in accordance with settler government regulations did not result in the nullification of Aboriginal title and rights. Thus, although Wet'suwet'en *yikh* stopped burning their berry patches following the provincial enactment of forestry regulations forbidding the use of burns as a land management practice, this did not invalidate a *yikh*'s connection to those lands. The court recognized colonial authorities have introduced environmental regulations that disrupted Indigenous peoples' ability to occupy their traditional lands. But the historical enforcement of provincial land laws of general application that interfered with Indigenous use did not erase the potential that an Indigenous people could renew that land use practice and use it as evidence of their Aboriginal title. Therefore, while continuity and present occupancy were required for Indigenous traditional use, the court did not require Indigenous peoples to possess an unbroken chain of continuity in their relations with their lands. The *Delgamuukw, Gisdaywa* decision thus spurred both the development of land use and occupancy studies and a push for Indigenous communities to revitalize traditional land use and occupancy as evidence of their ongoing relationship with their territories.

The increasing recognition of the relevance of Indigenous land use studies in resource management processes led to a proliferation of applied research on Indigenous geographies. Various formal governmental devices now call forth research on Indigenous relations to the land, requiring Aboriginal traditional knowledge to be included within regulatory reviews. A 2003 amendment to the Canadian Environmental Assessment Act directed environmental assessment processes to consider the effects of development on Indigenous peoples and their traditions.[36] This legislation was repealed in 2012 and replaced by a new Canadian Environmental Assessment Act that sought in part to ease barriers to pipeline project approvals. However, the new act still listed the promotion of "communication and cooperation with aboriginal peoples with respect to environmental assessments" as one of its underlying purposes; included regulatory consideration of project impacts to

Aboriginal health, socio-economic conditions, heritage, and traditional land use; and indicated that an "environmental assessment of a designated project may take into account community knowledge and Aboriginal traditional knowledge."[37] Similarly, the 2012 National Energy Board filing manual required that proponents provide detailed information about Indigenous land use if the project "would be located on, or traverse, Crown land or the traditional territory, reserve land or settlement area of an Aboriginal group"; if it "may adversely affect the current use of lands and resources by Aboriginal people"; or if "there is outstanding concern about this element of the project [i.e., effects on Indigenous land use], which has not been resolved through consultation."[38]

The emergence of management regimes integrating Indigenous peoples and their knowledge has been conditioned by the legal reasoning of colonial juridical authorities and the practical rationalities of colonial governmental apparatuses. As Paul Nadasdy has described in the Kluane territories of the Yukon, restricted notions of Indigenous traditions in resource governance work situate local Indigenous peoples' "place at the table" by reinforcing an a priori set of normative colonial relationships. This approach, Nadasdy argues, has the effect of "preventing rather than fostering meaningful change by ensnaring participants in a tangle of bureaucracy and endless meetings."[39] Despite rhetorics of empowerment, Nadasdy suggests that studies of Indigenous environmental knowledge foreclose on real possibilities of addressing power relations in the colonial present. Positioning Indigenous territorial knowledge as simply more data for governing management bureaucracies results in the distortion of Indigenous political geographies. Bureaucracies necessarily frame and screen the shape and content of Indigenous knowledge to make it fit within institutional knowledge management practices.[40] This obscures the holistic and contextual value that traditional knowledge experts often stress makes Indigenous knowledge unique. It also fundamentally serves to empower colonial centres of calculation, which work through the possession of abstract, quantified knowledge that allows them to act at a distance. In so doing, it reconstitutes the territoriality of the capitalist nation-state oriented to the extraction of resources from its peripheral regions.

The practical rationalities undergirding settler resource management processes thus continue to condition the terms on which Indigeneity is recognized. Resource management processes assume space can be segmented into a linear coordinate system. Cartesian imaginaries conceptualize the cultural and ecological landscape as a discrete and exclusive plane, and within this paradigm cultural sites are imagined as discrete and exclusive.[41] As J.B. Harley reminds us, the power-knowledge relations implicit in maps function as forms of political discourse in which the inclusion and exclusion of entities and relations work in accordance with particular interests.[42] Cartesian schema neglect the interrelation of sites throughout a territory. Thus, when such schema define one site worthy of protection against development, they simultaneously project others as empty spaces where development can proceed. The cartographic delineations implicit in recognizing sites of Indigenous cultural significance through Cartesian mapping work to define the spaces *without* Indigeneity, reproducing the mythological *terra nullius*.[43] The recognition of Indigenous traditions thereby continues to relegate Indigenous peoples to a past and restrict their claims to modern jurisdiction. This regularizes the relation to nature encoded in colonial ideas of development and renders subaltern alternative articulations of socio-natural relations within Indigenous societies.

Responding to the constraints of mapping in resource governance processes, Richard W. Stoffle and Michael J. Evans have documented the consistent bifurcation of Indigenous research strategies as they participated in environmental impact assessment processes in the United States.[44] Mirroring the institutionalization of consideration for Indigenous interests in Canadian resource governance process, the United States National Environmental Policy also requires American Indian cultural resource studies to be included in environmental assessment processes. Stoffle and Evans argue that there have been two broad trajectories of how Indigenous communities have sought to advance their interests in cultural resource studies: cultural triage and holistic conservation.

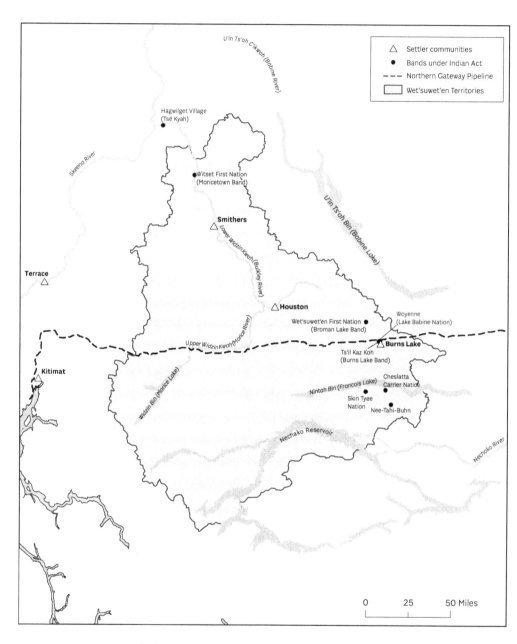

MAP 2: Enbridge Northern Gateway Pipeline, Wet'suwet'en territories, Indian Act bands, and settler communities.

The strategy of cultural triage seeks to identify sites of particular importance and prioritize the protection of these sites from development impacts. In contrast, the strategy of holistic conservation refuses the development consensus and instead posits Indigenous relations to the world as irreconcilable with the expansion of capitalist resource extraction. These two trajectories of response highlight the different ways in which Indigenous peoples continue to strategically negotiate their relationships with colonial power, as well as the different ways their claims seek to modify or offset extractive developments. Both strategies have been used by different Wet'suwet'en-led organizations to navigate and respond to colonial resource development on their lands.

### A Pipeline across Overlapping Sources of Indigenous Authority

Five years after the final decision in the *Delgamuukw, Gisdaywa* case, Enbridge began preliminary examination of the potential for a pipeline connecting the Athabasca tar sands to the Northwest Coast. The proposed Northern Gateway project, if constructed, would have crossed traditional territories claimed by the Wet'suwet'en hereditary chiefs and followed a course adjacent to numerous Wet'suwet'en reserves. It would have also impacted numerous other Indigenous nations. Under the operant legislation at the time, the project required certification by the National Energy Board and environmental assessment under the Canadian Environmental Assessment Act. In accordance with this legislation and the emergent jurisprudence around Aboriginal title and rights, project governance needed to address and mitigate its potential impact on Indigenous land interests. Thus, the regulatory review of the project included consideration of project impacts on Indigenous land interests, prominently including those of the Wet'suwet'en. As part of its application for project approval, Enbridge prepared detailed information on Aboriginal traditional land use and occupancy, conducting collaborative research with Indigenous communities, and providing independent funding for Indigenous communities to conduct or contract their own studies and submit information on traditional land use for regulatory consideration.

In this section, I seek to position these studies within the context of negotiations between Enbridge and different Wet'suwet'en band and hereditary authorities. Focusing first on Enbridge, I outline the broad course of its program of Aboriginal community engagement and research on Aboriginal traditional knowledge. I then situate these engagements within the duties guiding the conduct of different Wet'suwet'en authorities. Gesturing to the complexity of overlapping forms of contemporary Indigenous authority, I highlight the evolution and organization of two particular Wet'suwet'en groups: the band of Skin Tyee and the Office of the Wet'suwet'en. Both groups engaged in forms of traditional land use and occupancy research with regard to the Northern Gateway project; however, they oriented to the research in very different ways, following the responsibilities associated with the lawful conduct of their authority in relation to, respectively, the Indian Act and the obligations of the hereditary chiefs to uphold the territorial responsibilities of their *yikh* and *dïdikh*. On the one hand, the Skin Tyee study showcases how Indigenous interests can be accommodated in development planning. On the other, the research conducted by the Office of the Wet'suwet'en presents concerns about territorial use and possession that put in question whether the knowledge-gathering elements of environmental reviews lead to sufficient protection of Indigenous territories.

In 2002, Enbridge hired consultants to begin examining the feasibility of what was then called the Gateway Project. They contracted community engagement specialists who began contacting potentially impacted Indigenous communities. Over the next three years, the company would consider various routes and options for a pipeline connecting the Athabasca tar sands to Pacific ports. During this period, the company notified 171 Indigenous groups of its activities through a mailed brochure and introductory letter; following up this initial contact, the company also conducted meetings, had telephone conversations, and issued further letters clarifying central concerns.[45] Of the Indigenous groups that would be potentially impacted along the pipeline route, Enbridge consultants contacted the Office of the Wet'suwet'en hereditary chiefs as well as five Wet'suwet'en bands: Burns Lake Band (renamed

Ts'il Kaz Koh in 2013), Hagwilget Village, Wet'suwet'en First Nation (formerly the Broman Lake Band), Nee-Tahi-Buhn, and Skin Tyee (which broke away from Nee-Tahi-Buhn in 2000).[46] They also engaged the Carrier Sekani Tribal Council, with which the bands of Ts'il Kaz Koh and Wet'suwet'en First Nation remained affiliated.

In 2005, after defining its 1,170 kilometre project corridor between Bruderheim, Alberta, and Kitimat, British Columbia, Enbridge focused its engagement activities on Indigenous groups with reserves or traditional lands located within 80 kilometres of the project corridor.[47] At this point, the company formalized its Aboriginal engagement criteria. It engaged Indigenous authorities in accordance with the ways in which both the settler state and the court system recognized Indigeneity: it reached out to groups formally recognized "as a 'Band' as defined in the *Indian Act* and recognized by the Department of Indian and Northern Affairs Canada" as well as groups with claims to "protected Aboriginal rights, lands, and land uses as defined by s.35 of the Constitution Act, 1982."[48] In its project application, Enbridge identified and engaged with forty-two Indian Act bands, seven tribal council or band confederacies, and twenty-five Métis or non-Status Indian organizations along the pipeline route.[49] Two hereditary chiefs' organizations were also included on the company's engagement list: those of the Gitxsan and Wet'suwet'en. In its initial community outreach, "communities expressed concern over their lack of capacity to fully participate in the engagement process."[50] To address these concerns, Enbridge began providing capacity funding to Indigenous organizations along the pipeline corridor "to facilitate their participation in the engagement process."[51] The company used the engagement process, in part, to determine which Indigenous groups had land interests that needed to be accounted for in the project application.

To facilitate the collection of Indigenous land use and occupancy data for its regulatory submissions, Enbridge provided financial support for what it referred to as Aboriginal traditional knowledge (ATK) research. Indigenous communities were offered the choice between conducting ATK research in collaboration with company consultants or conducting it independently (either through their own offices or by contracting an independent consultant). Attempting to reflect the breadth of land use and occupancy studies, Enbridge funded two types of ATK research: traditional use studies and traditional ecological knowledge studies. As the company outlined in its project application, traditional use studies collected information on activities and sites or areas of cultural significance for Aboriginal peoples within their traditional territories. These types of activities, sites, or areas were classified under four categories: travel (trails, waterways, landmarks), harvesting (registered traplines, resource use areas, fish camps, berry-picking areas, medicinal plant collection areas), habitation (occupation sites, gathering places, camp sites, cabins), and spiritual (burial sites, sacred sites, sacred landscapes). Multi-use sites fell under more than one category. Traditional ecological knowledge, in contrast, was understood to be "the wisdom and understanding of a particular natural environment that has accumulated over countless generations."[52] Enbridge treated traditional ecological knowledge as supplemental to the research collected for the environmental assessment. It provided "additional context to baseline descriptions and the analysis of potential project effects."[53] In their application, Enbridge suggested ATK was incorporated into its project design and planning processes. In particular, Enbridge emphasized how locating traditional use sites and areas aided the company in its constraints mapping, rerouting assessments, and watercourse crossing analysis.

Once Enbridge had determined that an ATK study was required for a community, it sent consultants, which it referred to as ATK facilitators, to negotiate the scope of the research with that community. The ATK facilitators would discuss the Canadian regulatory requirements and Enbridge's objectives for the studies, as well as whatever research objectives that Indigenous community had. The ATK facilitators then collaborated with Indigenous community representatives to define the scope of and timeline for the research program. After these studies were completed, Enbridge summarized the results in the ATK volume of its project application and subsequent updates to this component of its application. From the company's perspective, the primary aim of ATK research was to collate Indigenous concerns about the impact of pipeline development on their lands and implement measures to mitigate these impacts. In theory, documenting this process would enable federal regulators to determine whether project planning had adequately accounted for and accommodated Indigenous interests. More simply put, it allowed regulators to determine whether the company had effectively integrated Indigenous knowledge into its project planning.

Wet'suwet'en band and hereditary entities adopted a range of approaches to conducting land use and occupancy studies to document the potential impacts of the Enbridge Northern Gateway project on their interests. These approaches are best understood along a spectrum. At one end of the spectrum lie band authorities who sought to secure the well-being of their members by providing information to Enbridge, and ultimately to regulators. Through research participation, these authorities sought to both minimize project impacts on valued land use sites and highlight ways that the project could support the retention of community traditions. At the other end of the spectrum are Indigenous organizations that used traditional use and occupancy studies to challenge not only the project, but also the forms of colonial territorial jurisdiction that permitted it under settler law. These different approaches to traditional knowledge research in part reflect broader questions about jurisdiction—and what duties different Wet'suwet'en authorities interpreted as guiding their conduct. To understand different community responses to corporate outreach and project proposals, it is therefore necessary to engage with the norms that guide the conduct of different forms of Indigenous legal authority.

Bands are constituted under the federal Indian Act, and the conduct of band authorities continues to be directed by the fiscal logics of the Canadian government. As Shiri Pasternak compellingly details, under the federal structures orienting the conduct of elected band officials, "financial solvency became a primary object of governance."[54] As I discussed in chapter 1, the historic and ongoing dispossession of Indigenous peoples has left their communities increasingly reliant on federal transfer payments. Colonial land thefts have enriched settler society while leaving Indigenous peoples relegated to a condition of dependency on reserve. Nevertheless, federal Indian policy consistently positions band authorities as responsible for addressing economic conditions among their members, depicting poor band governance as the cause of financial crises on reserve. On this basis, the federal government threatens to suspend the autonomy of any band it considers financially irresponsible, placing it into "third party management" where authority over band finances is transferred to a private accounting company.[55] This makes the issue of underdevelopment appear to be a problem fundamentally about band financial accountability. To maintain their political autonomy, band authorities are pressured to resolve "welfare dependency," typically by facilitating new economic opportunities for band members "with entrepreneurial and employment opportunities through resource extraction."[56] This pressure is particularly acute for band officials administering remote reserve communities, where band members have historically born the burden of industrial impacts on traditional lifeways while being largely excluded from economic development benefits. Although colonial dispossessions impacted all Wet'suwet'en communities, circumstances on different band reserves and among distinct band memberships varied.

In 2000, there were six bands with primarily Wet'suwet'en membership: Ts'il Kaz Koh, Nee-Tahi-Buhn, Skin Tyee, Wet'suwet'en First Nation, Hagwilget, and Moricetown (which would be renamed Witset in 2017). Ts'il Kaz Koh and Wet'suwet'en First Nation are among the smallest bands, with on-reserve populations of, respectively, 48 and 96, and total registered band memberships of 128 and 242.[57] Although the members of both these bands have long struggled to overcome racial discrimination, Ts'il Kaz Koh and Wet'suwet'en First Nation are adjacent to the major road and railway transportation corridor in the region and their members possess greater access to services in the nearby settler communities than those on more remote reserves. Moreover, both bands remain affiliated with the Carrier Sekani Tribal Council and have access to further services and support through it.

In contrast, the Nee-Tahi-Buhn and Skin Tyee bands, at the southern reaches of Wet'suwet'en territory, are far from the major transportation corridor along the railway. That region of Wet'suwet'en territories, in close proximity to the giant Nechako Reservoir created by the Kenney Dam in the 1950s, has endured some of the greatest impacts of industrial development.[58] While they live near one of the largest water infrastructure projects in Canadian history, they remain isolated, separated from the main population corridor along the railway line by Nïntah Bin (Francois Lake), the second longest natural lake in British Columbia. To access the nearest settler community with more than a 1,000 people, one must drive thirteen to fourteen kilometres from the Nee-Tahi-Buhn and Skin Tyee reserves to the MV Francois Forester ferry at Southbank, which runs across the lake hourly during the day, and then drive an additional 24 kilometres north to the municipality of Burns Lake. On the south side of the lake, the bands' regional population is sparse. The total membership of the Wet'suwet'en bands of Skin Tyee and Nee-Tahi-Buhn is, respectively, 166 and 323.[59] In both bands, most members live off reserve.[60] The most significant on-reserve population in the area is the Dakelh band of Cheslatta Carrier, which has 181 of its 351 members living on its reserves.[61] Until 2003, all of these communities lacked access to water services. In order to build community capacity and address local water problems, the Nee-Tahi-Buhn, Skin Tyee, and Cheslatta Carrier bands had to partner with the local settler community to pump water 44 kilometres south from Nïntah Bin.[62] Similar partnerships have been required to secure the other services, such as healthcare, in these communities, as well.[63]

The other two Wet'suwet'en bands, Hagwilget and Witset, are associated with the larger historic villages of the same names. With reserve lands set aside at seasonal fishing grounds along the Widzin Kwah, they remain on the major transportation corridor established by the railway, which followed the river. The total band membership of Witset is 2,043; in Hagwilget, it is 794.[64] Their combined membership of 2,837 constitutes 77 percent of the registered Status Indian population of Wet'suwet'en bands. Like many bands in

Canada, the off-reserve population of these bands has ballooned in the last half-century as the government has lifted many of the restrictions that prevented Status Indians from living off reserve.[65] Nevertheless, they remain the two largest on-reserve Wet'suwet'en centres, with 672 people currently residing on the Witset reserves and another 194 people living in Hagwilget Village.

Beyond population, Witset and Hagwilget have a number of characteristics that distinguish their communities from the four bands to the south. Witset and Hagwilget remain central to enduring practices of Wet'suwet'en hereditary governance through the *balhats*. These villages are the historic sites where all the Wet'suwet'en *yikh* congregated in the summer to fish and feast together. The *balhats* continue to be a central institution regulating social life in these communities. While historically the Wet'suwet'en families associated with the southern bands would have seasonally returned to renew their kinship relations in Witset and Hagwilget, in more recent years many of the residents of the southern reserves have grown isolated from the centres of *balhats* governance. The historic separation of Wet'suwet'en bands between two different Indian agencies is still felt in entrenched divisions between Witset and Hagwilget in the north and the bands in the south. In the 1970s and 1980s, the Witset and Hagwilget bands belonged to the Gitksan-Carrier Tribal Council, which supported the hereditary chiefs in launching the *Delgamuukw, Gisdaywa* litigation. While tensions remain over relations between hereditary and band governance, the band governments at Witset and Hagwilget have historically focused on administering services to band members and not land claims.

The southern bands, in contrast, historically affiliated with the Carrier Sekani Tribal Council (CSTC), which advanced territorial claims in the name of its member bands rather than hereditary title holders. Incorporated as a non-profit organization, the CSTC was created to negotiate land claim agreements on behalf of its affiliated bands. The organization is governed by a board of directors composed of elected band chiefs and headed by a tribal chief elected at general assemblies. Over time, the CSTC mandate has expanded to include helping coordinate natural resource governance activities with its member bands. The CSTC framework thus situates territorial concerns under band jurisdiction. This approach continues to influence the bands of Ts'il Kaz Koh and Wet'suwet'en First Nation, which remain affiliated with the CSTC, but also Skin Tyee and Nee-Tahi-Buhn, which left the tribal council to operate independently.

The hereditary chiefs also created a body, the Office of the Wet'suwet'en, to represent their territorial interests in negotiations with the state. Like the CSTC, the Office of the Wet'suwet'en is incorporated as a non-profit organization under the British Columbia Societies Act and is governed by a board of directors. Unlike the CSTC, the directors of the Office of the Wet'suwet'en represent the different *yikh* and *dïdikh*, not Indian Act bands. Typically, the *yikh* and *dïdikh* representatives are the hereditary chiefs themselves; when a hereditary chief is ill or dies, however, a *yikh* may be represented by one of its subchiefs or the leader of another *yikh* in the same *dïdikh*. Originally named the Wet'suwet'en Treaty Office, the Office of the Wet'suwet'en was founded to support and navigate contemporary land claim negotiations with the provincial and federal governments. These talks stalled when the provincial government refused to negotiate shared jurisdiction across Wet'suwet'en territories and the hereditary chiefs were unwilling to negotiate the extinguishment of their Aboriginal title and rights. The hereditary chiefs' organization subsequently expanded its mandate; the Office of the Wet'suwet'en now represents the *yikh* and *dïdikh* in a range of areas, from child and family services to natural resource governance.

The Office of the Wet'suwet'en can be understood as a bridging institution that aims to link settler-colonial regimes to Indigenous governance practices. On the one hand, it runs under provincial regulations for non-profit societies and conducts various activities in accordance with a matrix of legal agreements with state agencies. On the other hand, it follows unwritten codes of lawful conduct within the hereditary system, referred to as *'anuc niwh'it'en* in Witsuwit'en. Functionally, day-to-day operations are organized into different departments administered by paid staff, reflecting the bureaucratic traditions of settler-state and corporate governance.

To a significant extent, these departments are structured to mirror the organization of state agencies and how they conduct governance. For instance, the Department of Natural Resources in the Office of the Wet'suwet'en coordinates responses to proposed resource developments. The office also seeks to work in accordance with Wet'suwet'en legal traditions. For instance, it organizes community engagement processes around the *dïdikh*. Hereditary chiefs direct the office and have sought to affirm the territorial declarations that guide its natural resource governance work through the *balhats*.

This is the governance terrain that Enbridge entered when it began approaching Indigenous peoples along its proposed pipeline route in the mid-2000s. Among the different Indigenous governing bodies, there was a relatively high degree of Indigenous engagement in Aboriginal traditional knowledge research. By the end of 2009, Enbridge reported seventeen ATK community reports had been completed and another thirteen were underway, with most other Indigenous groups along the proposed pipeline route engaged in discussion over the potential for ATK studies.[66] The Carrier Sekani Tribal Council conducted independent research, publishing its study in 2006.[67] By the time Enbridge submitted its project application for regulatory review in 2010, Skin Tyee had completed a collaborative study with the Enbridge ATK facilitators, while Ts'il Kaz Koh had completed an independent study and Nee-Tahi-Buhn had an independent study underway.[68] Enbridge never engaged with Witset and did not continue engaging Hagwilget after making preliminary inquiries. The Office of the Wet'suwet'en would eventually complete its own independent study, which it submitted to federal regulators in January 2012.[69]

By sharing knowledge through ATK research, both Skin Tyee and the Office of the Wet'suwet'en sought to protect their interests with regard to the Northern Gateway project, although they conceptualized and conveyed their interests in different ways. Collaborating with Enbridge ATK facilitators, Skin Tyee focused on documenting particularly important traditional land uses that they wished to be conserved, while also articulating opportunities where partnership with Enbridge could advance community concerns.

Preparing an independent traditional use and occupancy study, the Office of the Wet'suwet'en challenged not only the Enbridge Northern Gateway proposal but the authority of settler-state-appointed regulators to approve the project without the Wet'suwet'en hereditary chiefs' consent. Thus, the Office of the Wet'suwet'en made the question of territorial sovereignty rather than land use central to their submission. They also called into question the superficiality of the environmental research conducted by Enbridge, particularly challenging gaps in its fisheries assessments. These contrasting interventions highlight the breadth of Indigenous responses to development proposals, but they also highlight different ways that Indigenous peoples remain active participants in shaping development trajectories, both reshaping proposals to better reflect their community concerns and challenging the broader logics of development itself.

### Permitting Pipelines: Collaborative Approaches to Research

Enbridge conducted collaborative research with Skin Tyee in 2009 to document its Aboriginal traditional knowledge and how pipeline development could accommodate their concerns. The company had first engaged the band in 2002 and began formal discussions about conducting Aboriginal traditional knowledge research in November 2005.[70] Skin Tyee had limited ability to conduct an independent study. It was a relatively impoverished community and in 2009, when the federal review of the Northern Gateway project began, it had only 148 registered band members, with just 31 residents living on Skin Tyee reserve lands.[71] Thus, the community decided to participate in collaborative research on their traditional land use. Through meetings with ATK facilitators, they agreed to a work plan for the research in April 2009.

Research advanced through three stages. First, interviews were conducted. Traditional knowledge holders were "provided with a general project description, including project-specific and regional maps."[72] Semi-directed discussions focused on baseline conditions (i.e., air and water quality, health and abundance of fish and wildlife), the potential effects of the project on traditional use areas, and any possible mitigation measures the company could take to lessen these potential effects. Based on the interviews, traditional use sites were marked on the maps. The interview process served to determine sites for field visits. In the second stage, field site visits enabled research participants to see the location of the project development area in relation to traditional use areas. ATK facilitators documented traditional and culturally important ecological sites with photographs, GPS pinpoints, notes, and sketch maps. The ATK facilitators then compiled reports based on their interviews and field surveys, "including maps of sites and areas discussed during interviews and recorded during field visits."[73] In the third stage, Enbridge ATK facilitators provided research participants and community representatives an opportunity to review the information in the reports to ensure its accuracy and suitability for release to the public. Skin Tyee approved this workplan in April 2009. Interviews were conducted with Skin Tyee members in May, field visits occurred in July, the draft report was reviewed with the community in November, and final revisions were made in December. The information from the ATK study was then incorporated into the Enbridge project application, which the company submitted to federal regulators in May 2010.[74]

By participating in this study, Skin Tyee was able to protect and advance its interests, to the extent that this was possible through pipeline development. The ATK research helped mitigate the impacts of pipeline development on Skin Tyee land use by, for example, delineating particular campsites and trails to be protected. Further, through the research collaboration, Skin Tyee was able to highlight modifications to the process of pipeline construction that would promote the maintenance of its members' traditional land use activities. However, the study did not simply engage in cultural triage. Skin Tyee also sought to modify development plans so that pipeline construction could improve the well-being of its population. Particularly, the Skin Tyee study leveraged a connection to the land, and an analysis of the cumulative impacts of development, to ensure pipeline construction created opportunities to improve transportation services on reserve, support the intergenerational transmission of Skin Tyee culture, distribute the financial benefits of the project to the community, and provide jobs to Skin Tyee members.

The research collaboration between Skin Tyee and Enbridge worked to define a field of Indigenous interests that could be accommodated in pipeline planning. Examining this collaboration, my aim is not to critique the fidelity of its translation of Skin Tyee traditional knowledge. Instead, I want to examine its intended political and economic effects—that is, how the land use and occupancy study sought to mediate relations between industry and Indigenous people. My point is not to criticize Skin Tyee but to use Enbridge's research engagements with Skin Tyee as an example of the company's approach to integrating Indigenous knowledge into project planning. I want to emphasize the repeatable ATK research methods that it demonstrates, tacitly modelling routinized practices of translating Aboriginal traditional knowledge into project planning. I use this example to underline how these knowledge translations both modify and extend the colonial systems of power-knowledge enabling development.

While the motivation to include ATK in project planning stems from Indigenous activism and critical academic work that sought to challenge the historic lack of consideration of Indigenous interests in resource management processes, the inclusion of traditional knowledge within governmental processes continues to be framed by colonial relationships of power-knowledge. Elements of Indigenous knowledge are selectively screened to fit within Enbridge's ATK submissions. The Skin Tyee traditional knowledge data collected and summarized in the Northern Gateway application served to demarcate the geography of Skin Tyee traditions—to fix it on the map and provide opportunities to route development around it while offering avenues to integrate contemporary Skin Tyee interests into development through employment and compensation programs.

In their study, Skin Tyee community members collaborated with corporate research facilitators to map their traditional use. This mapping elided broader Wet'suwet'en territorial claims. The definitional geography for the research was not Wet'suwet'en territory or even Skin Tyee geographies of land use but rather the regional effects assessment area defined by the proposed pipeline right-of-way. Development impacts were only considered in areas within 80 kilometres of the proposed pipeline right-of-way. Approximately 325 kilometres of the pipeline right-of-way crossed land considered to be within the regional effects assessment area associated with Skin Tyee traditional use.[75]

Skin Tyee research participants provided an extensive list of areas of traditional use, animal habitat, and ecological concern. They identified numerous multi-use and harvesting areas important to the community that would be intersected by, or adjacent to, the pipeline development corridor. The largest area of concern was potential impacts to sensitive watersheds. The proposed Northern Gateway Pipelines would run in close proximity to Ts'ëlkiy' Kwah (Lamprey Creek) and the upper Widzin Kwah (Morice River). Skin Tyee members stressed that the Widzin Kwah and its surrounds are intensively used for fishing, camping, hunting, and plant gathering. Other areas of concern named in the report included Bïwinï (Owen Lake), Bïwinï Kwah (Owen Creek), Misdzï Kwah (Parrott Creek), Natl'ënlï Bin (Nadina Lake), and Netanlï Bin (Skins Lake). Skin Tyee members also identified two hunting areas and six trails that were either crossed by or adjacent to the proposed right-of-way. Their study highlighted that the community's primary concerns involved the impact of potential pipeline spills on the health of fish populations. To mitigate these impacts, the study recommended routing the pipelines in ways that would minimize the risk that spills would reach the Widzin Kwah. Specifically, it recommended situating the pipeline away from the water on a geomorphological bench, a long, narrow strip of level land that is bounded by distinctly steeper slopes. Further, the report stressed the need to route the pipelines in ways that would avoid "spawning grounds of all fish including non-commercial species such as pacific [sic] lamprey eel."[76]

The Skin Tyee research also highlighted how documenting Indigenous land use sites is a necessary ingredient in tempering impacts on these sites by giving pipeline planners crucial information about locations around which to reroute projects. For example, the Enbridge project had the potential to affect traditional trails used by Skin Tyee members. To ensure a certain degree of protection for the trails, the community ATK report recommended establishing buffers between these trails and the pipelines. Similarly, the community report recommended avoiding "hunting camps with a 75 m. buffer."[77] Skin Tyee members also indicated a number of plant-gathering areas would be impacted by pipeline development. To mitigate the impact on traditional plant use, they recommended that, "if healthy cottonwood trees are cut down and are of 1.5 m or more in circumference," Enbridge provide the community with the logs.[78]

The Skin Tyee research suggested a number of other modifications to the Northern Gateway construction process with the aim of further protecting their traditional land use. For instance, the research indicated that plants used traditionally, such as berry patches, may not return after being disturbed by development because they have a hard time competing with other species. This would lead to a reduction in availability of traditional plants. The Skin Tyee report thus recommended replanting areas that would be disturbed by pipeline construction, such as the project right-of-way, "with the same species of plants that were removed."[79] Similarly, to mitigate soil disturbances, the report suggested that the soils and plants replaced after pipeline installation "match what was there as much as possible."[80] Based on their experience with the impacts of logging roads on their territories, Skin Tyee members noted that roads installed for pipeline construction and maintenance would impact water flows and thus alter vegetation. To avoid undue increases in runoff and changes in drainage patterns associated with project roads, the Skin Tyee research recommended that Enbridge "use existing roads as much as possible," and specifically that they "reclaim any access or roads that are not needed long-term; replant with trees."[81] To mitigate the possible effect of pipeline construction on deer, moose, elk, and caribou migrations, the community report recommended planning spring and fall construction around animal migrations. The report also recommended minimizing food contamination by managing the plants on the project right-of-way "without the use of chemical sprays."[82]

The Skin Tyee study additionally highlighted a number of ways that pipeline development could act as a vehicle for the maintenance of community traditions. Rather than presuming pipeline development was antithetical to the maintenance of Indigenous traditional land use, the study emphasized how funding from the project could support the revitalization of traditional practices. "Elders expressed a desire to teach the younger generation cultural values and traditions, to transfer...skills, knowledge, language, culture and pride to the young people."[83] With agricultural and resource development disrupting traditional lands, band members had to travel greater distance at greater cost to access hunting or trapping areas, limiting elders' ability to share traditional knowledge. The Skin Tyee study suggested that Enbridge could contribute to the establishment of a one-week culture camp that would support the intergenerational transmission of knowledge by providing "annual financial support ($20,000)."[84] The study further suggested that Enbridge could facilitate greater community access to traditional resources by providing each Skin Tyee reserve with a truck or van. These vehicles would provide territorial access for community members "who are too poor to afford vehicles, and cannot make use of the land as much as they used to as a result."[85] Transportation would enable Skin Tyee members to go "out into the bush to gather food and prepare for the winter."[86] Transportation would also serve to ensure vital medical transportation for isolated reserve residents, helping to secure the health of the reserve population.

The study recommended that the company hire community members to monitor construction to ensure that the potentially adverse effects of development were minimized. To address concerns about potential watershed impacts, the report suggested Skin Tyee members should be hired "to monitor streams and conduct clean-up (trees and debris). Streams that need to be cleaned are Trout Creek, Parrott Creek, and Lund Creek."[87] These environmental monitoring positions further served to address economic concerns around the high unemployment rate for the band. Without expertise or training in pipefitting, Skin Tyee members were best suited for entry-level positions, such as environmental monitoring, brushing, and reclamation work. The Skin Tyee report recommended Enbridge "provide direct awards (employment) through the band office with first refusal to STFN [Skin Tyee First Nation] on work within the traditional territory."[88]

The Northern Gateway project interlinked with long-term processes that were environmentally degrading Skin Tyee's traditional economy. At the same time, it offered Skin Tyee an opportunity to begin addressing their economic insecurity by siphoning a portion of the project's economic returns into the community. By the time of the Enbridge Northern Gateway proposal, the traditional Skin Tyee economy was already severely diminished due to other historic and enduring impacts of development. This context was made explicit by Enbridge, which noted in their application that Skin Tyee members "are no longer able to make a living hunting and trapping as a result of decreased wildlife and furbearer populations."[89] Of course, the construction of Northern Gateway would exacerbate these conditions. Removal of forest cover to prepare the project right-of-way would contribute to declining wildlife. The introduction of new roads would create avenues for both predatory animals and non-resident hunters to access wildlife populations, thereby increasing competition for a limited resource. To address these concerns, the community report recommended that Enbridge consult with the Skin Tyee chief, council, and elders to determine an appropriate amount of compensation to "administer to band members on a monthly basis."[90] As chapter 4 will highlight in further detail, Enbridge also offered Indigenous communities the opportunity to purchase an equity stake in the project.

Alongside all of the methods of mitigation and compensation listed in the community report were a number of disturbing issues that the pipeline would not ameliorate or address. For instance, the report identified numerous aquatic animals that were already suffering from poor water quality. It also described troubling health conditions on reserve, with Skin Tyee members experiencing elevated rates of "heart conditions, cancer and diabetes. Diabetes is attributed to a change from the traditional diet."[91] The Enbridge Northern Gateway project provided no plans to address these alarming environmental and health concerns because they took these conditions as baseline, and thus not requiring a project-specific mitigation strategy.

While Skin Tyee's participation in Enbridge's ATK studies contributed to allaying some of the impacts of the proposed Northern Gateway project on their community, it nonetheless also contributed to rationalizing the unfolding of capitalist extractive infrastructure, fragmenting Indigenous geographies according to a piecemeal territorial logic that does not recognize Indigenous traditional land use on its own terms. The discursive effects of the report were all the more poignant alongside other community ATK submissions, which continually repeated similar recommendations. Taken in combination, the effect of these suggestions was to normalize the supposed sufficiency of specific modifications to construction practices—for instance, avoiding the use of pesticides on the pipeline right-of-way—to address Indigenous concerns. The abstracting and compartmentalizing spatial formulae that Enbridge ATK facilitators employed to depict Skin Tyee land use reappeared in Enbridge's accounts of other Indigenous communities' concerns.[92] It reflected a standard mode of using land use studies to fragment Indigenous geographies into a patchwork of sites of intense use. This mapping elided Indigenous peoples' traditions of resource governance over large areas, limiting recognition of the geography of Indigenous traditions to small, intensively occupied areas such as village sites, cultivated or enclosed fields, fishing sites, and burial grounds. Efforts to account for sites of Indigenous cultural importance in Enbridge's collaborative ATK research effectively effaced interconnections between people and territory by focusing narrowly on charting specific bounded locations around which to route development.

By defining particular sites of Indigenous traditional interest, Enbridge was able to determine the spaces where interference with Indigenous traditions would, apparently, be minimal. This constrained approach to recognizing cultural traditions incarcerated Indigeneity in the local. Within the ontological presumptions of empire, as Jodi Byrd theorizes, "the Indian is left nowhere and everywhere."[93] Collaborative community ATK reports systematically reduced

Indigenous spatialities to an economic interest in local land that could be effectively and profitably sublated into a developing industrial economy through employment opportunities and equity agreements. This problem was, however, not unique to the collaborative research. Enbridge also abstracted information from independent reports, such as the critical traditional use and occupancy research conducted by the Carrier Sekani Tribal Council, into the same framework.[94] Other companies employed resonant techniques to assess impacts of other pipeline projects in British Columbia.[95] It is precisely this confined imagination of Indigeneity that corporate actors sought to define in order to permit development. However, as the Office of the Wet'suwet'en demonstrate, land use and occupancy studies are not constrained to this bounded conception of Indigeneity that leaves the universal knowledge claims of corporate science and resource management intact.

### Writing Back: Oppositional Politics in Regulatory Reports

Responding the Enbridge Northern Gateway project proposal, the Office of the Wet'suwet'en prepared an independent traditional use and occupancy study, challenging not only the proposed pipelines but the authority of Canadian regulators to determine the conditions shaping the project without Wet'suwet'en consent. The Office of the Wet'suwet'en vested their submissions in a reading of the legacy of the *Delgamuukw, Gisdaywa* litigation, titling their written submissions to the federally appointed Joint Review Panel for the Enbridge Northern Gateway Project (JRP) "Wet'suwet'en Rights and Title and Enbridge's Northern Gateway Pipelines Project."[96] Their submission focused on Wet'suwet'en territorial traditions of actively governing the land.

> *The Wet'suwet'en have never relinquished or surrendered Wet'suwet'en title and rights to the lands and resources within Wet'suwet'en territory and continue to occupy and use the lands and resources and to exercise existing title and rights within the territory. We have an inherent right to govern ourselves and our territory according to our own laws, customs, and traditions.*[97]

Invoking the tradition of the *Delgamuukw, Gisdaywa* case, the hereditary chiefs' organization challenged the frames of knowledge that Canadian regulatory bodies called forth, stressing the neglect for Wet'suwet'en sovereignty, the cumulative effects of decades of development, and the need to plan for ecological restoration.

The Office of the Wet'suwet'en hereditary chiefs raised a number of concerns with pipeline governance processes. First, approving pipelines without the hereditary chiefs' support disrespected their jurisdiction and undermined their ability to uphold their responsibilities to protect the territory. Second, the project-specific approach to regulation failed to adequately consider the cumulative effects of generations of development—including forestry, mining, and agriculture—degrading Wet'suwet'en territories. Third, there was insufficient consideration of the potential impacts on endangered and threatened salmon stocks on which the Wet'suwet'en have relied since time immemorial.

Focusing on the question of Wet'suwet'en territorial jurisdiction, the Office of the Wet'suwet'en forwarded the political question of who decides whether development happens. Thus, their intervention centred on the Wet'suwet'en hereditary chiefs' claims that they are a counter-authority to the authority of federal regulators. The Office of the Wet'suwet'en sought to strategically employ their independent traditional use and occupancy study as a wedge to open discussion of Wet'suwet'en territoriality, which had been absent in the outcomes of the corporate-community collaborative studies with Skin Tyee. The Office of the Wet'suwet'en sought to use their traditional use and occupancy study as a tool to challenge not simply a pipeline project but the underlying regimes of power-knowledge on which governmental regulation relied.

Foundationally, the Office of the Wet'suwet'en study pluralized the territorialities involved in development by shifting the frame of study from geographies of traditional land use to *yikh* territorial jurisdiction. This both narrowed and expanded discussions. While Skin Tyee based their assertions on an extensive geography of land use (which included ever more distant lands as development forced hunters to travel greater distances), the hereditary chiefs focused specifically on those lands to which they maintained an ancestral connection. Where the Skin Tyee traditional use study documented that the pipeline right-of-way would impact approximately 325 kilometres of the lands that Skin Tyee members used for hunting, gathering, and cultural activities, the Office of the Wet'suwet'en indicated that just 170 kilometres of the proposed Northern Gateway project was within the territories of Wet'suwet'en *yikh*. "The proposed corridor, including its resources, was traditionally occupied by Wet'suwet'en Clan [*dïdikh*] and House [*yikh*] members, who exercised land and stewardship rights, prerogatives, and responsibilities; these Wet'suwet'en traditions continue into the present."[98] Instead of simply mapping the geographies of Wet'suwet'en land use, the Office of the Wet'suwet'en began by laying out the *yikh* and *dïdikh* territories transected by the Northern Gateway project. From east to west, the proposed pipelines would enter the *yin tah* of Kwanbeahyax, a *yikh* of the Laksilyu; transit the Djakanyax *yin tah* of the Tsayu; travel through the *yin tah* of Anaskaski, Kiyaxwinits, and Cas Yex, the three *yikh* of the Gitdumden; cross the Widzin Kwah and enter the *yin tah* of Yex T'sa Wilk'us (also called Unist'ot'en), a *yikh* of the Gilserhyu; transect another Djakanyax *yin tah*; and finally skirt the edge of the Sayax *yin tah* of the Laksamshu.[99] The Northern Gateway project would thus impact territories belonging to all five Wet'suwet'en *dïdikh*.

In its approach to studying land use and occupancy, the Office of the Wet'suwet'en privileged the latter, emphasizing the need for colonial authorities and Enbridge to understand occupancy with respect to their territorial authority. Occupancy research builds upon geographies of land use but goes further, seeking to document how Indigenous peoples hold possession of a territory and therefore a legal claim to title. Echoing the evidence presented in the *Delgamuukw, Gisdaywa* case, the Office of the Wet'suwet'en explained that *yikh* authority over the *yin tah* was embodied in the figure of a hereditary chief, who held particular responsibilities to maintain the integrity of the land.

> *Hereditary Chiefs are entrusted with the stewardship of territories by virtue of the hereditary name they hold, and they are*

*the caretakers of these territories for as long as they hold the name. It is the task of a head Chief to ensure the House territory [yin tah] is managed in a responsible manner, so that the territory will always produce enough game, fish, berries and medicines to support the subsistence, trade, and customary needs of house members. The House [yikh] is a partnership between the people and the territory, which forms the primary unit of production supporting the subsistence, trade, and cultural needs of the Wet'suwet'en.*[100]

Thus, the Office of the Wet'suwet'en continued to advance claims based on their legal traditions. Using the study as a means of articulating their own claim to territorial jurisdiction, the Office of the Wet'suwet'en reiterated a claim to authority competing with that of colonial authorities.

In addition to articulating territorial claims in terms of Wet'suwet'en law, however, the Office of the Wet'suwet'en also continually invoked the language of the Supreme Court of Canada decision in *Delgamuukw, Gisdaywa*—specifically, the court's validation of Indigenous traditions as a form of evidence—as a validation of their traditional legal order. The Office of the Wet'suwet'en argued that their territorial claim needed to be understood in association with Wet'suwet'en regimes of ordering social life and territorial knowledge.

*The Wet'suwet'en's special relationship to the land, grounds and affirms our title. The Wet'suwet'en express their special relationship through how we organize ourselves on the land, through our governance system, our laws, feast, clans, houses, chiefs, our people's identification with the territory through our crests, Kungax [cin k'ikh], totem poles and Baht'lats [balhats]. Individually and together these expressions of our special relationship to the land are integral to our distinctive Wet'suwet'en culture, and our title includes exclusivity and incorporates present-day needs.*[101]

In their submissions, the Office of the Wet'suwet'en stressed that the project lay "within Wet'suwet'en Territory over which the Wet'suwet'en maintain Aboriginal Title and Rights."[102] Thus, the Office of the Wet'suwet'en leveraged the legacy of *Delgamuukw, Gisdaywa* to further advance their territorial claim.

The Office of the Wet'suwet'en report stressed that the Supreme Court of Canada had recognized that "Aboriginal title is based on and informed by the Aboriginal people's special attachment or relationship to the land."[103] The report used Aboriginal title—a bridging concept translating between colonial jurisprudence and Indigenous legal orders—to communicate and translate the meaning of Wet'suwet'en sovereignty.

> *Our Aboriginal title provides us with the right to occupy and use the land exclusive of all others. It provides us with an exclusive right to decide whether and how land and resources will be occupied and used according to our cultural values and principles, exclusive not only of Enbridge and its investors but also of the JRP. It provides us alone—exclusive of Enbridge and its investors—with right to develop and benefit from the economic potential of our land and resources. Development and use that is irreconcilable with the nature of the Wet'suwet'en's special attachment to the land is precluded.*[104]

Thus, the authors of the Office of the Wet'suwet'en report appropriated Chief Justice Lamer's discourse on the requirement that the occupation of Aboriginal title lands exclude other organized societies, arguing that this exclusivity should extend to corporate entities and settler-colonial authorities. The translation of Indigenous traditions through the land use and occupancy study here sought to disrupt normalized settler-colonial claims to sovereignty over Wet'suwet'en lands.

Moreover, pressing their concerns before federal regulators, the Office of the Wet'suwet'en stressed the need to consider the project within the legacy of colonial resource mismanagement. For settler authorities to act honourably with reference to history, they asserted that development proposals needed to be situated within a critical understanding of the impacts "resulting from 150 years of settler activity."[105] From their perspective, project-based assessments were inadequate, as they normalized decades of environmental degradation. Resource development needed instead to be regulated with respect to the cumulative impacts of generations of forestry, mining, commercial fishing, and agricultural development on "aquatic and terrestrial ecosystems...adversely impact[ing] water, fish, wildlife, plants and Wet'suwet'en cultural heritage."[106]

The Office of the Wet'suwet'en particularly stressed that the project application had not adequately dealt with the concerns around the sustainability of fisheries that deeply entwined with their Aboriginal rights. Their submission stressed that salmon lie at the core of Wet'suwet'en relations to the land and "utilization of the abundant and predictable salmon stocks formed the foundation of the economy."[107] Their analysis particularly emphasized the importance of sockeye stocks, "the most desirable fish for the Wet'suwet'en owing to a fat content that facilitates smoke-drying."[108] Wet'suwet'en oral history recounts a time when the salmon remained abundant, but colonial resource exploitation has resulted in declining salmon stocks. Salmon populations have been negatively impacted by coastal overharvesting by commercial fishers and habitat alterations that have eroded water quality and stream channels.

The Office of the Wet'suwet'en stressed the importance of restoring the vitality of salmon stock for their communities and their independence. They expressed concern that the future of fisheries remains uncertain, drawing upon the analysis of local fisheries scientists Allen S. Gottesfeld and Ken A. Rabnett.

*The abundance, productivity, and carrying capacity status of Morice sockeye are rated as poor. The current decline of Morice-Nanika sockeye due to high exploitation rates and low-productivity issues in Morice Lake has deeply impacted the Wet'suwet'en...The Morice-Nanika Sockeye Recovery Plan appears to be stalled due to a lack of strategic direction and commitment. Morice-Nanika sockeye are rated as threatened and will become endangered if limiting factors are not reversed.*[109]

Since the 1980s nadir of sockeye returns in the Widzin Kwah, when annual average returns were 2,500 fish, Indigenous involvement in fisheries management coincided with a tenfold increase in returns in the 1990s.[110] However, in the early years of the new millennium, returns again faltered, impacting the ability of Wet'suwet'en community members to conduct a subsistence fishery: "Since 2001, the Wet'suwet'en have not directed a food fishery on the Morice-Nanika sockeye stocks."[111] To address these conditions and improve the stewardship of the land, the Office of the Wet'suwet'en stressed the need for more engaged, collaborative planning.

The Office of the Wet'suwet'en has actively pursued opportunities to implement shared jurisdiction with settler authorities in environmental governance. For instance, they participated in the establishment of the Morice Water Management Area as a component of the Morice Lands and Resource Management Plan in 2007. This involved a significant compromise: agreeing to plan on the basis of watershed rather than Wet'suwet'en territorial boundaries. The hereditary chiefs have sought to conduct integrated planning across their *yin tah* and long struggled to overcome the colonial imposition of distinct administrative boundaries and frames. However, committed to fisheries restoration, the Office of the Wet'suwet'en decided to participate in this provincial watershed planning process. They supported the intent of the program to "maintain hydrological integrity, including water quality and quantity" within the area, in order "to ensure that the habitat and water quality supporting salmon and other fish is not negatively impacted."[112] Through such initiatives, the Office of the Wet'suwet'en has sought to advance the ecological restoration of their *yin tah*, damaged by the devastating impacts of decades of extractive development. These efforts, however, have been undermined by the fragmentary nature of settler governance regimes, which silo regulatory consideration to particular projects and industries without comprehensive, holistic environmental plans.[113]

The Office of the Wet'suwet'en stressed that the project represented another episode within the enduring history of colonial resource mismanagement. Enbridge had failed to provide federal regulators with the information they needed to uphold their own administrative duties, and had therefore not conducted the required environmental research for an analysis of the impacts of Northern Gateway. The Office of the Wet'suwet'en charged that the sections of the project application "dealing with baseline information, impact assessment, and mitigation are inadequate," and the company had simply not performed the necessary "detailed baseline studies to support the effects analysis."[114] Specifically, the Office of the Wet'suwet'en contended that Enbridge had failed to model the behaviour of dilbit—the substance formed when viscous bitumen from the Athabasca tar sands is diluted with condensate in order to make it sufficiently fluid for pipeline transport—in the event of a spill. They argued that dilbit was not equivalent to conventional oil, and it remained unclear whether dilbit would retain its hybrid character or split in its constituent elements in the event of a spill. The Office of the Wet'suwet'en expressed concern that spilled dilbit would separate, with condensate evaporating and spilled bitumen becoming embedded "deep into stream sediment," depositing a heavy residue that could have "potential significant residual effects on aquatic life" over both the short and long term.[115] Thus, they argued that it was necessary to better model the fate of spilled dilbit—including the distinct pathways that its constituent bitumen and condensate may follow—in the environment after a potential spill.

The Office of the Wet'suwet'en opened their submission with a claim to Indigenous sovereignty that exceeded the terms of reference for the JRP. It concluded by demonstrating that Enbridge had failed to provide federal regulators with the necessary information for them to uphold their own administrative duties. The Office of the Wet'suwet'en submissions pointed to substantive deficiencies in the information that Enbridge had provided on salmon, the lack of detailed modelling of salmon population dynamics, and the failure to account for the behaviour of spilled bitumen. They contested the economic imaginary of progress that Enbridge proposed through its pipelines, stressing Enbridge's lack of consideration for the value of traditional sustenance resources, particularly fisheries. Working to advance a list of particular complaints commensurate with the terms of colonial resource governance and simultaneously challenging these terms, the Office of the Wet'suwet'en sought to defend their interests within the colonial process while challenging the legitimacy of that process itself.

### On the Undecidability of Translations

The Skin Tyee and Office of the Wet'suwet'en land use and occupancy studies are markedly different. The two research endeavours show how the multivalence of Indigenous land use and occupancy studies simultaneously offer opportunities to mitigate the impacts of resource development, negotiate the terms of Indigenous integration into development projects, and assert a claim to sovereign authority over determining the course of development. The two studies show the breadth of strategies that Indigenous communities use to articulate their interests within and mount challenges to colonial governance processes. The Enbridge ATK program highlights the ways that corporate and colonial regimes seek to relegitimize their programs of development through the provision of minimal consideration to Indigenous communities' concerns. But these two studies also showcase how Indigenous assertions reconfigure dominant systems of meaning. The Skin Tyee study sought to modify the trajectory of infrastructure construction and offset the most dramatic impacts on their community members, while the Office of the Wet'suwet'en tried to challenge the basic logics of Canadian energy governance and block the pipeline. As Boaventura de Sousa Santos describes, the law presents both regulatory and emancipatory dimensions, enabling victories as Indigenous peoples appropriate legal instruments and discourses to advance their claims while simultaneously exposing themselves to regimes of regulation.[116]

Indigenous traditional use and occupancy studies should not be understood as innately colonial or decolonial but rather as a method for expressing Indigenous concerns within power-laden spaces of settler governance. Intellectual histories and policy studies chart the recent development of Indigenous knowledge as an object of intellectual interest to the corporate consultant and the state bureaucrat; however, it remains necessary to critically and explicitly consider how the techniques of land use and occupancy studies sit within broader relations of power-knowledge between Indigenous peoples, corporate capital, and settler authorities. The political impetus to integrate ATK into resource management practices emerges from decades of Indigenous political activism. But power relations still set discursive and material terms for knowledge translation. Particular practical rationalities guide both the constitution of Indigenous knowledge as an object of scientific investigation and regulatory intervention. However, strategies of engagement and knowledge translation remain plural, shaped by different projects of becoming in the world. While corporate and colonial techniques of engaging Indigenous peoples seek to enframe consideration of their relations to the land within the unfolding of colonial extractive regimes, the engagements of Indigenous peoples with colonial authorities are not foreclosed to a set domain. Indigenous interventions do not just meekly sit within governance processes. They have the puissance to disrupt the terms of those conversations.

While traditional use and occupation studies are often projected as a technique for replacing the original presence of Indigenous territorial orders within the space of settler sovereignty, they are configured by a deeper aporetic relation between Indigenous and colonial authorities. Counter-cartography relies on translations between Indigenous and colonial systems of knowledge. Despite power imbalances, the relation between Indigeneity and colonialism has never been decided, and Indigenous peoples not only insert a counterpoint within colonial government discourses, but also appropriate and reinterpret its frames, actively transforming it. Examining relations between modes of written and oral expression, Jacques Derrida has highlighted that a single mode cannot be privileged as the definitive source; rather knowledge circulates between different systems of signification.[117] Similarly, there is an undecidable relationship in translations between Indigenous traditional modes of ordering territorial knowledge and the modes of encoding them in traditional use and occupancy studies for consideration by settler-state authorities.

The process of representation is necessarily ambivalent. On the one hand, the need for land use and occupancy studies within governance processes signifies a lack: the unintelligibility of Indigenous traditional systems of ordering power-knowledge with Canadian resource governance processes. The existence of traditional use and traditional knowledge studies is premised on the (often implicit) supposition that Indigenous territoriality can only become present within the context of coloniality by rendering itself legible through said studies. The traditional use and occupancy study, as substitute for Indigenous territoriality itself, "is not simply added to the positivity of a presence, it produces no relief, its place is assigned in the structure by the mark of an emptiness."[118] On the other hand, the addition of written studies as supporting evidence of enduring Indigenous territorial jurisdiction can be understood as a method of ensuring Indigeneity is afforded a fuller measure of presence within governance considerations than it otherwise would be. In the reassertion of the absent presence of Indigenous traditions, land use and occupancy studies disrupt the fiction of colonial sovereignty as complete.[119] Indigenous presence demonstrates that settler authority is not total and unfettered, but imperfect and burdened by the weight of colonial history. Traditional use and traditional knowledge studies thus exist in an unresolved relation to the Indigenous territorialities they seek to encode, accreting inscriptions that codify Indigeneity as a presence reshaping colonial resource governance and its regimes of power-knowledge, and simultaneously standing as substitute for and thereby displacing Indigenous traditions of ordering territorial knowledge. Stated differently, there is an ambivalence to traditional use and occupancy studies as a technology that seeks to empower Indigenous territoriality but aims to do so through casting Indigenous territorial knowledge within the frames of a colonial discourse founded on the suspension of Indigenous territorialities.

Applying these theoretical frames to the land use and occupancy studies submitted in response to the Enbridge Northern Gateway project showcases this duality. First, a critical reading of corporate collaboration with Indigenous communities in constructing its ATK submissions demonstrates how colonial power relations are reproduced through the consideration of Indigenous interests.

The codification of Indigenous knowledge enables companies to include said knowledge in their project planning and allows state regulators to consider it in the exercise of their jurisdiction. However, this form of consideration separates Indigenous territorial knowledge from the contemporary exercise of Indigenous sovereignty. The constrained frame of ATK within bureaucratic discourse works to structure the spaces that Indigenous peoples are seen to occupy and to which they may lay claim. Within settler regulatory discourse, this works to define the language of contention, framing a legitimate set of bounded geographies for which Indigenous people can lobby, and inscribing a set of knowledges about what it means to be Indigenous. By delineating particular Indigenous sites for protection, ATK studies mark Indigeneity as traditional and localized, incapable of reworking global flows. Marking Indigenous knowledge as local continually effaces the way in which its locality is the product of implicit (and sometimes explicit) contrasts to networks that continually accumulate knowledge in particular centres of calculation, empowering contemporary colonial agents to act at a distance on sites and peoples demarcated as distinctly local. Similarly, marking Indigenous knowledge as traditional within the colonial present elides the ways that colonial discourse positions Indigeneity in the past and normalizes the settler possession of the present and future. These frames contain the recognition of Indigenous being, stabilizing and naturalizing the territorialization of the settler state and the forms of capitalist resource extraction that it facilitates. Thus, even as Indigenous land use and occupancy studies emerge out of a tradition of counter-research aimed at pressing back against colonial impositions, the practical rationalities of colonial governance continue to enclose notions of Indigenous traditions and being.

Through strategic interventions such as those of the Office of the Wet'suwet'en, however, Indigenous peoples also appropriate settler governance discourses to make claims to a form of counter-jurisdiction. Appropriating the language of settler courts, they continue to stress the importance of recognizing not only Aboriginal rights but also the systems of territorial jurisdiction within Indigenous legal orders that give Aboriginal title and rights meaning. They insist that Indigenous obligations to their kinship with the more-than-human world need to be the primary framework for making decisions in territorial governance. The Office of the Wet'suwet'en stressed in their report to Enbridge that the hereditary chiefs who remain wedded to the spirit of the land are the proper authorities to determine the course of development. However, they also, pragmatically, made very particular arguments and demands related to the insufficiency of the information that Enbridge provided. Thus, they interlaced conflicting political demands—those that are incommensurable with development, in the form of holistic conservation, and those that are commensurable with development, in the form of cultural triage. Stoffle and Evans contend that this is a productive strategy for inserting Indigenous concerns into settler resource governance processes.[120] On the one hand, political challenges of incommensurability—assertions that refuse to accord with the development consensus and posit a politics of Indigenous being and becoming in excess of the ontology of resource development—destabilize the development consensus, opening spaces of negotiation. On the other hand, assertions of commensurable site-specific demands create the basis for integrating Indigenous interests in the realignment of development agendas. To understand the broader political conflicts and political effects of these processes, however, one must ask after the worlds that resource governance processes are seeking to call into being.

# 4

# Indigenizing Infrastructure
*New Industrial Partnerships*

WHILE ABORIGINAL RIGHTS JURISPRUDENCE required consideration of the impacts of pipeline development on Indigenous traditional land use, Enbridge emphasized the benefits that the Northern Gateway project could bring Indigenous communities. The project website advertised that "Northern Gateway is more than an infrastructure project for the energy industry. It is a partnership between First Nations and Enbridge and can be considered an important bridge between Aboriginals and industry for mutual long term benefit." On the site, Enbridge acknowledged that "some Aboriginal groups have concerns about the Northern Gateway," but committed to engaging those communities "to find solutions." However, it principally directed conversation of solutions not towards environmental protection or routing development around Indigenous sites of concern, but to the possibilities of Indigenous economic integration. The company emphasized its commitment to ensuring "maximum participation of Aboriginal communities in economic opportunities that arise from the project, including equity ownership, directed procurement and employment." It particularly lauded the opportunity it provided for Aboriginal equity ownership, offering impacted Indigenous peoples, collectively, a 10 percent share in the project. With Northern Gateway originally valued at $5.5 billion, later to be reassessed at above $7.9 billion, this offered significant value to some of the most impoverished communities in Canada. Rather than simply juxtaposing industrial and Indigenous interests, the company sought to forge a new relationship of corporate-community partnership. "Becoming an owner in this project means Aboriginal groups are going to see cash flow within the first year of operations. Through equity ownership, Aboriginal people will be able to generate a significant new revenue stream that could help achieve the priorities of their people." In contrast to the long history of industrial displacement that marginalized Indigenous interests, corporate partnership was offered as a mode of empowerment. Enbridge boasted that the Northern Gateway Pipelines would distribute "approximately $280 million in net income to neighbouring Aboriginal communities, over the first 30 years."[1]

This chapter examines Enbridge's offer of corporate partnership as an example of how new corporate regimes aim to secure Indigenous well-being by integrating them in the industrial economy. Corporate aims to secure developments from Indigenous protest have, I argue, converged with Indigenous aims to escape economic dependency on the settler state. This partially resonates with longstanding colonial designs to assimilate Indigenous peoples into the settler political economy. However, the disciplinary apparatuses of these new private partnerships, often referred to as impact benefit agreements (IBAs), do not aim to erase Indigeneity. Rather, these corporate-community agreements establish a new contractual apparatus to secure a place for Indigenous peoples in development, specifically on the basis of their Indigeneity.

Operating beyond a simple binary of colonial oppression and Indigenous resistance, Indigenous peoples have established new spaces of negotiation with corporate power. Critical analysis, as Jean Dennison argues, should "avoid either ignoring or empowering the colonial forces with which colonized peoples must contend."[2] Court recognition of Aboriginal rights required the reconciliation of historic Indigenous territorial relationships to the contemporary settlement and development of the land; efforts to resolve relationships through treaty negotiations, however, quickly found themselves at an impasse. While the government approach to contemporary land claims sought to unburden settler sovereignty of its obligations to Indigenous peoples and thereby secure colonial developmental futures, the majority of Indigenous peoples, including the Wet'suwet'en hereditary chiefs, remain committed to maintaining relationships to the land and sharing territorial jurisdiction with the settler state.[3] Because the matter of Aboriginal title remains unresolved, corporations have increasingly partnered with Indigenous peoples to clear away political-legal obstacles for specific capitalist resource developments. Settler-state authorities have come to support these partnerships as a means of both securing capitalist development and reducing the burden of state support to marginalized Indigenous communities.

IBAs have modified the political economy of resource extraction, reordering relationships between corporate entities, settler authorities, and Indigenous peoples.[4] For Indigenous peoples long burdened by the effects of resource developments, negotiating IBAs provides a mechanism to ensure that some of the benefits of industrial development are distributed to their communities. Indigenous peoples, as Dennison argues, "have long understood the colonial process as at once devastating and full of potential." Drawing on the metaphor of Osage ribbon work, in which European materials are taken to produce distinctly Indigenous forms of cultural expression, she argues that "it is possible to create new and powerful forms out of an ongoing colonial process."[5] In the Canadian case, Indigenous aspirations to secure a livelihood have been linked to corporate designs to secure development projects from potential disruptions associated with Indigenous protests and litigation. These private contracts intersect with the assemblage of state authorities overseeing development, as corporations leverage IBAs to demonstrate how project development may benefit Indigenous communities in ways that offset potential economic impacts on traditional land use.[6]

In practice, Enbridge's efforts to reconcile Indigenous and industrial interests involved a plethora of contracts, covering the diversity of potentially impacted Indigenous groups at the various stages of development. As discussed in the previous chapter, Enbridge initiated discussions with Indigenous communities in 2002. By 2005, the company had begun negotiating cooperation agreements with Indigenous communities as a basis for communication around project impacts and benefits while using standard service agreements to ensure subcontracting consultants hired local Indigenous assistants. As their planning progressed, Enbridge also began contracting directly with Indigenous businesses for support services. Alongside the formal submission of their project application for regulatory review, Enbridge began arranging financing so Indigenous communities could purchase equity in the project. The specific Indigenous signatories to these private agreements were generally not publicly disclosed, and the exact considerations that led different Indigenous groups to their decision are not matters of public record. However, in making their case for the Northern Gateway project, Enbridge did provide detailed descriptions of what it referred to as its Aboriginal Economic Benefits Package, arguing that the benefits of pipeline development for Indigenous communities—including access to training, employment, and contracting opportunities, as well as project equity and a share of project revenue—outweighed any potentially negative impacts on Aboriginal rights.

Enbridge's efforts to create industry-Indigenous partnerships through its Aboriginal Economic Benefits Package complement its Aboriginal traditional knowledge research program, described in chapter 3. In contrast to efforts to preserve space for Indigenous traditional life projects within the interstices of development, however, such newly evolving techniques of industry-Indigenous partnership aimed to link the livelihoods and well-being of Indigenous people to pipeline development. This chapter stresses five avenues through which Enbridge sought to forge industry-Indigenous partnerships: training, employment, subcontracting, equity investments, and community funding. Through these avenues, Enbridge aimed to make pipelines integral to Indigenous livelihoods and thereby suspend the conflict between Indigeneity and industrial infrastructure projects. Enbridge sought to facilitate the emergence of new modes of Indigenous empowerment, not in traditional land-based activities, but through inclusion in industrial development activities on their traditional lands. This initiative had a dual impetus: both securing development against Indigenous protest and offering to secure the well-being of the Indigenous population through industrial involvement. In this, the Enbridge offer fit within the broader milieu of corporate strategies for securing development investments on unceded Indigenous lands.

## The Convergence of Industry and Indigenous Peoples

While the Supreme Court of Canada decision in the *Delgamuukw, Gisdaywa* case held that the settler state possesses the sovereign authority to ultimately render decisions in the public interest, it burdened the government with obligations to respect Indigenous land interests. The juridical codification of a government duty to consult Aboriginal title claimants and regulate development to protect their interests has provided Indigenous communities with leverage to negotiate for a share of economic benefits from development.[7] As Indigenous claims created friction that inhibited the flow of extractive resources, industry began developing strategies to secure Indigenous support for development and thereby mitigate the risks that Indigenous movements posed to industry investments.

In order to legally justify infringement of Aboriginal title and rights, settler authorities must demonstrate, first, that the infringement serves a compelling and substantial governmental objective and, second, that they acted honourably with regard to their fiduciary duties to Aboriginal peoples. The court was "fairly broad" in its description of the "legislative objectives that can justify the infringement of aboriginal title." These objectives included "the development of agriculture, forestry, mining, and hydroelectric power, the general economic development of the interior of British Columbia, protection of the environment or endangered species, the building of infrastructure and the settlement of foreign populations to support those aims."[8] Despite the court's broad definition in this regard, the government still needed to uphold its fiduciary duties to Aboriginal peoples. These duties required that government authorities consult Indigenous communities "in good faith, and with the intention of substantially addressing the concerns of the aboriginal peoples whose lands are at issue."[9] Settler authorities needed to consider Indigenous input and demonstrate that an infringement was necessary to achieve a compelling governmental objective, that it went no further than required to achieve the objective, and that the adverse impacts on Indigenous interests caused by the infringement did not outweigh the benefits flowing from it. The court also recognized that Aboriginal title included an economic component, meaning that "fair compensation will ordinarily be required when aboriginal title is infringed."[10]

Thus, in governing Aboriginal title lands, settler authorities needed to ensure that development benefits were distributed to Indigenous peoples and were proportionate to the impacts of development on their land interests. Of course, these requirements remained only conceptual, as the court had made no finding with regard to the Gitxsan and Wet'suwet'en hereditary chiefs' title claim due to Justice McEachern's mishandling of Indigenous traditional knowledge at trial. The 1997 Supreme Court decision in *Delgamuukw, Gisdaywa* spurred treaty negotiations with Indigenous peoples forward, but left the question of the interim status of claimed Aboriginal title lands unresolved.[11] Initially, provincial authorities, who had jurisdiction over developments on provincial lands under the constitution, treated consultation as a theoretical obligation for still-undefined, state-recognized Aboriginal title lands.

While *Delgamuukw, Gisdaywa* spurred the development of a modern treaty process in British Columbia, the advance of Aboriginal rights triggered racist backlash. White settler resentment of Indigenous claims was particularly pronounced in rural resource communities, where white workers and their families has assumed their entitlement to possession of the land.[12] When the first modern treaty in British Columbia, the Nisga'a Final Agreement, came into effect in 2000, leaders of the opposition Liberal Party sued the Nisga'a, provincial, and federal governments, seeking to overturn the agreement as unconstitutional. The courts dismissed the suit on the grounds that Aboriginal rights had been constitutionalized and the treaty was enacted in congruence with these constitutional guarantees.[13] Nonetheless, the 2001 election led to the victory of the racially revanchist Liberals and a hardening of government opposition to Aboriginal rights. The Liberal government selected Geoff Plant, the former counsel for the province against the Gitxsan and Wet'suwet'en hereditary chiefs in *Delgamuukw, Gisdaywa*, as the new attorney general for the province. Plant circumscribed any potential recognition of distinct Indigenous rights to land and self-government, overseeing a provincial referendum that justified hardline opposition to treaties that could significantly alter colonial relationships.[14]

Subsequent Indigenous litigation would challenge the staunch provincial government refusal to meaningfully engage Indigenous communities. In the 2004 *Haida Nation v. British Columbia* case, the Supreme Court of Canada found, in a unanimous decision, that the government had a duty to consult and accommodate Indigenous interests, which extends along a spectrum based on the strength of the claim to Aboriginal title and potential impact of the infringement. At the low end of the spectrum, little more than communication was required. However, where Indigenous peoples have a strong prima facie case for Aboriginal title, and where the risk of noncompensable damage is high, substantive engagement may be required.

> *While precise requirements will vary with the circumstances, the consultation required at this stage may entail the opportunity to make submissions for consideration, formal participation in the decision-making process, and provision of written reasons to show that Aboriginal concerns were considered and to reveal the impact they had on the decision.*[15]

The court was clear that in the case of claimed Aboriginal title lands, settler authorities are duty bound "to balance societal and Aboriginal interests in making decisions that may affect Aboriginal claims."[16] Where substantial risks to Indigenous interests existed, settler authorities were required to regulate development "to avoid irreparable harm or to minimize the effects of infringement, pending final resolution of the underlying claim."[17] The court also required that Indigenous people not adopt "unreasonable positions to thwart government from making decisions or acting in cases where, despite meaningful consultation, agreement is not reached."[18] In other words, the courts denied Indigenous peoples a right to decide against a given development project.

In the wake of the *Haida Nation* decision, the government of British Columbia adopted a more conciliatory approach to Indigenous peoples. The provincial government dropped its staunch opposition to Aboriginal rights, signing a new vision statement with the leadership of the three major Indigenous organizations in the province—the BC Assembly of First Nations, First Nations Summit, and Union of BC Indian Chiefs—which it called the New Relationship. In contradistinction to the provincial government's earlier focus on extinguishing Indigenous claims, the New Relationship framework sought to explicitly recognize an ongoing relationship between Indigenous peoples and the provincial government.[19] The vision statement began by repeating the final line of the Supreme Court of Canada's decision in *Delgamuukw, Gisdaywa*: "We are all here to stay."[20] The vision of this new relationship broadly oriented Indigenous peoples and the provincial government towards a process of mutual recognition and accommodation to effect the "reconciliation of Aboriginal and Crown titles and jurisdictions."[21] In adopting this new approach, the province did not fundamentally revise the stalled provincial treaty negotiations framework. Instead, it expanded negotiations around interim agreements specific to particular industries or industrial projects and sought to greatly expand programs to support Indigenous integration into the industrial economy.

The province recognized that the irreconciled relationship between the government and Indigenous peoples was impacting resource industry investments. It therefore dedicated substantial funding to the task of improving relations. As Roger Hayter and Trevor Barnes describe, Indigenous movements have created substantial friction for the flow of resources from British Columbia.[22] A Fraser Institute survey of mining companies found nearly one-third (31%) indicated that uncertainty associated with Indigenous claims was a strong investment deterrent.[23] Creating mechanisms to reconcile Indigenous claims with extractive projects was necessary to securing the province's resource-extractive economy. To accomplish this goal, the provincial government created a new, independent agency, the New Relationship Trust Corporation, with $100 million of funding to actualize the vision of a new relationship with Indigenous peoples. Over the summer of 2006, the agency commissioned a province-wide Indigenous engagement process to orient its activities. In the sessions, participants endorsed four core objectives of the New Relationship Trust: enhancing Indigenous governance, developing Indigenous capacity, improving Indigenous land and resource management, and improving the economic status of Indigenous communities.[24]

The *Haida Nation* case and declaration of the New Relationship did not directly require that resource companies change their approach to engaging Indigenous communities, but they did introduce new regulatory considerations into resource governance processes. This changed the types of information that companies would be expected to supply in regulatory applications. The court was exceedingly clear that ultimate responsibility for consultation and accommodation was the duty of the colonial sovereign: "The honour of the Crown cannot be delegated."[25] The court also stated, however, that settler authorities could "delegate procedural aspects of consultation to industry proponents seeking a particular development; this is not infrequently done in environmental assessments."[26] Thus, while the settler state was duty bound to ensure that adequate consultation and accommodation ultimately occurred, the actual process of community engagement and negotiation around the balance of project impacts and benefits could, in practice, be led by corporate development proponents. The Canadian courts had also recognized that Aboriginal title possessed an inescapable economic component, meaning that the government had a further duty to ensure that Indigenous peoples were fairly compensated for any infringement of their Aboriginal title. To ensure that Indigenous communities were fairly compensated, settler-state authorities asked companies to provide new forms of evidence regarding the economic impacts of their proposed development on Indigenous peoples.

For development proponents, demonstrating that their projects advanced Indigenous economic interests became increasingly important to gaining regulatory approval. IBAs served as contractual offsets for development impacts on Indigenous communities, guaranteeing Indigenous access to project benefits and demonstrating

Indigenous support of development on the negotiated terms. By signing IBAs, corporations could insulate their project proposals from legal entanglements over a potential infringement of claimed Aboriginal title and rights. The shifting landscape of Aboriginal law in Canada did not strictly define how companies needed to engage Indigenous people, but legal precedents around Aboriginal title and the duty to consult cast a shadow over development proposals that incentivized companies to engage in private negotiations with Indigenous communities.[27] Thus, in dynamic relationships around resource development, the aspirations of Indigenous peoples, state agents, and industry were becoming entangled in new ways. Dennison's assessment of Osage negotiations with contemporary colonialism in the United States rings true here, as well: Indigenous peoples manoeuvre "within this entanglement, attempting to bring about their own vision."[28]

To better secure their investments in the resource sector, companies employed private contracting strategies to gain social licence. Canadian mining company executive Jim Cooney first coined the term *social licence* in 1997 at a World Bank forum reflecting on the challenges facing the extractive industry over the next quarter-century. Employed at the time as Director of International and Public Affairs at Placer Dome (now Barrick), Cooney was responsible for managing corporate risk exposure in developing countries. Reflecting on political dynamics in postcolonial countries, Cooney stressed the need for extractive companies to not only abide by governmental permit requirements, but also "maintain an ongoing positive relationship with local communities and their allies... acting in a manner consistent with local expectations and demands."[29] In his account, globalization had a double movement: on the one hand, it was opening up new opportunities for foreign investment for the first time since the wave of resource nationalizations that accompanied Third World decolonization in the 1960s and 1970s; on the other hand, new global social movements had provided local communities with unprecedented levels of knowledge and extensive networks of political and economic leverage. While extractive industries continued to partner with authoritarian governments and employ paramilitary forces when convenient, companies also developed new techniques for privately contracting with local communities to secure their support for development.[30] Cooney made a case for the latter set of approaches, arguing that the extractive industry should adopt new practices of corporate social responsibility and sustainable development to ensure their extractive enterprises did not become social movement targets.[31] His arguments found broad resonance in international economic institutions such as the World Bank, which sought to secure development trajectories in the Global South. Social licence and social responsibility quickly became catchwords in corporate governance discussions.

As resource companies sought to grapple with the shifting political context of Indigenous movements in Northwest British Columbia, they drew upon their established strategies for securing social licence. Beyond state permitting processes, companies had normalized the use of private negotiations with local movements, such as allying with local militias and tribal communities in Nigeria, to secure their support for extractive developments.[32] In 2006, Michael McPhie, the former head of the Mining Association of British Columbia, published an opinion piece in the *Vancouver Sun* entitled "A Social Licence to Operate," in which he reflected on the path forward for industry following the *Haida Nation* decision and declaration of the New Relationship. In the piece, McPhie argued that the future of the extractive industry "rests on our ability to secure strong and productive relationships between our industry and the communities in which we operate."[33] Contracting directly with impacted communities provided companies with an avenue to secure development trajectories on contested British Columbia lands in the absence of treaties. As Cooney originally articulated, this process ran in parallel to the state permitting processes. Companies still operated within the constraints of government regulatory regimes, though they also lobbied extensively for reforms to these processes in efforts to limit the extent of their public obligations and shorten the timelines for regulatory review. However, corporations no longer simply deferred to the state to cultivate local support. Instead, they directly engaged local political authorities, movements, and rights claimants as potential investment risks to manage.[34]

Corporations solicited new Indigenous partners by appropriating the rhetoric of Indigenous movements, posing integration into the global circuits of capitalism as a solution to their communities' dependency on colonial systems. Within this frame, Indigenous integration into resource development schemes appeared to create, as Gabrielle Slowey suggests, "new models of self-determination through market partnerships designed to improve socioeconomic conditions."[35] Calvin Helin proposes that, through industrial partnerships, Indigenous people can realize a form of market freedom that alleviates conditions of colonial dependency that have left individual Indigenous people reliant on social assistance and Indigenous communities financially reliant on federal government transfers.[36] Several authors have argued that industry-Indigenous partnerships are more responsive to community concerns than negotiations with the settler state, as the former enable communities to negotiate directly with industrial developers.[37] This narrative, however, oversimplifies the historic relationship between capitalism and colonialism and fails to adequately account for the ways this relationship is being transformed.

In the peripheries of the settler state, the expansion and intensification of corporate regimes of resource exploitation has long been tied to colonialism. The emergence of industry-Indigenous partnerships has inflected this relationship in new ways, but capitalist integration does not erase exploitative colonial relations.[38] Over the last century, settler regimes have conventionally sought to clear the grounds for capitalist development by simply displacing Indigenous peoples—effecting colonial sovereignty to enable the unfolding of extractive relations. However, under earlier regimes of colonial exploitation in the fur trade, corporations operating in the name of the imperial sovereign had sought to partner directly with Indigenous peoples to facilitate the flow of resources from their lands. In recent years, companies have effectively renewed these older colonial strategies as they have begun to adopt new approaches to risk mitigation that focus on Indigenous community concern and securing local support to manage their project risk profile. But unlike fur trade negotiations, which followed Indigenous custom, contemporary industry-Indigenous partnerships reflect the corporate legal traditions encoded in the laws of the settler state.[39] Corporate contracting serves not to decolonize Indigenous peoples but to address a defect in colonial sovereignty in order to secure extractive resource flows.

Industry-Indigenous partnerships are not simply a mechanism of economic inclusion; they integrate Indigenous peoples within the structure of a colonial legal order that approaches the land as a commodity to exploit. At the core of the relationship between colonialism and capitalism is the reimagination of the land "as a resource," as Leanne Betasamosake Simpson argues. "The act of extraction removes all of the relationships that give whatever is being extracted meaning. Extracting is taking."[40] Colonialism underpins the very *form* of law, as China Miéville argues, "with unequal coercive violence implied in the very commodity form. This unequal coercion is what forces particular content into the legal form."[41] Private negotiations are premised on an economic imaginary of rights as commodities that one can exchange. Thus, contracts rely on the assumption that the economic component of Indigenous land interests can be commodified as a form of property within the capitalist market. Promises for employment, subcontracting opportunities, investment options, or revenue sharing are not an instance of corporate gift-giving, but a form of rent or exchange for the use of Indigenous lands. The discourse of corporate social responsibility, in effect, implies that companies are fairly compensating Indigenous peoples for the exploitation of their claimed lands. However, the capitalist commodification of relations, including relationships to the land itself, is part of the colonial process of displacing Indigenous territorial connections. Corporate-community agreements are not decolonizing; indeed, they continue to be underpinned by settler legal regimes governing private transactions. They are the culmination of colonial processes that integrate Indigenous peoples into a legal order based on the commodity.[42]

As people are increasingly employed to negotiate these contracts (and to conduct the studies discussed in the previous chapter), the process of reconciliation itself has emerged as a new domain of economic activity.[43] As settler regulatory processes aim to calculate the balance of Indigenous interests, and as they ask both industry and Indigenous peoples to make submissions about how effectively development projects address these interests, the process of documenting and quantifying different forms of Indigenous interests becomes a field not only of study but of paid work. Companies hire consultants to conduct Indigenous land use and occupancy studies and to negotiate corporate-community agreements. As Indigenous peoples seek to advance their own interests through both livelihoods in the industrial economy and protections for traditional land use, they also contract people to perform studies, provide legal advice, and conduct negotiations. Both companies, such as Enbridge, and regulators, such as the National Energy Board, provide Indigenous communities with capacity funding to do this work (although this funding is generally inadequate to the task of documenting the full depth of Indigenous relations to the land).

The emergent economies of reconciliation are necessarily transcultural, shaped not only by colonial extractive development agendas but also the translation of Indigenous territorial concerns, including those centred on cultural revitalization and environmental protection. The documentation of Indigenous traditional land use and the monitoring of environmental and cultural effects of resource developments on Indigenous lands have resulted in the creation of new employment and contracting opportunities in project planning processes. Moreover, Indigenous engagements with industry do not simply subsume Indigeneity to colonial capital. In important ways, capital is also Indigenized, as communities redirect financial resources to support processes such as Indigenous cultural revitalization and language preservation.[44] Partnering with industry has thus created routes for Indigenous peoples to become both increasingly connected to Indigenous traditions and reconciled with resource development regimes.

Despite such complexities, several critical commentators have argued that reconciling Indigenous peoples with development through corporate partnerships does more to provide certainty to development than justice to Indigenous peoples. Critics have particularly suggested that effecting reconciliation through corporate contracts represents a privatization of state duties to protect Aboriginal rights, removing negotiations over the specific terms of industrial development from the public domain.[45] These critiques rightly observe many of the negative effects of these agreements. They can, for instance, stifle Indigenous opposition to development and hinder Indigenous peoples' ability to influence decision-making.[46] They can also unequally distribute benefits within and across Indigenous communities.[47] These issues are not accidental defects or imperfections of private agreements, but are reflective of the settler regimes governing development.

The settler authorities who oversee emergent industry-Indigenous relations have applied modern techniques of governing economic life, broadly guiding the conduct of private negotiations rather than directly dictating their terms. Private industry-Indigenous partnerships do not challenge this governmental order; settler authorities rely on these private agreements to evaluate whether project planning has adequately accommodated Indigenous interests and provided fair compensation for any potential impacts on Aboriginal title and rights. In concert with the arts of liberal government, settler regulatory action has sought to maintain the general course of development by addressing irregularities in the market that could block the circulation of commodities. As Aboriginal rights jurisprudence has evolved, settler authorities have been burdened with legal responsibilities to protect Indigenous interests that can politically entangle development. Corporations have responded by codifying the development benefits that Indigenous communities can access. When these initiatives are sufficiently substantive, they create vital evidence of the Indigenous extractive empowerment that settler authorities need to effectively discharge their legal responsibilities to meaningfully reconcile development with Indigenous interests. When corporate benefit initiatives are less substantive than required, however, settler authorities can also impose conditions on development to ensure that projects meet the legal standards of accommodating Indigenous interests. While industry-Indigenous partnerships reflect a change in how relationships to the land are organized in settler law, they do not fundamentally undermine the exercise of settler jurisdiction, in which settler authorities are not responsible for directing the specific content of economic activities, but for addressing contradictions or conflicts that limit the capacity of economic forces to realize their potential.

**Learning to Share**

Education has taken an increasingly prominent role in efforts to build a new relationship among settler authorities, corporate entities, and Indigenous peoples. Schools function as a central mechanism for transmitting cultural knowledge and skilling future generations. It is in schools, colleges, and universities that people are formed into the citizenry of powerful political imaginaries.[48] As Marxist critics Samuel Bowles and Herbert Gintis have suggested, education serves to discipline students for the workforce and inculcate dominant capitalist norms.[49] While it's true that the forms of discipline working through education function as a process of subjectification for market participation, it is also true that they are productive of new relations, integrating Indigenous interests alongside those of capital.[50]

Indigenous peoples have long pursued increased access to education as a means of improving conditions in their communities. Historically, as settlement extended across the West, Indigenous communities sought to secure government commitments to support Indigenous education and provide future generations with the essential skills to participate in the emerging economy.[51] In response, settler authorities created Indian residential schools, a federally funded, church-run system that focused more on the annihilation of Indigenous culture than on effectively skilling youth for the modern economy.[52] As described in chapter 1, these schools sought to effect the targeted destruction of Indigenous culture, taking children from their families in order to rupture the intergenerational transmission of knowledge.[53] Addressing the legacy of the Indian residential school system has been central to the resurgence of Indigenous politics over the last half-century.

In response to the 1969 assimilationist White Paper, Indigenous leaders issued a counterproposal that they called "Citizens Plus," or the Red Paper. The counterproposal emphasized that Indigenous peoples needed to have access to and control over education programs. Originally drafted by the Indian Chiefs of Alberta, and subsequently adopted by the National Indian Brotherhood, the Red Paper challenged the logic of an assimilationist approach to annulling Indian status, instead proposing that Indigenous marginalization would be best addressed through expanding educational programming in Indigenous communities under Indigenous control. They argued that expanding education opportunities for Indigenous people under the jurisdiction of local Indigenous authorities offered "a means for many Indians to find economic security and self-fulfillment."[54] The Red Paper called for job training that reflected available employment opportunities and economic realities, but also stressed the importance of providing basic adult education that reaffirmed the value of Indigenous language and traditions. To ensure student success, they emphasized the need for increased education funding and for counselling services designed for and operated by Indigenous authorities to address addiction issues in their communities. Following the National Indian Brotherhood's demand for Indian control of Indian education in 1973, the federal government devolved control over on-reserve education, as well as administration of financial assistance programs for Status Indian adult learners, to Indigenous bands. However, in the absence of adequate funding for these programs and effective reorientation of major industries toward training and hiring Indigenous workers, devolution remained a token gesture that failed to ameliorate the marginalization of Indigenous peoples.[55]

Education again emerged as a major theme in 2006, during discussions over the terms of the declared New Relationship between Indigenous peoples and the British Columbia government. In Indigenous engagement sessions conducted across the province, Indigenous community members ranked education as their top priority by a wide margin."[56] Further, as detailed in the summary report on these discussions, "most respondents identified the lack of trained people as the highest barrier to positive change."[57] Session participants suggested the two areas in which communities were most in need of additional training were traditional knowledge and trades. Following these New Relationship discussions, the British Columbia Ministry of Advanced Education launched the Aboriginal Post-Secondary Education Strategy and Action Plan in 2007, investing significant funding in training Indigenous adult learners to encourage their incorporation into the developing economy and society. This supplemented existing federal educational support programs for Status Indian learners.

Approaching Indigenous communities, Enbridge integrated educational concerns into their early program of Indigenous engagements. They began offering educational opportunities to Indigenous communities in 2006, well in advance of regulatory approval. Janet Holder, vice president of western access at Enbridge and the executive responsible for overseeing the Northern Gateway project, described the importance of early engagement with Indigenous educational concerns.

> *I think we are taking a different approach than has historically been taken by proponents...in that we are starting that skills development before we know we have a project. Most organizations will wait until they know they have the project, have the permitting in place and then they start working on skills and development of skills and training. In our case, we're actually starting that very early on in the process.*[58]

The company sought to reflect Indigenous priorities by emphasizing education and beginning to develop training initiatives in its early community engagements.

Substantial resources were devoted to skills and training programs associated with the Northern Gateway project. Between 2006 and 2013, Enbridge "spent over $1 million on skills and training in Alberta and British Columbia."[59] In fact, the company created a $1.5 million education and training fund in 2011 for Northern Gateway "to develop an efficient funding mechanism for costs associated with pipeline, oil and gas and construction sector training initiatives."[60] In December 2012, the value of this fund was doubled to $3 million. Pipeline company representatives worked with Indigenous bands who administered federal and provincial educational funding programs to fill educational funding gaps using Northern Gateway's education and training fund. By February 2013, the company had skill development initiatives in place with fourteen Indigenous communities, ranging from essential skills training and upgrading for high school equivalency to trades programs preparing workers for employment in environmental monitoring, surveying, and welding.[61] Enbridge also reported that it was discussing skills development programs with another fifteen Indigenous communities. The company was responsive to community education goals. Catherine Pennington, senior manager of community partnerships and sustainability with the Northern Gateway project, described how a principal ambition and effect of the education funding and partnerships was to "help us design and follow through with education and training programs really as a mechanism to get people to employment now."[62] Thus, the education program sought to nurture the resubjectification of members of Indigenous communities impacted by development as pipeline workers.

Approaching the development of education and training programs, Enbridge stressed the importance of partnering with Indigenous communities to determine appropriate training supports. Pennington explained the company approached and developed its educational strategies based on the recognition that communities were the experts in evaluating their own needs.

> *Communities know what they need, they know who they are, they know what their interests are, they know who their partners are. And they are fundamentally the leader in the process. So we really have worked hard to ensure that that includes things like open dialogue and listening and full engagement and taking the direction of the community, recognizing that they're going to know best what they need for the short, medium and long-term.*[63]

Rather than prioritizing their workforce needs, the company emphasized that the goal of their Indigenous education and training fund was to effect a reconciliation of development activity with the needs and ambitions of Indigenous communities. In her testimony before the Joint Review Panel for the Northern Gateway Project (JRP), Pennington emphasized the importance of community educational plans developed in dialogue with the community: "Those plans are an individual plan depending on the community because each community will be different. The demographics, the population, the interest, there's a whole host of items that will change at the community level."[64] Thus, Enbridge sought to make skills assessments and design training programs based on each community's distinct educational needs and desires. "We really try to listen to communities and implement skills and training programs that will meet their needs," Pennington stressed. "This is not a cookie cutter program."[65]

While customizing educational initiatives to communities, Enbridge acted to fund and facilitate education rather than offer programming itself. Enbridge did not directly train employees to develop pipelines for the company. Instead, it relied upon a complex network of institutional partnerships and pipeline project subcontracting. Rather than directly dictating the content of either education or employment programs, it coordinated a network of training regimes to skill workers for its various contractors. Educational programming was primarily delivered by local public colleges. As corporate subcontracting drove activity in local pipeline construction and servicing markets, Enbridge project planning dictated the shifts in local effective demand for skilled pipeline workers. Corporate representatives engaged "local colleges in Alberta and British Columbia to ensure that they [were] aware of the upcoming labour need in energy pipeline and construction sectors."[66] The company also served as a central conduit for information to subcontracting firms about local labour markets and hiring opportunities. To communicate with potential contractors, the company held "contractor readiness sessions or 'boot camps,'" which included discussion of skills and training considerations relevant to project employers.[67]

Thus, implementation of education and training programs involved a composite governmental apparatus, linking Indigenous band governments, state agencies, corporate initiatives, and public educational institutions. In line with modern modes of market governance, settler-state, corporate, and band authorities did not directly define the particular content of education or act on individual workers. Rather they set funding priorities that could support individual learners. At the intersection of economic strategies and educational policies, a governmental apparatus emerged to effect a form of reconciliation aimed at ensuring the economic security and well-being of the Indigenous population. As Michel Foucault described, governmental strategies do not target individual subjects but aim to work on a population.[68] Rather than seeking to control individual bodies, as is the case with disciplinary regimes, the art of government works to foster the life of the population through the apparatuses of security.

Directed in coordination with local bands, funding supported individual Indigenous community members to attend local colleges, linking the governmental regulation of employment and training to the particular disciplinary apparatuses of subjectification through schools. In the local college, educational programming focused on disciplining individual students, and particularly Indigenous students, so their capabilities could be effectively honed to work for industry.[69] Education gave students the knowledge and skills to integrate into related jobs. As Foucault described in his classic work on disciplinary power, education functions through surveilling and controlling the individual body by constituting perceptual grids and structuring physical routines.[70] School discipline aligns students' dispositions, inculcating normalized ways of acting. In the discipline instilled through educational programs designed for Indigenous peoples, economic and political imperatives are coupled. Discipline works to ensure the development of skills, and thereby ensures increased productivity. At the same time, the inculcation of obedience intensifies students' subjection. Much as corporate traditional knowledge studies work to enframe Indigenous traditions to enable their integration into resource governance, training regimes work to discipline Indigenous community members to facilitate the incorporation of their livelihood strategies into industrial labour. The regimes of power-knowledge within disciplinary regimes of education reflect the composite character of government rationalities that bring together Indigenous aspirations with designs for resource extraction. Such educational regimes foster the subjectification of Indigenous students as extractive industry workers.[71]

As a constituent element of contemporary colonial governmentality, industry training has served not only to discipline labourers but also to simultaneously foster the reconciliation of Indigenous populations to industrial development. Through both private and public investments in education, the college as a public institution was oriented to advance the political economic agenda of reconciliation, resecuring the grounds for resource development. The form of tutelage provided in local colleges served to choreograph programs of conduct for Indigenous students to achieve self-actualization through employment in industrial development projects.[72] This tutelage aimed to transform Indigenous polities, reconfiguring conflicts over territorial jurisdiction into problems about access to training and employment. In so doing, new education and training programs sought to reverse the legacy of residential schooling and its goals of assimilating Indigenous peoples. Rather than seeking to induce youth to repress their Indigeneity (as Indian residential schools had done), these new training regimes sought to effect a culturally modified form of capitalist subjectification that could prepare Indigenous people qua Indigenous workers for participation in the resource-extractive economy. These regimes of education do not erase Indigeneity but inculcate students with a particular version of Indigenous subjectivity reconcilable with and employable within industrial development. Notably, these programs had the potential to advance Indigenous economic interests irrespective of whether communities remained politically uncertain or opposed to the project. As Pennington expressed, regardless of the current stance of an Indigenous community with respect to Northern Gateway, "the understanding that we have is that there remains an interest to think about skills and training and employment opportunities."[73] Thus, training regimes offered

Indigenous communities an opportunity to make extractive development the source of their economic well-being regardless of their political will or desire to do so.

### Building Industrial Livelihoods and Indigenous Entrepreneurship

Upon the foundation of expanding Indigenous industrial knowledge and capacity, the core of new corporate-community collaborations focused on ensuring Indigenous access to economic opportunities. The two principal mechanisms for enrolling Indigenous people into development were, first, corporate policies that sought to secure privileged Indigenous access to employment on the pipelines and, second, the business opportunities associated with project procurement and services. These two mechanisms were the most valued components of the Aboriginal Economic Benefits Package that Enbridge offered to Indigenous communities along the pipeline. It included an estimated $100 million in employment income on the project, $300 million in business opportunities for goods procurement and pipeline-construction-related services, and $200 to $300 million in contracts for marine and tunnel construction services.[74] To create these openings for economic inclusion, Enbridge developed company policies that directed subcontractors to hire Indigenous workers and provided targeted opportunities for Indigenous contractors to bid on project contracts. Through these economic opportunities, Enbridge sought to make the success of the pipeline project synonymous with the enhancement of Indigenous well-being.

Impoverished Indigenous peoples have used negotiations with resource-extractive companies to secure both livelihoods in the industrial economy and protections for traditional land use. As Ciaran O'Faircheallaigh has described in analogous negotiations with mining companies in Australia, Aboriginal peoples "want to get jobs both to supplement incomes that are often low and as a way of achieving personal autonomy and self-respect." Economic opportunities are desired as ways of ameliorating "problems of substance abuse, incarceration and, often a grim reality in Aboriginal communities, suicide."[75] Indigenous peoples do not universally oppose industrial development on principle and can indeed become strong supporters of it when industrial activity interlinks with programs of Indigenous empowerment. As historical scholarship has repeatedly pointed out, there is an extended history of Indigenous labour in resource industries in British Columbia that was only suppressed through processes of racial exclusion from industry labour markets in the latter half of the twentieth century.[76] In its engagements with Indigenous communities, Enbridge sought to emphasize how participation in the industrial economy could again become a route to the empowerment of Indigenous peoples.

Much as Enbridge initiated Indigenous training programs early in its project planning, it also began extending opportunities for Indigenous employment in the preliminary studies it conducted to prepare its regulatory applications. Thus, as the company began conducting baseline environmental studies in 2005 and 2006, it also sought to coordinate employment opportunities for local Indigenous workers with the biophysical consulting firms it contracted. Orchestrating these connections, the company used standard language in its service agreements that directed the consulting firms it contracted to hire workers from local Indigenous communities. As described in Enbridge's application for federal regulatory approval of the Northern Gateway project, the structure of these agreements created "the contractual foundation for including local assistants in fieldwork."[77] Enbridge communicated job opportunities to Indigenous communities with whom it had already formalized memoranda of understanding or cooperation agreements to facilitate community engagement processes. This network of contractual arrangements facilitated the employment of fifty-five Indigenous people from fourteen distinct communities by consultants collecting data for the Northern Gateway project in the 2005 and 2006 field seasons.[78] The project proposal was paused in 2007, but Enbridge renewed its engagements with Indigenous communities in 2008, replacing earlier cooperation agreements with the new protocol agreements.[79] By 2009, the company had signed thirty protocol agreements with thirty-six Indigenous groups.[80] The company continued to use standard service agreements to direct contractors to hire local Indigenous assistants. Ray Doering, the director of project services for the Northern Gateway project, testified in March

2013 that the company had ensured Indigenous employment in "a lot of environmental monitoring and field crew support work. We have had Aboriginal support on some of our earlier geotechnical programs and we expect, as we move forward with additional environmental field work and geotechnical fieldwork, that we'll continue to build off of that."[81]

In their regulatory arguments justifying the need for the project, Enbridge emphasized that the Northern Gateway Pipelines "would provide real jobs for a significant number of Canadians."[82] They estimated the project would provide direct employment to between 2,000 and 3,000 workers in peak pipeline construction periods. Once operational, Northern Gateway would only result in the direct employment of 104 regional residents. However, in their regulatory submissions and publicity materials, Enbridge further emphasized how project activity would echo beyond direct project employment through the broader economy, as business transactions would create additional indirect employment and the household spending of workers would induce further economic activity. The company estimated that the pipelines "would generate about 1,200 long term jobs (direct, indirect and induced)."[83]

As part of the Aboriginal Economic Benefits Package offered to communities impacted by Northern Gateway, the company established an Aboriginal employment target of 15 percent of construction labour and 10 percent of overall construction-related employment.[84] These targets would apply both to labourers directly employed by the Northern Gateway project and to contracted service providers. Enbridge also committed to ensuring that 20 percent of the 104 regional positions for direct employment in the operational pipelines would go to Indigenous candidates.[85] Enbridge claimed these targets, for the company and its subcontractors, would be "reasonably attainable based on recent empirical experience with projects of similar scope and scale and applying practices Enbridge has developed over time to improve rates of Aboriginal participation in its major projects."[86]

The company would not explicitly dictate how contractors were to meet these targets, but would instead require that contractors submit plans to be considered as part of their bids for project contracts: "Northern Gateway will require all potential primary contractors, as part of the competitive bid process, to submit a detailed Aboriginal participation plan, which would describe how they plan to include an Aboriginal workforce and provide details on the number of local and Aboriginal employees, jobs, duration, and so forth. It would also require contractors to report the Aboriginal participation rate as requested by Northern Gateway."[87] Tom Fiddler, the senior manager of safety and construction with the Northern Gateway project, attested to the company's experience and past success with such plans. He told the JRP, "The development and use of Aboriginal participation plans is not something unusual for us at Enbridge. In fact, many of our projects in Northern Alberta, but also as we go east across the Prairies, have involved the development of such plans."[88]

To bridge relationships between contractors and local Indigenous communities, Enbridge hired Aboriginal liaisons. "The use of Aboriginal liaisons is again a routine that we have employed, and very strategically," Fiddler explained. Aboriginal liaisons, in his account, had been "very effective" in ensuring Indigenous participation in project-related opportunities. With greater "cultural acceptance and...trust and respect" in the Indigenous community, these liaisons provided a key resource person that could be "leveraged by both our contractors and our construction management folks as well as the Aboriginal leaders."[89] These Aboriginal liaisons would work with the project contractors, industrial labour unions, and Indigenous communities and organizations to ensure a minimum 15 percent of construction and 10 percent of construction-related jobs were held by Aboriginal workers.[90]

Enbridge sought to build these relationships so Indigenous people could be employed in pipeline development on their lands. Explaining the goals of local Indigenous hiring, Fiddler was clear: "Our first premise is that to the extent participation is desired and we can facilitate it appropriately, we will involve First Nations in the areas of interest relative to their traditional territory."[91] Enbridge's approach to Aboriginal employment aimed to rework rather than simply replace Indigenous connections to the land. Recent efforts to Indigenize industrial labour, as Lindsay Bell describes, resonate with the long history of colonialism in the North, in which company agents historically harnessed the characteristics of Indigenous locality to the territorialization of space as a resource-extractive frontier.[92] While twentieth-century settler land policies had sought to contain Indigenous space, these new industrial employment regimes worked to reconstruct prior bonds between Indigenous people and the land, reconstructing Indigenous territorial relationships in sync with the requirements of capitalist resource-extractive development. These new employment regimes called into being a new form of industrial Indigeneity by creating opportunities to reconcile development with the economic component of claimed Aboriginal title to the land.

There were, however, also limits on the reconciliation that industrial employment could offer. Enbridge could facilitate opportunities for Indigenous employment and justify this as fair compensation for any impacts to their traditional territories, but they could not make Indigenous peoples consent to this exchange or take the jobs. As Janet Holder, Enbridge's vice president of western access, said,

> *I think there's only one qualifier: Aboriginal groups have to be willing. This is our aspiration, as we put it, but—and we're doing everything in our power to encourage Aboriginal groups to engage with us so that that is easily met. But if the Aboriginal groups choose not to engage, then it may be a difficult target.*[93]

Moreover, Indigenous opportunities for economic advancement through temporary and often unskilled labour were relatively limited. As Tom Fiddler noted at the JRP hearings, particular jobs tended to match the skills of Indigenous community members. For instance, "a key one would be...clearing and timber salvage work."[94] But as economic geographer Suzanne Mills has documented, construction trades unions and contractors have typically used skills definitions to limit Indigenous job access in spite of employment provisions of IBAs, and to ensure that local Indigenous employment on a specific project does not transfer to opportunities on projects beyond their territories.[95] Thus, while project-related employment offers could provide Indigenous workers with jobs for a set period, they typically do not provide community members with enduring economic security. Enhancing Indigenous economic gains requires more than jobs; it requires business opportunities.

The extension of subcontracting opportunities offered another avenue for Indigenous empowerment through participation in industrial development. Alongside providing individual employment opportunities, Enbridge argued that the Northern Gateway project would create opportunities for the advancement of Indigenous business ventures, in the form of either community-owned enterprises or privately owned corporations. These opportunities constituted the greatest portion of the proposed $1 billion Aboriginal Economic Benefits Package that Enbridge presented to Indigenous communities. Enbridge split discussions of Indigenous business opportunities between those associated with the construction of the pipelines and those associated with the marine terminal and shipping. For the pipelines, the company had set "a target of $300 million for Aboriginal procurement." It sought to distribute this money across the route. In the Northwest Interior of British Columbia, the company established the Burns Lake Aboriginal Communities Working Group "to develop strategies to maximize the participation of Aboriginal communities and their members in business, economic and social opportunities relating to the development, construction and operation of the Project." The company also supported "communities to design individual community plans in advance of construction to identify the steps required for each community to participate meaningfully in employment and business opportunities."[96]

To support these opportunities, Enbridge adopted corporate policies that would facilitate increased contracting with Indigenous businesses. Fiddler described how the corporation sought to structure opportunities to secure support services for pipeline construction from Indigenous operators.

> The plans include pre-qualification by Enbridge of subcontractor entities that have a predominant interest held by Aboriginal parties. It also talks about certain scopes of work where we've

*pre-qualified or worked with the community on assessing skills and interests and involvement in support as a subcontractor or as skilled labour or unskilled labour to certain aspects of the work.*[97]

Doering, responsible for securing support services for Northern Gateway, described how they were seeking to maximize opportunities for Indigenous businesses or joint ventures "piecing out the construction elements of the project."[98] He described discussions about breaking out particular elements of major pipeline construction contracts, creating smaller specific components "where we can achieve success with the Aboriginal communities and their joint ventures."[99] To better identify and coordinate the business capacity of local Indigenous enterprises, as well as the skillsets of available Indigenous workers, Enbridge began developing a regional skills and business inventory database.

As it had with training and employment, Enbridge began contracting with Indigenous businesses in the research phase that preceded its regulatory application. In addition to involvement in traditional land use fieldwork, small Indigenous consulting firms conducted specific environmental studies. Jeff Green, a consultant contracted as technical coordinator for the Northern Gateway environmental assessment, noted that Indigenous communities in British Columbia often "have resource management groups with trained biologists, sometimes BSc or Master degree biologists as well as technicians that can undertake a number of the different surveys that are required."[100] Noting that, as of March 2013, Enbridge had contracted approximately thirty such enterprises, Green highlighted the capacity of Indigenous firms along the pipeline to do "air monitoring, water quality monitoring, wildlife work, plant works, [and] centre line surveys."[101]

The company was also actively negotiating business relationships in advance of project approval. Moving forward, Doering emphasized the potential for Indigenous business firms, "particularly around the camps and catering element for the project."

*There's actually a very high dollar potential value to that component of the pipeline and facility construction and that's one area that we're really exploring, some very relevant and current Aboriginal businesses that are actually in that particular service. But there are probably a dozen other categories of potential contracting opportunities that we're looking at along pipeline construction, anywhere from some of the traditional activities like road building and clearing and logging and salvage opportunities, fuel supply, trucking contracts, concrete weights for pipeline buoyancy control, skids and mats for pipeline construction, stockpiling, surveying, reclamation activities, a variety of other consumables.*[102]

Across this range of activities, Enbridge sought to facilitate the integration of Indigenous people into the industrial development of their traditional territories. Contracting for these services, as Samuel Rose describes, depoliticizes economic activity and "promotes the insidious notion that capitalist exploitation…is wrong only when it is without collaboration with and acceptance by the indigenous community." Celebratory discourses of economic integration presented capitalist exploitation of land and labour as "acceptable (if not preferred) when it is Indigenous people exploiting the land and each other, or at least providing the legal acquiescence for exploitation for outside firms."[103]

Enbridge thus sought to resolve the conflict between industry and Indigenous peoples through the subsumption of Indigenous livelihoods to the pipeline industry as both labourers and contractors. Doing so modified colonial regimes that had previously relied on simple accumulation by dispossession. Rather than simply displacing Indigenous people from the land, this new regime of recognition sought to resignify Indigenous attachments to their traditional lands, reterritorializing Indigeneity to serve the requirements of capital. These industry-Indigenous partnerships were a marked contrast to twentieth-century settler-colonial regimes that simply sought to erase Indigeneity; however, they relied on the effects of earlier colonial interventions. The impact of Indian residential schools, decades of employment discrimination, and the degradation of the land by previous resource development had left many Indigenous people alienated from their land with high rates of dependence on government social assistance programs. Through its offers to support Indigenous employment and entrepreneurship, Enbridge sought to create avenues for Indigenous people to leverage their residual legal territorial claims to realize a form of empowerment through participation in pipeline development.

**Investing in Indigenous Equity**

The final components of Enbridge's proposed Aboriginal Economic Benefits Package were initiatives that aimed to effect financial inclusion. These mechanisms of inclusion represented a marked contrast to those that sought to integrate Indigenous people into the production of pipeline infrastructure through Indigenous training, hiring, and contracting practices. There is a concrete materiality to the production of the infrastructure for resource extraction. Thus, even relatively abstract knowledge work, such as documenting Indigenous traditional land use or conducting environmental baseline studies, occurs in relation to sets of material relations in the world. Financial processes, in contrast, operate at a greater degree of abstraction, centrally involving the circulation of symbols of value. Financial processes, of course, have real effects, and indeed are vitally necessary to managing delays in return on investment.[104] Commodity production, circulation, and exchange take time, and during this time, the capital involved in them is fixed. Finance—forms of investment and lending—is necessary to ensure that money continues to flow while capital is fixed. The abstract nature of money gives forms of financial reconciliation with Indigenous peoples a distinct character. In contrast to economic initiatives such as training and employment, financial inclusion is more structurally embedded within the financialized global flows of commodities and reliant on returns from expanding extractive developments.

Forty-five Indigenous groups were offered an opportunity to purchase equity prior to the completion of the review hearing process with twenty-six taking the offer.[105] In its public regulatory disclosures, Enbridge did not identify the Indigenous signatories to private agreements, instead simply listing the groups who had received the offer. Among the Wet'suwet'en, offers were provided to the Office of the Wet'suwet'en, Ts'il Kaz Koh, Nee-Tahi-Buhn, Skin Tyee, and Wet'suwet'en First Nation.[106] Alongside these Wet'suwet'en groups, the neighbouring Gitxsan Treaty Office, Cheslatta Carrier Nation, and Lake Babine Nation, as well as dozens of other groups and communities along the pipeline route, were offered opportunities to purchase an equity stake.

Critical scholarship on Indigenous relations to capitalism has typically emphasized questions of territory rather than finance.[107] However, as Alyosha Goldstein stresses, an entwining of land and finance, of settler colonialism and financial capitalism, is evident in "contemporary efforts to foreclose the lineages of historical injustice."[108] Anxieties about exposure to financial risks have driven resource-extractive companies to pay greater attention to the claims of historically oppressed communities, as is evident in discussions around social licence. They are guided to address Indigenous issues by a desire for investment security (rather than justice).[109] At the same time, dynamics in the oil and gas sector, like much of the broader economy, are becoming increasingly financialized, with financial markets increasingly dictating approaches to production management.[110] Financial capital has come to dominate productive capital such that production decisions are often responses to financial market signals rather than productive relationships. In this context, companies have increasingly explored financial strategies to reconcile Indigenous peoples and development. As Melanie Sommerville has described, a particular financialized discourse of reconciliation positions Indigenous financial inclusion as the remedy for colonialism's historic exclusions.[111]

Two particular initiatives constituted Enbridge's offer for Indigenous inclusion in the financial flows entwined with the project: encouraging Aboriginal equity ownership in the pipelines after approval and creating a community investment fund. The first initiative—Aboriginal equity ownership—was the most significant. In preparing its pipelines proposal, Enbridge set Northern Gateway up as a limited partnership to build and operate the pipelines. Enbridge was the only shareholder at the time of project application and intended to remain majority shareholder after project approval.

However, in order to finance the cost of the project's regulatory application process and to integrate Indigenous partners in the project, Enbridge had structured specific investment opportunities into the project. It raised $140 million to develop the project proposal from a mix of energy companies—including Cenovus, Nexen, Suncor, MEG Energy, and Total SA—who would hold options for shipping capacity and ownership shares if the project was developed. It also set aside 10 percent of the equity for Indigenous project partners.

Enbridge offered to provide an aggregate loan to all participating Indigenous partners of approximately $235 million to purchase equity in the project. Indigenous partners were to repay this loan "through the dividends they receive as equity owner for their 10% share."[112] The loan would amortize over thirty years from 2016 to 2046, accumulating debt at a rate of 7.75 percent while providing an 11 percent return on equity. Based on these projections, Enbridge expected equity ownership "to generate approximately $280 million in net, after-expense income to participating Aboriginal communities, over the first 30 years."[113] The company stated that equity ownership constituted "approximately one-third of the total potential Aboriginal benefits Northern Gateway is proposing."[114] Although the specific participating Indigenous groups were not publicly disclosed, Enbridge indicated that fifteen of the eighteen offers tendered in Alberta, and eleven of the twenty-seven tendered in British Columbia, had been signed.[115]

In contrast to the other elements of the Aboriginal Economic Benefits Package, the equity offer was not tailored to suit the particular needs and capacities of the community. The equity offer, as Enbridge explained in the Aboriginal Economic Benefits Package documents that it distributed to eligible communities, "is being made to provide sustainable benefit to neighbouring communities, irrespective of their current capacity to participate in other project benefits such as procurement and employment."[116] Enbridge determined on a case-by-case basis which groups qualified as "Eligible Aboriginal Investors," and its decisions were in part based on where a group was located. The company began with the list of Indigenous groups that had lands located within 80 kilometres of the project corridors, which it had previously used to focus its engagement activities. The province in which a group was located also mattered. In Alberta, where the Canadian government had signed historic land cession treaties with Indigenous peoples, Enbridge only made equity offers to communities who had expressed an interest in participating in the economic opportunities associated with the pipeline in its earlier engagement process; in British Columbia, where the majority of the land remained unceded, communities were eligible for the equity offer whether or not they had previously been receptive to participating in the economic opportunities related to the project. Once a group had been identified as an eligible investor, it had the opportunity to decide whether to sign onto the ownership agreement. Time was a factor at this stage. Communities who signed before the end of March 2011 were deemed "Early Equity Partners." After the original equity offer expired at the end of April 2011, unallocated equity would be redistributed among the early partners in that province.[117]

Signing on as an equity partner deepened the bond between Indigenous communities and pipeline development, entangling the interests of signatory communities with the pipelines and restricting their capacity to directly resist the project. After signing onto the project, equity partners could still participate in the regulatory review process and provide input on mitigation measures, but they were "expected to not oppose the Northern Gateway project and to cooperate with...the regulatory and environmental assessment process."[118] Equity partners had limited voting rights in governance, and those that they had were largely token as Enbridge would remain the voice of majority owner. Only one Indigenous leader in British Columbia, from the Gitxsan Treaty Office, publicly disclosed signing the offer. This announcement provoked widespread community denunciation as a violation of the hereditary chiefs' obligations to protect the territories and uphold traditional governance practices.[119] Conflict over pipeline development became internalized within the Gitxsan community, and dissident Gitxsan hereditary chiefs and community members occupied the treaty office for months.

These were not the only disciplinary effects that flowed from the agreements. Although Indigenous partners were to be beneficiaries of project profits, they were also bonded as project partners. This exposed them to additional liabilities under the contract if they later decided to oppose the project.[120] Similarly, there were asymmetrical relations of debt associated with Enbridge's offer of financial inclusion. Indigenous partners occupied a position of long-term indebtedness to the venture, reliant on project success not only to secure earnings but to repay the loans financing equity purchases. Thus, while equity partnership in Northern Gateway was marketed as an Indigenous benefit, it was also a substantial risk. For an Indigenous equity partner to successfully repay the loans for their equity purchase, the project needed to remain profitable over the course of three decades. Indigenous partners were locked in. Once construction began, signatories' interests were bound to the pipeline. If the pipeline was shut down or became financially unviable after construction because of a disaster, or the belated adoption of climate change mitigation measures in Canada, or some other reason, they had substantial financial exposure as debt-financed investors.

The second mechanism of financial inclusion that Enbridge proposed, a community investment fund, was not as restrictive but incredibly vague. The foundational concept was that Enbridge would withhold 1 percent of pre-tax earnings from the Northern Gateway project and set it aside for a community fund. "The proceeds from the Community Investment Fund would be distributed toward programs deemed to be of benefit to Aboriginal and non-Aboriginal groups along the Project corridor."[121] Enbridge estimated the value of this fund would exceed $100 million over the economic life of the Northern Gateway project. In contrast to other elements of its Aboriginal Economic Benefits Package, applications for community grants from the Community Investment Fund would be open to any community along the project route, regardless of ethnicity or support for the pipelines. The exact purpose of the fund was unclear. In their arguments to the review panellists, Enbridge suggested the fund "would be established to build strong communities."[122] The company deferred enunciating exactly what constituted a fundable, strong community-building event or program, suggesting this would be determined through community dialogue. John Carruthers, president of the Northern Gateway project, explained, "There'd be principles of what would qualify, generally fairly broad, and again representing the needs of the communities and then involving the communities in the allocation of those funds to directly go to what they see as a positive and value-added."[123] There were similarly few specifics on how the fund would be structured or distributed, with Carruthers equivocating over whether it would function as a trust, distribute funds geographically, or include needs assessments.[124] On top of its vague conception, the community fund, like equity partnership, was contingent on the viability of the project.

While some aspects of the Aboriginal Economic Benefits Package, such as training, hiring, and contracting, linked Indigenous well-being to particular, short-term activities around the material construction of the pipeline, Enbridge's efforts to effect Indigenous inclusion in the financial gains flowing from permitted pipelines made Indigenous project partners dependent on project profitability in the long term. Beyond simply being built, the pipeline needed to successfully integrate tar sands into global markets for the project to realize returns, and for Indigenous project partners to see the benefits of their investment. Conversely, access to cash would provide Indigenous communities with capital to invest according to their priorities. Thus, financial inclusion, particularly in the form of equity partnership, more deeply entangled Indigenous peoples with pipeline futures while offering participating communities the potential of greater financial capacity to pursue their own development goals.

**The Limits of Enbridge's Offer**
After decades of resistance to colonial impositions, Indigeneity has now gathered profound significance within regimes governing industrial development in northern resource peripheries. Composite public and private strategies to reconcile Indigenous peoples and development recast Indigenous critiques of colonial history,

marshalling the discourse of the New Relationship to create social licence for expanding extractive developments. This is a vital revision: where prior colonial policies sought to genocidally enfranchise Indigenous peoples into the settler citizenry, new regimes of Indigenous economic empowerment recognize Indigenous territorial relationships as the basis for integrating Indigenous people into resource-extractive projects. The new relationship between Indigenous peoples, corporations, and the state has reconstituted the challenge that Indigenous jurisdiction presented to settler authority in *Delgamuukw, Gisdaywa* into a series of problematics related to integrating Indigenous people into contemporary industrial development. With the uncertainties associated with Indigenous claims now being subject to calculation, resource-extractive corporations have expressed an increasing willingness to recognize elements of Indigenous aspirations. Thus, one of the most significant effects of *Delgamuukw, Gisdaywa* has been its effects on private contractual negotiations between resource companies and Indigenous peoples.

As Indigenous assertions reshaped resource governance processes, the relation also worked in reverse. The integration of Indigenous interests in the public and private processes governing resource development reshaped Indigeneity. Colonial frameworks defined a range of acceptable difference within which industrialized Indigeneity could be called into being. New forms of industry-Indigenous partnership appear to respond to Indigenous demands, but Indigenous aspirations were funnelled into an economic agenda centred on resource extraction. Corporate capital claims to cultivate a convergence between capitalist extractive development and Indigenous life projects, but channelling the expression of Indigeneity into forms of livelihood reconcilable with resource-extractive development ultimately links Indigenous aspirations for self-determination to the processes of accumulation by dispossession. But if the offer to participate in the destruction of one's traditional territories seems perverse, it can nonetheless be attractive for people whom colonial policies have long relegated to the past and denied a stake in the colonial present.

Interrogating these designs for Indigenous empowerment via industrial exploitation exposes how contemporary colonial capitalism continues to relegitimize itself through appropriating dissident voices and constructing new structures to regulate resistance. While Indigenous peoples are invited to join project partnerships, they are not recognized as possessing the inherent authority to refuse development on their territories. Instead, they are offered a narrower set of options. On the one hand, they can choose to participate in extractive development that erodes their traditional land with some negotiated share of the benefits. On the other hand, they can risk having dispossession forced upon them absent any palliatives. Thus, industry-Indigenous contracts reproduce in modified form elements of the political economy of the colonial present. These contracts recognize an Indigenous role in development, but do not meaningfully extend Indigenous political autonomy or protect the possibility of lives delinked from capitalist extractivism. Within the paradigm of corporate partnership, Indigenous peoples lack the power to decide against development. They are restricted to raising reasonable issues through consultation processes and negotiations.

The appropriation of the legacy of Indigenous resistance is thus selective, eliding elements of Indigenous struggle that challenge the underlying logics of resource-extractive capitalist relations. Locking Indigenous communities into the circuits of expanding hydrocarbon infrastructure, the promises of partnership continue to be haunted by the spectre of climate calamity. This is most evident in the most loudly trumpeted financial elements of industry-Indigenous partnership: equity offers. While Enbridge did offer this type of financial partnership to Indigenous communities, it did so on the grounds of requiring partners to abandon broader concerns about climate change and environmental justice. In order to realize returns on pipeline development, diluted bitumen needed to flow across Indigenous territories. Tar sands exploitation needed to expand. The paradigm of partnerships between industry and Indigenous peoples was political, even if it regularly restricted discussions to the private domain. In tying Indigenous empowerment to pipeline development, Enbridge sought to subsume Indigenous political and community life to the logics of fossil capital. If pipeline projects like Enbridge's realize their potential, operating to maximum capacity over their anticipated economic lifetimes, the global community will fail to control the climate crisis.[125] Industry-Indigenous partnerships purport to remedy historical injustice of colonialism through offers to build a more inclusive present and future when in fact these offers of collaborative development seek to lock Indigenous people into the cataclysmic trajectory of contemporary fossil capitalism and the unfolding climate emergency that it has created.

# III

Indigenous Resurgence and Enduring Conflicts over Territorial Sovereignty

# 5

# Sovereignty's Returns

IN THE 1980S, as the contest between the British Columbian government and the Gitxsan and Wet'suwet'en hereditary chiefs advanced through the courts in the *Delgamuukw, Gisdaywa* litigation, there were simultaneous negotiations playing out between provincial foresters and the hereditary chiefs in the woods. Despite the legal contestation of its jurisdiction, the province continued to materialize its territorial claim, issuing forest licences to log land claimed by the Gitxsan and Wet'suwet'en. The hereditary chiefs protested this development, asserting competing authority to determine the course of development.[1] Authorities from the Ministry of Forests met the hereditary chiefs in Hazelton to address the disputed governance of the territory. At the meeting, the epistemological and ontological divide between the foresters and hereditary chiefs was rendered explicit. The hereditary chiefs struggled to understand colonial claims to the territory through forest maps. One Gitxsan hereditary chief condensed his discomfort into a question: "If this is your land...where are your stories?"[2]

Negotiations were impaired by a communicative disjuncture between colonial cartographies and Indigenous orders of territorial power-knowledge. The provincial foresters and the hereditary chiefs not only used different languages to discuss the land—employing distinct discourses and practices to cognize territory—but also related to the land and its governance through fundamentally different forms of territorial sovereignty. Settler regimes approached the land as a resource to be exploited and relied upon cartographic technology to exercise power at a distance.[3] The embodied performances of Gitxsan *adaawk* and Wet'suwet'en *cin k'ikh*, in contrast, presented distinct genealogies of territorial sovereignty.[4] Meaning constantly slipped between interlocutors who were talking about and involved in different—if coextensive, frictional, and entangled— processes of enacting territorial authority. Scholars have often discussed the uncontrolled equivocation of Indigenous stories and settler maps as a product of the epistemic differences between cultural interpretations of the world.[5] However, these slippages can be better understood as the product of the disjunction between overlapping ontologies, between different ways of enacting relations to the world.[6] To analyze these ontological politics, it is necessary to call into question how different frameworks of encoding Indigenous knowledge interlink with different enactments of political authority.

This chapter continues to examine governance responses to the Enbridge Northern Gateway project discussed in chapters 3 and 4. Whereas there I sought to survey efforts to reconcile Indigenous peoples and development, here I turn directly to the competing political claims at stake in determining the fate of the Enbridge Northern Gateway project. In doing so, I return to the questions of sovereignty first explored in chapters 1 and 2, and the ways in which Wet'suwet'en hereditary chiefs have, through their interventions within spaces of settler governance, continued to enact forms of Indigenous jurisdiction in excess of colonial containments. Settler-state regulators continually mistook Wet'suwet'en articulations of political ontology—statements about the relations of authority that are being enacted—for simply cultural expressions. Colonial frames of regulatory recognition thus reduced Indigeneity to a different way of knowing, not a way of enacting territorial jurisdiction. While colonial authorities sought to constrain the legibility of Aboriginality within the domain of settler sovereignty, there were multiple coexistent enactments of Indigenous sovereignty. To recognize this plurality, I seek to present a contrapuntal account of the resource governance process. *Contrapuntal*, a term I borrow from the postcolonial literary theorist and trained classical musician Edward Said, refers to a musical performance that involves two distinct, indeed independent, melodies. Said used the term to describe the necessity of interpreting European cultural traditions against the backdrop of empire and the anti-colonial struggles to narrate the world otherwise.[7] I extend this metaphor to think about competing enactments of territorial authority. On the one hand, I aim to expose the workings of a colonial will to contain the world within a singular ontology of development; on the other hand, I document competing Indigenous assertions of an independent sovereign will to decide the course of development on their traditional territories. I argue that governance conflicts over pipelines involve more than simply the boundaries of recognized Indigenous traditions within settler-state law. The performances of Wet'suwet'en authority in the hearing chambers of a federal regulatory review process involved a contest between Canadian and Indigenous legal orders.

There is not only one law operating in Wet'suwet'en territories. Law is not subsumable into a singular system but has multiple origins in different communities of practice, including the conduct of Indigenous authorities.[8] As Audra Simpson articulates, Indigenous sovereignty did not disappear at the scene of the settler sovereign's emergence, and although it has become "nested" within the sovereignty of the settler state, "Indigenous political orders prevail within and apart from settler governance." She argues that the continued existence of Indigenous sovereignty "has implications for the sturdiness of nation-states" and requires that scholars engage "*critically* with Indigenous politics and how they challenge what most perceive as settled."[9] The conflict of the Enbridge pipelines, I argue, involved a deep ontological antagonism in which competing regimes attempt to determine what can or cannot be.

### Opening with a Song
On January 16, 2012, the federally appointed Joint Review Panel for the Enbridge Northern Gateway Project (JRP) convened a community hearing in Smithers, British Columbia. The community hearings sought to collect oral information from interveners for the review of the proposed Enbridge Northern Gateway project. The federal government had tasked the review panellists with evaluating the

FIGURE 5.1 Sue Alfred, who holds the Wet'suwet'en hereditary title Wilat in the dïdikh of Tsayu, at the Joint Review Panel hearings for the Enbridge Northern Gateway project. (Used with permission from Pat Moss.)

environmental impacts of the proposed pipeline, possible measures to mitigate adverse environmental impacts, the broader national interest served by the project, and public and Aboriginal concerns. The panel designed the community hearings to facilitate the consideration of knowledge best conveyed in an oral format, particularly the oral testimony of Indigenous traditional knowledge holders.

The oral evidentiary hearings were constituted in the name of the Canadian colonial sovereign. At the JRP hearing held at the Hudson Bay Lodge in Smithers, however, members of the Wet'suwet'en community performed a competing claim to sovereign authority. They opened the oral evidentiary hearing by singing a song specially composed for the occasion by Sue Alfred, a Tsayu hereditary chief holding the name Wilat, and two of her daughters, Dolores Alfred and

Marjorie Dumont. The song expressed the depth of the Wet'suwet'en connection to their territory, declaring in the chorus, *"noh' y'in tah way atsaan tsun"*—our territory is our livelihood.[10] The song also clearly expressed Wet'suwet'en determination to block the pipeline, closing with the unequivocal directive "Enbridge *noh' y'in tah wagga way sow' ye'h"*—don't step onto our land. This song and its performance enunciated a Wet'suwet'en sovereign will to decide the path of development on Wet'suwet'en territories. It was an assertion of Wet'suwet'en law.

From the perspective of federal government regulators, the Wet'suwet'en song was beyond the pale of conduct appropriate to the hearings process. The articulation of a Wet'suwet'en sovereign will to determine the course of development on their traditional territories worked in excess of the terms of the federal joint review process: it asserted jurisdictional claims competing with those of the colonial state, and thus challenged the frames of colonial sovereignty. From the perspective of Canadian officials, however, this amounted to disrespecting the review process. The JRP quietly handled the challenge of Wet'suwet'en articulations as a matter of protocol and an issue of defining the appropriate bounds for Indigenous cultural expressions. "Culture as a modifier de-politicizes resurgence," Leanne Betasamosake Simpson writes; the language of culture denies the political content of challenges to colonial sovereignty.[11]

The official JRP transcript elided the political content of the Wet'suwet'en opening performance, only inscribing bracketed mention of an "(Opening Ceremony and Prayer)."[12] Rendered mere ceremony, settler officials situated the performance as preamble to proceedings. This silenced the way in which Wet'suwet'en claims to sovereignty troubled the territorial jurisdiction of state, asserting a competing form of Indigenous territoriality. The Wet'suwet'en opening performances exceeded the bounds of appropriate conduct in a colonial regulatory discourse, both in terms of content and form. The issuance of an Indigenous sovereign will to determine the course of development on Wet'suwet'en lands exceeded the conditions within which colonial regulatory authorities would grant hearing. More than this, the form of expression—a song in

Witsuwit'en—was unintelligible to colonial authorities as a part of a governmental process. As a performance that could not be accounted for in its political character, the Wet'suwet'en song was transcribed in the colonial record as simply a cultural opening.

Julie Cruikshank explains that Indigenous accounts of territorial relations are often interpreted as culturally distinct expressions "rather than paradigms based on long-term, engaged relations with other active beings."[13] By registering Wet'suwet'en performances as cultural rather than political—bringing Indigeneity within colonial registers—the JRP transcript effectively erased Wet'suwet'en sovereignty from the panel's purview. Sheila Leggett, the JRP chair, effectively confirmed this in her opening comments: "The record includes all of the information that the Panel will consider in making our decisions. We will not consider any information that is not in the record."[14] The inclusion of Indigenous cultural difference purportedly signalled the generosity of colonial power, offering forms of inclusion and acknowledgement to Indigenous Others. Including recognition of Wet'suwet'en articulations as cultural expressions rather than political assertions, however, effected a consolidation of settler jurisdiction over Wet'suwet'en subjects and territories within colonial registers. It was a form of epistemic silencing: the subaltern could sing in the hearing chamber, but the performance of Wet'suwet'en law through song would not be heard. This silencing represents a rift between colonial and Wet'suwet'en epistemologies and ontologies. More than this, though, the framing of Wet'suwet'en law as cultural performance represents a false presumption on the part of colonial authorities of the primacy of settler processes of relating to the world.

As a further enactment of a colonial will to determine the shape of the hearings, representatives of the National Energy Board indicated that they did not want the Wet'suwet'en to open with an anti-Enbridge song again at the Burns Lake hearings in the Island Gospel Fellowship Church on January 17. While the review panellists justified their attempt to silence the song on the grounds of respect for Enbridge in this state-administered process, the Wet'suwet'en hereditary chiefs perceived the attempt to dictate the terms of traditional opening ceremonies as an affront to their

FIGURE 5.2 *Wet'suwet'en hereditary chiefs entering the Joint Review Panel hearings in Burns Lake. (Used with permission from Nikki Skuce.)*

authority in their own territories. The Wet'suwet'en did not cede control of the opening. The panel was convened to hear their testimony and would begin in accordance with their process. The chiefs again entered the church gymnasium in Burns Lake in full regalia; they again assembled before the crowd; they again performed their oppositional anthem. The details of this performance were again, unsurprisingly, quieted in the official panel record as the "(Opening Ceremony)."[15]

In her opening remarks in Burns Lake, Leggett noted how "that word 'respect'" had been repeated in each community they visited: "We talked about it yesterday; we've talked about it every day."[16] At the hearing session in Smithers, British Columbia, on January 16, 2012, George Williams, who holds the name Sa'un in the *didikh* of Tsayu, told the panel in Smithers, "Wakoos [*wiggus*] means respect. It is our job, Tsayu, Laksilyu, Gilseyhu, Laksamshu, to protect our territories. Our language, our culture comes from the territories."[17] Wet'suwet'en presenters spoke fervently about the need for *wiggus* to ensure that people acted with humility in relation to the land, recognizing the obligation to preserve the land for future generations. The meaning of *wiggus* as described by Wet'suwet'en representatives differed from the concept of respect invoked by Leggett. By leaning on the transliterated term *respect*, Leggett shifted the sense of *wiggus* from the registers of Indigenous legal orders to those of the state, reminding presenters "to be respectful of all parties involved in this proceeding in their evidence."[18] Though colonial and Wet'suwet'en authorities both used the same term, there was a communicative disjuncture as they talked of respecting different sets of relationships. While Indigenous presenters spoke of the need for the government and industry to respect Wet'suwet'en law, Leggett employed the term as a thinly veiled criticism of Indigenous peoples' failure to comply with the mandated bounds of the state-defined process. The issue was not one of linguistic difference per se, but rather distinct discourses associated with heterogeneous ways of being in the world.

Colonial practices of listening to evidence enframed the Indigeneity that regulators heard within the chambers. Leggett stressed that the hearing was convened "to listen to the Oral Traditional Knowledge that you [Indigenous peoples] have to share with us."[19] The way that Legget called forth Indigenous testimony, however, was an attempt to orchestrate acceptable articulations of Aboriginal oral traditional knowledge and ensure that they fit within colonial governance practices. She encouraged presenters to focus on describing the value of "historical perspectives...about hunting for the berries, about the spirituality that's involved in going fishing."[20] The review panellists sought, in other words, to conceptually enframe Wet'suwet'en being with a particular colonial imagination of Indigeneity, a move reminiscent of what Audra Simpson critiques in anthropology: settler authorities "dealt almost exclusively with Indigenous peoples in an ahistorical and depoliticized sense."[21]

Wet'suwet'en presentations were contrapuntal, playing off colonial arrangements. Rather than simply articulating their subjectivity in the frames of the colonial state, Wet'suwet'en performances were always already interpellated within Indigenous legal orders. Although Wet'suwet'en performances in the hearing chambers were called forth by the colonial structure of the hearings, Wet'suwet'en authorities maintained an independent rhythm within the chambers, voicing counterpoints to performances of colonial sovereignty. The performances of the Wet'suwet'en opening song present a metonym for a broader political performance of Indigenous sovereignty in the evidentiary hearings. In their testimony, Wet'suwet'en witnesses spoke to the depth of their connection to their territories, and moreover expressed political claims to sovereignty over those lands.

While the hearings were ostensibly constructed to facilitate settler governmental consideration of Indigenous oral traditions, the regulatory hearing continued to constrain Indigenous performances to fit the structure of colonial aurality. Although in *Delgamuukw, Gisdaywa* the Supreme Court of Canada had recognized the validity of Wet'suwet'en *cin k'ikh* as a form of evidence, the colonial traditions that Justice McEachern had described as his judicial tin ear continued to shape reception of Wet'suwet'en evidence. "Engagement with Indigeneity," as Sarah Hunt argues, "involves the establishment of ontological limits around what knowledge is and is not legible—the establishment of boundaries of meaning, the creation of categories, and making them real through their use."[22] The official Canadian governmental records of the hearing silenced Wet'suwet'en songs but recorded their speeches. The practice of colonial aurality within the hearing process, selectively listening to and codifying information, distorted Wet'suwet'en performances at the hearings. The issue here was not simply one of translation; the competing Wet'suwet'en and Canadian authorities were hearing fundamentally different things.[23] Colonial authorities constricted their hearing, deeming Wet'suwet'en performances to be simply cultural rather than political expressions. In contrast, within Wet'suwet'en political ontology, the hereditary chiefs' performances gave voice to a competing Wet'suwet'en sovereign will. Thus, Canadian officials projected the colonial sovereign right to decide as a solo, while the Wet'suwet'en counterpoint pluralized the political ontology of the hearings chamber. As Jodi Byrd writes, "the state—in contradistinction to indigenous peoples' own ontologies of relationship and power—enacts sovereignty as ontological possession."[24] By incarcerating Indigenous being within colonial frameworks of understanding, the JRP effectively did just that: it universalized a colonial political ontology, relying upon and reproducing a colonial conception of sovereignty as the singular possession of settler authorities. This masked the ontological and legal pluralism that characterized a geography simultaneously defined as Canada and as Wet'suwet'en territory. It covered over how multiple processes of becoming in relation to heterogenous assemblages of the world coexist, overlap, and conflict. Settler authorities elicited a political world with a singular truth. They presented themselves as the singular arbiters of that truth, naturalizing the enactment of a colonial sovereign authority to enforce binding decisions regarding the disposition of lands. Yet Indigenous performances in excess of these settler frames continued to contest the projection of a universal colonial jurisdiction over Wet'suwet'en *yin tah*.

Both Indigenous peoples and settler authorities continue to enact a sovereign right to determine the course of development and define limits that may not be exceeded. The coextensive articulation and overlap of colonial and Indigenous political communities and articulations of sovereign power results in friction. For instance, when Indigenous peoples assert a jurisdictional claim that threatens the flow of resources, colonial authorities have increasingly responded by approaching Indigenous peoples as a threat to the security of settler society.[25] Conversely, when the enactment of the colonizing power of settler sovereignty is achieved through the suspension of Indigenous legal orders, the settler state constitutes a threat to the political community of the Wet'suwet'en. These conflicting sovereignties have at times resulted in the imposition of one legal order on the other—typically with colonial authorities imposing their will on Indigenous peoples.[26] Critics of colonial biopolitics have highlighted how this has involved the violent inscription of the force of settler law on Indigenous bodies and territories, which are transformed through the materialization of extractivist designs.[27] It is important to register that such colonial sovereign power relations are not simply violent. In establishing the boundaries of warranted subaltern being, they are also productive, constituting particular forms of recognition of subaltern peoples with profound political effects.[28]

**Colonial Arts of Listening**
Thinking critically about colonial arts of listening highlights the broader problematic of settler-state recognition for Aboriginal title and rights. Canadian court rulings and government policies no longer simply seek to suspend Indigeneity. Colonial judges and bureaucrats have increasingly recognized a role for Indigenous peoples in resource governance on their traditional territories. But these emergent regimes of recognition also represent a series of expulsions that continually suspend recognition of Indigenous sovereignty.[29] While Indigenous counterclaims regularly evoke Indigenous legal frameworks in excess of the constrained recognition offered by the settler state, the performance of colonial authority as the ultimate arbiter of Indigenous concerns continually enacts the supersession of settler sovereignty over Indigenous polities. Interrogating how settler resource governance agencies incorporate consideration of Indigenous peoples thus exposes the exclusionary workings of settler jurisdiction.

Canadian court acknowledgement of Aboriginal title and rights has been celebrated as the foundation of a movement to reconcile Indigenous claims with the colonial settlement and development of the land. However, it also exemplifies a record of continual expansion of settler authority over Indigenous legal traditions. Within the framework of Canadian law, Aboriginal rights are restricted to the customs, practices, and traditions that a particular group of Aboriginal people exercised at the time of contact and that they have continued to exercise through to the present. This constrained notion of legitimate Aboriginal rights eschews recognition of Indigenous practices that lie outside colonial conceptions of being Aboriginal.[30] It is unsurprising, then, that the vast majority of Aboriginal rights court cases have involved hunting and fishing, basic sustenance activities that accord with colonial imaginations of Aboriginal peoples. Perhaps of utmost concern, however, is the Canadian court's conceptualization of Aboriginal title as a burden on the underlying title of the Crown. In this framing, the imagined dominance of colonial sovereignty—based on the suspension of Indigenous jurisdictional claims—serves as the only basis for a recognition of Aboriginality.[31]

The regulatory inclusion of Aboriginality in colonial resource governance processes—including oral evidentiary hearings—thus works by defining the conditions under which Aboriginal being is deserving of settler-state recognition. Drawing on the principles of reconciliation established, in part, through *Delgamuukw, Gisdaywa*, the Supreme Court has steadily advanced a doctrine that requires that settler authorities to consult with Aboriginal peoples. In the 2004 *Haida Nation* case, Chief Justice McLachlin, writing for a unanimous court, found that the Crown has a "duty to consult with Aboriginal peoples and accommodate their interests."[32] The Supreme Court grounded this duty in the honour of the Crown, suggesting that settler authorities must act in good faith through consultation. Moreover, the court indicated that the duty of the colonial sovereign applied even in the absence of proven Aboriginal title. As with earlier judgments, this advance in Aboriginal law served to further institutionalize a conception of settler-state agencies as the bodies capable of acting in the name of sovereign power. The court left unquestioned the basis for the jurisdiction of settler authorities, focusing its consideration not on questions of authority but rather on what would constitute the metric for determining the extent of the colonial sovereign duty to consult Indigenous peoples. This metric, it decided, was the prima facie strength of an Indigenous community's claim to Aboriginal title and the potential impacts of proposed development on Indigenous interests.[33] In Aboriginal title and rights cases, settler sovereignty is again taken for granted, and the burden of proof placed on Indigenous peoples.[34]

Furthermore, the Supreme Court has yoked Indigenous communities with a requirement to be reasonable when participating in the exercise of consultation. In *Taku River Tlingit First Nation v. British Columbia*, a second case decided alongside *Haida Nation*, the Supreme Court found that settler authorities' duty to consult did not involve considering steadfast Indigenous opposition to a proposed project. Again writing for a unanimous court, Chief Justice McLachlin found that "there is no ultimate duty to reach agreement."[35] The court refused to cognize the possibility that Indigenous peoples were capable of simply deciding against a given development project, as such a position would reflect an unreasonable attempt by Indigenous peoples to thwart development, which would violate the requirement that they participate in consultations in good faith. Simply put, the court presumed the monopoly of state sovereignty and refused to consider an Indigenous exercise of sovereignty that competes with settler-state jurisdiction.

Instead of recognizing an Indigenous right of refusal, settler authorities have a narrower duty requiring that "Aboriginal concerns be balanced reasonably with the potential impact of the particular decision on those concerns and with competing societal concerns. Compromise is inherent to the reconciliation process."[36] In cases such as *Taku River Tlingit*, in which the court sees Indigenous peoples as acting unreasonably and refusing to compromise their interests, settler authorities could lawfully force the terms of reconciliation upon them. While the Taku River Tlingit had a strong prima facie claim to Aboriginal title, and despite the substantial risks associated with the proposed reopening of a mine in Tlingit territory, the government merely needed to balance its public governmental objectives with its duties to protect the interests of Indigenous communities. If regulatory conditions minimize impacts on Aboriginal title and rights and ensure that development provides opportunities to offset potential impacts to Indigenous economic interests in the land, settler authorities have discharged their responsibilities, regardless of Indigenous authorities' position on a project. In *Taku River Tlingit*, because provincial authorities had consulted the Taku River Tlingit and ensured adequate accommodation of their interests in the eyes of the court, they had upheld the honour of the Crown. In the context of the Canadian legal system, abrogating Taku River Tlingit sovereignty and denying them the right to determine the course of development on their traditional lands was consistent with the exercise of settler sovereignty.

While jurisprudence on the duty to consult is often celebrated as grounds to reconcile Aboriginal claims, the court decisions are ambivalent, both expanding protections for Aboriginal rights and exemplifying the continual expansion of state authority over Indigenous legal traditions.[37] The basic presumptions of state sovereignty and Indigenous subjugation in settler courts continue to inform the practices of accommodating Indigenous land use and traditional knowledge in settler government permitting processes. Prevailing approaches to incorporating Indigenous concerns within the domain of state decision-making continue to naturalize colonial territorial sovereignty. Such forms of recognition work to reify Aboriginality within the categories of settler-state law. The frame of Aboriginal rights in Canadian law is thus a screen that blocks from view other possibilities for becoming a subject within Indigenous legal orders. The dominant colonial frame governing the constrained incorporation of Indigeneity necessarily relies upon the foreclosure of any recognition of Indigenous traditions as bodies of law constituting competing forms of territorial sovereignty.

It is precisely such a limited conception of Indigenous claims and territorial relationships that review hearings call forth as evidence in the form of traditional knowledge. In response to evolving Canadian legal duties to reconcile state processes with Indigenous concerns, aspects of the duty to consult have been integrated into various governmental bodies and practices. Section 8(1) of the agreement between the National Energy Board and the Canadian Minister of the Environment that established the Joint Review Panel for the Northern Gateway Project mandated the panel to "receive information from Aboriginal peoples related to the nature and scope of potential or established Aboriginal and treaty rights that may be affected by the project and the impacts or infringements that the project may have on potential or established Aboriginal and treaty rights." On this basis, the panel could issue "recommendations for appropriate measures to avoid or mitigate potential adverse impacts or infringements on Aboriginal and treaty rights and interests." Section 8(2) further delineates the panel's reporting requirements in relation to information collected about Aboriginal rights.

> *8.2 The Panel shall reference in its report:*
> *a) the information provided by Aboriginal peoples regarding the manner in which the Project may affect potential or established Aboriginal and treaty rights; and*
> *b) in the case of potential Aboriginal rights, the information provided by the Aboriginal groups regarding the Aboriginal groups' strength of claim respecting Aboriginal rights.*[38]

Clearly, while the primary purpose of the agreement was to coordinate the assessments of environmental effects required under the Canadian Environmental Assessment Act and of public convenience required under the National Energy Board Act, the government also sought to use the review process to discharge the state duties to consult and accommodate Aboriginal peoples.[39]

In their orchestration of Indigenous presentations of oral evidence in community hearings, the review panellists sought to constrain the terms under which Indigenous peoples could speak. In her direction to presenters in Smithers, panel chair Leggett noted that "oral evidence is information that is relevant to the matters the Panel will be considering, as stated in the List of Issues in the Hearing Order, but that cannot be provided as written evidence."[40] For Indigenous peoples, these issues included potential impacts on Aboriginal interests including treaty rights, asserted and proven Aboriginal rights (including title), and socio-economic matters. The socio-economic matters under consideration by the panel included human occupancy and resource use, heritage resources, traditional land and resource use, social and cultural well-being, human health, infrastructure and services, and employment and economy. Issues related to consultation with Aboriginal groups and the public on the project also registered on the list. However, in procedural directions for the oral evidentiary hearings, the panel clearly indicated that these hearings were for oral traditional knowledge, not "recommendations to the Panel on whether or not to approve the Project or terms and conditions that should be applied if the Project were to proceed."[41] Following the logic of the court in *Delgamuukw, Gisdaywa*, the JRP considered Indigenous oral knowledge to be a valid source of evidence of their connection to the land; declarations regarding the disposition of the lands, however, constituted a form of argument, not evidence. Indigenous knowledge was engaged as a source of information but denied recognition as a potential framework through which a decision could be rendered. The panel thus winnowed the meaning of Indigeneity and fundamentally denied the vitality of Indigenous traditions in the moment of their recognition.

In the procedural direction for the oral evidentiary sessions, the review panellists clarified that the hearings were designed to hear oral traditional knowledge, particularly that of Indigenous peoples, as well as knowledge and personal experiences relevant to understanding the effects of the Northern Gateway project. The directive clearly stated that several types of evidence were not appropriate for these hearings. These included accounts expressing presenters' opinions about the project. The directive also stated that it was not appropriate in the oral evidentiary hearing to provide recommendations to the panel about whether to authorize the project, nor about the terms and conditions that should be binding if such authorization was deemed appropriate. The procedural direction forbade questioning the legitimacy of the purported authority of the panel. All of these directions are examples of how contemporary state processes of including Aboriginality in resource governance continue to vitalize the exclusion of Indigenous sovereignty through the filtered incorporation of difference.

The panel derived its authority from prior enactments of colonial sovereign power over Indigenous life, and reproduced this power through its activities. The theatre of the colonial sovereign was repeatedly enacted through, for example, the announcement of review agreements by federal ministers, the appointment of the review panellists, the issuance of hearing orders by the appointed panel, and the panel chair's opening remarks. In a tautology of the state, the JRP based its authority on the claimed authority of colonial sovereignty and constantly acted in its name while bracketing the question of how both the panel and colonial sovereignty were constituted. Working within their own solipsistic logics, colonial government processes, including the JRP for Northern Gateway, approach Indigeneity as a problem to be solved rather than as a sovereign peer. By reducing Indigeneity to fragmentary collections of Aboriginal customs, practices, and traditions that belong to particular people and places, settler authorities localize Indigenous interests and presume that the settler sovereign has the exclusive authority to determine the relationship between localized Indigenous interests and broader national interests in expanding tar sands extraction infrastructure.

The Wet'suwet'en witnesses who presented to the JRP had to reckon with the presumptions of settler authority and make their presentations within colonial processes of regulatory decision-making. Wet'suwet'en presenters sought to protect their traditional territories by documenting their connections to them. However, they also regularly challenged the limits of settler-state recognition and exceeded the enframing of their relationship to their territories as a frozen tradition.

**A Contrapuntal Hearing**

Wet'suwet'en concern with upholding their responsibilities under their own body of law was central to the evidence Wet'suwet'en witnesses provided. Wet'suwet'en presentations continually questioned the colonial sovereign's legitimacy, advancing the hereditary chiefs' competing claims to authority on their traditional territories. In their evidence, Wet'suwet'en witnesses forwarded arguments about Wet'suwet'en law and jurisdiction and centred their testimony on the dictates and responsibilities of their own legal order—not the delimited frames of the JRP. On the basis of the Wet'suwet'en legal order, the hereditary chiefs made two things very clear. First, they had responsibilities to protect their land and the traditional lifeways of their people. Second, they had decided that the proposed Enbridge Northern Gateway Pipeline project could not proceed.

Darlene Glaim, who then held the name Gyolo'ght in the *dïdikh* of Gitdumden, spoke first, as the hearing was located on Cas Yex territory for which she was responsible.[42] Rather than addressing the Canadian review panellists, she began by addressing the hereditary chiefs assembled in the room. She opened, "*dinï ze', ts'akë ze', skiy ze'*," remarks that recognize the authority of the hereditary lineages in the room, including both the chiefs present and their children—understood to include not only direct matrilineal descendants but broader networks of kinship within a *yikh*—who would inherit their hereditary names.[43] This address was quieted from the record of the JRP, which simply bracketed that Glaim began by "(speaking in native language)."[44] The subsequent message she delivered in English, however, was clearly recorded: "As Gyolo'ght, I come back here before your Panel today, respectfully, to speak about our laws, language and culture, our social structure."[45] Glaim began, as the vast majority of the Wet'suwet'en speakers to follow would, by recognizing the lineage of her name, and how her authority accrued on the basis of her knowledge of her genealogy and its connection to her *yin tah*. She recognized that the title Gyolo'ght had been previously held by her uncle, and how the name was transferred to her through the *balhats*: "As a Gitdumden clan [*dïdikh*] member, I've been holding feasts [*balhats*] and living among our Nation here through our form of government, which is the feast and clan system, and I held the feast in Moricetown...as all our clans do."[46] Thus, Glaim—holding the authority of the title Gyolo'ght in Cas Yex, a subchief in the *yikh* responsible for the territory around Smithers—stressed the centrality of the chiefs' jurisdiction under the *balhats*.

Glaim also described her responsibilities to maintain the vital connection between their lineage and the land. She explained that the crest blanket she wore before the panel symbolized these connections: "It holds our laws, our strength and our power behind the name that I hold, and it is related to the land here. This is Gyolo'ght territory."[47] Other Wet'suwet'en witnesses would similarly emphasize the importance of kinship and the sacred bond between a lineage and the land. Speaking for the Gilserhyu, Elsie Tiljoe emphasized how members of her *dïdikh* learned from their elders about their responsibilities to maintain the territories for future generations. She recounted the instructions of their grandmother, Christine Holland: "She said to us many times, 'Look after my territory. When you get married and have children and then take them out, show them where our territory is. When they grow up, they'll look after our territory.'"[48]

Emphasizing how traditional relationships to territory are embedded in distinct Wet'suwet'en frames, numerous Wet'suwet'en witnesses chose to testify in the Witsuwit'en language. Even when Wet'suwet'en witnesses presented in English, their presentations were peppered with Witsuwit'en terms that possess no English equivalent. Witsuwit'en words provide more than another set of names for the world; they are part of a distinct conceptual apparatus through which Wet'suwet'en people render the world meaningful and maintain relations to it. Wet'suwet'en translators assisted in the interpretation of Witsuwit'en language testimony for the JRP records, which were maintained in the official languages of Canada, English and French. But translations are never perfect. It is important to recognize the necessary slippage in meaning that occurs as terms shift from the conceptual registers of Witsuwit'en to those of English or French. While a gloss can be provided in translation, the structure of a language is entwined with how people conceptualize and relate to their world. Moreover, despite the availability of translators to aid the process of correctly transcribing their evidence, the transcription of the JRP hearings remained incomplete and did not, as we have seen, include all evidence presented in Witsuwit'en. For instance, when Frank Alec, a Wet'suwet'en trapper who held the title Dunen in the Gitdumden, described how he received rights to use particular territories, this was absented from the official record. "I'm what they refer to as (speaking in Native language). That means, 'I am given this piece of land, given this responsibility to manage a piece of land from our Hereditary Chief.'"[49] The transcriber never asked speakers or translators to spell terms in their own language, instead regularly dropping terms from the record and occasionally interjecting seemingly random phonetic attempts to capture concepts.

Nevertheless, the fundamental jurisdictional claim underpinning Wet'suwet'en oral presentations was clear. In Elsie Tiljoe's words, "If they put the pipelines through our territory, it will ruin our territory completely."[50] Tiljoe's husband, Russell Tiljoe, who held the title Likhdïlye in the Gitdumden, reiterated the central jurisdictional aspect of the hereditary chief's territorial claim. His testimony, delivered in Witsuwit'en, was translated by Victor Jim, who held the name Misalos in the Tsayu. In translation, Tiljoe said: "It is our tribal law that we look after our territories."[51] A member of Anaskaski, a *yikh* of Gitdumden, Tiljoe explained Wet'suwet'en opposition to Enbridge in terms of enduring *yikh* responsibilities to the land: "We did not give up our territories to anyone and our ancestors as well did not sign the Wet'suwet'en territories away. That is why we say no to Enbridge, absolutely no. They will not touch our territories."[52]

Wet'suwet'en performances also served to render the space of the hearing uniquely legible within their own legal orders. At the Burns Lake hearing, after the Wet'suwet'en delegation entered singing "Enbridge *noh' y'in tah wagga way sow' ye'h*," Damien Pierre, who holds the title Gu'a'dik' in the Gitdumden, performed a sacred ceremony to open proceedings. In opening remarks before this ceremony, Frank Alec explained:

*Guests, the National Energy Board, Government of Canada and citizens of Burns Lake and the surrounding areas.*

*The next portion is very important to us; for every gathering, for every ceremony that we plan a year ahead there is a ceremony called "the Rattle." It signifies the start of serious business of talking straight and talking in an appropriate manner.*

*Along with the rattle cry is the feather, the plume when it rises, and it rises in a gathering like this; that means whatever that has been spoken about, that whatever that is mentioned needs to be listened to.*

*The feather is very sacred to us when it rises the way you will witness it today. And the rattle cry itself is very sacred to us as well; it signifies the start of serious business. And when I say serious business, it means that there is work behind all of what is going to be talked about, what is going to be mentioned.*

*In our culture, most of the work that has been done for over a year, all the planning that we've been doing on the land, the trapping, the hunting, the fishing, all the resources that come from the land is what signifies the rattle cry and the feather when it rises and when we're going to be talking serious business.*

*And we're doing it here because this is serious business.*[53]

This ceremony, as Alec described, not only signalled the initiation of formal legal discussions in Wet'suwet'en society, but specifically situated proceedings with relation to the source of Wet'suwet'en authority in the land. Invoking Wet'suwet'en connections to the seasonal rhythms of the *yin tah* and the movements that connected people to the life of the land, Alec placed discussions in the context of Wet'suwet'en obligations to a more-than-human world.

This sacred ceremony invoked Wet'suwet'en law. "The rattle cry, *sinelh*, is a highly valued clan [*didikh*] song performed only by and for persons of high rank," say Jo-Anne Fiske and Betty Patrick. "This sacred music should never be used for entertainment, outside the territory, or outside of an appropriate ceremony."[54] The *sinelh* "sanctions the event and the words of the chief." Similarly, the plume of feathers, or *cis*—a cloud of feathers blown into the air—is used to signify "the opening of the main business of the *balhats* and reminds all present that the event will unfold according to time-honoured laws and customs...It is the most significant symbol of the chiefs' power and of the sacred intent of the *balhats*."[55] Invoking these sacred symbols, the Wet'suwet'en signalled the beginning of formal proceedings under Wet'suwet'en law.

The audibility of Wet'suwet'en law qua law before the JRP was, however, inhibited by the panel's presumption of underlying colonial sovereignty. While panel chair Leggett recognized the possibilities for cross-cultural learning that listening to Wet'suwet'en authorities afforded the assemblage of govenment officials, she addressed Pierre's opening *sinelh* ceremony as a cultural rather than legal performance.

> *Thank you very much for the welcoming and for joining us for this Joint Review Panel Community Hearing for the Enbridge Northern Gateway Project.*
>
> *I was particularly struck with some of the opening comments. This is a tremendous opportunity of learning, certainly for this Panel, of a variety of cultural ways and one of the things that struck me was the explanation, which I appreciated, about the rattle cry and how that signifies straight talk and serious business.*[56]

Transliterating the *sinelh* across legal orders, Leggett affected a potent gesture of inclusive exclusion, denying the legal aspect of the performance of Wet'suwet'en law in the moment of its recognition by Canadian regulators. Colonial regimes of recognition thus conditioned what forms of Aboriginality could be heard within Canadian regulatory processes. The invocation of a discourse of Wet'suwet'en law through the *sinelh* and *cis* marked an excess that was inaudible in the regulatory hearings of the JRP.

Leggett's opening remarks articulated the constrained terms on which the panel invited Indigenous peoples to speak: "Sharing your personal knowledge and views on the impacts that the proposed project may have on you and your community and how any impacts could be eliminated or reduced is of great help to us, and we appreciate that you've chosen to be here today."[57] By consistently regarding Wet'suwet'en legal discourse as simply cultural expressions, colonial regulators denied how Wet'suwet'en songs and ceremony situated discussions within a different modality of relating to the world. Regulators only interpreted the significance of performances within the framework of a colonial ontology. Wet'suwet'en territorial jurisdiction, enacted through the *balhats* and embodied in practices of following seasonal rhythms, remained surplus to the spatial ontology of the capitalist nation-state. The review process did not consider Wet'suwet'en sovereignty to be one of the Indigenous traditions that would be affected by project. The JRP excluded any meaningful consideration of a form of Wet'suwet'en sovereignty that may compete with that of the settler state. Narrowing discussion to technical details of "evidence," the panel sought to foreclose the question of the politico-legal constitution of the hearing and sovereignty. Yet while this foreclosure of the political was a settler ambition, it has remained a colonial fantasy that has been constantly challenged by Indigenous mobilizations.

Indigenous movements assert that settler sovereignty has never been perfected. Its enactment is constantly perforated by Indigenous counterclaims. While Canadian federal policies seek to define the appropriate trajectory for pipeline development, life always unfolds in forms that exceed efforts to police it. Within this context, numerous critical scholars have sought to conceptually differentiate the techniques of governing within an existing order from political interventions that transform a given order. Slavoj Žižek insists that politics involves the "the art of the impossible," reconfiguring "the very parameters of what is considered 'possible' in the existing constellation."[58] Erik Swyngedouw similarly describes politics as "the space of litigation" for those excluded from the state order. "A true political space is always a space of contestation for those who have no name or no place," he writes.[59] Political interventions thus become political through addressing the constitutive exclusions of the present order, calling forth the potential for alternative forms of becoming. Concurring with Swyngedouw and Žižek on the primacy of a transformative antagonism in politics, I argue that Indigenous politics can productively rupture an existing colonial order. However, Indigenous politics cannot be simply interpreted within the frames of the existing colonial order. Critical accounts of Indigenous law must address the logics of Indigenous orders beyond the dominant frames of Canadian law.

Within the context of the JRP oral evidentiary hearings, Wet'suwet'en hereditary chiefs explicitly set discussion in terms of political and legal conflict between Indigenous peoples and settler territorial jurisdiction imposed in the name of colonial sovereignty. They refused to contain their evidence to the confines of existing settler-state policies governing the consideration of oral traditional knowledge. This is what Audra Simpson calls a politics of refusal: the Wet'suwet'en insisted "on being and acting as peoples who belong to a nation other than the United States or Canada."[60] John Ridsdale, who holds the Tsayu chiefly title Na'Moks, succinctly tied the enactment of the *sinelh* to the hereditary chiefs' obligations to protect the relationship between a lineage and the land for future generations.

> *I want to thank Danny and Pierre [sic; Damien Pierre] for doing our syneth [sinelh]. He stated that it's our national anthem. Canadians, they have one, too. In there, it states it's "our home and native land." This is our home in Wet'suwet'en land. For centuries, the Wet'suwet'en, as it's been stated before, we protected our lands from any form of incursions, whether it be from other nations and now, with this threat that's on hand.*[61]

Ridsdale stressed that his authority came from his place in his lineage and its relationship to the land. "I am Wet'suwet'en. I carry the name of Namox [Na'Moks] and I know my authority. I know my rights and I know our title."[62] Ridsdale's adamancy found resonance with the Northern audience, who loudly applauded. Trying to reassert the authority of the panellists, JRP Chair Leggett sought to interject: "Chief—."[63] Ridsdale, however, continued unabated.

> *I'm going to speak on our survival on the land, how we become Chiefs, how we get from boys to men and how we do that when we're teenagers; how we set ourselves up to carry names in the future; how we know to speak on our lands; how we know to respect our Elders; how we know to respect the guests on our territory. With a couple of minutes, that's a quick view that I can give you.*
>
> *We're going to speak on the mountains where we were raised, where we did our winter; Tsalit Mountain, Nadina Mountain. I wanted to speak on Wetzin'kwa [Widzin Kwah]. Wetzin'kwa means blue-green waters. The threat to our territories and to our waters. We'd have to change the name of our rivers, the name of our mountains, the name of our creeks, the name of our stories, the name of our names.*
>
> *When we speak in the feast hall, we tell the truth. When I swore on the Rattle, the Rattle is hundreds of years old. I did not plan on coming here and telling lies. I did not plan on coming*

*here and saying these are things that we will allow. I did plan on coming here and tell you that this threat to our territories, to our lands, to our culture, to our people is cultural genocide, and we would not allow that.*[64]

The assembled crowd at the hearing again broke into applause, vocally backing Ridsdale, who briefly paused before concluding:

*I did come here to state that, as the Wet'suwet'en Chief, we were taught right on how to look after our lands, how to respect our laws, how to look after our youth and make sure that the promises we made to our grandchildren were never broken.*

*We do not own the land. We're only borrowing it from our grandchildren. It is of the utmost importance that we return the land to our grandchildren in better condition than when we walked on it.*

*This proposed project endangers our promises to our grandchildren that we would look after our land, our culture, our people for them. We cannot break this promise to our grandchildren.*[65]

Ridsdale did not cede to the claimed sovereignty of settler society. In fact, he made no direct mention of the panel beyond the implied disrespect of its terms of reference to Wet'suwet'en law. Instead, he pronounced his solemn commitment to uphold his responsibilities under Wet'suwet'en law.

Henry Alfred, who held the title Wah Tah K'eght as hereditary chief of Tsee K'al K'e Yex within the Laksilyu, spoke in the Witsuwit'en language about the chiefs' authority to control activities on their *yin tah*.[66] Ron Austin, who holds the title T'sek'ot in the Laksilyu, translated for him.[67] Alfred, who passed away in 2018, was one of the elder statesmen of the Wet'suwet'en at the time, having held his chiefly title since 1967. He was the last surviving Wet'suwet'en hereditary chief who had testified to the court in the *Delgamuukw, Gisdaywa* case.[68] "In the old days, they were strict about their territories, trespass," he remembered. Austin summarized a story Alfred told about his grandfather, a predecessor in the lineage of Wah Tah K'eght, "who caught a person trespassing."[69]

*FIGURE 5.3 John Ridsdale, Wet'suwet'en hereditary chief Na'Moks of the Tsayu, at the Joint Review Panel hearings for the Enbridge Northern Gateway project. (Used with permission from Pat Moss.)*

> *The first time he gave him a feather and, then, the next season, his grandfather came back, the person was trapping again on his territory, so he told him to stop, gave him a second feather. I don't—he told the person "I don't want to hurt you."*
>
> *Third season, Wah tah K'eght went into his territory, again, the person was still on the trap line so he took a rope out of his pack—the person didn't know he was coming—wrapped it around his neck, killed him and tossed him into the river. They were strict about their territory.*[70]

Alfred then described how he did not want a pipeline through his territories. "If the water is contaminated in our territory, my grandchildren will never know what it's like to have clean water and to enjoy the territories."[71] His position on the proposed pipeline was clear: "We say 'No' to Enbridge. 'Don't spoil our territory.'"[72] Wah Tah K'eght closed his presentation stating, "If this pipeline goes through, the succession of names will be ruined, the succession of lands that are handed down to Chiefs will also be ruined."[73]

A claim to political sovereignty emerges in the moment when a form of collective identity or difference is constelled as the basis for implementing a sovereign will or decision. Members of a political community constitute themselves as such in deciding on an issue related to their security and taking action to implement this decision. It is the willingness of a people to fight for themselves as a people that grounds their claim to sovereignty, that forms the foundation of their political existence as a people. Legal theorist Giorgio Agamben has stressed how sovereign authority relies upon the definition of a political authority beyond the law, capable of acting to determine states of exception in which rights can be suspended and particular individuals are placed outside the law. Such individuals can be subsequently banned, incarcerated, or killed. Agamben argues that the state of exception lies at the foundation of every legal order, constituting the "structure in which law encompasses living beings by means of its own suspension."[74] Sovereign authority is enacted through the suspension of subjects from the rule of law to realize the force of law. This structure is constantly reproduced as an effect of operationalizing authority to determine the status of particular rights.[75] Thus, sovereignty is not simply the underpinning of a claim to authority within a given territory but constantly effected through the implementation of decisions to exclude, prohibit, and even terminate particular forms of life. As long as a people possesses a collective identity strong enough to motivate its members to defend the security of the collective by suspending the rights of others, it is capable of sustaining a claim to sovereignty. A people, constituted as a political collective with a claim to sovereignty, makes assertions on the basis of a constitutional framework that they call into existence. Notably, the structure of sovereignty that Agamben describes is not unique to European legal traditions or legal orders based on a written code; it is a description of what enables any political authorities to institute a legal order.

If sovereignty is something that is continually enacted through decisions over when rights are recognized or suspended, it is necessarily inchoate. Indigenous transgressions into the domain of what is politically considered "settled" territory demonstrate this fact by calling into question the assumed complete, final, and perfect monopoly of settler sovereignty.[76] Sovereignty is neither absolute nor the sole possession of settler authorities. Indigenous authorities, too, enact claims to sovereignty when they render and implement decisions on who possesses rights on their territories and what forms of livelihood need to be suspended in the name of protecting the security of their collective. This is certainly true of Wet'suwet'en hereditary chiefs. As Henry Alfred described, "they were strict about their territory."[77] Wet'suwet'en law established circumstances in which hereditary chiefs could act as sovereigns in their territories, exercising the authority to decide on the rights of others. The chiefs could do more than extend land use rights in their territories; they could also determine when such rights would be suspended, forbidding particular activities and even acting to enforce their authority through taking a person's life. In the JRP hearings, it was this type of claim to authority that the hereditary chiefs asserted.

The Wet'suwet'en hereditary chiefs thus participated in the review process without accepting its presumption of settler supremacy. Wet'suwet'en community members continually resisted incarceration within delimited notions of tradition and overloaded the governmental processes regulating development with assertions of their own sovereignty and right to decide what happens on their territories. In so doing, they pluralized enactments of who has jurisdiction, asserting their own right to fight to determine what forms of development are prohibited from their lands. The Wet'suwet'en hereditary chiefs articulated forms of authority, subjectivity, and territory surplus to those associated with colonial frames. In excess of the Aboriginality imagined by settler-colonial disciplinary and governmental regimes, Wet'suwet'en authorities advanced claims to sovereignty that problematized those of the colonial sovereign and opened new spaces of negotiation.

## With the Weight of a Feather

The Canadian government sought to contain recognition of Indigenous geographies and construct British Columbia's Northwest Interior as a landscape of industrial development, but for the members of Wet'suwet'en *yikh* and *dïdikh*, the region never ceased to exist as Indigenous territory under Indigenous jurisdiction. As a result of conflicts over development, the Wet'suwet'en have had to enunciate the presence of their territory and sovereignty ever more forcefully. This presence, as theorized by Leanne Simpson, presents the potential for "flight paths out of colonialism and into magnificent unfolding of Indigenous place-based resurgences and nationhoods."[78] The Witsuwit'en word for territory is *yin tah*. The root term, *yin*, refers to earth, but in *yin tah* this root is modified to denote not only a physical landscape but the interconnection of that landscape with a people.[79] As Jodi Byrd writes about the Chickasaw political order, "the intersubstantiations of sovereignty and relationship that connect community to ancestral place and belonging arise from the ontologies of reciprocal complementarity."[80] In Witsuwit'en, the concept of *yin tah* is multifaceted. *Yin tah* connotes relations that pertain to modes of resource ownership and regimes governing use, but it also signifies continuities in enactments of Wet'suwet'en jurisdiction that span across generations. The practices of enacting Wet'suwet'en territory and jurisdiction have continued to evolve over the centuries, responding to developments both internal and external to Wet'suwet'en society.

In August 2010, the political significance of Wet'suwet'en traditional territories became a focal point of negotiations between representatives of Enbridge and Wet'suwet'en activists. Hagwilakw and Toghestiy, two members of the *dïdikh* Laksamshu, issued formal notice that Enbridge was trespassing on their unceded *dïdikh* lands and did not have permission to build a pipeline on their *yin tah*.[81] On August 24, 2010, Enbridge sent representatives Michelle Perret and Kevin Brown to present an update to the town council of Smithers on their proposed Northern Gateway Pipelines. The council meeting was packed. As the Enbridge representatives moved to the front of the room, a delegation of Wet'suwet'en activists greeted them with a war song. Perret gave a short presentation, outlining how Enbridge was cleaning up its recent pipeline spill into the Kalamazoo River in Michigan and then emphasizing the thousands of jobs that the Northern Gateway Pipeline construction would create. At the end of Enbridge's presentation, Warner Naziel took the floor. Naziel held the title Toghestiy in the Laksamshu. He reminded the Enbridge representatives that jurisdiction over Wet'suwet'en lands lay with the Wet'suwet'en people, not the municipal government of Smithers. He stated that Enbridge did not have permission to be on Laksamshu territories and had already been warned that they were trespassing. Naziel and Antoinette Austin, who held the title Hagwilakw, then hand-delivered an eagle feather to the Enbridge representatives. This constituted, as Naziel explained, their final warning. To cheers from the assembled crowd, he stated, "further trespass will be dealt with under Wet'suwet'en law."

The feathering was an issue of considerable contention. The Wet'suwet'en activists that conducted the 2010 feathering were associated with the Lhe Lin Liyin, a guardian or warrior society that was organizing a grassroots campaign within the Wet'suwet'en community against pipeline development. The group, which formed in response to what grassroots activists considered the overly bureaucratic response of the Office of the Wet'suwet'en to industry's attack on Wet'suwet'en territories, sought to revitalize ancient Wet'suwet'en laws and construct vehicles for their enforcement. The feathering did not have the authorization of the Office of the Wet'suwet'en hereditary chiefs, nor had it been approved by the *dïdikh* chiefs in advance. It was rationalized on the basis of grassroots members' dreaming. As Antonia Mills describes, there are dual sources of authority in Wet'suwet'en society, one originating "from the assumption of the highest chiefs' titles," the other "from individual contact with the spirit realm through dreams, medicine-dream sickness, and visionary experiences."[82] While the Lhe Lin Liyin had coordinated a protest action when they learned of Enbridge's planned visit, the feathering emerged organically. One group member brought the feathers in response to a compulsion that they might be needed. When she arrived with the feathers, the others responded to the call to action. Naziel and Austin, who held esteemed

Laksamshu titles but were not hereditary chiefs that headed *yikh* within their *dïdikh*, determined that it was appropriate to issue the warning of trespass and performed the feathering at the close of the evening's events. Thus, the Lhe Lin Liyin projected a claim to represent the sovereignty of the Wet'suwet'en on the basis of their connection to the spirit power of the people.

Enbridge did not regard Wet'suwet'en articulations of their sovereign will to determine and enforce limits to the development of their territories as merely cultural forms of expression. In an Enbridge update on Aboriginal engagement, submitted as written evidence to the JRP, the company referred to the 2010 feathering as "a setback" in relations with the Wet'suwet'en.

> *Evidence of a shift and cooling of communications was apparent to all who witnessed two Northern Gateway representatives receive a feather trespass warning in August of 2010 at a meeting convened with the mayor and council of the Town of Smithers, BC. At this meeting, the two Northern Gateway representatives present each received an eagle feather from two Wet'suweten [sic] hereditary chiefs, conveying notice of trespass upon the Likht'amisyu [Laksamshu]...clan's territories. This feathering incident occurred shortly after the Wet'suwet'en gathered at the meeting sang a traditional war song, and was followed by an explanation from the hereditary chiefs issuing the notice that this was the second warning of trespass issued to Northern Gateway, and that further acts of trespass by Northern Gateway would be dealt with under traditional Wet'suwet'en laws.*[83]

Enbridge's statement reflects its confusion around who among the Wet'suwet'en holds the authority of a full hereditary chief; it assumes that the subchiefs who had conducted the feathering at Smithers were hereditary chiefs. The company therefore failed to accurately position the feathering within Wet'suwet'en society. The feathering at Smithers involved a particular faction of the Wet'suwet'en and was not explicitly authorized by the chiefs of the *yikh* of Laksamshu, nor by the Office of the Wet'suwet'en hereditary chiefs. Nevertheless, Enbridge interpreted it as a sign of the deteriorating relationship between the company and Wet'suwet'en hereditary chiefs writ large.

This shift in relations highlighted how the Wet'suwet'en were steadily articulating and strengthening their position as a sovereign people capable of deciding whether a pipeline should transect their territory. But different collectives of the Wet'suwet'en have adopted distinct strategies for engaging colonial power and articulating their territorial relationships. At one extreme, the band of Skin Tyee collaborated with industry. At the other extreme, the Lhe Lin Liyin refused to participate in the colonial regulatory process, enacting claims to Wet'suwet'en sovereignty external to the formal Canadian review process. The Office of the Wet'suwet'en, which organized the testimony at the JRP hearings, fell somewhere in the middle. It participated in the review process, but did so in an effort to articulate its own claims to jurisdiction, even if these claims exceeded the JRP's terms of reference.

In contrast to Skin Tyee's collaboration, which operated within the limits of colonial governance structures, Enbridge interpreted the Lhe Lin Liyin's and Office of the Wet'suwet'en's assertions of Wet'suwet'en sovereign will to determine the course of development on their territories as extra-legal threats. In the company's account, enactments of Wet'suwet'en law disrespected and violated the spirit of good faith negotiations and reasonable conduct mandated by Canadian law. Enbridge did not differentiate the actions of the Office of the Wet'suwet'en at the JRP hearings from those of the *dïdikh* members associated with the Lhe Lin Liyin at the Smithers town council meeting. Despite the two groups' markedly different approaches, Enbridge paralleled the Lhe Lin Liyin feathering with the Office of the Wet'suwet'en's *cis* ceremony that opened the Burns Lake oral evidentiary hearing in the Island Gospel Church. In a submission to the JRP, Enbridge wrote:

> *Following a ceremonial incantation addressed to the "northern gods," a Wet'suweten [sic] Elder blew a myriad of tiny feathers over a Northern Gateway representative in attendance. These feathers covered the hair and clothing of the Northern Gateway*

*representative targeted by this feathering incident. Following this incident, it was explained by one of the registered Wet'suwet'en speakers at the JRP hearing session that breach of traditional Wet'suwet'en laws could result in banishment from the community, or death, and that Wet'suwet'en trespass laws were just as strictly enforced as those other offenses described by the speaker which were punishable by death.*[84]

Invocations of the spirit of Wet'suwet'en law violated what Enbridge believed should be the norms of civil discourse in a liberal legal process. These Wet'suwet'en actions also disregarded the Canadian regulatory expectation that Indigenous people provide reasonable evidence of their concerns and not seek to thwart development. Enbridge viewed the Wet'suwet'en hereditary chiefs as acting to undermine the regulatory decision-making of the settler authorities reviewing the pipeline. The Office of the Wet'suwet'en, through its witnesses at the hearings, had made presentations "clearly articulating its opposition to the Project." Because of this, Enbridge dissolved an agreement that the two parties had made around communications protocol, stating that it "no longer reflected the interests of the parties."[85]

The Enbridge submission to the panel regarding the *cis* ceremony was a document of considerable debate during the JRP hearings. The Office of the Wet'suwet'en forwarded a motion that Enbridge's depiction of this sacred ceremony, which invokes their law, as "an incantation to 'northern gods'" be stricken from the record because it used language that was "appalling and abusive."[86] Writing on behalf of the Office of the Wet'suwet'en, Mike Ridsdale, John Ridsdale's brother, clarified that the Wet'suwet'en possessed no "northern gods." The JRP recognized that evidence could be removed "if it is prejudicial," but found that "although the evidence in question may be viewed as offensive to the Wet'suwet'en people it does not meet the legal threshold for removal."[87] This ruling reflected the distance between Wet'suwet'en authorities and Canadian regulators.

But Enbridge's depiction of events at the Island Gospel Church is notable for more than its antiquated language. It also confused the feathering at the Smithers town council meeting with the spreading of feathers at Burns Lake. The two events used different types of feathers and distributed feathers in distinct ways. Although in both cases the feathers symbolize an invocation of Wet'suwet'en law, the types of feathers and their modes of distribution have different meanings. The long eagle feathers that Naziel and Austin handed the Enbridge representatives in the Smithers council chambers were distributed as a mark of shame. These feathers were presented in the context of trespass; they denoted a body rendered bare life and subject to killing without consequence. Naziel clarified the significance of the feathering in a speech about trespass when Enbridge received the feathers. The Laksamshu members, backed by the Lhe Lin Liyin, threatened to impose the force of Wet'suwet'en law if Enbridge returned to develop their lands, and indicated that Enbridge was no longer subject to the protection of Wet'suwet'en law. Traditionally, in the case of a person, further trespass meant death. However, the way in which corporations are cognized and treated within Wet'suwet'en law remains unclear. When I questioned Naziel about this, he suggested that if the corporate entity, Enbridge, continued to disrespect the order to stay off Laksamshu lands, the *dïdikh* would have to meet to determine an appropriate response. Nonetheless, the long eagle feather is a mark that externalizes bodies, individual or corporate, from the traditional protections of Wet'suwet'en law.

This is not the meaning of the *cis* ceremony, in which a plume of eagle down rises in the air from the head of a dancer and sacralizes proceedings as determinative of the terms of peace. As Frank Alec described to the review panellists, eagle down, the emblem of Wet'suwet'en law, is distributed to demonstrate that "whatever that is mentioned needs to be listened to."[88] Antonia Mills, in her book on the Wet'suwet'en legal order, *Eagle Down Is Our Law*, says that the *cis* ceremony signifies the opening of formal governance proceedings. *Cis* distributed in the feast hall signals that the decisions are the binding terms of peace.[89] As Mike Ridsdale stressed in the Office of the Wet'suwet'en written motion to remove Enbridge's prejudicial discussion of feathering from the JRP record, the performance of the *cis* ceremony was actually "a prayer to allow the spirit power to guide the JRP Hearing." He elaborated, "This expression is important, when eagle down is distributed the peace is binding and retaliation is stopped, unless that peace is broken by the outsider or offending party."[90] The Wet'suwet'en presenters, although clearly articulating their opposition to Enbridge's proposed pipeline, offered peace with the company if they respected the sovereign decision of the Wet'suwet'en. The framework of the *cis* ceremony is therefore one of respect, not shame. It establishes the terms and conditions of lawful conduct and right relationships, the terms on which reconciliation can occur. Historically, this framework referred to establishing peace between *yikh* and *dïdikh*, not corporations or states. But in performing this ceremony in the context of the Northern Gateway review, the Wet'suwet'en hereditary chiefs extended Wet'suwet'en legal obligations to protect the land to contemporary colonial actors: Canadian energy regulators and pipeline companies. They thus presented the rejection of the Enbridge pipeline as the foundation for reconciling the Wet'suwet'en community and Canada, as well as the Wet'suwet'en community and Enbridge.

On April 20, 2013, John Ridsdale, carrying the hereditary title Na'Moks, hosted a Tsayu *balhats* in which his *dïdikh* publicly displayed their opposition to all pipeline development in the feast hall. The review panellists refused to consider a written record of that feast in its review process "as the evidence has little probative value and could be prejudicial to some parties as they prepare for final argument."[91] While the corporate derogation of Indigenous legal traditions did not meet the prejudicial standard of Canadian regulators, the panel determined that a *balhats* exerting the territorial authority of Wet'suwet'en hereditary chiefs over corporate enterprises was an unjust form of prejudice.

Despite the disrespect of Canadian regulators, the Tsayu did not abandon their claim. Instead, Ridsdale mobilized his traditional territorial responsibilities as a chief in his *dïdikh*, making further counterclaims to Canadian state sovereignty and bringing them to bear on the Enbridge corporation. He travelled to Enbridge's annual general meeting in Calgary on May 8, 2013. Wearing traditional regalia bearing symbolic connections to his territories, he brought them notice of the final Tsayu decision on the Enbridge pipeline. Rather than simply juxtaposing local Indigenous traditions with global dynamics of resource development, this movement worked to reterritorialize the geographies of resource development. It did this within the traditional body of Wet'suwet'en law through stretching the geographic responsibilities of Wet'suwet'en law to encompass the geographies of capital penetrating Wet'suwet'en territories. This movement is yet another example of how Wet'suwet'en hereditary chiefs have sought to offset the authority of the colonial sovereign to decide on development projects on Wet'suwet'en territories and to establish a sovereign demand that no pipeline development proceed. It has also begun to reconcile the position of the hereditary chiefs with the grassroots activists who dreamed of a future in which their territories remain intact and their traditions vital.

**Between Overlapping Enunciations of Law**
To understand the action of Indigenous sovereign claims against the state, it is necessary to theorize a condition of ontological and legal pluralism within settler-colonial states. Rather than accept colonial efforts to totalize the sphere of settler jurisdiction as complete, it is necessary to recognize that Indigenous peoples continue to contest not only the terms of their inclusion within the colonial state but also the legitimacy of the state sovereign itself. Examining the indeterminacy of the encounter between contestant articulations of territorial authority demonstrates the possibilities inhering to a condition of overlapping sovereignties. Sovereign action cannot be reduced to a singular state-centred system. It has multiple sources, which may complement, overlap, or offset one another. This is not to suggest that competing sovereignties constitute autonomous fields that evolve without interaction. Through constant interaction, the language and idioms of Indigenous and settler sovereignty are transliterated into other frames. The conflict here is ontological: different regimes aim to implement a sovereign will to decide, to suspend particular political claims, and to call others into being.

This ontological conflict extends into the space of governance hearings. A hearing is not a neutral medium for receiving knowledge, but a structured way of perceiving the world that is always already inflected by one's ontological investments in a particular worlding. Hearings can, therefore, be a frontier between legal orders, a place of struggle, advances, and retreats. Despite efforts by settler authorities to constrain the terms on which subaltern people may speak and be heard by colonial sovereignty, Indigenous peoples nevertheless refuse these binds, speaking back to the colonial sovereign and asserting parallel jurisdiction to it.

This vantage sheds light on how Indigeneity cannot simply be understood within the terms of a colonial order that seeks to domesticate Aboriginality. Indigenous claims function as an interruption and challenge to the existing settler order. Performances of Indigenous authority may supplement the original absence of Indigenous sovereignty within colonial legal discourse. As Lindsey Te Ata O Tu MacDonald and Paul Muldoon express, "recognition is demanded from the state at the same moment that its authority is disavowed."[92] Like a pharmakon, these articulations of Indigeneity possess the potential of both a poison and cure to colonialism, both an irruption into and a repair for state sovereignty. By placing state practices of recognition in parallax with the articulations of Indigenous law, it is possible to think about the state's "traditions" and how they continue to reproduce colonial relations in the present. While the confines of colonial recognition imagine a foreclosure of Indigenous being to the past and refuse the possibilities of a contemporary Indigeneity, shifting perspective brings into view Indigenous contestations of settler sovereignty's exclusions and highlights Indigenous relations to territory and tradition as activated contemporary forces.

Though settler-state recognition seeks to subjugate Indigenous peoples under the name of the colonial sovereign, Indigenous claims continue to call into question colonial sovereignty and assert unreconciled claims to Indigenous sovereignty. Indigenous movements voice a demand to reorder colonial regimes. Indigenous claims create a space of litigation for colonized peoples excluded from the settler order. As was demonstrated in the Hudson Bay Lodge, Island Gospel Fellowship Church, and Town of Smithers Council Chambers, traditional Wet'suwet'en authorities continue to enact relationships to the land and forms of jurisdiction incommensurate with the terms of state recognition. While new governmental regimes that attempt to incorporate Indigenous peoples within them have emerged, these newly inaugurated regimes never end the struggle, once and for all, over who has the authority to decide on issues of territorial governance, including resource development. Who decides the course of development and exercises legitimate authority to enforce decisions over a particular territory remains an actively contested question.

Sovereignty is not a fait accompli but an ongoing set of plural enactments. Indigenous claims work to reassert the basic antagonism undergirding settler law and informing its application. These claims are political insofar as they return discussion to the original and normalized suspension of their legal orders. As Indigenous peoples confront the presumptions underpinning settler authority, they challenge not only the question of who possesses authority but also the prerogatives that guide the conduct of that authority. The question is not only who decides but also what are the appropriate responsibilities that guide that decision-making.

Struggles over jurisdiction open spaces of possibility and negotiation, disrupting the normalization of colonial sovereignty and the presumed reasonability of endless, intensifying extractivism. To a certain extent, answers to questions of authority and responsibility around resource development are already being negotiated through the articulation of new doctrines encumbering the exercise of the sovereign authority of the Crown in Canada with, for instance, the duty to consult Aboriginal peoples. But if Canadian regulatory records of such moments result in the recapture of Indigeneity within the sphere of a colonial doctrine of Aboriginal law—which they do—I nevertheless want to hold open the possibilities that assertions of Indigenous sovereignty present to colonial legal orders. Such assertions are by necessity unreconciled in the colonial present. They force an order founded in the suppression of Indigenous law to reckon with Indigenous assertions that are beyond the purview of colonial discourse. Doing so, they expand the horizon of possibilities within the colonial present to include real possibilities for decolonial futures.

# 6

# The Ongoing Cycle of Struggle

ON FEBRUARY 10, 2020, police raided a Wet'suwet'en blockade against pipeline construction in Northwest British Columbia, arresting seven people. The project at the centre of the dispute was the Coastal GasLink project, a liquefied natural gas pipeline to be constructed and operated by TC Energy (previously named TransCanada). Northern Gateway, rejected almost four years prior, seemed a distant memory; tar sands infrastructure discussions had long faded from the scene. Instead of federal regulators at the National Energy Board, it was provincial officials who were responsible for project approvals and ensuring the reconciliation of Indigenous peoples with development. At question was not a national economic strategy of tar sands development but provincial plans to accelerate unconventional gas production and export. Aside from the Wet'suwet'en, the actors had changed. But in the broadest outline, the conflict continued to resonate with the tensions that had underpinned Northern Gateway. The Coastal GasLink Pipeline was a massive infrastructure project tied to expanding extraction of unconventional gas reserves accessible through new fracking techniques in the Montney Basin in Northeast British Columbia. It linked to the $40 billion LNG Canada export terminal, the largest private sector investment in Canadian history. Again, the Wet'suwet'en were taking a prominent role in the fight over the expansion of fossil capitalism, and in so doing also sought to address broader questions about Indigenous-settler relations and how we govern the land responsibly. It was the latest iteration of generations-long negotiations between Wet'suwet'en and settler authorities. When the arrests triggered a cascade of solidarity actions across the country that ground the national economy to a halt, federal officials were pulled into the dispute. British Columbia and Canada were again called to account for their relationship to colonial legacies. People across the country demanded that these governments clearly articulate how they envisioned reconciling development with Indigenous peoples. Like Northern Gateway before it, Coastal GasLink again raised the question of who has the authority to determine the course of development on unceded Indigenous territories.

So far, I have sought to track the Indigenous-settler relationships that have emerged after *Delgamuukw, Gisdaywa* in the absence of certainty over land title. Focusing on the Northern Gateway project, I have highlighted how pipelines have become entangled with Indigenous mobilizations. I have examined the friction that Wet'suwet'en claims to territory and jurisdiction created for Enbridge and its efforts to install infrastructure to facilitate a greater flow for hydrocarbon exports. I have illustrated the central role that Indigenous movements play in shaping the future of fossil capitalism. But the story has always been about more than pipelines. The movement of resources in settler societies, such as Canada, relies upon the continued dispossession of Indigenous peoples, and the contest over pipelines has always centred on the question of who controls the land. Corporations seeking to secure the colonial extraction of resources have sought to forge agreements with impacted Indigenous communities, while settler authorities at both the provincial and federal levels have sought to regulate development to secure the flow of resources. In this, Northern Gateway remains paradigmatic: settler authorities and their corporate partners sought to smooth the pipeline path by routing the project around sites of Indigenous traditional land use while creating opportunities for Indigenous people to participate in economic development. These solicitations have proven attractive to some, but others have continued to refuse consent. The Wet'suwet'en hereditary chiefs, in particular, have long fought against the extension of colonial relations in the present and future. Their mobilizations continue to unsettle the colonial resource economy, throwing into question who has authority over resources. In this struggle, they have proven themselves a powerful contemporary force shaping the dynamics of development.

I will close the book by reiterating the cyclical and uncertain movements between colonial dispossession, Indigenous resistance, and regulatory reconciliation. Against the concept of a final resolution, I suggest that relationships between Indigenous and settler authorities are necessarily open, constantly subject to contestation and realignment. The uncertainty of these relationships means that development is not shaped by a singular will but entangled with the interplay of different life projects. This is evident in the final chapters of the Northern Gateway story, as regulatory efforts to reconcile Indigenous peoples and pipeline development failed. These failures remain significant. Despite efforts to learn from the Northern Gateway experience, the basic structure of reconciliation that regulators sought to effect in that case continues to be repeated in subsequent pipeline projects. Many of the tensions that undermined the Northern Gateway project remain in more recent contentious pipeline proposals in British Columbia, such as the Trans Mountain and Coastal GasLink projects. In fact, tensions have tended to significantly intensify as pipeline development has advanced. In the wake of the Northern Gateway failure, government and corporate strategies have sought to divide Indigenous communities and fracture resistance. But continued Indigenous resistance has also opened new negotiations, including initial provincial government gestures towards formalizing shared jurisdictional arrangements. It is too soon to evaluate the effects of these new strategies to both divide and cooperate with Indigenous communities, but it is clear that future forms of development will be shaped by their relations to Indigenous peoples.

**Requiem for a Pipedream**

The final chapters of the Northern Gateway project unwound over a series of years with long delays punctuated by contentious decisions and stark reversals. Ultimately the project died; its failure to reconcile Indigenous interests with pipeline development proved fatal. There has been considerable debate about the nature of this failure. Midway through the regulatory review process, the federal government intervened to rewrite the rules guiding it, further delimiting the extent to which Enbridge needed to consider Indigenous and environmental concerns. Within these delimited frames, the final report of the JRP examining the project explicitly addressed the impacts of the Northern Gateway project on Aboriginal traditional land use, economic interests, and ability to practice self-governance. Indigenous communities disputed the substance of government consideration of their interests. The Wet'suwet'en in particular began to erect infrastructure to block pipeline development. Ultimately, the courts determined that the governmental consultation over Northern Gateway had left too many Indigenous and environmental concerns undocumented. Indigenous interests extended beyond a few scattered sites around which development needed to be routed. Settler authorities needed to effectively document Indigenous concerns and ensure adequate economic compensation for development impacts. These technicalities led to the eventual defeat of Enbridge, but they never resolved the broader challenge to settler sovereignty. Indeed, within this legal and political discourse, the question of Indigenous sovereignty remains unaddressed.

The Enbridge Northern Gateway proposal began as a set of bureaucratic proceedings distant from general public concern. It became national news in 2012. In April of that year, in response to oil and gas lobbyists, the federal Conservative government introduced an omnibus budget bill, dubbed the Jobs, Growth, and Long-Term Prosperity Act, to narrow the scope of review. This bill was rapidly forced through the legislature, receiving royal ascent in June, barely two months after its first reading. The act radically altered Canadian legislative frameworks, particularly around energy and environmental governance, rewriting the governing legislation for both the Canadian Environmental Assessment Agency and the National Energy Board.[1] It weakened the powers of the National Energy Board, which previously had the capacity to reject project proposals, allowing it to only issue recommendations to the federal cabinet. Within technical proceedings, the legislation narrowed the scope of reviews. For instance, assessments of fisheries impacts were narrowed to only consider fish species of human commercial interest or subsistence needs. Review processes now operated under strict time limits that would provide greater certainty for investors. These legislative amendments were applied to the Northern Gateway review process despite the fact that the Northern Gateway review had been formally initiated in in January 2012, and these new regulations would prejudice the capacity of impacted communities to convey their concerns. The Northern Gateway review was subsequently required to conclude no later than the end of 2013. In December 2013, a second omnibus bill, the Jobs and Growth Act, made further sweeping legislative changes, including amending the Navigable Waters Protection Act to remove thousands of lakes and streams from federal protection. Under the banner #IdleNoMore, organizers launched a national campaign of protests against the steady derogation of constitutional requirements to protect Indigenous rights.[2] The Enbridge Northern Gateway project review proceeded under the highly politicized circumstances of these reforms and counter-protests.

Nevertheless, the review panellists assigned to the project sought to present themselves as an expert panel guided by technical concerns, including effectively balancing national economic interests with the protection of the environment and Aboriginal rights. In its final report, the JRP determined that the company had effectively integrated consideration of Aboriginal traditional land use. Specifically, the panel validated the methodology that had been used in community-based research on Aboriginal traditional knowledge. Although it noted that Indigenous communities, including the Wet'suwet'en, had expressed concerns about project impacts on vital salmon fisheries, the panel dismissed these concerns.

> *The Panel does not agree with the view of some Aboriginal groups that the effects associated with this project during construction and routine operations would eliminate the opportunity for Aboriginal groups to maintain their cultural and spiritual practices and the pursuit of their traditional uses and activities associated with the lands, waters, and their resources.*[3]

Instead, the panel concurred with the company's view, stating that "during construction and routine operations, there would not be significant adverse effects on the lands, waters, or resources in the project area." Equating Indigenous territorial interests with the environment, the panel extrapolated that "there would not be significant adverse effects on the ability of Aboriginal people to utilize lands, waters, or resources in the project area for traditional purposes." The panel found spills, though possible, would be unlikely and would have only temporary, if significant, impacts. Such an event could disrupt Indigenous access to their traditional lands, waters, and resources, including traditional foods. Thus, a major spill could present a significant burden on impacted Indigenous groups, restricting their ability to practice their traditional activities. However, the panel determined this risk was acceptable, as "such interruptions would be temporary."[4]

While the reviewers determined Enbridge's approach to traditional land use research was appropriate, they also found that the company had failed to effectively engage Indigenous communities at times. It wrote, "The company could have done more to clearly communicate to some Aboriginal groups how it considered, and would continue to consider, information provided." There were also concerns about information gaps in the accounting for Aboriginal traditional land use, though in the view of the panel, these gaps did not fatally impair the project. As it viewed Aboriginal traditional land use as inherently localized, the panel concluded that impacts could be addressed through adjustments in the routing and surveying of the pipelines. This was codified in one of the recommended panel conditions on project approval: "To address concerns regarding site-specific traditional land use information...the Panel requires Northern Gateway to continue to consult with Aboriginal groups and engage them on detailed route-walks and centreline surveys." The panel held settler authorities as arbiters of the adequacy of accommodation of Indigenous interests, and the permitting condition required that the company report any additional impacts it identified and propose mitigation measures to state regulators.[5]

Evaluating the broader merits of the project in terms of its economic and environmental impacts, the panel stressed the "significant potential benefits to local, regional, and national economies associated with the project."[6] Regarding the integration of Indigenous economic interests into project construction, the panel was particularly laudatory of the corporate measures "to encourage and support the participation of interested Aboriginal groups and businesses in the project, and to assist local and Aboriginal business and individuals to qualify for the opportunities that would be available." In their final report, the panellists expressed their opinion that Enbridge's "commitments break new ground by providing an unprecedented level of long-term economic, environmental, and social benefits to Aboriginal groups." They particularly extolled the company's "commitment to provide equity participation to eligible Aboriginal groups, its commitment to meet or exceed 15 per cent Aboriginal employment for construction and operation of the project, and its proposed programs to support education and training for interested Aboriginal individuals and businesses."[7]

The panel did mention the potential effect of Northern Gateway on Indigenous self-determination, but ultimately determined that the unquantifiable nature of this broader question meant that it, the panel, could not assess project impacts and benefits for Indigenous self-determination. The panellists recognized that Indigenous groups had repeatedly "described how their cultural practices and values are integral to their traditional forms of governance and their concern that the project may affect their ability to make decisions related to the use of lands, waters, and resources."[8] Specifically, the panel acknowledged that the Office of the Wet'suwet'en had made extensive arguments about traditional governance and intangible aspects of their relationship to the land. The reviewers recognized that the Wet'suwet'en hereditary chiefs had stressed the importance of "how they look after their traditional territories because as a people they are a part of the land," as well as how "arrangements for management of the fishery are deeply interconnected and woven into the fabric of Wet'suwet'en culture."[9] The panel observed that the Office of the Wet'suwet'en connected these relationships to the lineage of their *yikh* and *di̇dikh*, which were ceremonially renewed through the *balhats* as "the time when laws are determined, names are taken and responsibilities are passed on to future generations."[10] The Wet'suwet'en had argued that a potential spill could rupture the constitutional relationships that linked a lineage and the land. In its project application for Northern Gateway, Enbridge provided no accounting or mitigation plans for these impacts because they could not be economically quantified. Responding to these concerns, the panel concurred that "some aspects of cultural activity cannot be described in economic terms." The panel then rationalized that, like Northern Gateway, it would not address these concerns; it was responsible for accounting for cultural impacts only "to the extent that activities contribute to a culture, and monetary values can be attributed to these activities."[11] Federal regulators restricted regulatory consideration to only fungible cultural attributes. Inalienable Indigenous rights to self-determination or responsibilities to the land were disappeared in the context of Canadian natural resource governance. They were beyond the pale of a colonial framework that reduced environmental governance to the calculation and balancing of economic rationales.

The JRP ultimately recommended that Northern Gateway be approved, subject to 209 conditions. Where uncertainty existed, it did not recommend precaution and delays to enable further investigation. Instead, the panel simply recommended that the company develop additional plans and conduct further studies to address unresolved Indigenous and environmental concerns. From the view of the panellists, the basic framework of reconciliation proffered through the review process was acceptable, and the details could be subsequently managed as technical matters. The panel recommended, for instance, that Enbridge be required to conduct further studies on traditional land use and develop detailed routing and design plans to mitigate pipeline impacts on that use. To address consultation issues, they recommended the company also be required to provide further documentation of its engagements with Indigenous communities. Similarly, Enbridge would be required to file plans and reports documenting how it would implement programs to advance Indigenous economic interests through training and education, employment, contracting, and procurement. Finally, to address some of the unquantified issues around environmental impacts in its original application, Enbridge was to develop a compensation plan for project impacts on freshwater fish and fish habitat. It also needed to conduct a research program to more effectively determine whether spilled dilbit had a greater propensity to sink in water than conventional oil, and how that would impact environments and environmental remediation efforts in spill events.

Following the release of the JRP report, the federal government conducted further consultations with impacted communities to determine if the panel's proposed accommodations adequately protected Indigenous interests. As consultation remained a duty of the colonial sovereign, Canadian officials were responsible for meaningfully engaging with impacted Indigenous communities to ensure the adequacy of the environmental assessment process and consider any project-related concerns that exceeded its scope. In these consultations, Indigenous communities again flagged substantial concerns that had not been resolved in the JRP's restricted timeline and terms of reference. As the panel's 209 recommended project conditions made clear, Northern Gateway still needed to clarify numerous aspects of the project's impacts and benefits for Indigenous peoples, along with fundamental scientific concerns about environmental impacts. While some of the conditions recommended by the panel required further refinements to project planning, many simply required conducting studies around fisheries or spill behaviour to gauge impacts after pipelines began operating. Thus, it remained impossible to adequately assess the social and environmental effects of the project on Indigenous interests. Indigenous communities asked for additional data on fisheries impacts and dilbit spill modelling so they could better understand how the pipelines could affect their territories and communities, but federal government officials did not seek to collect the requested additional information. They effectively ignored both Indigenous community concerns and their duty to ensure that project impacts on Indigenous peoples were appropriately accommodated. On June 17, 2014, the Canadian government approved the Northern Gateway project, subject only to the conditions suggested by the JRP.

Less than two weeks later, on June 26, 2014, the Supreme Court of Canada issued its first finding of Aboriginal title in *Tsilhqot'in Nation v. British Columbia*. In the decision, the court drew heavily on the definition of Aboriginal title in *Delgamuukw, Gisdaywa*. It also clarified the forms of Indigenous land use necessary to demonstrate title, and thus its potential extent. Provincial government lawyers had argued that land occupation required an intensity of use reminiscent of the British common law traditions, where people could claim home and harvesting sites but not larger hunting territories. The court determined this to be an ethnocentric approach to Aboriginal title. Instead, following *Delgamuukw, Gisdaywa*, the justices indicated that "a culturally sensitive approach to sufficiency of occupation [is] based on the dual perspectives of the Aboriginal group in question—its laws, practices, size, technological ability and the character of the land claimed—and the common law notion of possession as a basis for title."[12] Assessing a claim to Aboriginal title required considering that Indigenous peoples "might conceive of possession of land in a somewhat different manner than did the common law." Specifically, the court found that "a culturally sensitive approach suggests that regular use of territories for hunting, fishing, trapping and foraging is 'sufficient' use to ground Aboriginal title."[13] Although the Tsilhqot'in were not on the Northern Gateway route and thus not directly impacted by the project, the decision challenged the parsimonious and fragmentary approach to understanding Aboriginal traditional land use and occupancy that Enbridge and regulators had employed in evaluating the impact of Northern Gateway. The site-specific approach to cataloguing and accommodating Indigenous interests failed to attend to the broader set of territorial concerns.

The *Tsilhqot'in Nation* decision also reaffirmed the utility of project-specific negotiations to accommodate Indigenous interests. While in *Delgamuukw, Gisdaywa* the court had directed the government to negotiate comprehensive land claims directly with Indigenous communities, in *Tsilhqot'in Nation* the justices now suggested that more localized negotiations could present an effective avenue for reconciling Indigenous peoples and development: "Governments and individuals proposing to use or exploit land, whether before or after a declaration of Aboriginal title, can avoid a charge of infringement or failure to adequately consult by obtaining the consent of the interested Aboriginal group."[14] This normalized the proliferation of mechanisms that sought to reconcile Indigenous peoples with extractive development through forms of economic inclusion. In contrast, *Delgamuukw, Gisdaywa* had emphasized that the inalienable aspect of Aboriginal title required that Indigenous communities cede the land to the colonial sovereign in order to allow its use for a purpose irreconcilable with the nature of Aboriginal title. In place of a political solution to inalienable Aboriginal title, the court now approached Indigenous interests as increasingly fungible, subject to forms of private reconciliation through project-specific negotiations over impacts and benefits. In the wake of the *Tsilhqot'in Nation* decision, the International Energy Agency reduced its projections for Canadian hydrocarbon production growth, suggesting that pipeline projects that crossed British Columbia would face additional burdens to "obtain the consent of the title-holder."[15]

Nevertheless, the court could hardly be seen as decolonizing. It reiterated the authority of the colonial sovereign to infringe Aboriginal title when substantive governmental objectives warranted. Here the requirements echoed those articulated in *Delgamuukw, Gisdaywa*. Government authorities needed to justify the need for the project, minimize impacts on Aboriginal title lands, and ensure that Indigenous peoples were fairly compensated. In effect, the *Tsilhqot'in Nation* decision expanded the breadth of Aboriginal title recognition but further regularized economic calculations over its infringement. The case normalized reconciliation through economic inclusion, potentially without regard to Indigenous desires. But it also gave hope to Indigenous peoples who sought to use the court to force settler authorities to recognize their interests.

Indigenous communities led by the coastal Gitxaala and Haisla did just this, challenging the federal government's approval of Northern Gateway in court. Both nations were threatened by the impacts of the development of the pipelines and related shipping activity. Known as the people of the open ocean, the Gitxaala are the furthest west of the fourteen Tsimshian bands and live on an island that would be impacted by tanker traffic. The marine terminal for the Northern Gateway project would be on Haisla territories, immediately west of Wet'suwet'en territories. The court challenges spanned a wide range of procedural issues, from an insufficient formal environmental assessment process to problematic Indigenous community consultations. The Gitxaala and Haisla charged that the Canadian program of consultations with Indigenous communities, which followed the formal public review process, amounted to token and empty gestures. Their counsel argued that plans for the proposed Enbridge project had inadequately catalogued Indigenous land interests, and that there were still gaps in even the most basic information about the potential for a spill and how it would be addressed. Community requests for additional information on fisheries dynamics and the fate of bitumen in water had gone unanswered since the release of the project review. In court, government representatives did not contest the suggestion that Indigenous communities had been told that they needed to accept the conclusions of the JRP report. Positions on the pipeline hardened.

Parallel to the litigation, the Wet'suwet'en were making preparations to assert their territorial jurisdiction to block the pipeline on the ground. In 2009, the Office of the Wet'suwet'en established a cabin-building program along the pipeline route, reasserting their occupation of the territories. The first cabin to be completed was on the Gilserhyu territory of the *yikh* led by Knedebeas, a name then held by Warner William.[16] Beginning in 2011, members of that *yikh*, known both as Unist'ot'en and Yex T'sa Wilk'us, began hosting an annual direct-action training, called the Unist'ot'en Camp, on their traditional territories at the point on the Widzin Kwah where the pipelines would cross the river.[17] In the succeeding years, the Unist'ot'en Camp became a permanent Wet'suwet'en presence on the territories, occupying them year-round.[18] The Unist'ot'en exercised their jurisdiction over who could access the territories by establishing a checkpoint.[19] In 2015, the hereditary chiefs of all the *dïdikh* declared their opposition to all new pipelines on their territories, enacting a form of jurisdiction over their territories that remained unreconciled with settler authorities acting in the name of colonial sovereignty. By materializing their territorial jurisdiction at the Unist'ot'en checkpoint, Wet'suwet'en hereditary authority presented an additional barrier to pipeline development should the Gitxaala and Haisla litigation fail.

The approval of Northern Gateway in 2014 thus did not resolve the question of pipeline construction but incited its further politicization. Energy and infrastructure, already prominent in national discussions, became central to political debates in the 2015 federal election. In the election campaign, Liberal leader Justin Trudeau critiqued the review process around Northern Gateway, arguing that the Conservative government of Stephen Harper had weakened public support for pipeline projects. In an August party leaders' debate in Toronto, Trudeau laid out his argument.

> *Harper continues to say we can't do anything for the environment because it will hurt the economy...He has hurt the economy. People don't trust this government to look out for our long-term interests. He hasn't convinced communities of the rightness of his pipelines, of the proposals he supported. He hasn't been working with First Nations and the kinds of partnerships that are needed if we're going to continue to develop natural resources. But the job of the Prime Minister is to get those resources to market.*[20]

Trudeau repeated this assessment in a September debate in Calgary, arguing that the Conservatives' unabashed prioritization of fossil extractivism pitted the economy against the environment and bolstered resistance to pipeline projects. "He hasn't gotten pipelines built," Trudeau concluded of Harper.[21] In the October vote, Trudeau swept Harper from power.

In June 2016, with Trudeau's Liberals in government, the Federal Court of Appeal quashed the Northern Gateway approval on the basis of the Harper government's failure to adequately consult Aboriginal communities. In its decision, the court highlighted the impossibility of meaningful consultation without adequate information about Indigenous interests or the potential effects of the project on them. Reviewing the consultation process, the federal court overturned project approval, ruling that the Canadian government "offered only a brief, hurried and inadequate opportunity...to exchange and discuss information and to dialogue." The court was blunt in its assessment of the consultation process: "The inadequacies—more than just a handful and more than mere imperfections—left entire subjects of central interest to the affected First Nations, sometimes subjects affecting their subsistence and well-being, entirely ignored."[22] The government had failed to uphold its duty to ensure "the honourable treatment of Canada's Aboriginal peoples and Canada's reconciliation with them."[23] As the issue was specific to the constitutional duties of the colonial sovereign to Indigenous peoples rather than to the broader public, it was not necessary to conduct another public review of the project. Settler authorities did, however, need to take more time to gather information related to Indigenous concerns, provide that information to communities, and then carefully consider community feedback in project decision-making. The newly elected Liberals had three options: reject the project, re-engage Indigenous communities, or restart the public review process.

On November 29, 2016, Trudeau announced that he had chosen the first option, directing the National Energy Board "to dismiss the application for the Northern Gateway Pipelines Project." Explaining the decision, he stated that the project had failed to meet the "strict criteria" that his government sought to uphold in its commitments to protect the environment. "It has become clear that this project is not in the best interests of the local affected communities, including Indigenous peoples." Specifically, the Liberal government had determined that the remote northern pipeline was unjustifiable in a region dependent on an ecosystem that "thrives with diverse wildlife, and supplies an abundant and sustainable economy to the tens of thousands of people who depend on its health."[24] Almost a decade after the Energy Summit against pipelines in Witset, the alliance of small, northern Indigenous communities opposed to Northern Gateway had slayed the multi-billion-dollar behemoth. The project rejection represented the victory of an Indigenous will to shape the trajectory of development, demonstrating the capacity of Indigenous peoples to change the future of fossil capitalism.

## The Enduring Violence of Reconciliation

While the Liberal government juxtaposed its approach to reconciliation to that of the Conservatives, the two approaches shared many fundamental principles. At its foundations, the Liberals' approach to reconciling Indigenous interests with pipeline development was not qualitatively different from the Conservatives' approach. Their criticism did not challenge the basic structure of the latter's approach, only the extent to which it had been implemented. The Liberals sought to enhance the degree to which Indigenous interests were documented and accommodated, but not to stop the expansion of fossil fuel infrastructure.

The Conservatives had provided minimal consideration to Indigenous interests, speeding up review processes to serve the needs of industry and deferring substantial documentation of Indigenous interests to project implementation. This had, in the Liberal view, created pipeline delays in the form of opposition and court challenges. The Liberals suggested that pipeline development could be smoothed through more systematic consideration and finer application of the calculus of fair compensation. This suggestion did not involve rethinking the mechanisms with which those calculations had historically been made, and which I have documented throughout this book. Aboriginal land use studies and economic integration into project benefits remained the core features of their purported revisioning of the processes to reconcile development with Indigenous peoples. Federal government officials still elided broader consideration of Indigenous jurisdiction and refused to recognize Indigenous authority to decide the course of development. Indigenous mobilizations still challenged the silencing of their authority. These mobilizations were beyond the pale of colonial consideration and became the subject of police repression. Thus, in spite of the patina of improved consultation, the reconciliation proposed by the Liberals continued to rely on the suspension of Indigenous rights and the application of the force of law to impose colonial extractive designs.

The Liberal assertion that their approach departed from the Conservatives' earlier disregard for Indigenous peoples was duplicitous. This duplicity was evident in the Liberals' rejection of the Northern Gateway project in 2016. This announcement was buried in a press conference following another announcement about the approval of a different contentious pipeline project, Kinder Morgan Trans Mountain. The government's termination of Northern Gateway was not a recognition of the need to secure Indigenous consent for extractive projects, but instead a way of emphasizing that the government had raised its regulatory standards. But the goal those standards were meant to achieve—ensuring the legal foundation for extractivist development through necessary accommodation of Aboriginal interests—remained unchanged.

The Trans Mountain project, like Northern Gateway, aimed to expand the export infrastructure for bitumen mined in the Athabasca tar sands. Through Trans Mountain, Trudeau, like Harper with Northern Gateway before him, sought to extend the extractive resource relations that form the foundation of the colonial present. As Robert MacNeil and Matthew Paterson assert, Trudeau's government has continued "to normalize the oil sector and make imagining something beyond it seem impossible."[25] Trudeau's approval of Trans Mountain alongside the rejection of Northern Gateway was meant to reassure the oil industry of his ongoing support. He rationalized his government's support for Trans Mountain on the basis that it was the government's responsibility to ensure that the tar sands could be developed to the full extent possible: "There isn't a country in the world that would find billions of barrels of oil and leave it in the ground while there is a market for it." His approach contrasted with that of the Conservatives in its rhetorical commitment to balancing economic and environmental objectives, as well as the suggestion that his government would use tar sands exploitation to create the economic returns necessary to fuel a "transition to a clean energy economy."[26] But the Liberal offer was not a break with fossil capitalism and its basis in resource dispossession of Indigenous peoples. It simply sought to better mediate environmental,

Indigenous, and industry interests in order to rationalize pipeline development.

Despite this supposed better mediation of conflicting interests, development of the Trans Mountain project has faced many of the same hurdles faced by Northern Gateway. In particular, regulators have still faced the challenge of unreconciled Indigenous political claims. The original Trans Mountain expansion project application was filed with the National Energy Board in December 2013. The pipeline proposal aimed to twin an existing Trans Mountain Pipeline, which had been built in 1952, increasing capacity from 300,000 to 890,000 barrels per day. It aimed to be in service within six years. Trans Mountain's route through southern British Columbia to port in the metro-Vancouver area traversed more highly developed and environmentally degraded lands than Northern Gateway's proposed route. Nevertheless, it faced challenges from communities along its route that opposed its development. In 2014, as contractors began conducting environmental fieldwork to collect information for the project application, a mass civil disobedience campaign caused constant disturbances to the work, leading to more than one hundred arrests. As it crossed unceded territories, Indigenous peoples again prominently led the resistance. Along the coast, the Tsleil-Waututh Nation released an independent assessment of the project in May 2015, determining it to be unacceptable under their laws.[27] When Trudeau took office in October 2015, he committed to reforming governance processes to provide more consideration of environmental and Indigenous interests with the goal of securing social licence for development. He did not achieve this goal. After Trans Mountain's 2016 approval, the project found itself increasingly entangled in litigation and direct-action campaigns.[28] In 2018, Kinder Morgan announced that resistance to Trans Mountain had so delayed the project that its development had become financially unviable. The company sold Trans Mountain to the Canadian government for $4.5 billion in May 2018.[29] The project immediately saw further delays when the Federal Court of Appeal overturned Trudeau's original approval, ruling that neither the regulatory review nor the Indigenous consultation process had been properly completed.[30]

Following this setback, Trudeau's government renewed its efforts to legitimize the project. The National Energy Board undertook a new environmental assessment to address shipping issues ignored in the first review process. In 2019, the National Energy Board recommended approval of the project again, subject to new conditions, and the federal government again approved the pipeline.[31] The courts upheld this approval.[32]

However, the government vastly underestimated the array of political and environmental forces that would interfere with pipeline development. In British Columbia's Lower Mainland, mass protests and arrests accompanied the start of project construction, once again causing delays.[33] In the Southern Interior, the Secwépemc began to establish a series of tiny homes along the pipeline route, further entangling the pipeline development with the prosecution of Indigenous land defenders in court.[34] Further shutdowns were caused by the onset of the COVID-19 pandemic in 2020 and an atmospheric river event in 2021 that caused record rainfalls, flooding, and mudslides. Economic uncertainties cascading from these disasters, including a supply chain crisis and rampant inflation, continued to complicate construction.[35] The cost of building the Trans Mountain Pipeline extension, which was originally estimated at $5.4 billion, had ballooned to $30.9 billion by March 2023.[36]

Meanwhile, tar sands expansion is increasingly reliant on Trans Mountain's completion. Energy East and Keystone XL, two other major pipeline proposals meant to connect the Alberta tar sands to Québec and Oklahoma, were cancelled in 2017 and 2021, respectively. Trans Mountain is the last remaining major proposal to expand the tar sands' access to market. The federal government, in order to reconcile what it sees as necessary oil infrastructure development with impacted Indigenous peoples, continues to engage more than 129 potentially impacted Indigenous groups to negotiate their inclusion in the project's forecast economic benefits. As with Northern Gateway, this inclusion will be administered through mechanisms of employment and training, contracting and procurement, funding for community services and infrastructure, and pipeline revenue sharing, including purchases of equity stake in the project.[37]

While the Wet'suwet'en have remained peripheral to proceedings around Trans Mountain, their pipeline resistance has continued. Following Northern Gateway, no additional tar sands pipelines have been proposed in Northwest British Columbia. However, there have been numerous liquefied natural gas pipeline proposals that aim to connect another unconventional hydrocarbon, fracked gas, from the Montney Formation in Northeast British Columbia to the coast for global distribution. As these are not interprovincial pipelines, they are under provincial governmental jurisdiction (although the export terminals on the coast are under federal jurisdiction, and the federal government's approval of these ports implies its tacit support for the pipelines).[38] Two particular pipeline projects, the Pacific Trails Pipeline (originally owned by Chevron and Woodside Petroleum, purchased by Enbridge in January 2022) and the Coastal GasLink project (owned by TC Energy, formerly TransCanada), threaten Wet'suwet'en territories. As critical Canadian conversations around fossil capitalism in the new millennium initially focused on the tar sands, both of these liquefied natural gas projects had seen far less scrutiny or public attention than Northern Gateway by the time they received project approvals, in 2008 and 2014 respectively.

Wet'suwet'en presence, however, remains strong. The Pacific Trails Pipeline and Coastal GasLink project will overlap with Northern Gateway's once-proposed route across Wet'suwet'en territories, meaning the cabin development on the Unist'ot'en *yin tah*, which would have impeded Northern Gateway, will be along the path of these new pipelines as well. Although the Pacific Trails Pipeline was approved first, Chevron and Woodside Petroleum delayed committing to a final investment decision, and TC Energy's Coastal GasLink was the first of the two projects to advance to development. The Unist'ot'en asserted Wet'suwet'en jurisdiction to control movements on their *yin tah* by installing a checkpoint on the bridge over the Widzin Kwah next to their cabins. The checkpoint controlled access to the Unist'ot'en *yin tah*, and

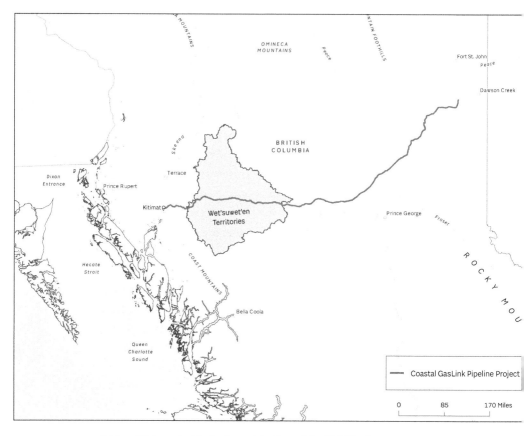

MAP 3: *Wet'suwet'en Territories and the Coastal GasLink Pipeline.*

limited pipeline employees' and contractors' ability to survey routes and prepare for pipeline construction.[39] The situation that emerged was a conflict of laws. The Unist'ot'en, led by Warner William who holds the title Knedebeas, asserted Aboriginal title to their traditional lands and argued that they maintain territorial jurisdiction under Wet'suwet'en law.

Having learned from the Northern Gateway experience, both the provincial government and pipeline companies intensified their efforts to build pipeline partnerships with local bands and undermine the hereditary chiefs. Under Harper, federal cuts to program funding had eroded services on reserve. Despite the fact that Aboriginal peoples and lands were under federal jurisdiction, the government of British Columbia sought to take advantage of federal funding shortfalls by providing funds to bands to engage in planning processes to evaluate the benefits that a pipeline could bring to their community.[40] In 2014, the consulting firm Good Medicine Group facilitated the provincially funded community planning process in Moricetown (known today as Witset, home to the band in which the majority of the Wet'suwet'en are members). Led by Marc Storms, a former social worker in Northwest British Columbia, the Good Medicine Group marketed itself as a capacity-building organization that helped communities plan "to engage in economic growth activities that translate into financial, social and wellness outcomes that will benefit all members." Although the consulting group is now defunct, its former website emphasized that energy projects provide "a means of economic opportunity through participation and negotiating impact benefit agreements (IBAs) and Joint Ventures with industry."

By 2018, five of the six Wet'suwet'en bands had signed agreements with Coastal GasLink, including Skin Tyee, Nee-Tahi-Buhn, Burns Lake, Wet'suwet'en First Nation, and Witset.[41] The bands also signed pipeline agreements with the province to "develop an effective long-term working relationship that includes Moricetown and the Wet'suwet'en sharing benefits associated with the Natural Gas Pipeline Project and supporting the development of the Natural Gas Pipeline Project."[42] Unlike the other bands, the village of Hagwilget supported the hereditary chiefs' authority over Wet'suwet'en territories and did not sign onto the pipeline.

The province also partnered with TC Energy (then TransCanada) and LNG Canada to fund a dissident movement within the hereditary system. In 2016, the government provided $60,000, with matching support from the energy-extraction companies, to a group called the Wet'suwet'en Matrilineal Coalition to engage community members and communicate the economic benefits of resource development.[43] The group was led by three Wet'suwet'en women, Darlene Glaim, Gloria George, and Theresa Tait-Day. Glaim, who previously held the title Gyolo'ght and was responsible for the Cas Yex territory around Smithers, inherited the hereditary chiefdom of Cas Yex in the Gitdumden and the title of Woos after the passing of the *yikh*'s previous chief, Roy Morris.[44] Gloria George took the title Smogelgem as the hereditary chief of Sayax in the Laksamshu after the passing of the *yikh*'s previous chief Leonard George (although some members of the Wet'suwet'en community never recognized this title transfer as legitimate, as they viewed the *balhats* she hosted as unequal to the name). Finally, Theresa Tait-Day claimed to be the spokesperson for Kwanbeahyax of the Laksilyu after the passing of Frank Patrick, the previous holder of Wah Tah Kwets, the chiefly title for the *yikh*. Darlene Glaim, who had led the Gitdumden testimony in opposition to Northern Gateway, was now actively supportive of the potential for economic reconciliation of Wet'suwet'en interests with liquid natural gas pipelines. The Wet'suwet'en Matrilineal Coalition, Glaim explained, was "formed with the intent to negotiate a benefit agreement...with the TransCanada Coastal Gas Link Project."[45]

The Wet'suwet'en Matrilineal Coalition did not effectively foster support for the pipeline among the *dìdikh*. In Glaim's assessment, the coalition "caused much turmoil amongst our people and leadership."[46] For causing this disharmony and bringing their *yikh* into disrepute, the other hereditary chiefs "feathered" the principal women involved in the coalition in 2019, annulling their standing in the *balhats* because of their violation of their traditional duties to protect the land.[47] They were banned from conducting business on behalf of their *yikh* unless they cleansed their names within the *balhats*. Thus shamed, they could no longer speak with the authority of hereditary chiefs. The hereditary chief names Woos and Smogelgem were subsequently taken by Frank Alec and Warner Naziel, who both worked with their respective *dïdikh* of Gitdumden and Laksamshu to oppose the Coastal GasLink project.

The government and industry sought to divide the Wet'suwet'en community with promises of project revenues, and in some respects they did. But their methods also deepened resistance, much as had occurred with Northern Gateway. Unlike Northern Gateway, however, the Coastal GasLink project advanced to construction, leading to pronounced conflicts among the Wet'suwet'en, the British Columbia government, and TC Energy over who had the capacity to determine what development would be permitted, and what would be forbidden. As they were preparing for construction in 2018, TC Energy obtained court injunctions to remove the Unist'ot'en checkpoint.[48] In solidarity with the Unist'ot'en, the Gitdumden and Laksamshu *dïdikh* also established camps on their own *yin tah*, and activists associated with these camps were also targeted by injunctions. The police enforcement of injunctions against Wet'suwet'en *dïdikh* led to arrests in 2019 and 2020, demonstrating how the settler state sought to enact its authority through the suspension of Indigenous mobilizations against the pipeline. But here again the decisions of settler authorities were not final. Indeed, they only heightened the conflict between Wet'suwet'en and settler law.

The police efforts to suppress the Wet'suwet'en *dïdikh* in early 2020 triggered solidarity actions across the country that shut down ports and train traffic. Dennis Darby, CEO of Canadian Manufacturers and Exporters, estimated that the blockades stranded $425 million worth of goods each day.[49] This vast network of supporters, acting in the name of protecting Wet'suwet'en territorial sovereignty, served to demonstrate not only a will to govern the land that competed with the colonial sovereign, but also a capacity to control economic movement across Canada. The situation was unresolved when the COVID-19 pandemic emerged in March 2020, shutting down mobilizations in the name of public health and safety.

Under the cover of the coronavirus crisis, pipeline construction resumed. With most of the world cloistered away to restrict the spread of the coronavirus, the oil and gas industry quickly lobbied for construction crews to be labelled essential workers.[50] The government complied, and pipeline work continued on both Coastal GasLink and Trans Mountain, but the opportunity to construct contentious projects without oversight or interference was brief.

Pipeline conflicts now seem endemic, and the costs of resistance continue to add up. Chevron put its stake in the Pacific Trails Pipeline up for sale in December 2019 but initially failed to find a buyer. In 2021, they announced that they would no longer fund the project, leading Woodside Petroleum to also sell its stake.[51] Enbridge re-entered the scene in 2022, buying up the near-abandoned project, but its future remains uncertain.[52] Coastal GasLink has also been slowed by enduring resistance, as well as problems of corporate irresponsibility. There have been ongoing protests interfering with project development, and there have been instances of sabotage.[53] The Unist'ot'en *yikh* and Gitdumden *didikh* have monitored pipeline development and notified provincial regulators when the company has violated its environmental permits.[54] After repeated Coastal GasLink violations, particularly in relation to allowing sediment erosion into sensitive waterways, the British Columbia Environmental Assessment Office issued a series of stop-work orders for non-compliance with environmental requirements.[55] The continual delays have led to escalating project costs. Originally estimated at $6.6 billion, TC Energy now projects Coastal GasLink to cost $14.5 billion.[56]

Indigenous resistance has undeniably been a major factor in transforming the financial viability of fossil capitalism in the Canadian North. While the broader future for pipeline development on Wet'suwet'en territories remains uncertain, it is clear that the Wet'suwet'en will remain a force on their lands.

**Fighting for Future Generations**

Indigenous mobilizations challenge not only the forms of authority embedded within Canadian state institutions, but also the logic that guides how that authority is conducted. Canadian law does not simply regularize settlement; it installs a legal order that normalizes commodity relations and the unfolding of a political economy focused on expanding extractive infrastructure to maximize profits. This is what critical geographers have discussed as time-space compression, a constant drive to build communication and transportation infrastructure to make an ever more connected world of growing consumption.[57] This is the impulse underlying pipeline development and the rationality underpinning why settler authorities permit it. By contesting these projects, the Wet'suwet'en hereditary chiefs have sought to demonstrate a different logic—one embedded within the continual renewal of connections through practices of gifting that stretch reciprocal obligations into the past and future. The Wet'suwet'en challenge to settler society is, in other words, about more than any particular pipeline. It is about the relationships that are valued within society and the assumptions that underpin legal norms. Most fundamentally, the Wet'suwet'en hereditary chiefs raise the question of what principles should guide the lawful conduct of authorities in governing the land.

This question seems abstract, but actually invites a deeper grounding of law in obligations to place. Colonial discourse normalizes property regimes based on the possession and enclosure of lands in order to produce commodities. At the same time, it constructs Indigenous peoples, in contradistinction to these norms, as nomads, simply wandering the forest.[58] As Edward Chamberlin notes, however, the construction of Indigenous peoples as ungrounded and settlers as emplaced is backwards.

> *For millennia, farming people have roamed around the world looking for new places and dreaming of the home they left behind, moving on after a generation or so to other new places. And we call these people..."settlers"? The other people, the indigenous people who have lived in the same place for tens of thousands of years...we call Them "wanderers"?*[59]

Despite the terms of colonial discourse, it is Indigenous people who are deeply rooted in place, constantly renewing connections to the more-than-human world that surrounds them.[60] The Gitxsan neighbours of the Wet'suwet'en refer to white settlers as *amxsiwaa*, a term for driftwood that has lost its colour from long travel.[61] This concept beautifully captures the definitional aspect of out-of-placeness that underpins settler relations to colonized lands.

Wet'suwet'en seasonal movements through the territories, in contrast, create a distinct awareness of the rhythms of the land and the continual renewal of intergenerational relations.[62] These cyclic movements, through the seasons and generations, between distinct *yikh* territories and central fishing villages, vitally inform the meaning of reciprocal gifting within Wet'suwet'en *balhats*. As Rauna Kuokkanen discusses in her theorization of Indigenous gifting, the land is part of the "reciprocity practiced in life-renewing ceremonies and gift-giving rituals."[63] She stresses how practices of reciprocity continually reassert "the bonds of relationships in the world simply because according to the worldviews from which these bonds stem, our very existence depends on it."[64] Richard Daly, an anthropologist who studied the Gitxsan and Wet'suwet'en in the 1980s and served as an expert witness on their behalf in the *Delgamuukw, Gisdaywa* trial, describes how practices of reciprocal gifting serve to distribute risk across a community dependent on "the uncertainties of salmon runs, wild produce, weather patterns, gambling risks, and political enmities."[65]

Situating lawful conduct within the framework of the gift establishes a moral economy focused on maintaining kinship relations and linkages to ancestors for future generations.[66] The logic of Indigenous gift-giving is best understood with reference to inalienable possessions, such as lands held by matrilineal kinship groups.[67] More than seeking to gain status, the central role of gifting in Wet'suwet'en society is renewing sacred connections to the land. In the *Delgamuukw, Gisdaywa* trial, Sarah Layton, who then held the Unist'ot'en hereditary chiefly title Knedebeas, gave evidence on how her participation in the case was motivated by her concern for future generations. She explained her reasoning in her 1988 court testimony.

> *Our ancestors...lived off the land, now there is nothing to live off in there...I don't want no money...I want it back the way—the way the territory was in the past for our future children's use, our grandchildren, and our great-great grandchildren, so they will be able to use it the way our ancestors have in the past.*[68]

Her testimony highlighted the concept of intergenerational responsibility that underpins the conduct of Wet'suwet'en authorities. On behalf of their *yikh*, hereditary chiefs are responsible for protecting the land so that it can be transferred to future generations.

It is these relationships that are being symbolically reenacted in the *balhats*, renewing ancestral relations to the land before the broader community. Thus, instead of the logic of time-space compression that drives capitalist expansion and continual investments in extractive infrastructure, the Wet'suwet'en legal order is directed by a logic of place-time extension.[69] Rather than constantly seeking to effect the annihilation of space by time, the lawful conduct of Wet'suwet'en authorities seeks to extend time through place, continually renewing connections to human and more-than-human kin. Maintaining genealogical lineages in the *balhats* reaffirms connections to the land that stretch from time immemorial to future generations.

It is, however, actually being on the land itself that connects Wet'suwet'en *yikh* members to their ancestral lineage. In the *Delgamuukw, Gisdaywa* trial, Layton described how she learned about the territory from her grandmother, Christine Holland, who had held the title Knedebeas before Layton, and led the Unist'ot'en from the 1950s until her passing in 1980.

> *We stayed out in the territory trapping, except for possibly three months during the summer when we went to Hagwilget to put up fish and go fishing...When we went out in the territory trapping before Christmas we would trap for marten, squirrels, and weasel, and then towards the springtime we would trap for beaver...They would smoke the beaver meat to use at a potlatch for the summer months, muskrats also.*[70]

Holland raised her family, including her grandchildren on Unist'ot'en territory, and it was these experiences that qualified Layton to become chief after her grandmother's passing.

Through their generations-long stable associations with particular territories, Wet'suwet'en *yikh* have knowledge about the land that allows them to observe the cumulative impacts of development in ways that settler processes of resource governance, which fragment regulatory oversight between different projects, agencies governing specific industries, and provincial and federal authorities, cannot.[71] As Kuokkanen argues, Indigenous epistemes are not simply remnants of the past but remain "indispensable tools for the pursuit of knowledge."[72] In their submissions to the JRP, the Office of the Wet'suwet'en stressed the importance of cumulative impact assessment, as "the additional impacts posed by the pipelines project would irreversibly and seriously damage territories and a people that have already been made vulnerable by development in the form of mines, forestry, pipelines, railways, highways and other roads, agriculture, and the privatization of lands."[73] For the Wet'suwet'en, these long-term environmental changes are particularly concerning because they erode the capacity of *yikh* to continue to use and maintain their relationships to their territories. This underpins why the Office of the Wet'suwet'en had not only fought against pipelines but also engaged in initiatives to improve the stewardship of the land, such as the establishment of the Morice Water Management Area. This dual impulse towards both land protection and restoration informed the creation and activities of the Unist'ot'en Camp.

At the Unist'ot'en Camp, Wet'suwet'en community members are supported to contribute to both the rejuvenation of the land and their own connection to the land. Freda Huson became heavily involved in the camp in order to reconnect to the territory where her great-grandmother and former hereditary chief of Unist'ot'en, Christine Holland, had raised her family. After a few years of splitting her time between the Unist'ot'en Camp and her job in Witset, Huson decided to move into the cabin by the Widzin Kwah to reestablish a permanent presence on the territory. The camp had a dual purpose: it served to block the route of proposed pipeline development and it created a space for Unist'ot'en and other Wet'suwet'en to reconnect with life on the land. The Unist'ot'en Camp protected the headwaters of the Widzin Kwah, key spawning grounds for the salmon that the Wet'suwet'en have harvested seasonally since time immemorial. As Leanne Betasamosake Simpson writes, "blockades are both a refusal and an affirmation." Speaking of the Wet'suwet'en hereditary chiefs, she describes these mobilizations as regenerative and affirmative: "An affirmation of a different political economy. A world built upon a different set of relationships and ethics. An affirmation of life."[74]

As the Unist'ot'en Camp has become more established, it has expanded with additional housing, gardens, and a healing lodge. Huson's niece, Karla Tait, serves as the director of clinical programming for the Unist'ot'en Healing Centre. Tait's doctoral research focused on working with Indigenous communities to build culturally appropriate psychological interventions. The intergenerational trauma caused by colonialism has been devastating: there are higher rates of unemployment, incarceration, addictions, and suicide among Indigenous people than the general public. The legacy of residential schooling and child apprehensions by provincial child and family welfare officials has disrupted kinship networks, severing connections between generations.[75] As Tait argues, "legacies of colonization disconnected [the Wet'suwet'en] from who we are as Indigenous people." Through the healing lodge, she hopes to help Indigenous people "return to some of our traditional teachings and land-based wellness practices of our ancestors."[76] Living onsite, clients have opportunities to reconnect to the land, harvesting medicines and picking berries in summer, trapping and tanning hides in winter. More than this, they have an opportunity to be immersed in a place celebrating the Witsuwit'en language, songs, stories, and dances. At its core, the Unist'ot'en Healing Centre aims to validate people's Indigenous identity and guides them to practice greater care for themselves, other community members, and the land.

Reconnecting with life on the land has served to renew kinship with past generations and the more-than-human world. "It's amazing," Tait describes, "the power that this land has, that the water has, the presence we can feel of our ancestors on this territory."77 Huson echoes the mutuality of land and cultural healing: "If we take care of our land, then the land will take care of us."78 Huson's late father, Dan Michell, who held the title Wigetimschol in the Tsayu, elaborated the importance of this type of connection to the land in the *Delgamuukw, Gisdaywa* trial: "We are brought up in those territory [sic] which we know that we belong to the land and the land belong to us. That's one way of putting it...And that is why we are taught to respect the land and everything that's in it."79 Indigenous resurgence, as Leanne Simpson theorizes, "must be concerned with the reattachment of our minds, bodies, and spirits to the network of relationships and ethical practices that generates grounded normativity."80 It also needs to guide the conduct of authorities who, Tait stresses, need "to not make a decision for the present that's going to hurt your future. We're always borrowing from our future generations."81

The Unist'ot'en Camp reasserts the vitality of ancestral connections to the land. Although it began as an initiative associated with a single *yikh* under the guidance of its hereditary chief Knedebeas, it has seeded effects that disseminate beyond their *yin tah*. As Tait describes, the camp's engagement with the intergenerational obligations guiding the conduct of Wet'suwet'en authorities has invited community members to think about the long-term impacts of development.

> *There's a lot of incentives for our communities to look at these industry partnerships for things like LNG or tar sands. It comes at a huge cost, and it's a cultural cost, it's an identity cost, essentially. It's asking communities who are at a disadvantage, really, to sign on for short term opportunities to feed their children, without allowing them to consider the impacts on their grandchildren, and the next generations to really have those opportunities to embrace their identity, and who they are, because so much of that, for us, is based on our land and our connection to the land and all the teachings.*82

The example of the Unist'ot'en Camp has incited broader conversations among the Wet'suwet'en that have led other *yikh* and *dïdikh* to publicly declare their opposition to pipelines in the *balhats*.

It also provided inspiration to the broader environmental movement, which has increasingly centred an analysis of colonialism in its activism.[83] As Clayton Thomas-Müller explains, Indigenous peoples are "the keystones in a hemispheric social movement strategy that could end the era of Big Oil and eventually usher in another paradigm from this current destructive age of free-market economics."[84] Indigenous mobilizations, including those of the Wet'suwet'en, invite people to rethink the geographies of responsibility that orient the conduct of environmental governance processes. As an embodiment of an Indigenous system of territorial governance that normalizes actions that uphold intergenerational responsibilities to the land rather than those that seek profit maximization in the short term, the Unist'ot'en are inspiring broader conversations about how Indigenous law can provide everyone with an alternative framework for relating to the land.

Of more immediate concern for the Wet'suwet'en, the Unist'ot'en Camp has pressed both the federal and provincial government to rethink how they approach the hereditary chiefs. In February 2020, Huson and Tait were among those arrested as the police enforced the injunction against Wet'suwet'en interference with the Coastal GasLink development.[85] Their arrest triggered national protests that ultimately forced the federal and provincial governments to engage in new negotiations with the Wet'suwet'en hereditary chiefs. In order to lift the solidarity blockades across the nation, the governments of British Columbia and Canada negotiated a new memorandum of understanding with the hereditary chiefs in which the signatories committed to negotiating shared jurisdiction. Thus, while the Coastal GasLink project is being built, governance relationships remain unsettled and under negotiation.

The 2020 memorandum of understanding was the first instance in which provincial authorities indicated their willingness to move away from the British Columbia treaty framework that sought to secure certainty for resource development through the effective extinguishment of Aboriginal title to the majority of the land base. The memorandum recognized the hereditary chiefs' authority over the territories and outlined a process for negotiating shared jurisdiction. In the agreement, the provincial and Canadian governments specifically affirm recognition that Wet'suwet'en traditional authorities hold territorial title and rights "under their system of governance."[86]

However, settler government recognition of the hereditary chiefs has been controversial. Elected band governments have vocally opposed the new framework, which would affect their capacity to negotiate pipeline agreements.[87] As their communities remain underfunded and their memberships remain underemployed, pipeline agreements represent a potentially vital source of revenue for band services and infrastructure, as well as the employment of band members. The industry-backed dissidents, who had earlier sought to sign project impact agreements through the Wet'suwet'en Matrilineal Coalition, continue to vocally oppose the hereditary chiefs, although they are a minority voice among the *diдikh*. The memorandum indicated that negotiating industry-Indigenous partnerships with Indian Act bands may not be sufficient to reconcile Indigenous interests with development. The memorandum also signalled a new settler government willingness to engage Indigenous governance traditions not simply as a historic residue to be removed, but as part of the future of resource management in British Columbia.

Going forward, monumental questions remain to be resolved, both among the different Wet'suwet'en sources of hereditary and band authority and between settler and Wet'suwet'en authorities.[88] It is uncertain how settler modes of government conduct, based on the normalization of commodity relations, can be melded with those of the hereditary chiefs and their obligations to past and future generations. It is an open question how legal paradigms that treat natural resources as commodities can be married to Wet'suwet'en responsibilities to the spirit of the land. Balancing the principles of Wet'suwet'en and Canadian law requires more than simply altering the distribution of benefits from resource exploitation. The hereditary chiefs have invited the Canadian and provincial governments to begin to reimagine their relationship to the land. The unfolding climate crisis shows that it is incumbent upon us to begin to shift our focus to long-term sustainability rather than short-term profitability. In this context, the hereditary chiefs' offer to incorporate settlers into shared jurisdiction with respect to Wet'suwet'en law can be understood as a gift; it is an invitation for all Canadians to build a more reciprocal relationship to the land that can be sustained into the future.

**Rethinking Development through the Wet'suwet'en Encounter**
Throughout this book, I have sought to demonstrate that the politics of development are not simply reducible to a colonial will. Instead, what emerges as development must be understood in terms of the entanglement of colonial power with Indigenous strategies of resistance and self-determination that work both against and alongside colonialism. Development has been contoured within a topography of Indigenous political claims as well as the more conventional colonial drives to accumulate wealth through the appropriation of nature. There is an extensive web of relations between various agents—including judges and hereditary chiefs, corporate ATK facilitators and Indigenous lands departments, pipeline contractors and Indigenous dreamers, educators and industrial labourers—that shapes development. This has resulted in the entwining of Indigeneity and colonialism, and the constitution of composite strategies to both secure regimes of resource extraction and ensure Indigenous well-being. However, the conjoining of colonial development and Indigenous empowerment remains a fragile assemblage based on a selective recognition of Indigenous claims. Although settler colonialism relies upon and reproduces particular logics of development, Indigenous peoples interject their own political projects to mobilize or block particular courses of development. Indigenous interventions have served to modify, reform, and even offset colonial development strategies, playing an important role in contouring the topography of actually existing development. The integration of Indigenous regimes of knowledge and practice within colonial regimes relies on screening out articulations of Indigeneity that are incommensurate with colonial plans for industrial

development. This excess Indigeneity presents latent possibilities for transcending the limits of circumscribed colonial development strategies.

Through investigations into different initiatives and forms of collective action related to courtroom litigation, traditional use research, industrial partnership, resource governance hearings, and political struggle, I have diagramed how new relationships are being forged and contested through diffuse networks. These relationships, while often acting to constrain or condition Indigenous life projects along particular avenues, have not simply acted to repress Indigeneity. Instead through constituting spaces of negotiation between Indigeneity and colonialism, contemporary power relations have been both productive and coercive. Reformed colonial regimes have opened avenues to recognize and revivify particular forms of Indigenous authority, territoriality, and subjectivity. Conversely, Indigenous peoples have worked to levy conditions on development that protect their interests in new development projects on their lands. They have also fought to stop development when they determine a development project is irreconcilable with the world that they want to build.

My study has focused on Wet'suwet'en relations to colonial power. However, the Wet'suwet'en struggle with settler colonialism has much to say about the entanglements of colonial power and Indigeneity in general. In this book, I have sought to think through the complex relations between the infrastructures of fossil capitalism, settler governmental mechanisms of reconciling Indigenous peoples to development, and the resurgence of Indigenous legal orders. Critical scholarship needs to approach accumulation by dispossession—an immanent condition of possibility for capitalism in settler colonies—as ongoing, both facilitated and mediated by settler legal frameworks. Fundamentally, settler governance is driven by the production of opportunities for accumulation, and the subsumption of questions of securing the well-being of the population to the expansion of capital and commodity flows. It relies upon continually effecting accumulation by dispossession, displacing Indigenous peoples from their lands. To do this, settler authorities need to replace Indigenous legal orders, which relate to the world as embedded within networks of kinship, with a colonial legal order that approaches the natural world as an economic resource to exploit. But the imposition of settler law has never been complete; it is imperfect, inchoate, insecure. Indigenous people remain and continue to advance challenges that alter the workings of contemporary capitalism; therefore, accumulation by dispossession is not a fait accompli. Its enactment in the present must confront Indigenous contestation. In such contests, there is not simply one law but multiple, and the conflicts among these laws are constitutive of political economic relations.

Theoretically and methodologically, my approach is informed by an appreciation for ontological pluralism. I have attempted to place colonial and Indigenous life projects and practices of worldmaking in parallax. From one angle, I have examined the colonial exercise of distinct yet interpenetrated modalities of sovereign prohibition, disciplinary prescription, and governmental regulation. Colonial sovereign power works to suspend processes of Indigenous political becoming beyond defined limits; disciplinary power normalizes particular forms of Indigenous being; governmental regulation works both to minimally protect a geography of Indigenous traditions and to foster emergent processes of Indigenous becoming congruent with the ontology of capitalist development. Responding to Indigenous demands, colonial regimes have been remade, altering the responsibilities associated with colonial forms of authority, the processes of territorial governance, and the operations of regimes of subjectification.

However, Indigeneity is not bound to colonial frames, and there are distinct trajectories of Indigenous becoming in the present, endlessly opening spaces of negotiation. Forms of Indigenous conduct remain unreconciled with colonial regimes of discipline and governmentality. This state of irreconciliation constitutes a foundation for Indigenous authorities to advance claims that problematize those of settler authorities acting in the name of the colonial sovereign. The spaces of negotiation and the demands for recognition produced through Indigenous activism have worked to call forth new colonial strategies of engagement. Throughout the book, I have brought forward examples of how relations between the settler state and Indigeneity are punctuated by moments of both resistance and reconciliation. This cyclic movement is, I argue, configured through the interaction and imbrication of colonial regimes of authority, territoriality, and subjectification with those of Indigenous peoples. It is a cycle of consultations, contestations, and convergences that remains necessarily unfinished, endlessly emerging to constitute the present and future.

Resource extraction is thus regulated not simply through state interventions into the domain of political economy to secure the circulation of goods, but also through the interpolation of Indigenous concerns into resource governance. This has resulted in the entwining of Indigeneity and colonialism, and the constitution of composite strategies to both secure regimes of resource extraction and ensure Indigenous well-being. An emergent regime of knowledge associated with Indigenous traditions has served to condition development, providing protections for these traditions in the interstices of development, albeit within a framework of resource governance that continues to prioritize mobilizing resource flows over protecting Indigenous territories. Further, the settler governmental apparatuses regulating development have required industry to integrate Indigenous peoples into industrial labour processes. Disciplinary regimes train Indigenous workers to participate in industrial development projects. The contemporary integration of Indigenous labour finds echoes in the earlier reliance of colonial economies on Indigenous labour in the fur trade, as well as in early resource economies.

However, the crafted convergence of Indigeneity with strategies for resource extraction has not placed questions of sovereignty in abeyance. The conjoining of colonial development and Indigenous empowerment remains a fragile assemblage constituted on the basis of a selective recognition of Indigenous claims, ignoring those that are irreconcilable with colonial extractivism. This excess Indigeneity, I argue, remains both a foundational exception—that which must be excluded to permit the unfolding of fossil capitalism in a settler society—and the immanent possibility for different modes of life. Indigeneity is not simply displaced. It remains as a potent force creating possibilities for a different future, one that values intergenerational connections over accelerating processes of resource extraction. As development plans aim to traffic resources from and through Indigenous territories, Indigenous peoples continue to raise questions regarding who possesses the sovereign authority to decide the course of development on their traditional lands. The absent presence of Indigenous sovereignty demands that we examine the constraints of the strategies of convergence that have been crafted by settler authorities. It also continues to open spaces of negotiation through which new relations can emerge. There is no simple succession in which a new relationship finally settles old conflicts over colonial sovereignty.

Fundamentally, *Indigenous Legalities, Pipeline Viscosities* insists on the need to overturn entrenched colonial frames that position Indigenous peoples solely in relation to the time before contact. It is true that the Wet'suwet'en *yikh* have lineages stretching back thousands of years, but their relationship to colonialism is of relatively recent vintage, and it is active. Colonialism does not simply disappear Indigenous peoples or traditions, but it does make Aboriginal rights appear in controlled ways. "Aboriginality" is the name of the political condition produced through the submergence of Indigenous peoples within colonizing states. State recognition is not decolonizing; Leanne Simpson describes it as "superficial dances of reconciliation and dialogue" that allow Indigenous peoples to "negotiate for the cheap gifts of economic and political inclusion."[89] As I have demonstrated, colonial politics of recognition can in fact serve to relegitimize processes of extractive development and Indigenous dispossession. The solution is not an imagined return to an imagined precolonial purity of Indigenous traditions. Instead, it requires renewing Indigenous practices of jurisdiction in the present and ending the presumption of settler supremacy over Indigenous authorities. Decolonial challenges assert different modes of lawful conduct and create ongoing spaces of negotiation to reformulate relationships, potentially opening horizons for futures beyond the colonial present of fossil capitalism.

# Appendix 1

*The Five Wet'suwet'en Dïdikh and Their Yikh, Chiefs, and Other Hereditary Titles*

DÏDIKH AND YIKH FORM THE BASIC STRUCTURE of Wet'suwet'en governance through the *balhats*. To each *yikh* belongs a chiefly title that is inherited by *yikh* members along kinship lines. Other hereditary titles are similarly inherited.

Where an older spelling was used in legal proceedings or other official documents, the older spelling is given first, with Hargus orthography in parentheses. Note that other spellings may exist.

| Dïdikh | Yikh | Chief | Selected Other Dïdikh Hereditary Titles |
|---|---|---|---|
| Gilserhyu (C'ilhts'ëkhyu) | Kayax (K'iy Yikh) | Samooh (Simuyh) | Satsan (Sats'an) |
|  | Yex T'sa Wilk'us / Unist'ot'en (Yikh Tsawilhggis) | Knedebeas (Nedïbïs) |  |
|  | Yat'sowitan (Yikh Ts'iwit'an') | Goohlaht (Gguhlat) |  |
| Gitdumden (Gidimt'en) | Anaskaski (Insggisgï) | Medeek (Midïk) | Dunen |
|  | Cas Yex (Cas Yikh) | Woos (Wos) | Gu'a'dik' |
|  | Kiyaxwinits (Këyikh Winïts) | Gisdaywa (Gisdewe) | Gyolo'ght (C'oligit) Likhdïlye |

| Dïdikh | Yikh | Chief | Selected Other Dïdikh Hereditary Titles |
|---|---|---|---|
| Laksilyu (Likhsilyu) | Ginehklayax (C'inegh Lhay Yikh) | Hag Wil Negh (Hagwilnekhlh) | Maxlaxlex (Mikhlikhlekh) T'sek'ot (Dzïggot) |
| | Kwanbeahyax (Kwin Begh Yikh) | Wah Tah Kwets (Ut'akhkw'its) | |
| | Tsee K'al K'e Yex (Tsë Kal K'iyikh) | Wah Tah K'eght (Ut'akhgit) | |
| Laksamshu (Likhts'amisyu) | Medziyax (Misdzï Yikh) | Kloumkhun (Lho'imggin) | Hagwilakw (Hagwil'awh) Toghestiy (To Ghestiy) |
| | Sayax (Sa Yikh) | Smogelgem (Smogilhgim) | |
| Tsayu | Djakanyax (Tsa Kën Yikh) | Kweese (Kw'is) | Lilloos (Lilus) |
| | Namox Yax (Namoks Yikh) | Namox (Namoks; John Ridsdale, who holds this title in 2023, spells this Na'Moks) | Misalos Sa'un (Sa'on) Wigetimschol (Wigidimsts'ol) Wilat |

Adapted from Morin, *Niwhts'ide'ni Hibi'it'en*, 393; McCreary, *Shared Histories*, 29.

# Appendix 2
## Wet'suwet'en Bands

BANDS ARE GOVERNANCE GROUPS designated and recognized by the Canadian government under the Indian Act. Band names are given in current usage first, with relevant previously used names in parentheses.

| Band | Notes |
| --- | --- |
| Nee-Tahi-Buhn | Established 1984; originally an amalgamation of the families associated with the Francois Lake, Uncha Lake, and Skin Tyee reserve lands. In 2000, a group broke away from Nee-Tahi Buhn and became the Skin Tyee band. |
| Omineca Band | Established 1959; an amalgamation of the families associated with the Broman Lake, Burns Lake, Decker Lake, Francois Lake, Maxan Lake, Uncha Lake, and Skin Tyee reserve lands. Omineca dissolved in 1984, becoming the Broman Lake Band and Nee-Tahi-Buhn. |
| Skin Tyee | Broke away from Nee-Tahi-Buhn in 2000. |
| Ts'il Kaz Koh (Burns Lake Band) | Reserves initially surveyed 1906. They were reviewed and reduced in size by the Royal Commission in 1915–1916. |

| Band | Notes |
| --- | --- |
| Hagwilget Village (Tsë Kyah) | Historic village established in the 1820s. In 1891, it was surveyed by the Indian Land Commissioner and designated as reserve land. |
| Wet'suwet'en First Nation (Broman Lake Band) | Established 1984; an amalgamation of the families associated with the Broman Lake, Decker Lake, and Maxan Lake reserve lands. |
| Witset First Nation (Moricetown Band) | Historic village dating back thousands of years. In 1891, it was surveyed by the Indian Land Commissioner and designated as reserve land. |

# Glossary

*Wet'suwet'en Place Names, Witsuwit'en Terms,
and Gitxsanimaax Terms*

**Wet'suwet'en Place Names**

Names are given in the Hargus orthography.

Bïwinï: Owen Lake
Bïwinï Kwah: Owen Creek
C'iggiz: Broman Lake
C'inu'iy Ïkwah: Canyon Creek
Honcagh Bin: Uncha Lake
Misdzï Kwah: Parrott Creek
Natl'ënlï Bin: Nadina Lake
Netanlï Bin: Skins Lake
Nin: Babine Lake area
Nïntah Bin: Francois Lake
Tacot: Tyee Lake
Tasdlegh: Maxan Lake
Tselh K'iz: Tsichgass Lake
Ts'ëlkiy' Kwah: Lamprey Creek
T'aco: Decker Lake
U'in Ts'ah C'ikwah: Babine River
Widzin Bin: Morice Lake
Widzin Kwah: Morice and Bulkley rivers

**Witsuwit'en Terms**

Terms are given in the Hargus orthography.

'anuc niwh'it'en: the proper conduct of lawful relations
balhats: feast, potlatch; traditional governance ceremonies through which *yikh* passed down responsibility for names and the *yin tah* to future generations
cin k'ikh (older: *kungax*): literally, a trail of song; the dramatization of a personal crest or name
cis: down feathers, plume; a symbol of the law
dïdikh: a clan; a matrilineal network of related *yikh* who cohost *balhats* together
sinelh: rattle cry; a sacred symbol for the law
wiggus: respect; a term that implies awareness of obligations and responsibilities to kin, including ancestors and future generations, and the land
Witsuwit'en: the people of the upper drainage, a contrast that distinguished the Wet'suwet'en from the Dakelh living to the south; in this book, the term is reserved to refer to the language of the Wet'suwet'en
yikh (older: *yex*): a house; a matrilineal kinship group that historically resided together; each *yikh*, along with other related *yikh*, belongs to a *dïdikh*
yin tah: territory; emphasizes the connection of people, through proper ceremonies, to territory, by modifying the root *yin*, which means earth, to highlight its connection to a particular people

**Gitxsanimaax Terms**

adaawk: oral history of a *wilp*
amxsiwaa: white settlers; a term for driftwood that has lost its colour from long travel
Gitxsanimaax: the language of the Gitxsan
limx'ooy: dirge song
p'teex: a clan; a *p'teex* is made up of two or more *wilp*
wilp: a house; two or more *wilp* are in a *p'teex*

# Notes

**Introduction**
1. Harper, "Address by Prime Minister."
2. Canadian Association of Petroleum Producers, *Canadian Crude Oil*, 2.
3. Harper, "Address by Prime Minister."
4. Hoberg, "Battle over Oil Sands."
5. Indigenous and Northern Affairs Canada, "Population Characteristics Witset First Nation."
6. Culhane, *Pleasure of the Crown*.
7. Quoted in Office of the Wet'suwet'en, "Event Galvanizes Opposition." Kloum Khun is how the hereditary chief's name is spelled in the press release. Lho'imggin is the updated spelling according to Sharon Hargus, following her work in *Witsuwit'en Grammar* and *Witsuwit'en Hibikinic*. From here forward, I will refer to Hargus's work simply as the Hargus orthography.
8. Sterritt, "Unflinching Resistance," 277.
9. Coulthard, *Red Skin, White Masks*, 7.
10. L.B. Simpson, *Dancing on Our Turtle's Back*; L.B. Simpson, *As We Have Always Done*.
11. Berger, *Northern Frontier*, 1.
12. Berger, *Northern Frontier*, xxii.
13. Limerick, *Legacy of Conquest*; Barman, *West Beyond the West*; Furniss, *Burden of History*; Perry, *On the Edge of Empire*; Edmonds, *Urbanizing Frontiers*.
14. Notably, Turner's version of American history focused on the distinctive break between American society and its European antecedence. This differed in important respects from contemporary Canadian accounts that positioned its national development explicitly within the legacy of British imperialism. However, classical American and Canadian traditions of frontier theorizing share presumptions about the finality of colonial displacements of Indigenous

peoples. Thinking beyond the methodological nationalism that conventionally separates US and Canadian studies, I want to emphasize shared investments in normalizing settler possession. For my purposes, Turner presents an iconic articulation of how frontier development was imagined in both settler states. F.J. Turner, "Significance of the Frontier"; F.J. Turner, "The West," 293.

15. R. White, *Middle Ground*.
16. Wolfe, "Settler Colonialism"; Coulthard, *Red Skin, White Masks*; A. Simpson, *Mohawk Interruptus*.
17. Berger, *Northern Frontier*, xxv.
18. Tennant, *Aboriginal Peoples and Politics*; C. Harris, *Making Native Space*.
19. Culhane, *Pleasure of the Crown*; P.D. Mills, *For Future Generations*; Hoffman and Joseph, *Song of the Earth*.
20. The standard legal citation of the case references it as *Delgamuukw v. British Columbia*. In the footnotes, I use standard citation practices so readers can more easily find my sources. The spelling of Gisdaywa in the extended case citation reflects the way it was spelled in court. Gisdewe is the updated spelling according to the Hargus orthography.
21. *Delgamuukw v. British Columbia*, [1997] 3 S.C.R. 1010, para. 186.
22. Lippert, *Beyond the Nass Valley*; McKee, *Treaty Talks in British Columbia*; Penikett, *Reconciliation*.
23. Blackburn, "Searching for Guarantees"; Connauton, "Reimagining BC Modern Treaties"; Woolford, *Between Justice and Certainty*; Manuel, *Unsettling Canada*.
24. McCreary and Turner, "Did the Protests Work?"
25. Popowich, "National Energy Board as Intermediary"; Mullan, "Supreme Court and the Duty to Consult"; Lambrecht, *Aboriginal Consultation*; Promislow, "Irreconcilable?"; Newman, *Revisiting the Duty to Consult*.
26. McGregor, "Coming Full Circle"; Christie, "Culture, Self-Determination and Colonialism"; Borrows, *Drawing Out Law*; Napoleon, Provost, and Sheppard, "Thinking About Indigenous Legal Orders."
27. A. Mills, *Eagle Down*; Brody, *Other Side of Eden*; Daly, *Our Box Was Full*.
28. Johnson, *Trail of Story*, 4.
29. Coulthard, *Red Skin, White Masks*, 13.
30. McCreary and Turner, "Contested Scales"; Temper, "Blocking Pipelines"; McCreary, "Between the Commodity and the Gift."
31. Blomley, "Shut the Province Down"; Napoleon, "Behind the Blockades"; Christie, "Indigenous Authority"; Pasternak, "Jurisdiction and Settler Colonialism"; Belanger and Lackenbauer, *Blockades or Breakthroughs?*; A.J. Barker and Ross, "Reoccupation and Resurgence."
32. Simpson theorizes this form of self-recognition specifically in relation to the work of Glen Coulthard. L.B. Simpson, *As We Have Always Done*, 65.
33. Bradshaw, *Global Energy Dilemmas*.

34. Haley, "From Staples Trap to Carbon Trap"; MacNeil, "Canadian Environmental Policy"; Fast, "Stapled to the Front Door"; MacNeil, "Decline of Canadian Environmental Regulation"; McCreary, "Beyond Token Recognition"; Peyton and Franks, "New Nature of Things?"
35. Pachauri et al., *Climate Change 2014*, 2.
36. International Energy Agency, *World Energy Outlook 2015*, 20.
37. The requirement for a 23 percent reduction in oil usage is calculated based a scenario in which global carbon dioxide emissions are capped at 450 parts per million. This would require a projected reduction in global oil consumption from 4,194 million tonnes in 2012 to 3,242 million tonnes in 2040. International Energy Agency, *World Energy Outlook 2014*, 56.
38. Hansen et al., "Target Atmospheric $CO_2$."
39. Charpentier, Bergerson, and MacLean, "Understanding the Canadian Oil Sands"; Swart and Weaver, "Alberta Oil Sands and Climate"; Englander, Bharadwaj, and Brandt, "Historical Trends in Greenhouse Gas Emissions"; Cai et al., "Well-to-Wheels Greenhouse Gas Emissions."
40. T. Mitchell, *Carbon Democracy*.
41. Huber, *Lifeblood*.
42. P.G. Harris, *What's Wrong with Climate Politics*; Harrison, "Federalism and Climate Policy Innovation."
43. Bradshaw, *Global Energy Dilemmas*.
44. International Energy Agency, *World Energy Outlook 2014*, 23.
45. Levant, *Ethical Oil*, 10.
46. Alberta Energy Regulator, *ST98*, 3.
47. Canadian Energy Research Institute, *Canadian Economic Impacts*, ix.
48. Bridge and Le Billon, *Oil*.
49. International Energy Agency, *World Energy Outlook 2013*, 421.
50. Bridge and Wood, "Less Is More."
51. D. Harvey, *Limits to Capital*, 87.
52. Angevine, "Canadian Oil Transport Conundrum," 20.
53. International Energy Agency, *World Energy Outlook 2014*, 62.
54. Chastko, *Developing Alberta's Oil Sands*; W. Marsden, *Stupid to the Last Drop*; Clarke, *Tar Sands Showdown*; Nikiforuk, *Tar Sands*; Carter, *Fossilized*.
55. J. Simpson, Jaccard, and Rivers, *Hot Air*.
56. Glenn and Otero, "Canada and the Kyoto Protocol."
57. Gibson, "In Full Retreat"; Kirchhoff and Tsuji, "Reading between the Lines"; MacNeil, "Canadian Environmental Policy"; McCreary, "Beyond Token Recognition"; Salomons and Hoberg, "Setting Boundaries of Participation"; Peyton and Franks, "New Nature of Things?"
58. Stanford, "Staples, Deindustrialization, and Foreign Investment"; Haley, "From Staples Trap to Carbon Trap"; Fast, "Stapled to the Front Door"; MacNeil, "Decline of Canadian Environmental Regulation."
59. International Energy Agency, *World Energy Outlook 2014*, 122.

60. Hoberg, "Battle over Oil Sands"; Le Billon and Vandecasteyen, "(Dis)Connecting Alberta's Tar Sands"; Veltmeyer and Bowles, "Extractivist Resistance."
61. Weis et al., "Introduction," 3.
62. McCreary, "Crisis in the Tar Sands."
63. Moore et al., "Catching the Brass Ring"; Galay, "Impact of Spatial Price Differences"; Galay, "Are Crude Oil Markets Cointegrated?"
64. Canadian Association of Petroleum Producers, "Canada's Role," 14.
65. Shervill, *Smithers*; Kruisselbrink, *Smithers*; McCreary, *Shared Histories*.
66. Glavin, *Death Feast in Dimlahamid*; Furniss, *Burden of History*.
67. McCreary, "Treaties Great Deal for Non-Natives"; McCreary, "Settler Treaty Rights."
68. Here I am gesturing to research that seeks to unveil the "weapons of the weak"—subaltern strategies of escaping the power of the state. Scott, *Weapons of the Weak*.
69. Kovach, *Indigenous Methodologies*; Wilson, *Research Is Ceremony*.
70. McCreary and Murnaghan, "Remixed Methodologies."
71. McCreary, *Shared Histories*.
72. Massey, "Global Sense of Place," 28.
73. Tsing, *Friction*, 1.
74. Fabian, *Time and the Other*; Rifkin, *Beyond Settler Time*; A. Mitchell, "Revitalizing Laws"; Gergan and McCreary, "Disrupting Infrastructures."

## 1 | The First Century

1. Limerick, *Legacy of Conquest*.
2. Snelgrove, Dhamoon, and Corntassel, "Unsettling Settler Colonialism."
3. King, "Godzilla vs. Post-Colonial," 185.
4. Paul, *We Were Not the Savages*, 7.
5. *Cin k'ikh* is often spelled *kungax* in older orthographies. A. Mills, *Eagle Down*, 122.
6. Brody, *Other Side of Eden*, 197.
7. Johnson, *Trail of Story*.
8. In the Hargus orthography, Satsan is spelled Sats'an.
9. George, "Foreword," vi.
10. Sterritt, "Unflinching Resistance," 267.
11. Whyte, "Indigenous Science (Fiction)," 229.
12. Sterritt, "Unflinching Resistance," 267.
13. Borrows, *Recovering Canada*, 88.
14. George, "Foreword," viii.
15. George, x.
16. Borrows, *Canada's Indigenous Constitution*.
17. Dorsett and McVeigh, *Jurisdiction*, 35.
18. Barkan, *Corporate Sovereignty*, 28.
19. Innis, *Fur Trade in Canada*.

20. Stern, "'Bundles of Hyphens,'" 23.
21. McCreary, "Historicizing the Encounter," 174.
22. Roberts, *Modern Firm*, 7.
23. Van Kirk, *Many Tender Ties*.
24. Venema, "Under the Protection of a Principal Man"; Milligan and McCreary, "Inscription, Innocence, and Invisibility."
25. Innis, *Fur Trade in Canada*, 134.
26. Ray, *Indians in the Fur Trade*.
27. J.R. Miller, *Compact, Contract, Covenant*.
28. Borrows, "Wampum at Niagara."
29. Borrows and Coyle, *Right Relationship*.
30. Rich, *Fur Trade and the Northwest*.
31. Campbell, *North West Company*, 1.
32. Roberts, *Modern Firm*.
33. Innis, *Fur Trade in Canada*.
34. Berland, *North of Empire*, 74.
35. Turkel, *Archive of Place*; Erickson, *Canoe Nation*; Dean, *Inheriting a Canoe Paddle*.
36. Mackenzie, *Voyages*.
37. Morice, *History of the Northern Interior*, 54-72.
38. Morice, 122.
39. The visit is documented in a fur trader's memoir. Peter Skene Ogden, a former Nor'Wester and HBC trader, was posthumously attributed authorship of this memoir, but the timelines don't line up. Ogden returned to London in 1822 to lobby for the retention of his job after the merger of the HBC and NWC. In 1823, he was appointed to the reorganized company and assigned to Spokane House. It is unlikely that he would have visited Witset in 1823. Fur Trader, *Traits of American-Indian Life*, 76-106; T.C. Elliott, "Peter Skene Ogden."
40. Ray, *Indians in the Fur Trade*.
41. Fisher, *Contact and Conflict*.
42. On Wet'suwet'en social relations, see Jenness, "Carrier Indians of the Bulkley River"; A. Mills, *Eagle Down*; Daly, *Our Box Was Full*; Morin, *Niwhts'ide'ni Hibi'it'en*. On the closely related Nedut'en, see Fiske and Patrick, *Cis Dideen Kat*. On the neighbouring Gitxsan, see Cove, "Gitksan Traditional Concept of Land Ownership"; P.D. Mills, *For Future Generations*. On the Tsimshian, see Roth, *Becoming Tsimshian*.
43. Daly, *Our Box Was Full*, 198.
44. The spelling of the *dïdikh* names here accords with those that were recorded in the *Delgamuukw, Gisdaywa* trial proceedings. Using the Hargus orthography, the names are respectively, Gidimt'en, C'ilhts'ëkhyu, Likhsilyu, Likhts'amisyu, and Tsayu.
45. Budhwa and McCreary, "Reconciling Cultural Resource Management," 200.

46. Daly, *Our Box Was Full*, 46.
47. Daly, 252–254.
48. Daly, 46.
49. Trusler, "Footsteps amongst the Berries," 54.
50. L.M.J. Gottesfeld, "Aboriginal Burning for Vegetation Management"; Trusler and Johnson, "'Berry Patch' as a Kind of Place."
51. McCreary, "Between the Commodity and the Gift."
52. Fur Trader, *Traits of American-Indian Life*, 96.
53. Fur Trader, 97.
54. This is almost certainly Smogelgem, or Smolgelgem as the name is spelled in the *Delgamuukw, Gisdaywa* proceedings. It is spelled Smogilhgim in the Hargus orthography. Fur Trader, 98.
55. Fur Trader, 92.
56. Daly, *Our Box Was Full*, 211–236.
57. Morin, *Niwhts'ide'ni Hibi'it'en*, 20.
58. Harrington, "Eulachon and the Grease Trails"; Ryan, "Territorial Jurisdiction."
59. Barbeau, *Pathfinders in the North Pacific*; Fisher, *Contact and Conflict*; S. Marsden and Galois, "Tsimshian, Hudson's Bay Company."
60. Hargus, *Witsuwit'en Grammar*.
61. A. Mills, *Eagle Down*, 120–34.
62. A. Mills, 123–25.
63. M. Cassidy, *Gathering Place*.
64. Mulhall, *Will to Power*, 55–56. Another name for Witset is Kyah Wiget, or Këyikh Wigit following the Hargus orthography, meaning old or abandoned village, referring to the long period during which it was unoccupied.
65. Ray, "Creating the Image of the Savage."
66. Quoted in Ray, "Fur Trade History," 303.
67. Ray, 305.
68. Warkentin, *Canadian Exploration Literature*.
69. Cail, *Land, Man, and the Law*; Bhandar, *Colonial Lives of Property*.
70. Barbeau, *Pathfinders in the North Pacific*; Clayton, *Islands of Truth*.
71. Hoogeveen, "Sovereign Intentions."
72. Ferguson, *James Douglas*.
73. Hoogeveen, "Sovereign Intentions."
74. Tennant, *Aboriginal Peoples and Politics*, 10–16.
75. J. Stevenson, *Trail of Two Telegraphs*; Mynett, *River of Mists*, 24–37.
76. R.G. Harvey, *Carving the Western Path*, 26; Mynett, *River of Mists*, 54–57.
77. Large, *Skeena*, 44–45; Mynett, *River of Mists*, 38–53.
78. McHarg and Cassidy, *Before Roads and Rails*.
79. Foster, "The Queen's Law."
80. Mynett, *Murders on the Skeena*.
81. M. Cassidy, *Skeena River Uprising*; Barbeau, *Downfall of Temlaham*.

82. Galois, "Gitxsan Law and Settler Disorder."
83. Cannon, "Revisiting Histories of Legal Assimilation."
84. Minutes of Decision: Hagwilget Indians, taken by P. O'Reilly, 19 September 1891, vol. 20, 107-111, UBCIC Federal Collection (hereafter cited as Minutes of Decision: Hagwilget); Minutes of Decision: Hazelton Indians, taken by P. O'Reilly, 29 September 1891, vol. 20, 113-114, UBCIC Federal Collection (hereafter cited as Minutes of Decision: Hazelton).
85. B. Barker and McCreary, "Any Indian Woman Marrying."
86. Bracken, *Potlatch Papers*.
87. R.E. Loring to Deputy Superintendent General of Indian Affairs D.C. Scott., 26 June 1919, RG10, vol. 7126, file 971/3-5, file pt. 1, LAC.
88. McCreary, *Shared Histories*, 61.
89. McCreary, 109-10.
90. Pasternak, "Fiscal Body of Sovereignty."
91. Cail, *Land, Man, and the Law*.
92. Gauvreau, "Exploration Survey of New Caledonia."
93. Gordon, *Made to Measure*.
94. Tennant, *Aboriginal Peoples and Politics*, 39-65; C. Harris, *Making Native Space*, 73-261.
95. Tennant, *Aboriginal Peoples and Politics*, 26-52; Galois, "History of the Upper Skeena," 139-65.
96. D.C. Harris, *Landing Native Fisheries*, 34-105.
97. Minutes of Decision: Hagwilget, vol. 20, 107-111, UBCIC Federal Collection.
98. Minutes of Decision: Hazelton Indians, vol 20, 113-114, UBCIC Federal Collection.
99. McCreary, *Shared Histories*, 38.
100. O'Reilly quoted in Morin, *Niwhts'ide'ni Hibi'it'en*, 284.
101. Galois, "History of the Upper Skeena," 140.
102. Loring quoted in M. Cassidy, *Gathering Place*, 24.
103. Sterritt, "Unflinching Resistance."
104. D.C. Harris, *Fish, Law, and Colonialism*, 14-78, 186-216.
105. Muszynski, *Cheap Wage Labour*.
106. D.C. Harris, *Fish, Law, and Colonialism*, 55-58.
107. D.C. Harris, 66.
108. D.C. Harris, 79-126.
109. Correspondence from A.W. Vowel, 2 June 1905, RG10 vol. 1583, file no. 129, LAC.
110. D.C. Harris, *Fish, Law, and Colonialism*, 111-13.
111. Talbot, *New Garden of Canada*, 249.
112. C. Harris, *Resettlement of British Columbia*, 183, 184.
113. Leonard, *A Thousand Blunders*.
114. Kruisselbrink, *Smithers*.
115. *Smithers: Grand Truck Pacific*, 9.

116. Shervill, *Smithers*.
117. D.C. Harris, *Fish, Law, and Colonialism*, 174-75.
118. Lutz, *Makuk*, 261.
119. Prince Rupert Forest District quoted in L.M.J. Gottesfeld, "Aboriginal Burning for Vegetation Management" 179.
120. Sinclair, Wilson, and Littlechild, *Honouring the Truth*.
121. Morin, *Niwhts'ide'ni Hibi'it'en*, 264-74.
122. Milloy, *A National Crime*.
123. Sinclair, Wilson, and Littlechild, *Honouring the Truth*.
124. Kelm, *Colonizing Bodies*, 66-67.
125. McCreary, *Shared Histories*, 62-63.
126. Fontaine, *Broken Circle*.
127. McCreary, *Shared Histories*.
128. Lutz, *Makuk*.
129. Lutz, 23.
130. Knight, *Indians at Work*, 125.
131. Tennant, *Aboriginal Peoples and Politics*, 96-98; Galois, "The History of the Upper Skeena," 152-153; C. Harris, *Making Native Space*, 228-248; P.D. Mills, *For Future Generations*, 52-54.
132. Morin, *Niwhts'ide'ni Hibi'it'en*, 175.
133. Morin, 308-309.
134. Morin, 311-312.
135. Sam, "Power and Equality."
136. Morin, *Niwhts'ide'ni Hibi'it'en*, 310.
137. Morin, 311.
138. Wah Tah Kwets is spelled Ut'akhkw'its in the Hargus orthography.
139. Royal Commission on Indian Affairs for the Province of British Columbia Meeting with the Moricetown Band, 26 April 1915, Babine Agency Testimony, 68, OHAB-UBCIC; Proceedings of the Supreme Court of British Columbia, 26 May 1989, 16897, UBC-OC *Delgamuukw*. (BC Supreme Court proceedings from this archive hereafter cited as BCSC Proceedings along with their date).
140. Royal Commission on Indian Affairs for the Province of British Columbia Meeting with the Moricetown Band, 26 April 1915, Babine Agency Testimony, 65-67, OHAB-UBCIC.
141. Peters, *Canyon Creek*, 28.
142. Morin, *Niwhts'ide'ni Hibi'it'en*, 303-4; McCreary, *Shared Histories*, 43.
143. Morin, *Niwhts'ide'ni Hibi'it'en*, 304-306; McCreary, *Shared Histories*, 43.
144. A. Mills, "Hang Onto These Words," 320, 322, 408-9.
145. Tennant, *Aboriginal Peoples and Politics*, 114.
146. Jenness, *Indians of Canada*, 368.
147. McDonald, "Nineteenth-Century Economy of the Tsimshian."
148. Lutz, *Makuk*, 210.
149. Lutz, 210.

150. Lutz, 216.
151. Groot et al., *Chronicles of Smithers*, 49-51; Morin, *Niwhts'ide'ni Hibi'it'en*, 317; McCreary, *Shared Histories*, 79-80.
152. Hudson, "Traplines and Timber," 141.
153. Mullins, "Changes in Location and Structure."
154. Hak, *Capital and Labour*, 36-37.
155. McCreary, *Shared Histories*, 80, 137.
156. McCreary, 76.
157. Daly, *Our Box Was Full*, 254-258.
158. A. Mills, *Eagle Down*, 70; Daly, *Our Box Was Full*, 254-256; A. Mills, "Hang Onto These Words," 53-58; Morin, *Niwhts'ide'ni Hibi'it'en*, 219-220; McCreary, *Shared Histories*, 76.
159. McCreary, *Shared Histories*, 82-83.
160. Daly, *Our Box Was Full*, 175.
161. Napoleon, "Ayook," 83-91.
162. Rossiter, "Producing Provincial Space."
163. McCreary, *Shared Histories*, 82.
164. Davenport-Hines, *Universal Man*.
165. Morin, *Niwhts'ide'ni Hibi'it'en*, 334.
166. Sam, "Power and Equality."
167. Sam, 41.
168. Fiske and Patrick, *Cis Dideen Kat*, 120.
169. Windsor and McVey, "Annihilation"; Gergan and McCreary, "Disrupting Infrastructures."
170. Lawton, "Kemano-Kitimat."
171. Boyer, "Kitimat, Canada's Aluminum Titan," 384.
172. J. Wood, *Home to the Nechako*, 41-43.
173. Troy quoted in Larsen, "The Micropolitics of Storytelling," 88.
174. Hartman, "Impacts of Growth in Resource Use."
175. B. Christensen, *Too Good to Be True*, 120.
176. Christensen, 121.
177. Morin, *Niwhts'ide'ni Hibi'it'en*, 333.
178. Robinson, *New Industrial Towns*.
179. Myers, "Incredible Bid for Aluminum," 3.
180. Boyer, "Kitimat, Canada's Aluminum Titan," 384.
181. BC Hydro Power Pioneers, *Gaslights to Gigawatts*.
182. Gergan and McCreary, "Disrupting Infrastructures."
183. A.S. Gottesfeld and Rabnett, "Skeena Fish Populations," 380.
184. Lutz, *Makuk*, 261-62; *Interior News*, "Indians Air Grievances"; *Interior News*, "Illegal Moose."
185. A.S. Gottesfeld and Rabnett, "Skeena Fish Populations," 66.
186. Hoffman and Joseph, *Song of the Earth*.
187. A.S. Gottesfeld and Rabnett, "Skeena Fish Populations," 115.

188. Braun, *Intemperate Rainforest*; Prudham, "Sustaining Sustained Yield."
189. Rajala, *Clearcutting the Pacific Rain Forest*.
190. Bernsohn, *Cutting Up the North*.
191. Hak, *Capital and Labour*.
192. McCreary, *Shared Histories*, 139-40.
193. Prudham, *Knock on Wood*.
194. Shervill, *Smithers*, 108; Kruisselbrink, *Smithers*, 148-49.
195. Barman, *West Beyond the West*, 281.
196. C. Harris, *Resettlement of British Columbia*, 193.
197. McCreary, *Shared Histories*, 132.
198. McCreary, 130-52.
199. Lutz, *Makuk*, 257-73.
200. N. McFarlane, Superintendent's Quarterly Report for the Period Ending September 30, 1967: Babine Indian Agency, RG10, 1987-88/007 VFRC, box no. 9, file no. 971/23-4, LAC.
201. Braun, *Intemperate Rainforest*; Prudham, "Sustaining Sustained Yield."
202. C. Harris, *Resettlement of British Columbia*, 185.
203. Lutz, *Makuk*, 270.
204. BC Legislative Assembly, *Annual Report of the Department of Social Welfare*, 46.
205. Beddows, *Report on the Smithers Indian Project*, 4.
206. McCreary, *Shared Histories*, 183-88.
207. Strong-Boag, *Fostering Nation?*, 116.
208. Morin, *Niwhts'ide'ni Hibi'it'en*, 277.
209. McCreary, *Shared Histories*, 183-84.
210. Wickham, "Initiating the Process of Youth Decolonization," 182.
211. Dickason, *Canada's First Nations*, 231.
212. Dickason, 387.
213. Cairns, *Citizens Plus*, 51-53.
214. Trudeau quoted in Cairns, 52.
215. Trudeau quoted in Francis, *The Imaginary Indian*, 217.
216. Makka and Fleras, *Politics of Indigeneity*, 189.
217. Government of Canada, "Statement on Indian Policy," 2.
218. Cardinal, *Unjust Society*.
219. Weaver, *Making Canadian Indian Policy*.
220. Dyck, *What Is the Indian "Problem,"* 108-18.
221. F. Cassidy and Bish, *Indian Government*.
222. Here I refer to the Nisga'a nation in accordance with its current spelling, while using the historic spelling of the Nishga Tribal Council to refer to that organization. Raunet, *Without Surrender*.
223. Foster, "We Are Not O'Meara's Children."
224. *Calder et al. v. Attorney-General of British Columbia*, [1973] S.C.R. 313.
225. Foster, Raven, and Webber, *Let Right Be Done*.

226. Many of these village names and their spelling have shifted over time. In current usage, the spelling of Kitwangak is now Gitwangak, Kitseguecla is Gitsegukla, and Sikadoak is Sik-e-Dakh (also known as Glen Vowell). Gitanmaax and Kispiox continue to be spelled the same way. Gitksan-Carrier Tribal Council, *Our Declaration*.

227. The spellings here reflect the historical spelling of the band names in the period. Kitwancool is now known as Gitanyow; Burns Lake is Ts'il Kaz Koh. Omineca no longer exists and has been split into three distinct bands.

## 2 | From Renunciation to Reconciliation

1. *Delgamuukw v. British Columbia*, 1991 CanLII 2372 (BCSC), 2.
2. BCSC Proceedings, 12 May 1987, 65, UBC-OC *Delgamuukw*.
3. BCSC Proceedings, 12 May 1987, 65–66, UBC-OC *Delgamuukw*.
4. *Delgamuukw v. British Columbia*, 1991 CanLII 2372 (BCSC), 21.
5. *Delgamuukw v. British Columbia*, [1997] 3 SCR 1010.
6. Blomley, "Text and Context," 526.
7. George, "Fire Within Us," 55.
8. In the wake of the trial decision, critics wrote extensive denunciations of Justice's McEachern's handling of evidence, particularly taking issue with the way he privileged written history as objective while dismissing Indigenous oral history as unreliable and community-based ethnographic research as biased. A sample of these critiques is available in F. Cassidy, *Aboriginal Title in British Columbia*; B.G. Miller, "Anthropology and History."
9. Although this decision opened Canadian courts to a fuller account of history, courts today still struggle to accord evidentiary weight to Indigenous oral histories. Borrows, "Listening for a Change"; Napoleon, "Delgamuukw"; B.G. Miller, *Oral History on Trial*.
10. Cove, "Gitksan Traditional Concept of Land Ownership"; A. Mills, *Eagle Down*; Sterritt et al., *Tribal Boundaries*; Overstall, "Encountering the Spirit in the Land"; Daly, *Our Box Was Full*.
11. Sparke, "A Map That Roared," 479.
12. T. Mitchell, *Colonizing Egypt*.
13. Sparke, "A Map That Roared," 472.
14. Sparke, 472.
15. Sparke, 471.
16. Pinder, *Carriers of No*, 5.
17. BCSC Proceedings, 27 May 1987, 670–671, UBC-OC *Delgamuukw*.
18. BCSC Proceedings, 27 May 1987, 673.
19. BCSC Proceedings, 27 May 1987, 673–674.
20. BCSC Proceedings, 11 June 1987, 1096.
21. In the Hargus orthography, Lilloos and Maxlaxlex become Lïlus and Mikhlikhlekh.
22. Commission Evidence of Emma Michell, 18 December 1986, vol. 5, 158, UBC-OC *Delgamuukw*.

23. Pinder, *Carriers of No*, 11–12.
24. *Delgamuukw v. The Queen*, 1987 CanLII 2980 (BCSC).
25. *Delgamuukw* 1987, para. 7.
26. *Delagumuukw v. British Columbia*, 1989 CanLII 2884 (BCSC), para. 32. The incorrect spelling "Delagumuukw" is the spelling used in the published decision.
27. *Delgamuukw v. British Columbia*, 1991 CanLII 2372 (BCSC), 149.
28. *Delgamuukw* 1991, 121.
29. *Delgamuukw* 1991, 146–147.
30. *Delgamuukw* 1991, 36.
31. Cruikshank, "Invention of Anthropology," 29.
32. Culhane, *Pleasure of the Crown*.
33. *Delgamuukw v. British Columbia*, 1991 CanLII 2372 (BCSC), 4.
34. Godlewska, "Napoleon's Geographers"; Edney, *Mapping an Empire*; Driver, *Geography Militant*; Branch, *Cartographic State*.
35. Bravo, "Ethnographic Navigation"; Milligan and McCreary, "Inscription, Innocence, and Invisibility"; Bernstein, *How the West Was Drawn*.
36. Ray, *Telling It to the Judge*.
37. *Delgamuukw v. British Columbia*, 1991 CanLII 2372 (BCSC), 739.
38. Henderson, "Context of the State of Nature."
39. *Uukw v. B.C. (Govt.)*, 1986 CanLII 795 (BCSC).
40. Özden-Schilling, "Technopolitics in the Archive."
41. Sparke, "A Map That Roared."
42. Wainwright and Bryan, "Cartography, Territory, Property"; Thom, "Reframing Indigenous Territories."
43. *Delgamuukw v. British Columbia*, [1997] 3 SCR 1010.
44. *Delgamuukw* [1997], para. 96.
45. *Delgamuukw* [1997], para. 98.
46. I borrow the concept of nested sovereignty from A. Simpson, *Mohawk Interruptus*.
47. Borrows, "Sovereignty's Alchemy."
48. BCSC Proceedings, 12 May 1987, 75, UBC-OC *Delgamuukw*.
49. BCSC Proceedings, 12 May 1987, 67.
50. Dorsett and McVeigh, *Jurisdiction*, 50.
51. Benton and Ross, "Empires and Legal Pluralism," 6.
52. Pasternak, "Jurisdiction and Settler Colonialism."
53. *Oxford English Dictionary Online*, "jurisdiction, n." accessed January 17, 2016, http://www.oed.com/view/Entry/102156.
54. Dorsett and McVeigh, *Jurisdiction*, 4.
55. Gisday Wa and Delgam Uukw, *Spirit in the Land*.
56. McCreary, "Burden of Sovereignty"; McCreary and Budhwa, "Core of the Wet'suwet'en Conflict"; McCreary and Turner, "Did the Protests Work?"
57. Jenness, "Carrier Indians of the Bulkley River," 540.

58. BCSC Proceedings, 14 May 1990, 26515–26526, UBC-OC *Delgamuukw*.
59. The spelling of Kitwancool has been updated to Gitanyow in current usage.
60. BCSC Proceedings, 13 May 1987, 146–147, UBC-OC *Delgamuukw*.
61. *Delgamuukw v. British Columbia*, 1991 CanLII 2372 (BCSC), 852–856.
62. *Delgamuukw* 1991, ix–x.
63. Following the Hargus orthography, Wigetimschol is spelled Wigidimsts'ol. The spelling of Na'Moks follows the preference of John Ridsdale, who holds this title in 2023. It appears as Namox in legal documents and is spelled Namoks in the Hargus orthography.
64. Following the Hargus orthography, Goohlaht is spelled Gguhlat and Samooh is spelled Simuyh.
65. Daly, *Our Box Was Full*, 62, 290.
66. *Delgamuukw v. British Columbia*, 1991 CanLII 2372 (BCSC), 584–585.
67. McCreary, "Burden of Sovereignty."
68. D.B. Cox, "Gitksan-Wet'suwet'en as Primitive Peoples"; Foster, "It Goes Without Saying"; Walters, "British Imperial Constitutional Law"; Doyle-Bedwell, "Legal Test of Extinguishment."
69. Borrows, "Sovereignty's Alchemy"; Christie, "Colonial Reading of Recent Jurisprudence"; Christie, "Indigenous Authority."
70. J.R. Miller, *Compact, Contract, Covenant*.
71. Gisday Wa and Delgam Uukw, *Spirit in the Land*.
72. Weber, "Politics as a Vocation," 76.
73. Anghie, *Imperialism, Sovereignty*.
74. Benton, *Search for Sovereignty*; Agnew, "Sovereignty Regimes"; Agnew and Oslender, "Overlapping Territorialities"; Benton and Ross, "Empires and Legal Pluralism"; McCreary and Lamb, "Political Ecology of Sovereignty."
75. *Delgamuukw v. British Columbia*, 1991 CanLII 2372 (BCSC), 652.
76. My use of the term *Native* here reflects how peoples indigenous to Southern Rhodesia were codified in imperial British law. *Re Southern Rhodesia*, [1919] AC 211.
77. *Delgamuukw* 1991, 626.
78. *Delgamuukw* 1991, 209.
79. *Delgamuukw* 1991, 210.
80. *Delgamuukw* 1991, 21.
81. Nadasdy, *Sovereignty's Entailments*, 4.
82. *Delgamuukw v. British Columbia*, 1991 CanLII 2372 (BCSC), 631.
83. *Delgamuukw* 1991, 21.
84. *Delgamuukw* 1991, 628.
85. *Delgamuukw* 1991, 535.
86. *Delgamuukw* 1991, xi.
87. *Delgamuukw* 1991, xi.
88. *Delgamuukw* 1991, 648, 649.
89. *Delgamuukw v. British Columbia*, 1993 CanLII 4516 (BCCA).

90. *Delgamuukw v. British Columbia*, [1997] 3 SCR 1010.
91. Borrows, "Sovereignty's Alchemy"; Christie, "Colonial Reading of Recent Jurisprudence."
92. A. Simpson, *Mohawk Interruptus*; L.B. Simpson, *As We Have Always Done*.
93. *Delgamuukw v. British Columbia*, [1997] 3 SCR 1010, para. 117.
94. Slattery, "The Metamorphosis of Aboriginal Title."
95. *Delgamuukw v. British Columbia*, [1997] 3 SCR 1010, para. 117.
96. *Delgamuukw* [1997], para. 128.
97. Borrows, "Sovereignty's Alchemy."
98. *Delgamuukw v. British Columbia*, [1997] 3 SCR 1010, para. 145.
99. Borrows, "Sovereignty's Alchemy," 558.
100. Christie, "Colonial Reading of Recent Jurisprudence," 46.
101. *Delgamuukw v. British Columbia*, [1997] 3 SCR 1010, para. 143.
102. *Delgamuukw* [1997], para. 143.
103. Christie, "Colonial Reading of Recent Jurisprudence."
104. Blomley, "Shut the Province Down."
105. Gitksan-Carrier Tribal Council, *Our Declaration*.
106. Sterritt, *Mapping My Way Home*, 308.
107. Glavin, *Death Feast in Dimlahamid*; Wild, *Blockade*; Blomley, "Shut the Province Down."
108. McKee, *Treaty Talks in British Columbia*, 62–63.
109. McKee, 63.
110. Mathias et al., *Report of the British Columbia Claims Task Force*.
111. *Delgamuukw v. British Columbia*, 1993 CanLII 4516 (BCCA).
112. McKee, *Treaty Talks in British Columbia*.
113. Morin, *Niwhts'ide'ni Hibi'it'en*, 340.
114. Thom, "Reframing Indigenous Territories"; C. Turner and Fondahl, "Overlapping Claims."
115. Carrier Sekani Tribal Council, "Statement of Intent."
116. Morin, *Niwhts'ide'ni Hibi'it'en*, 334.
117. Lake Babine Nation, "Statement of Intent"; Cheslatta Carrier Nation, "Statement of Intent."
118. Blackburn, "Searching for Guarantees."
119. Woolford, *Between Justice and Certainty*; Penikett, *Reconciliation*; J.R. Miller, *Compact, Contract, Covenant*.
120. Manuel, *Unsettling Canada*, 90.
121. Lockyer, "Gitksan Wet'suwet'en Sign Accord."
122. Eichstaedt and Donaldson, "Gitxsan, Wet'suwet'en Suspend Suit."
123. P.D. Mills, *For Future Generations*, 92.
124. *Delgamuukw v. British Columbia*, [1997] 3 SCR 1010, para. 129.
125. *Delgamuukw* [1997], para. 166.
126. Slattery, "Metamorphosis of Aboriginal Title."
127. Slattery, 262.

128. McKee, *Treaty Talks in British Columbia*, 95.
129. McKee, 95.
130. Scott, *Postcolonial Sovereignty?*
131. Woolford, *Between Justice and Certainty*; Penikett, *Reconciliation*.
132. Manuel, *Unsettling Canada*, 91.
133. P.D. Mills, *For Future Generations*.
134. A. Hunt and Wickham, *Foucault and Law*.
135. Foucault, *Security, Territory, Population*, 21.
136. Foucault, 21.

## 3 | Indigeneity on the Page

1. *Delgamuukw v. British Columbia*, [1997] 3 SCR 1010.
2. Tobias, *Chief Kerry's Moose*, 3.
3. Zent, "Genealogy of Scientific Representations."
4. Nahwegahbow, "Foreword," vii.
5. Galois, "History of the Upper Skeena."
6. Özden-Schilling, "Cartographies of Consignment."
7. Foster, Raven, and Webber, *Let Right Be Done*.
8. Sanders, "Nishga Case"; McConnell, "*Calder* Case in Historical Perspective."
9. Duff, "Contributions of Marius Barbeau"; Nowry, *Man of Mana*.
10. Barbeau, *Totem Poles of the Gitksan*; Barbeau and Beynon, *Tsimshian Narratives*.
11. Duffy, *Road to Nunavut*.
12. Freeman, "Looking Back—and Looking Ahead."
13. Freeman, *Inuit Land Use*; Brice-Bennett, *Our Footprints Are Everywhere*.
14. Tobias, *Chief Kerry's Moose*; Tobias, *Living Proof*.
15. Usher, Tough, and Galois, "Reclaiming the Land."
16. Berger, *One Man's Justice*.
17. Notzke, *Aboriginal Peoples and Natural Resources*; Notzke, "Aboriginal Natural Resource Management"; J. Christensen and Grant, "How Political Change Paved the Way."
18. Brody, *Maps and Dreams*.
19. Berger, *Northern Frontier*, 1.
20. Berger, xxi.
21. *Baker Lake (Hamlet) v. Canada (Minister of Indian Affairs and Northern Development)*, (1979) 107 D.L.R. (3d) 513 (FCTD).
22. Scottie, Bernauer, and Hicks, *I Will Live*.
23. Bickenbach, "*Baker Lake* Case"; D.W. Elliott, "*Baker Lake* and the Concept of Aboriginal Title."
24. McNeil, "Onus of Proof of Aboriginal Title."
25. *Western Arctic (Inuvialuit) Claims Settlement Act*, S.C. 1984, c. 24, sec 14(5).
26. Government of Northwest Territories, "Traditional Knowledge Policy."
27. M.G. Stevenson, "Indigenous Knowledge in Environmental Assessment."

28. *Delgamuukw v. British Columbia*, [1997] 3 SCR 1010, para. 143.
29. *Delgamuukw* [1997], para. 147.
30. McNeil, "Onus of Proof of Aboriginal Title."
31. McNeil, *Common Law Aboriginal Title*, quoted in *Delgamuukw v. British Columbia*, [1997] 3 SCR 1010, para. 149.
32. *Delgamuukw* [1997], para. 152.
33. *Delgamuukw* [1997], para. 149.
34. *Delgamuukw* [1997], para. 152.
35. *Delgamuukw* [1997], para. 152.
36. *Canadian Environmental Assessment Act*, S.C 1992 C. 37.
37. *Canadian Environmental Assessment Act*, S.C. 2012, C. 19, sec. 4(1)(d), sec. 5(1)(c), sec. 19(3).
38. National Energy Board, *Filing Manual*, 4A-29.
39. Nadasdy, "Anti-Politics of TEK," 224.
40. G. White, "Cultures in Collision"; Nadasdy, *Sovereignty's Entailments*.
41. Pearce and Louis, "Mapping Indigenous Depth of Place"; Johnson, *Trail of Story*.
42. Harley, "Deconstructing the Map."
43. McCreary and Milligan, "Pipelines, Permits, and Protests."
44. Stoffle and Evans, "Holistic Conservation and Cultural Triage."
45. Enbridge Northern Gateway Project Sec. 52 Application, 27 May 2010, ref. no. 2213, vol. 5A, 3-1-3-2, ENGP Records. (Hereafter cited as Enbridge Sec. 52 Application.)
46. Enbridge Sec. 52 Application, ref. no. 2213, vol. 5A, B-1-B-8, ENGP Records.
47. Enbridge Sec. 52 Application, vol. 5A, 2-5.
48. Enbridge Sec. 52 Application, vol. 5A, 2-5.
49. Enbridge Sec. 52 Application, vol. 5A, 2-6-2-8.
50. Enbridge Sec. 52 Application, vol. 5A, 3-2.
51. Enbridge Sec. 52 Application, vol. 5A, 3-2.
52. Enbridge Sec. 52 Application, vol. 5B, 4-3.
53. Enbridge Sec. 52 Application, vol. 5B, 4-3.
54. Pasternak, "Fiscal Body of Sovereignty," 326.
55. Pasternak, 321.
56. Pasternak, 327.
57. BC Assembly of First Nations, "First Nations in BC," entries on Ts'il Kaz Koh and Wet'suwet'en.
58. B. Christensen, *Too Good to Be True*.
59. BC Assembly of First Nations, "First Nations in BC," entries on Skin Tyee and Nee-Tahi-Buhn.
60. The listed on-reserve membership of Nee-Tahi-Buhn is 112. BC Assembly of First Nations, "First Nations in BC."
61. BC Assembly of First Nations, "First Nations in BC," entry on Cheslatta Carrier Nation.

62. Indigenous Business and Investment Council, "Cheslatta Carrier Nation."
63. Larsen, "Promoting Aboriginal Territoriality."
64. BC Assembly of First Nations, "First Nations in BC," entries on Witset First Nation and Hagwilget First Nation Government.
65. Respectively, Witset and Hagwilget have off-reserve populations of 1,371 and 600. Statistics Canada, "Aboriginal Peoples in Canada 2016"; BC Assembly of First Nations, "First Nations in BC."
66. Enbridge Sec. 52 Application, ref. no. 2213, vol. 5B, 1-4, ENGP Records.
67. Carrier Sekani Tribal Council, *Aboriginal Interests & Use Study.*
68. Enbridge Sec. 52 Application, ref. no. 2213, vol. 5B, 1-8, ENGP Records.
69. Office of the Wet'suwet'en—Presentation entitled "Wet'suwet'en Rights and Title," 9 January 2012, ref. no. 3477, ENGP Records. (Hereafter cited as OW Presentation.)
70. Enbridge Sec. 52 Application, ref. no. 2213, vol. 5A, 5-100, ENGP Records.
71. Tsiroulnitchenko and Hazell, "Economic Activity," appendix 2, 74.
72. Enbridge Sec. 52 Application, ref. no. 2213, vol. 5B, 4-8, ENGP Records.
73. Enbridge Sec. 52 Application, vol. 5B, 4-8.
74. Enbridge Sec. 52 Application, vol. 5A, 5-100.
75. Enbridge Sec. 52 Application, vol. 5B, 5-15.
76. Enbridge Sec. 52 Application, vol. 5B, C-280.
77. Enbridge Sec. 52 Application, vol. 5B, C-285.
78. Enbridge Sec. 52 Application, vol. 5B, C-311.
79. Enbridge Sec. 52 Application, vol. 5B, C-285.
80. Enbridge Sec. 52 Application, vol. 5B, C-278.
81. Enbridge Sec. 52 Application, vol. 5B, C-279.
82. Enbridge Sec. 52 Application, vol. 5B, C-284.
83. Enbridge Sec. 52 Application, vol. 5B, C-289.
84. Enbridge Sec. 52 Application, vol. 5B, C-289.
85. Enbridge Sec. 52 Application, vol. 5B, C-290.
86. Enbridge Sec. 52 Application, vol. 5B, C-309.
87. Enbridge Sec. 52 Application, vol. 5B, C-279.
88. Enbridge Sec. 52 Application, vol. 5B, C-290.
89. Enbridge Sec. 52 Application, vol. 5B, C-309.
90. Enbridge Sec. 52 Application, vol. 5B, C-309.
91. Enbridge Sec. 52 Application, vol. 5B, C-288.
92. McCreary and Lamb, "Political Ecology of Sovereignty"; McCreary and Milligan, "Pipelines, Permits, and Protests."
93. Byrd, *Transit of Empire*, xix.
94. McCreary and Milligan, "Pipelines, Permits, and Protests."
95. McCreary and Turner, "Contested Scales"; Milligan and McCreary, "Kitimat LNG Terminal"; McCreary and Milligan, "Limits of Liberal Recognition."
96. OW Presentation, ref. no. 3477, ENGP Records.
97. OW Presentation, para. 512.

98. OW Presentation, para. 3.
99. In the Hargus orthography, Kwanbeahyax becomes Kwin Begh Yikh; Djakanyax becomes Tsa Kën Yikh; Anaskaski, Kiyaxwinits, and Cas Yex become Insggisgï, Këyikh Winïts, and Cas Yikh; Yex T'sa Wilk'us becomes Yikh Tsawilhggis; and Sayax becomes Sa Yikh.
100. OW Presentation, ref. no. 3477, para. 6, ENGP Records.
101. OW Presentation, para. 7.
102. OW Presentation, para. 4.
103. OW Presentation, para. 7.
104. OW Presentation, para. 8.
105. OW Presentation, para. 44.
106. OW Presentation, para. 44.
107. OW Presentation, para. 12.
108. OW Presentation, para. 14.
109. OW Presentation, para. 25.
110. A.S. Gottesfeld and Rabnett, "Skeena Fish Populations," 380.
111. OW Presentation, ref. no. 3477, para. 184, ENGP Records.
112. BC Ministry of Agriculture and Lands, "Morice Land and Resource Management Plan," 112.
113. McCreary, "Between the Commodity and the Gift."
114. OW Presentation, ref. no. 3477, para. 41, ENGP Records.
115. OW Presentation, para. 51.
116. Santos, *New Legal Common Sense*.
117. Derrida, *Of Grammatology*.
118. Here I am drawing on Derrida's broader theorizations of the supplement. Derrida, 145.
119. Pasternak, "Jurisdiction and Settler Colonialism."
120. Stoffle and Evans, "Holistic Conservation and Cultural Triage."

## 4 | Indigenizing Infrastructure

1. Enbridge Northern Gateway Pipelines, "Benefits for Aboriginals."
2. Dennison, *Colonial Entanglement*, 7–8.
3. Woolford, *Between Justice and Certainty*; McCreary and Turner, "Did the Protests Work?"
4. Slowey, *Navigating Neoliberalism*; S. Mills and Sweeney, "Employment Relations."
5. Dennison, *Colonial Entanglement*, 7.
6. Caine and Krogman, "Powerful?"; McCreary, Mills, and St-Amand, "Lands and Resources for Jobs."
7. Lambrecht, *Aboriginal Consultation*; Heisler and Markey, "Scales of Benefit"; Galbraith, "Making Space for Reconciliation"; McCreary, Mills, and St-Amand, "Lands and Resources for Jobs."
8. *Delgamuukw v. British Columbia*, [1997] 3 S.C.R. 1010, para. 165.

9. *Delgamuukw* [1997], para. 168.
10. *Delgamuukw* [1997], para. 169.
11. McKee, *Treaty Talks in British Columbia*; Woolford, *Between Justice and Certainty*; Penikett, *Reconciliation*.
12. Furniss, *Burden of History*.
13. Campbell v. British Columbia (Attorney General), 2000 BCSC 1123.
14. P. Wood and Rossiter, "Fantastic Topographies."
15. Haida Nation v. British Columbia (Minister of Forests), [2004] 3 S.C.R. 511, para. 44.
16. *Haida Nation*, para. 45
17. *Haida Nation*, para. 47.
18. *Haida Nation*, para. 42.
19. P. Wood and Rossiter, "Unstable Properties."
20. *Delgamuukw v. British Columbia*, [1997] 3 S.C.R. 1010, para. 165; New Relationship Statement of Vision, accessed 19 June 2019, http://www2.gov.bc.ca/new_relationship_accord.pdf.
21. New Relationship Statement of Vision.
22. Hayter and Barnes, "Neoliberalization."
23. McMahon and Vidler, *Survey of Mining Companies*, 68.
24. New Relationship Trust Corporation, *Feedback Summary*.
25. Haida Nation v. British Columbia (Minister of Forests), [2004] 3 S.C.R. 511, para. 53.
26. *Haida Nation*, para. 53.
27. S. Mills and Sweeney, "Employment Relations"; McCreary, "Historicizing the Encounter."
28. Dennison, *Colonial Entanglement*, 7.
29. Cooney, "The Term 'Social Licence,'" 199.
30. Watts, "Economies of Violence"; Watts, "Righteous Oil?"; Watts, "Empire of Oil."
31. Cooney, "The Term 'Social Licence.'"
32. Watts, "Economies of Violence"; Watts, "Righteous Oil?"; Watts, "Empire of Oil."
33. McPhie, "Social Licence to Operate."
34. P. Bowles and MacPhail, "The Town That Said 'No.'"
35. Slowey, *Navigating Neoliberalism*, xviii.
36. Helin, *Dances with Dependency*; Helin, *Economic Dependency Trap*.
37. Galbraith, Bradshaw, and Rutherford, "Supraregulatory Approach"; O'Faircheallaigh, "Environmental Agreements"; Noble and Fidler, "Indigenous Community-Corporate Agreements."
38. McCreary, "Historicizing the Encounter."
39. Scott, "Extraction Contracting."
40. L.B. Simpson, *As We Have Always Done*, 75.
41. Miéville, *Between Equal Rights*, 178.
42. McCreary, "Between the Commodity and the Gift."
43. O'Faircheallaigh, "Aborigines, Mining Companies."

44. Cattelino, *High Stakes*.
45. Fidler and Hitch, "Impact and Benefit Agreements"; Cameron and Levitan, "Impact and Benefit Agreements"; Peterson St-Laurent and Le Billon, "Staking Claims and Shaking Hands."
46. Fidler and Hitch, "Impact and Benefit Agreements"; Caine and Krogman, "Powerful"
47. O'Faircheallaigh, "Community Development Agreements"; D. Cox and Mills, "Gendering Environmental Assessment."
48. McCreary, Basu, and Godlewska, "Critical Geographies of Education."
49. S. Bowles and Gintis, *Schooling in Capitalist America*.
50. Haig-Brown, *Taking Control*; McCreary, "Mining Aboriginal Success."
51. Dempsey, *Red Crow*; J.R. Miller, *Shingwauk's Vision*.
52. Haig-Brown, *Resistance and Renewal*; Milloy, *National Crime*.
53. Sinclair, Wilson, and Littlechild, *Honouring the Truth*.
54. National Indian Brotherhood, *Indian Control of Indian Education*, 12.
55. Lanceley-Barrie, "Devolution."
56. New Relationship Trust Corporation, *Feedback Summary*, 7.
57. New Relationship Trust Corporation, 7.
58. Joint Review Panel Hearing Transcript, 13 March 2013, Prince Rupert, BC, ref. no. 5235, paras. 24637–24638, ENGP Records. (All Joint Review Panel hearing transcripts can be found in the ENGP Records archive. They will be hereafter cited as JRP Hearing, along with date, place, and reference number.)
59. Dentons Canada LLP, counsel for Norther Gateway Pipelines Limited Partnership—Final Written Argument, 31 March 2013, ref. no. 5461, para. 1062, ENGP Records. (Hereafter cited as Northern Gateway Final Argument.)
60. Northern Gateway Final Argument, para. 1063.
61. Northern Gateway Final Argument, para. 1065.
62. JRP Hearing, 12 March 2013, Prince Rupert, BC, ref no. 5234, para. 24571, ENGP Records.
63. JRP Hearing, 18 March 2013, Prince Rupert, BC, ref no. 5254, paras. 30495–30496, ENGP Records.
64. JRP Hearing, 18 March 2013, para 30874.
65. JRP Hearing, 13 March 2013, Prince Rupert, BC, ref. no. 5235, para. 24666, ENGP Records.
66. Northern Gateway Final Argument, ref. no. 5461, para. 1066, ENGP Records.
67. Northern Gateway Final Argument, para. 1068.
68. Foucault, *Birth of Biopolitics*.
69. Taylor, Friedel, and Edge, "Pathways"; McCreary, "Mining Aboriginal Success"; S. Mills and McCreary, "Negotiating Neoliberal Empowerment."
70. Foucault, *Discipline and Punish*.
71. Lawrence, "Governing Warlpiri Subjects."
72. McCreary, "Mining Aboriginal Success."

73. JRP Hearing, 12 March 2013, Prince Rupert, BC, ref. no. 5234, para. 24544, ENGP Records.
74. Northern Gateway Final Argument, ref. no. 5461, para. 1088, ENGP Records.
75. O'Faircheallaigh, "Aborigines, Mining Companies," 3.
76. Lutz, *Makuk*; McCreary, *Shared Histories*; Hoffman and Joseph, *Song of the Earth*.
77. Enbridge Sec. 52 Application, ref. no. 2213, vol. 5A, 3-8, ENGP Records.
78. Enbridge Sec. 52 Application, vol. 5A, 3-9.
79. Enbridge Sec. 52 Application, vol. 5A, 3-4.
80. Enbridge Sec. 52 Application, vol. 5A, 3-5.
81. JRP Hearing, 18 March 2013, Prince Rupert, BC, ref. no. 5254, paras. 30454–30455, ENGP Records.
82. Northern Gateway Final Argument, ref. no. 5461, para. 1071, ENGP Records.
83. Northern Gateway Final Argument, para. 1071.
84. Northern Gateway Final Argument, para. 1073.
85. Janes Freedman Kyle Law Corporation on behalf of the Gitxaala Nation—Affidavit and Supporting Written Evidence of Elmer Moody, 20 December 2011, ref. no. 4700, pt. 2, 0243, Enbridge Northern Gateway Project—All Records, IACC-CIA registry no. 21799. (Hereafter cited as Affidavit supporting Elmer Moody.)
86. Northern Gateway Final Argument, ref. no. 5461, para. 1081, ENGP Records.
87. Northern Gateway Final Argument, para. 1078.
88. JRP Hearing, 22 November 2012, Prince George, BC, ref. no. 4948, para. 417, ENGP Records.
89. JRP Hearing, 22 November 2012, para. 420.
90. Northern Gateway Final Argument, ref. no. 5461, para. 1078, ENGP Records.
91. JRP Hearing, 22 November 2012, ref. no. 4948, para. 416, ENGP Records.
92. Bell, "In Search of Hope."
93. JRP Hearing, 16 March 2013, Prince Rupert, BC, ref. no. 5238, para. 29470, ENGP Records.
94. JRP Hearing, 22 November 2012, Prince George, BC, ref. no. 4948, para 418, ENGP Records.
95. S. Mills, "Geography of Skill."
96. Northern Gateway Final Argument, ref. no. 5461, paras. 1073, 1074, 1080, ENGP Records.
97. JRP Hearing, 22 November 2012, ref. no. 4948, para. 418, ENGP Records.
98. JRP Hearing, 18 March 2013, Prince Rupert, BC, ref. no. 5254, para. 30423, ENGP Records.
99. JRP Hearing, 18 March 2013, para. 30425.
100. JRP Hearing, 13 March 2013, Prince Rupert, BC, ref. no. 5235, para. 24826, ENGP Records.
101. JRP Hearing, 13 March 2013, para. 24823.

102. JRP Hearing, 18 March 2013, Prince Rupert, BC, ref. no. 5254, paras. 30423–30424, ENGP Records.
103. Rose, "Two Thematic Manifestations," 233.
104. D. Harvey, *Limits to Capital*.
105. Northern Gateway Final Argument, ref. no. 5461, 309, ENGP Records.
106. Northern Gateway Final Argument, 308.
107. Radcliffe, "Geography and Indigeneity III."
108. Goldstein, "Finance and Foreclosure," 43.
109. Stanley, "Resilient Settler Colonialism."
110. Labban, "Oil in Parallax."
111. Sommerville, "Naturalising Finance, Financialising Natives."
112. Affidavit supporting Elmer Moody, ref. no. 4700, pt. 2, 0246, ENGP Records.
113. Affidavit supporting Elmer Moody, pt. 2, 0242.
114. Northern Gateway Final Argument, ref. no. 5461, para. 1088, ENGP Records.
115. JRP Hearing, 18 March 2013, Prince Rupert, BC, ref. no. 5254, paras. 30830–30849, ENGP Records.
116. Affidavit supporting Elmer Moody, ref. no. 4700, pt. 2, 0247, ENGP Records.
117. This process was originally considerably more complicated and differentiated not only the provinces but also the geographic areas of the British Columbia Coast and Interior. However, no Indigenous equity partner ever emerged on the Coast, simplifying the reallocation process considerably. Affidavit supporting Elmer Moody, pt. 2, 0249.
118. Affidavit supporting Elmer Moody, pt. 2, 0250.
119. McCreary, "Historicizing the Encounter."
120. Pasternak, "Fiscal Body of Sovereignty."
121. Northern Gateway Final Argument, ref. no. 5461, para. 1058, ENGP Records.
122. Northern Gateway Final Argument, para. 1058.
123. JRP Hearing, 18 March 2013, Prince Rupert, BC, ref. no. 5254, paras. 30423–30354, ENGP Records.
124. JRP Hearing, 18 March 2013, paras. 30365–30383.
125. Malm, *How to Blow up a Pipeline*.

### 5 | Sovereignty's Return

1. Wild, *Blockade*; Blomley, "Shut the Province Down."
2. Chamberlin, *If This Is Your Land*, 1.
3. Latour, *Science in Action*; Harley, "Deconstructing the Map"; Godlewska and Smith, *Geography and Empire*; Edney, *Mapping an Empire*.
4. A. Mills, *Eagle Down*; Daly, *Our Box Was Full*; P.D. Mills, *For Future Generations*.
5. M.G. Stevenson, "Indigenous Knowledge in Environmental Assessment"; Zent, "Genealogy of Scientific Representations."
6. Blaser, "Ontology and Indigeneity"; Cadena, *Earth Beings*; Cadena and Blaser, *World of Many Worlds*.
7. Said, *Culture and Imperialism*.

8. Borrows, *Recovering Canada*.
9. A. Simpson, *Mohawk Interruptus*, 11.
10. I was kindly provided with a copy of the song lyrics and their English translation by staff of the Office of the Wet'suwet'en at the January 17, 2012, hearing of the JRP at Burns Lake. I am quoting the lyrics as they were presented to me and have not updated them to the Hargus orthography.
11. L.B. Simpson, *As We Have Always Done*, 50.
12. JRP Hearing, 16 January 2012, Smithers, BC, ref. no. 4529, ~para. 5419, ENGP Records. As the official transcript bracketed this performance as preamble, it had no designated paragraph number.
13. Cruikshank, "Glaciers," 246.
14. JRP Hearing, 16 January 2012, Smithers, BC, ref. no. 4529, para. 5437, ENGP Records.
15. JRP Hearing, 17 January 2012, Burns Lake, BC, ref. no. 4538, ~para. 6354, ENGP Records. Again, because this performance was bracketed, it has no designated paragraph number.
16. JRP Hearing, 17 January 2012, para. 6386.
17. JRP Hearing, 16 January 2012, Smithers, BC, ref. no. 4529, para. 6034, ENGP Records. Gilseyhu is another spelling of Gilserhyu, which, as already mentioned, is C'ilhts'ëkhyu in the Hargus orthography. Sa'un is Sa'on in the Hargus orthography.
18. JRP Hearing, 17 January 2012, Burns Lake, BC, ref. no. 4538, para 6389, ENGP Records.
19. JRP Hearing, 17 January 2012, para. 6385.
20. JRP Hearing, 17 January 2012, para. 6388.
21. A. Simpson, *Mohawk Interruptus*, 11.
22. S. Hunt, "Ontologies of Indigeneity," 29.
23. Here I am drawing on the conceptualization of uncontrolled equivocation from Viveiros de Castro, "Perspectival Anthropology."
24. Byrd, *Transit of Empire*, 22.
25. Pasternak and Dafnos, "Circuitry of Capital"; Dafnos, "Enduring Settler-Colonial Emergency."
26. Comack, *Racialized Policing*; Crosby and Monaghan, *Policing Indigenous Movements*; Ceric, "Beyond Contempt."
27. Muldoon, "Sovereign Exceptions"; Rifkin, "Indigenising Agamben"; Morgensen, *Spaces Between Us*; Morgensen, "Biopolitics of Settler Colonialism"; Pasternak, "Fiscal Body of Sovereignty."
28. Lund, "Fragmented Sovereignty"; McCreary and Lamb, "Political Ecology of Sovereignty."
29. Monture-Angus, *Journeying Forward*; Christie, "Colonial Reading of Recent Jurisprudence."
30. Borrows, "Trickster"; Borrows, "Frozen Rights in Canada"; Henderson, *First Nations Jurisprudence*.

31. Borrows, "Sovereignty's Alchemy"; Christie, "Colonial Reading of Recent Jurisprudence."
32. *Haida Nation v. British Columbia (Minister of Forests)*, [2004] 3 S.C.R. 511, para. 16.
33. Christie, "Colonial Reading of Recent Jurisprudence."
34. McNeil, "Onus of Proof of Aboriginal Title."
35. *Taku River Tlingit First Nation v. British Columbia*, 2004 SCC 74, para. 2.
36. *Taku River Tlingit First Nation*, para. 2.
37. Christie, "Colonial Reading of Recent Jurisprudence."
38. Joint Review Panel Agreement, 4 December 2009, ref. no. 2165, ENGP Records.
39. Lambrecht, *Aboriginal Consultation*.
40. JRP Hearing, 16 January 2012, Smithers, BC, ref. no. 4529, para. 5439, ENGP Records.
41. JRP Procedural Direction No. 4—Oral Evidence by Intervenors, 23 January 2012, doc. no. A2L3V6, REGDOCS.
42. In the Hargus orthography, Gyolo'ght is spelled C'oligit.
43. *Dinï ze'* refers to male chiefs, both singular and plural; *ts'akë ze'* refers to plural female chiefs; *skiy ze'* refers to all children of chiefs.
44. JRP Hearing, 16 January 2012, Smithers, BC, ref. no. 4529, para. 5473, ENGP Records.
45. JRP Hearing, 16 January 2012, para. 5473.
46. JRP Hearing, 16 January 2012, para. 5475.
47. JRP Hearing, 16 January 2012, para. 5476.
48. JRP Hearing, 16 January 2012, para. 5812.
49. JRP Hearing, 17 January 2012, Burns Lake, BC, ref. no. 4538, para. 6517, ENGP Records.
50. JRP Hearing, 16 January 2012, Smithers, BC, ref. no. 4529, para. 5818, ENGP Records.
51. JRP Hearing, 16 January 2012, para. 5540.
52. JRP Hearing, 16 January 2012, para. 5548.
53. JRP Hearing, 17 January 2012, Burns Lake, BC, ref. no. 4538, paras. 6354-6359, ENGP Records.
54. Fiske and Patrick, *Cis Dideen Kat*, 62.
55. Fiske and Patrick, 83.
56. JRP Hearing, 17 January 2012, Burns Lake, BC, ref. no. 4538, paras. 6380-6381, ENGP Records.
57. JRP Hearing, 17 January 2012, para. 6410.
58. Žižek, *Ticklish Subject*, 204.
59. Swyngedouw, "Impossible Sustainability," 194.
60. A. Simpson, *Mohawk Interruptus*, 2.
61. JRP Hearing, 17 January 2012, Burns Lake, BC, ref. no. 4538, paras. 6645-6646, ENGP Records.

62. JRP Hearing, 17 January 2012, para. 6647.
63. JRP Hearing, 17 January 2012, para. 6648.
64. JRP Hearing, 17 January 2012, paras. 6649–6651.
65. JRP Hearing, 17 January 2012, paras. 6652–6654.
66. In the Hargus orthography, Wah Tah K'eght and Tsee K'al K'e Yex become, respectively, Ut'akhgit and Tsë Kal K'iyikh.
67. Following Hargus, T'sek'ot is spelled Dzïggot.
68. McCreary, "Plaintiff Helped Win."
69. JRP Hearing, 17 January 2012, Burns Lake, BC, ref. no. 4538, para. 6608, ENGP Records.
70. JRP Hearing, 17 January 2012, paras. 6609–6610.
71. JRP Hearing, 17 January 2012, para. 6611.
72. JRP Hearing, 17 January 2012, para. 6612.
73. JRP Hearing, 17 January 2012, para. 6614.
74. Agamben, *State of Exception*, 3.
75. Lund, "Fragmented Sovereignty"; McCreary and Lamb, "Political Ecology of Sovereignty."
76. A. Simpson, *Mohawk Interruptus*; Pasternak, *Grounded Authority*.
77. JRP Hearing, 17 January 2012, Burns Lake, BC, ref. no. 4538, para. 6610, ENGP Records.
78. L.B. Simpson, *As We Have Always Done*, 193.
79. Morin, *Niwhts'ide'ni Hibi'it'en*, 1.
80. Byrd, *Transit of Empire*, 222.
81. In the Hargus orthography, Hagwilakw is spelled Hagwil'awh.
82. A. Mills, *Eagle Down*, 40.
83. Written Reply Evidence of Northern Gateway Pipelines, 20 July 2012, ref no. 4234, attachment 17, 6-65, ENGP Records. (Hereafter cited as Northern Gateway Written Reply.)
84. Northern Gateway Written Reply, attachment 17, 6-65.
85. Northern Gateway Written Reply, attachment 17, 6-66.
86. Office of the Wet'suwet'en—Notice of Motion—Aboriginal Engagement, 1 August 2012, ref no. 4179, ENGP Records. (Hereafter cited as OW Notice of Motion.)
87. Joint Review Panel—Ruling No. 83—Notice of Motion filed by the Office of the Wet'suwet'en, 29 August 2012, ref. no. 4311, ENGP Records.
88. JRP Hearing, 17 January 2012, Burns Lake, BC, ref. no. 4538, para. 6356, ENGP Records.
89. A. Mills, *Eagle Down*.
90. OW Notice of Motion, ref. no. 4179, 1, ENGP Records.
91. Joint Review Panel—Ruling No. 163—Notice of Motion filed by Office of the Wet'suwet'en, 1 May 2013, updated 13 May 2013, ref. no. 5396, ENGP Records.
92. Te Ata O Tu MacDonald and Muldoon, "Globalisation," 201.

## 6 | The Ongoing Cycle of Struggle

1. Gibson, "In Full Retreat"; Kirchhoff and Tsuji, "Reading between the Lines"; MacNeil, "Canadian Environmental Policy"; McCreary, "Beyond Token Recognition"; Salomons and Hoberg, "Setting Boundaries of Participation"; Peyton and Franks, "New Nature of Things?"
2. Kino-nda-niimi Collective, *Winter We Danced*; A.J. Barker, "Direct Act of Resurgence"; Callison and Hermida, "Dissent and Resonance."
3. Joint Review Panel for the Enbridge Northern Gateway Project, *Considerations: Report*, vol. 2, 307.
4. Joint Review Panel for the Enbridge Northern Gateway Project, vol. 2, 307.
5. Joint Review Panel for the Enbridge Northern Gateway Project, vol. 2, 307.
6. Joint Review Panel for the Enbridge Northern Gateway Project, vol. 2, 295.
7. Joint Review Panel for the Enbridge Northern Gateway Project, vol. 2, 296–297.
8. Joint Review Panel for the Enbridge Northern Gateway Project, vol. 2, 48.
9. Joint Review Panel for the Enbridge Northern Gateway Project, vol. 2, 268, 305.
10. Joint Review Panel for the Enbridge Northern Gateway Project, vol. 2, 305.
11. Joint Review Panel for the Enbridge Northern Gateway Project, vol. 2, 362.
12. *Tsilhqot'in Nation v. British Columbia*, 2014 SCC 44, para. 41.
13. *Tsilhqot'in Nation*, para. 42.
14. *Tsilhqot'in Nation*, para. 97.
15. International Energy Agency, *World Energy Outlook 2014*, 122.
16. Following Hargus's orthography, Knedebeas becomes Nedı̀bı̀s.
17. In the Hargus orthography, Yex T'sa Wilk'us is Yikh Tsawilhggis.
18. A.J. Barker and Ross, "Reoccupation and Resurgence"; Temper, "Blocking Pipelines."
19. McCreary and Turner, "Contested Scales."
20. *C-SPAN*, "Canadian Party Leaders Debate [Toronto]."
21. *C-SPAN*, "Canadian Party Leaders Debate [Calgary]."
22. *Gitxaala Nation v. Canada*, 2016 FCA 187, para. 325.
23. *Gitxaala Nation*, para. 329.
24. Trudeau, "Decisions on Major Energy Projects."
25. MacNeil and Paterson, "Trudeau's Canada," 384.
26. Trudeau, "Decisions on Major Energy Projects."
27. Clogg et al., "Indigenous Legal Traditions."
28. M. Simpson and Le Billon, "Reconciling Violence."
29. Chase, Cryderman, and Lewis, "Government to Buy."
30. *Tsleil-Waututh Nation v. Canada (Attorney General)*, 2018 FCA 153.
31. Canada Energy Regulator, "Conditions and Recommendations."
32. Killoran et al., "Significant Win."
33. M. Simpson and Le Billon, "Reconciling Violence."
34. Sze, *Environmental Justice*.

35. CBC News, "Cost of Trans Mountain."
36. Potkins, "Horrified."
37. Department of Finance, "What We Heard Report."
38. McCreary, "Between the Commodity and the Gift."
39. McCreary and Turner, "Contested Scales."
40. McCreary and Turner, "Did the Protests Work?"
41. Coastal GasLink, "Coastal GasLink Signs Agreements."
42. Coastal GasLink Pipeline Project Natural Gas Pipeline Benefits Agreement signed by Government of British Columbia and Moricetown Band, 23 January 2015, accessed 3 August 2023, https://www2.gov.bc.ca/assets/gov/environment/natural-resource-stewardship/consulting-with-first-nations/moricetown_band_pba_cgl_signed_bcr.pdf.
43. Wet'suwet'en Matrilineal Coalition, "Practicing Unity in Oral Traditions and Decisions Regarding Lands and Resources," grant application to the Government of British Columbia, released by the Government of British Columbia in response to a freedom of information request, http://docs.openinfo.gov.bc.ca/Response_Package_ARR-2017-71755.pdf.
44. Following Hargus, Woos becomes Wos.
45. Darlene Glaim to Theresa Tait-Day, resignation letter, 31 March 2017, released by the Government of British Columbia in response to a freedom of information request, http://docs.openinfo.gov.bc.ca/Response_Package_ARR-2017-71755.pdf.
46. Glaim to Theresa Tait-Day.
47. McCreary and Turner, "Did the Protests Work?"
48. *Coastal GasLink Pipeline Ltd. v. Huson*, 2018 BCSC 2343; *Coastal GasLink Pipeline Ltd. v. Huson*, 2019 BCSC 2264.
49. Canadian Manufacturers and Exporters, "Call on Federal Government."
50. McCreary and Wouters, "Pandemic Pipelines."
51. Canadian Press, "Woodside Petroleum."
52. T. Barker. "Enbridge Purchases Pacific Trail Pipeline."
53. Chan, "Violent Overnight Attack."
54. Hoekstra, "More Environmental Concerns."
55. Penner, "Coastal GasLink in Hot Water."
56. Potkins, "Coastal GasLink Price Tag."
57. D. Harvey, *Condition of Postmodernity*.
58. Bhandar, *Colonial Lives of Property*.
59. Chamberlin, *If This Is Your Land*, 30.
60. Larsen and Johnson, *Being Together in Place*.
61. Wale and Jack, "Gitxsan Dictionary."
62. Johnson, *Trail of Story*.
63. Kuokkanen, *Reshaping the University*, 38.
64. Kuokkanen, 37.
65. Daly, *Our Box Was Full*, 34.

66. Kimmerer, *Braiding Sweetgrass*.
67. Weiner, *Inalienable Possessions*; Godelier, *Enigma of the Gift*.
68. BCSC Proceedings, 2 March 1988, 4022, UBC-OC *Delgamuukw*.
69. McCreary, "Between the Commodity and the Gift."
70. BCSC Proceedings, 1 March 1988, 3971, UBC-OC *Delgamuukw*.
71. McCreary, "Between the Commodity and the Gift."
72. Kuokkanen, *Reshaping the University*, 139.
73. OW Presentation, ref. no. 3477, para. 97, ENGP Records.
74. L.B. Simpson, *Short History of the Blockade*, 56.
75. Blackstock, "Residential Schools"; Sinclair, Wilson, and Littlechild, *Honouring the Truth*.
76. Unist'ot'en Healing Centre, "Unist'ot'en Camp."
77. Unist'ot'en Camp, "Unist'ot'en Member Karla Tait."
78. Unist'ot'en Healing Centre, "Unist'ot'en Camp."
79. BCSC Proceedings, 17 February 1988, 3647, UBC-OC *Delgamuukw*. In the Hargus orthography, Wigetimschol is spelled Wigidimsts'ol.
80. L.B. Simpson, *As We Have Always Done*, 44.
81. Unist'ot'en Healing Centre, "Unist'ot'en Camp."
82. Unist'ot'en Healing Centre.
83. Davis, *Alliances*.
84. Thomas-Müller, "Native Rights-Based Strategic Framework," 243.
85. McCreary and Turner, "Did the Protests Work?"
86. Memorandum of Understanding between Canada, British Columbia, and Wet'suwet'en, 29 February 2020, updated 14 May 2020, https://www.rcaanc-cirnac.gc.ca/eng/1589478905863/1589478945624.
87. Bennett, "Critics Question Closed-Door Deal."
88. Bursey et al., "Memorandum of Understanding."
89. L.B. Simpson, *Short History of the Blockade*, 57.

# Bibliography

**Archival Sources**

*Delgamuukw* Trial Transcripts (UBC-OC *Delgamuukw*). University of British Columbia. Open Collections. https://open.library.ubc.ca/collections/delgamuukw.

Enbridge Northern Gateway Project—All Records (ENGP Records). Impact Assessment Agency Canada—Canadian Impact Assessment Registry no. 21799. https://www.iaac-aeic.gc.ca/050/evaluations/exploration?projDocs=21799.

Federal Collection of Minutes, Correspondence, and Sketches of the Indian Reserve Commission (Federal Collection UBCIC). Union of British Columbia Indian Chiefs Archive Research Collections. https://jirc.ubcic.bc.ca/.

Library and Archives Canada (LAC). https://library-archives.canada.ca/.

Our Homes Are Bleeding—Digital Archive (OHAB-UBCIC). Union of British Columbia Indian Chiefs Archive Research Collections. https://ourhomesarebleeding.ubcic.bc.ca/.

REGDOCS. https://apps.cer-rec.gc.ca/REGDOCS/.

**Court Cases**

*Baker Lake (Hamlet) v. Canada (Minister of Indian Affairs and Northern Development)*, [1979] 107 D.L.R. (3d) 513 (FCTD)

*Calder et al. v. Attorney-General of British Columbia*, [1973] S.C.R. 313

*Campbell v. British Columbia (Attorney General)*, 2000 BCSC 1123

*Coastal GasLink Pipeline Ltd. v. Huson*, 2018 BCSC 2343

*Coastal GasLink Pipeline Ltd. v. Huson*, 2019 BCSC 2264

*Delagumuukw v. British Columbia*, 1989 CanLII 2884 (BCSC)

*Delgamuukw v. British Columbia*, 1991 CanLII 2372 (BCSC)

*Delgamuukw v. British Columbia*, 1993 CanLII 4516 (BCCA)

*Delgamuukw v. British Columbia*, [1997] 3 S.C.R. 1010

*Delgamuukw v. The Queen*, 1987 CanLII 2980 (BCSC)

*Gitxaala Nation v. Canada*, 2016 FCA 187

*Haida Nation v. British Columbia (Minister of Forests)*, [2004] 3 S.C.R. 511

*Re Southern Rhodesia*, [1919] AC 211

*Taku River Tlingit First Nation v. British Columbia*, 2004 SCC 74

*Tsilhqot'in Nation v. British Columbia*, 2014 SCC 44

*Tsleil-Waututh Nation v. Canada (Attorney General)*, 2018 FCA 153

*Uukw v. B.C. (Govt.)*, 1986 CanLII 795 (BCSC)

**Bibliography**

Agamben, Giorgio. *State of Exception*. Chicago: University of Chicago Press, 2005.

Agnew, John. "Sovereignty Regimes: Territoriality and State Authority in Contemporary World Politics." *Annals of the Association of American Geographers* 95, no. 2 (2005): 437-461.

Agnew, John, and Ulrich Oslender. "Overlapping Territorialities, Sovereignty in Dispute: Empirical Lessons from Latin America." In *Spaces of Contention: Spatialities and Social Movements*, edited by Byron Miller, Justin Beaumont, Walter Nicholls, 121-140. Aldershot: Ashgate, 2013.

Alberta Energy Regulator. *ST98: Alberta's Energy Reserves & Supply/Demand Outlook*. Calgary: AER, 2015.

Angevine, Gerry. *The Canadian Oil Transport Conundrum*. Vancouver: Fraser Institute, 2013.

Anghie, Antony. *Imperialism, Sovereignty and the Making of International Law*. Cambridge: Cambridge University Press, 2004.

Barbeau, Marius. *The Downfall of Temlaham*. Edmonton: Hurtig Publishers, 1973.

Barbeau, Marius. *Pathfinders in the North Pacific*. Caldwell: Caxton Printers and Ryerson Press, 1958.

Barbeau, Marius. *Totem Poles of the Gitksan, Upper Skeena River, British Columbia*. Ottawa: F.A. Acland, 1929.

Barbeau, Marius, and William Beynon. *Tsimshian Narratives*. Edited by John J. Cove and George F. MacDonald. 2 vols. Ottawa: Canadian Museum of Civilization, 1987.

Barkan, Joshua. *Corporate Sovereignty: Law and Government under Capitalism*. Minneapolis: University of Minnesota Press, 2013.

Barker, Adam J. "A Direct Act of Resurgence, a Direct Act of Sovereignty: Reflections on Idle No More, Indigenous Activism, and Canadian Settler Colonialism." *Globalizations* 12, no. 1 (2015): 43-65.

Barker, Adam J., and Russell Myers Ross. "Reoccupation and Resurgence: Indigenous Protest Camps in Canada." In *Protest Camps in International Context: Spaces, Infrastructures and Media of Resistance*, edited by Gavin Brown, Anna Feigenbaum, Fabian Frenzel, and Patrick McCurdy, 199-220. Bristol: Policy Press, 2017.

Barker, Barbara, and Tyler McCreary. "Any Indian Woman Marrying Any Other Than an Indian Shall Cease to Be Indian: Sharon McIvor's Fight for Gender Equality in the Indian Act." *Briarpatch*, March 1, 2008.

Barker, Thom. "Enbridge Purchases Pacific Trail Pipeline from Chevron/Woodside." *Terrace Standard*, January 20, 2022. https://www.terracestandard.com/news/enbridge-purchases-pacific-trail-pipeline-from-chevron-woodside/.

Barman, Jean. *The West beyond the West: A History of British Columbia*. Toronto: University of Toronto Press, 1991.

BC Assembly of First Nations. "First Nations in BC." Accessed June 17, 2021. https://www.bcafn.ca/first-nations-bc.

BC Hydro Power Pioneers. *Gaslights to Gigawatts: A Human History of BC Hydro and Its Predecessors*. Vancouver: Hurricane Press, 1998.

BC Legislative Assembly. *Annual Report of the Department of Social Welfare for the Year Ended March 31st, 1959*. Victoria: Government Printer, 1960.

BC Ministry of Agriculture and Lands. *Morice Land and Resource Management Plan*. Victoria: Integrated Land Management Bureau, 2007.

Beddows, D.G. *Report on the Smithers Indian Project*. Book I. Smithers: Department of Social Welfare, 1965.

Belanger, Yale D., and P. Whitney Lackenbauer, eds. *Blockades or Breakthroughs? Aboriginal Peoples Confront the Canadian State*. Montréal: McGill-Queen's University Press, 2015.

Bell, Lindsay. "In Search of Hope: Mobility and Citizenship on the Canadian Frontier." In *Migration in the 21st Century: Political Economy and Ethnography*, edited by Pauline Gardiner Barber and Winnie Lem, 132–152. New York: Routledge, 2012.

Bennett, Nelson. "Critics Question Closed-Door Deal with Wet'suwet'en Hereditary Chiefs." *Prince George Citizen*, May 27, 2020. https://www.princegeorgecitizen.com/local-news/critics-question-closed-door-deal-with-wetsuweten-hereditary-chiefs-3740473.

Benton, Lauren. *A Search for Sovereignty: Law and Geography in European Empires 1400-1900*. Cambridge: Cambridge University Press, 2010.

Benton, Lauren, and Richard J. Ross. "Empires and Legal Pluralism: Jurisdiction, Sovereignty, and Political Imagination in the Early Modern World." In *Legal Pluralism and Empires, 1500-1850*, edited by Lauren Benton and Richard J. Ross, 1–17. New York: New York University Press, 2013.

Berger, Tom. *Northern Frontier, Northern Homeland: The Report of the Mackenzie Valley Pipeline Inquiry*. Ottawa: Ministry of Supply and Services, 1977.

Berger, Tom. *One Man's Justice: A Life in the Law*. Vancouver: Douglas & McIntyre, 2002.

Berland, Jody. *North of Empire: Essays on the Cultural Technologies of Space*. Durham: Duke University Press, 2009.

Bernsohn, Ken. *Cutting Up the North: The History of the Forest Industry in the Northern Interior*. North Vancouver: Hancock House, 1981.

Bernstein, David. *How the West Was Drawn: Mapping, Indians, and the Construction of the Trans-Mississippi West*. Lincoln: University of Nebraska Press, 2018.

Bhandar, Brenna. *Colonial Lives of Property: Law, Land, and Racial Regimes of Ownership*. Durham: Duke University Press, 2018.

Bickenbach, Jerome E. "The *Baker Lake* Case: A Partial Recognition of Inuit Aboriginal Title." *University of Toronto Faculty of Law Review* 38 (1980): 232-249.

Black, Toban, Stephen D'Arcy, Tony Weis, and Joshua Kahn Russell, eds. *A Line in the Tar Sands: Struggles for Environmental Justice*. Toronto and Oakland: Between the Lines and PM Press, 2014.

Blackburn, Carole. "Searching for Guarantees in the Midst of Uncertainty: Negotiating Aboriginal Rights and Title in British Columbia." *American Anthropologist* 107, no. 4 (2005): 586-596.

Blackstock, Cindy. "Residential Schools: Did They Really Close or Just Morph into Child Welfare?" *Indigenous Law Journal* 6, no. 1 (2007): 71-78.

Blaser, Mario. "Ontology and Indigeneity: On the Political Ontology of Heterogeneous Assemblages." *Cultural Geographies* 21, no. 1 (2014): 49-58.

Blomley, Nicholas. "Shut the Province Down: First Nations Blockades in British Columbia, 1984-1995." *BC Studies* 111 (1996): 5-35.

Blomley, Nicholas. "Text and Context: Rethinking the Law-Space Nexus." *Progress in Human Geography* 13, no. 4 (1989): 512-534.

Borrows, John. *Canada's Indigenous Constitution*. Toronto: University of Toronto Press, 2010.

Borrows, John. *Drawing Out Law: A Spirit's Guide*. Toronto: University of Toronto Press, 2010.

Borrows, John. "Frozen Rights in Canada: Constitutional Interpretation and the Trickster." *American Indian Law Review* 22 (1997): 37-64.

Borrows, John. "Listening for a Change: The Courts and Oral Tradition." *Osgoode Hall Law Journal* 39 (2001): 1-38.

Borrows, John. *Recovering Canada: The Resurgence of Indigenous Law*. Toronto: University of Toronto Press, 2002.

Borrows, John. "Sovereignty's Alchemy: An Analysis of *Delgamuukw v. British Columbia*." *Osgoode Hall Law Journal* 37 (1999): 537-598.

Borrows, John. "The Trickster: Integral to a Distinctive Culture." *Constitutional Forum* 8, no. 2 (1996): 27-32.

Borrows, John. "Wampum at Niagara: The Royal Proclamation, Canadian Legal History, and Self-Government." In *Aboriginal and Treaty Rights in Canada: Essays on Law, Equality and Respect for Difference*, edited by Michael Asch, 155-172. Vancouver: UBC Press, 1997.

Borrows, John, and Michael Coyle, eds. *The Right Relationship: Reimagining the Implementation of Historical Treaties*. Toronto: University of Toronto Press, 2017.

Bowles, Paul, and Fiona MacPhail. "The Town That Said 'No' to the Enbridge Northern Gateway Pipeline: The Kitimat Plebiscite of 2014." *The Extractive Industries and Society* 4, no. 1 (2017): 15–23.

Bowles, Samuel, and Herbert Gintis. *Schooling in Capitalist America: Educational Reform and the Contradictions of Economic Life*. New York: Basic Books, 1976.

Boyer, David S. "Kitimat, Canada's Aluminum Titan." *National Geographic* 110, no. 3 (1956): 376–398.

Bracken, Christopher. *The Potlatch Papers: A Colonial Case History*. Chicago: University of Chicago Press, 1997.

Bradshaw, Mike. *Global Energy Dilemmas: Energy Security, Globalization, and Climate Change*. Cambridge: Polity Press, 2014.

Branch, Jordan. *The Cartographic State: Maps, Territory, and the Origins of Sovereignty*. Cambridge: Cambridge University Press, 2013.

Bravo, Michael. "Ethnographic Navigation and the Geographical Gift." In *Geography and Enlightenment*, edited by David Livingstone and Charles W.J. Withers, 199–235. Chicago: University of Chicago Press, 1999.

Brice-Bennett, Carol. *Our Footprints Are Everywhere: Inuit Land Use and Occupancy in Labrador*. Nain: Labrador Inuit Association, 1977.

Bridge, Gavin, and Philippe Le Billon. *Oil*. London: Polity Press, 2012.

Bridge, Gavin, and Andrew Wood. "Less Is More: Spectres of Scarcity and the Politics of Resource Access in the Upstream Oil Sector." *Geoforum* 41, no. 4 (2010): 565–576.

Brody, Hugh. *Maps and Dreams: A Journey into the Lives and Lands of the Beaver Indians of Northwest Canada*. Vancouver: Douglas & McIntyre, 1981.

Brody, Hugh. *The Other Side of Eden: Hunters, Farmers and the Shaping of the World*. Vancouver: Douglas & McIntyre, 2000.

Braun, Bruce. *The Intemperate Rainforest: Nature, Culture, and Power on Canada's West Coast*. Minneapolis: University of Minnesota Press, 2002.

Budhwa, Rick, and Tyler McCreary. "Reconciling Cultural Resource Management with Indigenous Geographies: The Importance of Connecting Research with People and Place." In *A Deeper Sense of Place: Stories and Journeys of Indigenous-Academic Collaboration*, edited by Jay T. Johnson and Soren C. Larsen, 195–214. Corvallis: Oregon State University Press, 2013.

Bursey, David, Radha Curpen, Sharon Singh, and Charlotte Teal. "Memorandum of Understanding on Wet'suwet'en Rights and Title—An Ambitious Plan." *Bennett Jones*, June 3, 2020. https://www.bennettjones.com:443/Blogs-Section/Memorandum-of-Understanding-on-Wetsuweten-Rights-and-Title.

Byrd, Jodi A. *The Transit of Empire: Indigenous Critiques of Colonialism*. Minneapolis: University of Minnesota Press, 2011.

Cadena, Marisol de la. *Earth Beings: Ecologies of Practice Across Andean Worlds*. Durham: Duke University Press, 2015.

Cadena, Marisol de la, and Mario Blaser, eds. *A World of Many Worlds*. Durham: Duke University Press, 2018.

Cai, Hao, Adam R. Brandt, Sonia Yeh, Jacob G. Englander, Jeongwoo Han, Amgad Elgowainy, and Michael Q. Wang. "Well-to-Wheels Greenhouse Gas Emissions of Canadian Oil Sands Products: Implications for U.S. Petroleum Fuels." *Environmental Science & Technology* 49, no. 13 (2015): 8219–8227.

Cail, Robert E. *Land, Man, and the Law: The Disposal of Crown Lands in British Columbia, 1871–1913*. Vancouver: UBC Press, 1974.

Caine, Ken J., and Naomi Krogman. "Powerful or Just Plain Power-Full? A Power Analysis of Impact and Benefit Agreements in Canada's North." *Organization & Environment* 23, no. 1 (2010): 76–98.

Cairns, Allan. *Citizens Plus: Aboriginal Peoples and the Canadian State*. Vancouver: UBC Press, 2000.

Callison, Candis, and Alfred Hermida. "Dissent and Resonance: #Idlenomore as an Emergent Middle Ground." *Canadian Journal of Communication* 40, no. 4 (2015): 695–716.

Cameron, Emilie, and Tyler Levitan. "Impact and Benefit Agreements and the Neoliberalization of Resource Governance and Indigenous-State Relations in Northern Canada." *Studies in Political Economy* 93 (2014): 29–56.

Campbell, Marjorie W. *The North West Company*. New York: St. Martin's Press, 1957.

Canadian Association of Petroleum Producers. *Canada's Role in the World's Future Energy Mix*. Calgary: CAPP, 2018.

Canadian Association of Petroleum Producers. *Canadian Crude Oil Production and Supply Forecast 2006–2020*. Calgary: CAPP, 2006.

Canada Energy Regulator. "Conditions and Recommendations Overview—Trans Mountain Expansion Project Reconsideration Report. Government of Canada." CER. Updated August 5, 2022. https://www.cer-rec.gc.ca/en/applications-hearings/view-applications-projects/trans-mountain-expansion/conditions-recommendations-overview-trans-mountain-expansion-project-reconsideration-report.html.

Canadian Energy Research Institute. *Canadian Economic Impacts of New and Existing Oil Sands Development in Alberta (2014–2038)*. Calgary: CERI, 2014.

Canadian Manufacturers and Exporters. "CME & Presidents of Canada's Leading Manufacturers Call on Federal Government to Restore Rail Service." Posted Feb. 18, 2020. https://cme-mec.ca/blog/cme-presidents-of-canadas-leading-manufacturers-call-on-federal-government-to-restore-rail-service/.

C-SPAN. "Canadian Party Leaders Debate [Toronto]." Broadcast from Toronto, August 6, 2015. Video, 02:00:00. https://www.c-span.org/video/?327486-1/debate-canadian-party-leaders.

C-SPAN. "Canadian Party Leaders Debate [Calgary]." Broadcast from Calgary, Sep. 17, 2015. Video, 01:29:36. https://www.c-span.org/video/?328174-1/canadian-party-leaders-debate.

Canadian Press. "Woodside Petroleum Looks to Sell its 50 per cent Stake in Kitimat LNG Project." *Toronto Star*, May 18, 2021.

Cannon, Martin J. "Revisiting Histories of Legal Assimilation, Racialized Injustice, and the Future of Indian Status in Canada." In *Racism, Colonialism, and Indigeneity in Canada*, edited by Martin J. Cannon and Lina Sunseri, 88–97. Don Mills: Oxford University Press, 2011.

Cardinal, Harold. *The Unjust Society: The Tragedy of Canada's Indians*. Edmonton: Hurtig Publishers, 1969.

Carrier Sekani Tribal Council. *Aboriginal Interests & Use Study on the Enbridge Gateway Pipeline*. Prince George: CSTC, 2006.

Carrier Sekani Tribal Council. "Statement of Intent." BC Treaty Commission, submitted June 29, 1995. https://www.bctreaty.ca/carrier-sekani-tribal-council.

Carter, Angela V. *Fossilized: Environmental Policy in Canada's Petro-Provinces*. Vancouver: UBC Press, 2020.

Cassidy, Frank, ed. *Aboriginal Title in British Columbia:* Delgamuukw v. The Queen. Lantzville, BC: Oolichan Books; Montréal: Institute for Research on Public Policy, 1992.

Cassidy, Frank, and Robert L. Bish. *Indian Government: Its Meaning in Practice*. Lantzville, BC: Oolichan Books; Halifax: Institute for Research on Public Policy, 1989

Cassidy, Maureen. *The Gathering Place: A History of the Wet'suwet'en Village of Tse-kya*. Hagwilget: Hagwilget Band Council, 1987.

Cassidy, Maureen. "The Skeena River Uprising of 1888." *British Columbia Historical News* 16, no. 3 (1983): 6–12.

Cattelino, Jessica R. *High Stakes: Florida Seminole Gaming and Sovereignty*. Durham: Duke University Press, 2008.

CBC News. "Cost of Trans Mountain Expansion Pipeline Keeps Climbing, Now $30.9B." *CBC*, March 10, 2023. https://www.cbc.ca/news/canada/calgary/trans-mountain-pipeline-costs-1.6775415.

Ceric, Irina. "Beyond Contempt: Injunctions, Land Defense, and the Criminalization of Indigenous Resistance." *South Atlantic Quarterly* 119, no. 2 (2020): 353–369.

Chamberlin, J. Edward. *If This Is Your Land, Where Are Your Stories? Finding Common Ground*. Toronto: Vintage Canada, 2004.

Chan, Cheryl. "Violent Overnight Attack at Coastal GasLink Site Leaves Workers Shaken, Millions in Damage." *Vancouver Sun*, February 17, 2022. https://vancouversun.com/news/local-news/coastal-gaslink-site-attacked-overnight-with-millions-in-damage-to-equipment.

Charpentier, Alex D., Joule A. Bergerson, and Heather L. MacLean. "Understanding the Canadian Oil Sands Industry's Greenhouse Gas Emissions." *Environmental Research Letters* 4, no. 1 (2009): 014005.

Chase, Steven, Kelly Cryderman, and Jeff Lewis. "Trudeau Government to Buy Kinder Morgan's Trans Mountain for $4.5-billion." *The Globe and Mail*, May 29, 2018.

Chastko, Paul A. *Developing Alberta's Oil Sands: From Karl Clark to Kyoto*. Calgary: University of Calgary Press, 2004.

Cheslatta Carrier Nation. "Statement of Intent." BC Treaty Commission, submitted July 12, 1995. https://www.bctreaty.ca/cheslatta-carrier-nation.

Christensen, Bev. *Too Good to Be True: Alcan's Kemano Completion Project*. Vancouver: Talonbooks, 1995.

Christensen, Julia, and Miriam Grant. "How Political Change Paved the Way for Indigenous Knowledge: The Mackenzie Valley Resource Management Act." *Arctic* 60, no. 2 (2007): 115-123.

Christie, Gordon. "A Colonial Reading of Recent Jurisprudence: *Sparrow*, *Delgamuukw* and *Haida Nation*." *Windsor Yearbook of Access to Justice* 23, no. 1 (2005): 17-53.

Christie, Gordon. "Culture, Self-Determination and Colonialism: Issues around the Revitalization of Indigenous Legal Traditions." *Indigenous Law Journal* 6 (2007): 13-29.

Christie, Gordon. "Indigenous Authority, Canadian Law, and Pipeline Proposals." *Journal of Environmental Law and Practice* 25 (2013): 189-215.

Clarke, Tony. *Tar Sands Showdown: Canada and the New Politics of Oil in an Age of Climate Change*. Toronto: James Lorimer, 2008.

Clayton, Daniel. *Islands of Truth: The Imperial Fashioning of Vancouver Island*. Vancouver: UBC Press, 2000.

Clogg, Jessica, Hannah Askew, Eugene Kung, and Gavin Smith. "Indigenous Legal Traditions and the Future of Environmental Governance in Canada." *Journal of Environmental Law and Practice* 29 (2016): 227-256.

Coastal GasLink. "Coastal GasLink Signs Agreements With 100 Per Cent of B.C. Elected Indigenous Bands Along the Pipeline Route." *What's New* [Coastal GasLink blog], September 13, 2018. https://www.coastalgaslink.com/whats-new/news-stories/2018/2018-09-13coastal-gaslink-signs-agreements-with-100-per-cent-of-b.c.-elected-indigenous-bands-along-the-pipeline-route/.

Comack, Elizabeth. *Racialized Policing: Aboriginal People's Encounters with the Police*. Winnipeg: Fernwood, 2012.

Connauton, Joanne. "Reimagining BC Modern Treaties: A Critical Discourse Analysis of the Tsawwassen, Maa-nulth, and Tla'amin Final Agreements." Master's thesis, Royal Roads University, 2023. VIURRSpace. http://doi.org/10.25316/IR-19104.

Cooney, Jim. "Reflections on the 20th Anniversary of the Term 'Social Licence'." *Journal of Energy & Natural Resources Law* 35, no. 2 (2017): 197-200.

Coulthard, Glen Sean. *Red Skin, White Masks: Rejecting the Colonial Politics of Recognition*. Indigenous Americas, edited by Robert Warrior. Minneapolis: University of Minnesota Press, 2014.

Cove, John J. "The Gitksan Traditional Concept of Land Ownership." *Anthropologica* 24, no. 1 (1982): 3-17.

Cox, B. Douglas. "The Gitksan-Wet'suwet'en as Primitive Peoples Incapable of Holding Proprietary Interests: Chief Justice McEachern's Underlying Premise in *Delgamuukw*." *Dalhousie Journal of Legal Studies* 1 (1992.): 141–160.

Cox, David, and Suzanne Mills. "Gendering Environmental Assessment: Women's Participation and Employment Outcomes at Voisey's Bay." *Arctic* 68, no. 2 (2015): 246–260.

Crosby, Andrew, and Jeffrey Monaghan. *Policing Indigenous Movements: Dissent and the Security State*. Halifax: Fernwood, 2018.

Cruikshank, Julie. "Are Glaciers 'Good to Think With'? Recognising Indigenous Environmental Knowledge." *Anthropological Forum* 22, no. 3 (2012): 239–250.

Cruikshank, Julie. "Invention of Anthropology in British Columbia's Supreme Court: Oral Tradition as Evidence in *Delgamuukw v. B.C.*" *BC Studies* 95 (1992): 25–42.

Culhane, Dara. *The Pleasure of the Crown: Anthropology, Law and First Nations*. Vancouver: Talonbooks, 1998.

Dafnos, Tia. "The Enduring Settler-Colonial Emergency: Indian Affairs and Contemporary Emergency Management in Canada." *Settler Colonial Studies* 9, no. 3 (2019): 379–395.

Daly, Richard. *Our Box Was Full: An Ethnography for the* Delgamuukw *Plaintiffs*. Vancouver: UBC Press, 2005.

Davenport-Hines, Richard. *Universal Man: The Seven Lives of John Maynard Keynes*. London: William Colins, 2015.

Davis, Lynne, ed. *Alliances: Re/Envisioning Indigenous-Non-Indigenous Relationships*. Toronto: University of Toronto Press, 2010.

Dean, Misao. *Inheriting a Canoe Paddle: The Canoe in Discourses of English-Canadian Nationalism*. Toronto: University of Toronto Press, 2013.

Dempsey, Hugh A. *Red Crow: Warrior Chief*. Saskatoon: Fifth House, 1995.

Dennison, Jean. *Colonial Entanglement: Constituting a Twenty-First-Century Osage Nation*. Chapel Hill: The University of North Carolina Press, 2012.

Department of Finance. *What We Heard Report: First Step of Engagement Process on Indigenous Economic Participation in TMX*. Ottawa: Department of Finance, 2019.

Derrida, Jacques. *Of Grammatology*. Translated by Gayatri Chakravorty Spivak. Baltimore: Johns Hopkins University Press, 1997. First published 1967 as *De la grammatologie* by Éditions de Minuit (Paris).

Dickason, Olive Patricia, with David McNab. *Canada's First Nations: A History of Founding Peoples from Earliest Times*. 4th ed. Don Mills: Oxford University Press, 2009.

Dorsett, Shaunnagh, and Shaun McVeigh. *Jurisdiction*. New York: Routledge, 2012.

Doyle-Bedwell, Patricia E. "The Evolution of the Legal Test of Extinguishment: From *Sparrow* to *Gitskan*." *Canadian Journal of Women and the Law* 6 (1993): 193–204.

Driver, Felix. *Geography Militant: Cultures of Exploration and Empire.* Oxford: Blackwell, 2001.

Duff, Wilson. "Contributions of Marius Barbeau to West-Coast Ethnology." *Anthropologica* 6, no. 1 (1964): 63-96.

Duffy, R. Quinn. *The Road to Nunavut: The Progress of the Eastern Arctic Inuit since the Second World War.* Montreal: McGill-Queen's University Press, 2014.

Dyck, Noël. *What Is the Indian "Problem": Tutelage and Resistance in Canadian Indian Administration.* St. John's: Institute of Social and Economic Research, 1991.

Edmonds, Penelope. *Urbanizing Frontiers: Indigenous Peoples and Settlers in 19th-Century Pacific Rim Cities.* Vancouver: UBC Press, 2010.

Edney, Matthew H. *Mapping an Empire: The Geographical Construction of British India, 1765-1843.* Chicago: University of Chicago Press, 1997.

Eichstaedt, Carol, and Doug Donaldson. "Gitxsan, Wet'suwet'en Suspend Suit in Favor of Treaty Negotiations." *Windspeaker* 12, no. 18 (1994): 2.

Elliott, David W. "*Baker Lake* and the Concept of Aboriginal Title." *Osgoode Hall Law Journal* 18 (1980): 653.

Elliott, Thompson Coit. "Peter Skene Ogden, Fur Trader." *The Quarterly of the Oregon Historical Society* 11, no. 3 (1910): 229-278.

Enbridge Northern Gateway Pipelines. "Benefits for Aboriginals." Accessed May 29, 2013. http://www.northerngateway.ca/aboriginal-engagement/benefits-for-aboriginals/.

Englander, Jacob G., Sharad Bharadwaj, and Adam R. Brandt. "Historical Trends in Greenhouse Gas Emissions of the Alberta Oil Sands (1970-2010)." *Environmental Research Letters* 8, no. 4 (2013): 044036.

Erickson, Bruce R. *Canoe Nation: Nature, Race, and the Making of a Canadian Icon.* Vancouver: UBC Press, 2013.

Fabian, Johannes. *Time and the Other: How Anthropology Makes Its Object.* New York: Columbia University Press, 1983.

Fast, Travis. "Stapled to the Front Door: Neoliberal Extractivism in Canada." *Studies in Political Economy* 94 (2014): 31-60.

Ferguson, James H. *James Douglas: Father of British Columbia.* Toronto: Dundurn Press, 2009.

Fidler, Courtney R., and Michael Hitch. "Impact and Benefit Agreements: A Contentious Issue for Environmental and Aboriginal Justice." *Environments* 35, no. 2 (2007): 45-69.

Fisher, Robin. *Contact and Conflict: Indian-European Relations in British Columbia, 1774-1890.* 2nd ed. Vancouver: UBC Press, 1992.

Fiske, Jo-Anne, and Betty Patrick. *Cis Dideen Kat (When the Plumes Rise): The Way of the Lake Babine Nation.* Vancouver: UBC Press, 2000.

Fontaine, Theodore. *Broken Circle: The Dark Legacy of Indian Residential Schools.* Victoria: Heritage House, 2010.

Foster, Hamar. "It Goes Without Saying: The Doctrine of Extinguishment by Implication in *Delgamuukw*." In F. Cassidy, *Aboriginal Title in British Columbia: Delgamuukw v. The Queen*, 133–160.

Foster, Hamar. "The Queen's Law is Better Than Yours: International Homicide in Early British Columbia." In *Essays in the History of Canadian Law*. Vol. V, *Crime and Criminal Justice*, edited by Jim Phillips, Tina Loo, and Susan Lewthwaite, 41–111. Toronto: Osgoode Society for Legal History, 1994.

Foster, Hamar. "We Are Not O'Meara's Children: Law, Lawyers, and the First Campaign for Aboriginal Title in British Columbia, 1908–1928." In *Let Right Be Done: Aboriginal Title, the* Calder *Case, and the Future of Indigenous Rights*, edited by Hamar Foster, Heather Raven, and Jeremy Webber, 61–84. Vancouver: UBC Press, 2007.

Foster, Hamar, Heather Raven, and Jeremy Webber, eds. *Let Right be Done: Aboriginal Title, the* Calder *Case, and the Future of Indigenous Rights*. Vancouver: UBC Press, 2007.

Foucault, Michel. *The Birth of Biopolitics: Lectures at the College de France, 1978–1979*. Edited by Michel Senellart. Translated by Graham Burchell. New York: Palgrave Macmillan, 2008. First published 2004 as *Naissance de la biopolitique : Cours au Collège de France, 1978–1979* by Éditions du Seuil/Gallimard (Paris).

Foucault, Michel. *Discipline and Punish: The Birth of the Prison*. Translated by Alan Sheridan. New York: Vintage Books, 1979. First published 1975 as *Surveillir et punir* by Gallimard (Paris).

Foucault, Michel. *Security, Territory, Population, Lectures at the College de France, 1977–1978*. Edited by Michel Senellart. Translated by Graham Burchell. New York: Palgrave Macmillan, 2007. First published 2004 as *Sécurité, territoire, population: Cours au Collège de France, 1977–1978* by Éditions de Seuil (Paris).

Francis, Daniel. *The Imaginary Indian: The Image of the Indian in Canadian Culture*. Vancouver: Arsenal Pulp Press, 1992.

Freeman, Milton. ed. *Inuit Land Use and Occupancy Project*. Ottawa: Department of Indian Affairs and Northern Development, 1976.

Freeman, Milton. "Looking Back—and Looking Ahead—35 Years After the Inuit Land Use and Occupancy Project." *The Canadian Geographer* 55, no. 1 (2011): 20–31.

Furniss, Elizabeth. *The Burden of History: Colonialism and the Frontier Myth in a Rural Canadian Community*. Vancouver: UBC Press, 1999.

Fur Trader, A. *Traits of American-Indian Life and Character*. London: Smith, Elder, 1853.

Galay, Gregory. "Are Crude Oil Markets Cointegrated? Testing the Co-Movement of Weekly Crude Oil Spot Prices." *Journal of Commodity Markets* 16 (2019): 100088.

Galay, Gregory. "The Impact of Spatial Price Differences on Oil Sands Investments." *Energy Economics* 69 (2018): 170–184.

Galbraith, Lindsay. "Making Space for Reconciliation in the Planning System." *Planning Theory & Practice* 15, no. 4 (2014): 453-479.

Galbraith, Lindsay, Ben Bradshaw, and Murray B. Rutherford. "Towards a New Supraregulatory Approach to Environmental Assessment in Northern Canada." *Impact Assessment and Project Appraisal* 25, no. 1 (2007): 27-41.

Galois, Robert. "Gitxsan Law and Settler Disorder: The Skeena 'Uprising' of 1888." In *New Histories for Old: Changing Perspectives on Canada's Native Pasts*, edited by Theodore Binnema and Susan Neylan, 220-248. Vancouver: UBC Press, 2007.

Galois, Robert. "The History of the Upper Skeena Region, 1850 to 1927." *Native Studies Review* 9, no. 2 (1993): 113-183.

Gauvreau, N.B. "Exploration Survey of New Calendonia, Part II." In *British Columbia Crown Land Surveys for the Year Ending 31st December, 1891*, compiled by F.G. Vernon, 371-381. Victoria: Richard Wolfenden, 1891.

George, Herb (Satsan). "The Fire within Us." In F. Cassidy, *Aboriginal Title in British Columbia:* Delgamuukw v. The Queen, 53-57.

George, Herb (Satsan). "Foreword." In *Song of the Earth: The Life of Alfred Joseph*, by Ross Hoffman with Alfred Joseph, v-x. Smithers: Creekstone Press, 2019.

Gergan, Mabel D., and Tyler McCreary. "Disrupting Infrastructures of Colonial Hydro-Modernity: Lepcha and Dakelh Struggles against Temporal and Territorial Displacements." *Annals of the American Association of Geographers* 112, no. 3 (2022): 789-798.

Gibson, Robert B. "In Full Retreat: The Canadian Government's New Environmental Assessment Law Undoes Decades of Progress." *Impact Assessment and Project Appraisal* 30, no. 3 (2012): 179-188.

Gisday Wa and Delgam Uukw. *The Spirit in the Land: Statements of the Gitksan and Wet'suwet'en Hereditary Chiefs in the Supreme Court of British Columbia 1987-1990*, 2nd ed. Gabriola: Reflections, 1992.

Gitksan-Carrier Tribal Council. *Our Declaration*. Anspayaxw (Kispiox): GCTC, 1977.

Glavin, Terry. *A Death Feast in Dimlahamid*. Vancouver: New Star Books, 1990.

Glenn, Jane M., and José Otero. "Canada and the Kyoto Protocol: An Aesop Fable." In *Climate Change and the Law*, edited by Erkki J. Hollo, Kati Kulovesi, Michael Mehling, 489-508. Dordrecht: Springer, 2013.

Godelier, Maurice. *The Enigma of the Gift*. Chicago: University of Chicago Press, 1999.

Godlewska, Anne. "Napoleon's Geographers (1797-1815): Imperialists and Soldiers of Modernity." In *Geography and Empire*, edited by Anne Godlewska and Neil Smith, 31-55. Oxford: Blackwell, 1994.

Godlewska, Anne, and Neil Smith, eds. *Geography and Empire*. Oxford: Blackwell, 1994.

Goldstein, Alyosha. "Finance and Foreclosure in the Colonial Present." *Radical History Review* 2014, no. 118 (2014): 42-63.

Gordon, Katherine. *Made to Measure: A History of Land Surveying in British Columbia.* Winlaw: Sono Nis Press, 2006.

Gottesfeld, Allen S., and Ken A. Rabnett. *Skeena Fish Populations and their Habitat.* Hazelton: Skeena Fisheries Commission, 2007.

Gottesfeld, Leslie M.J. "Aboriginal Burning for Vegetation Management in Northwest British Columbia." *Human Ecology* 22, no. 2 (1994): 171–188.

Government of Canada. "Statement of the Government of Canada on Indian Policy." Ottawa: Department of Indian Affairs and Northern Development, 1969.

Government of Northwest Territories. "Traditional Knowledge Policy." Last modified March 10, 2005. https://www.gov.nt.ca/ecc/sites/ecc/files/documents/53_03_traditional_knowledge_policy.pdf

Groot, T., J. Warmerdam, M. Reitsma, B. Perry, L. McIntosh, D. Cromer, and D. Mendel. *Chronicles of Smithers: Our 100th Anniversary.* Smithers: self-published, Bulkley Valley Printers, 2013.

Haig-Brown, Celia. *Resistance and Renewal: Surviving the Indian Residential School.* Vancouver: Arsenal Pulp Press, 1988.

Haig-Brown, Celia. *Taking Control: Power and Contradiction in First Nations Adult Education.* Vancouver: UBC Press, 1995.

Hak, Gordon H. *Capital and Labour in the British Columbia Forest Industry, 1934-74.* Vancouver: UBC Press, 2007.

Haley, Brendan. "From Staples Trap to Carbon Trap: Canada's Peculiar Form of Carbon Lock-In." *Studies in Political Economy* 88 (2011): 97–132.

Hansen, James, Makiko Sato, Pushker Kharecha, David Beerling, Robert Berner, Valerie Masson-Delmotte, Mark Pagani, Maureen Raymo, Dana L. Royer, and James C. Zachos. "Target Atmospheric $CO_2$: Where Should Humanity Aim?" *The Open Atmospheric Science Journal* 2, no. 1 (2008): 217–231.

Hargus, Sharon. *Witsuwit'en Grammar: Phonetics, Phonology, Morphology.* Vancouver: UBC Press, 2007.

Hargus, Sharon. *Witsuwit'en Hibikinic: Witsuwit'en–English and English–Witsuwit'en.* Smithers: Wet'suwet'en Language and Cultural Society, 2022.

Harley, J.B. "Deconstructing the Map." *Cartographica* 26, no. 2 (1989): 1–20.

Harper, Stephen. "Address by the Prime Minister at the Canada-UK Chamber of Commerce." Prime Minister's Office, July 14, 2006. Accessed May 29, 2013. http://pm.gc.ca/media.asp?=1247.

Harrington, R. F. "Eulachon and the Grease Trails of British Columbia." *Canadian Geographical Journal* 74, no. 1 (1967): 28–31.

Harris, Cole. *Making Native Space: Colonialism, Resistance, and Reserves in British Columbia.* Vancouver: UBC Press. 2002.

Harris, Cole. *The Resettlement of British Columbia: Essays on Colonialism and Geographic Change.* Vancouver: UBC Press, 1997.

Harris, Douglas C. *Fish, Law, and Colonialism: The Legal Capture of Salmon in British Columbia.* Toronto: University of Toronto Press, 2001.

Harris, Douglas C. *Landing Native Fisheries: Indian Reserves and Fishing Rights in British Columbia, 1849-1925*. Vancouver: UBC Press, 2008.

Harris, Paul G. *What's Wrong with Climate Politics and How to Fix It*. Cambridge: Polity Press, 2013.

Harrison, Kathryn. "Federalism and Climate Policy Innovation: A Critical Reassessment." *Canadian Public Policy* 39, supplement 2 (2013): S95-S108.

Hartman, G.F. "Impacts of Growth in Resource Use and Human Population on the Nechako River." *GeoJournal* 40, no. 1-2 (1996): 147-164.

Harvey, David. *The Condition of Postmodernity: An Enquiry into the Origins of Cultural Change*. Oxford: Blackwell, 1989.

Harvey, David. *The Limits to Capital*. Oxford: Basil Blackwell, 1984.

Harvey, Robert G. *Carving the Western Path: By River, Rail, and Road through Central and Northern B.C.* Vancouver: Heritage House, 2006.

Hayter, Roger, and Trevor J. Barnes. "Neoliberalization and Its Geographic Limits: Comparative Reflections from Forest Peripheries in the Global North." *Economic Geography* 88, no. 2 (2012): 197-221.

Heisler, Karen, and Sean Markey. "Scales of Benefit: Political Leverage in the Negotiation of Corporate Social Responsibility in Mineral Exploration and Mining in Rural British Columbia, Canada." *Society & Natural Resources* 26, no. 4 (2013): 386-401.

Helin, Calvin. *Dances with Dependency: Indigenous Success through Self-reliance*. Vancouver: Orca Spirit, 2006.

Helin, Calvin. *The Economic Dependency Trap: Breaking Free to Self-Reliance*. St. Louis: Ravencrest Pub, 2011.

Henderson, James Y. "The Context of the State of Nature." In *Reclaiming Indigenous Voice and Vision*, edited by Marie Battiste, 11-38. Vancouver: UBC Press, 2000.

Henderson, James Y. *First Nations Jurisprudence and Aboriginal Rights: Defining the Just Society*. Saskatoon: Native Law Centre, 2006.

Hoberg, George. "The Battle over Oil Sands Access to Tidewater: A Political Risk Analysis of Pipeline Alternatives." *Canadian Public Policy* 39, no. 3 (2013): 371-391.

Hoekstra, Gordon. "More Environmental Concerns on Pipeline River Crossing in Northern B.C.: Wet'suwet'en Hereditary Chiefs." *Vancouver Sun*, January 31, 2023. https://vancouversun.com/business/more-environmental-concerns-on-pipeline-river-crossing-in-northern-b-c-wetsuweten-hereditary-chiefs.

Hoffman, Ross, with Alfred Joseph. *Song of the Earth: The Life of Alfred Joseph*. Smithers: Creekstone Press, 2019.

Hoogeveen, Dawn. "Sovereign Intentions: Gold Mining Law and Mineral Staking in British Columbia." *BC Studies* 198 (2018): 81-101.

Huber, Matthew. T. *Lifeblood: Oil, Freedom, and the Forces of Capital*. Minneapolis: University of Minnesota Press, 2013.

Hudson, Douglas R. "Traplines and Timber: Social and Economic Change among the Carrier Indians of Northern British Columbia." PhD Dissertation, University of Alberta, 1983. ERA. https://doi.org/10.7939/R3TQ5RK9H.

Hunt, Alan, and Gary Wickham. *Foucault and Law: Towards a Sociology of Law as Governance*. London: Pluto Press, 1994.

Hunt, Sarah. "Ontologies of Indigeneity: The Politics of Embodying a Concept." *Cultural Geographies* 21, no. 1 (2014): 27–32.

*Interior News*. "Illegal Moose Costly for Lakes Residents." Feb. 12, 1953.

*Interior News*. "Indians Air Grievances at Big Burns Lake Rally." May 1, 1952.

Indigenous and Northern Affairs Canada. "Population Characteristics Witset First Nation." First Nations Profiles. Updated December 7, 2021. https://fnp-ppn.aadnc-aandc.gc.ca/FNP/Main/Index.aspx.

Indigenous Business and Investment Council. "Cheslatta Carrier Nation." Accessed on June 14, 2021. https://www.bcibic.ca/success-stories/cheslatta-carrier-nation/.

Innis, Harold A. *The Fur Trade in Canada: An Introduction to Canadian Economic History*. Toronto: University of Toronto Press, 1964.

International Energy Agency. *World Energy Outlook 2013*. Paris: IEA, 2013. https://www.oecd-ilibrary.org/energy/world-energy-outlook-2013_weo-2013-en.

International Energy Agency. *World Energy Outlook 2014*. Paris: IEA, 2014. https://www.oecd-ilibrary.org/energy/world-energy-outlook-2014_weo-2014-en.

International Energy Agency. *World Energy Outlook 2015*. Paris: IEA, 2015. https://www.oecd-ilibrary.org/energy/world-energy-outlook-2015_weo-2015-en.

Jenness, Diamond. "The Carrier Indians of the Bulkley River: Their Social and Religious Life." *Bureau of American Ethnology* 133, no. 25 (1943): 469–586.

Jenness, Diamond. *Indians of Canada*. 6th ed. Ottawa: National Museums of Canada, 1967.

Johnson, Leslie M. *Trail of Story, Traveller's Path: Reflections on Ethnoecology and Landscape*. Edmonton: Athabasca University Press, 2010.

Joint Review Panel for the Enbridge Northern Gateway Project. *Considerations: Report of the Joint Review Panel for the Enbridge Northern Gateway Project*. 2 vols. Calgary: Publication Office of the National Energy Board, 2013.

Kelm, Mary-Ellen. *Colonizing Bodies: Aboriginal Health and Healing in British Columbia, 1900–1950*. Vancouver: UBC Press, 1998.

Killoran, Maureen, Olivia Dixon, Emily MacKinnon, and Sean Sutherland. "Significant Win at the Supreme Court of Canada: Leave to Appeal Trans Mountain Pipeline Decision Denied." *Osler* [blog], July 2, 2020. http://www.osler.com/en/about-us/press-room/2020/significant-win-at-the-supreme-court-of-canada-leave-to-appeal-trans-mountain-pipeline-decision-den.

Kimmerer, Robin W. *Braiding Sweetgrass: Indigenous Wisdom, Scientific Knowledge and the Teachings of Plants*. Minneapolis: Milkweed, 2013.

King, Thomas. "Godzilla vs. Post-colonial." *World Literature Written in English* 30, no. 2 (1990): 10–16.

Kino-nda-niimi Collective, ed. *The Winter We Danced: Voices from the Past, the Future, and the Idle No More Movement.* Winnipeg: ARP Books, 2014.

Kirchhoff, Denis, and Leonard J.S. Tsuji. "Reading between the Lines of the 'Responsible Resource Development' Rhetoric: The Use of Omnibus Bills to 'Streamline' Canadian Environmental Legislation." *Impact Assessment and Project Appraisal* 32, no. 2 (2014): 108–120.

Knight, Rolf. *Indians at Work: An Informal History of Native Indian Labour in British Columbia, 1858–1930.* 2nd ed. Vancouver: New Star Books, 1996.

Kovach, Margaret. *Indigenous Methodologies: Characteristics, Conversations, and Contexts.* Toronto: University of Toronto Press, 2009.

Kruisselbrink, Harry. *Smithers: A Railroad Town.* 2nd ed. Smithers: Bulkley Valley Historical and Museum Society, 2012.

Kuokkanen, Raunna. *Reshaping the University: Responsibility, Indigenous Epistemes and the Logic of the Gift.* Vancouver: UBC Press, 2007.

Labban, Mazen. "Oil in Parallax: Scarcity, Markets, and the Financialization of Accumulation." *Geoforum* 41, no. 4 (2010): 541–552.

Lake Babine Nation. "Statement of Intent." BC Treaty Commission, submitted December 17, 1993. https://www.bctreaty.ca/lake-babine-nation.

Lambrecht, Kirk. N. *Aboriginal Consultation, Environmental Assessment, and Regulatory Review in Canada.* Regina: University of Regina Press, 2013.

Lanceley-Barrie, Darlene. "The Devolution of Post Secondary Student Support to First Nations: I Am Not the Right Kind of Indian." Master's thesis, University of Saskatchewan, 2001. Harvest. http://hdl.handle.net/10388/etd-03122008-080513.

Large, R. Geddes. *Skeena: River of Destiny.* Vancouver: Mitchell Press, 1958.

Larsen, Soren C. "Promoting Aboriginal Territoriality through Interethnic Alliances: The Case of the Cheslatta T'en in Northern British Columbia." *Human Organization* 62, no. 1 (2003): 74–84.

Larsen, Soren C. "The Micropolitics of Storytelling in Collaborative Research: Reflections on a Mapping Project with the Cheslatta-Carrier Nation in British Columbia." In *A Deeper Sense of Place: Stories and Journeys of Indigenous-Academic Collaboration*, edited by Soren C. Larsen and Jay T. Johnson, 85–102. Corvallis, OR: Oregon State University Press, 2013.

Larsen, Soren C., and Jay T. Johnson. *Being Together in Place: Indigenous Coexistence in a More Than Human World.* Minneapolis: University of Minnesota Press, 2017.

Latour, Bruno. *Science in Action: How to Follow Scientists and Engineers through Society.* Cambridge: Harvard University Press, 1987.

Lawrence, Rebecca. "Governing Warlpiri Subjects: Indigenous Employment and Training Programs in the Central Australian Mining Industry." *Geographical Research* 43, no. 1 (2005): 40–48.

Lawton, F.L. "The Kemano-Kitimat Hydro-Electric Power Development." *Journal of the Royal Society of Arts* 101, no. 4912 (1953): 887–909.

Le Billon, Philippe, and Ryan Vandecasteyen. "(Dis)connecting Alberta's Tar Sands and British Columbia's North Coast." *Studies in Political Economy* 91 (2013): 35–57.

Leonard, Frank. *A Thousand Blunders: The Grand Trunk Pacific Railway and Northern British Columbia*. Vancouver: UBC Press, 1996.

Levant, Ezra. *Ethical Oil: The Case for Canada's Oil Sands*. Toronto: McClelland & Stewart, 2010.

Limerick, Patricia N. *The Legacy of Conquest: The Unbroken Past of the American West*. New York: W.W. Norton & Company, 1987.

Lippert, Owen, ed. *Beyond the Nass Valley: National Implications of the Supreme Court's* Delgamuukw *Decision*. Vancouver: Fraser Institute, 2000.

Lockyer, Debora. "Gitksan Wet'suwet'en Sign Accord." *Windspeaker* 12, no. 5 (1994): 2.

Lund, Christian. "Fragmented Sovereignty: Land Reform and Dispossession in Laos." *Journal of Peasant Studies* 38, no. 4 (2011): 885–905.

Lutz, John S. *Makuk: A New History of Aboriginal-White Relations*. Vancouver: UBC Press, 2008.

MacDonald, Lindsey Te Ata O Tu, and Paul Muldoon. "Globalisation, Neo-liberalism and the Struggle for Indigenous Citizenship." *Australian Journal of Political Science* 41, no. 2 (2006): 209–223.

Mackenzie, Alexander. *Voyages from Montreal, on the River St. Laurence, through the Continent of North America, to the Frozen and Pacific Oceans; in the Years 1789 and 1793. With a Preliminary Account of the Rise Progress, and Present State of the Fur Trade of that Country*. London: Cadell & Davies, 1801.

MacNeil, Robert. "Canadian Environmental Policy under Conservative Majority Rule." *Environmental Politics* 23, no. 1 (2014): 174–178.

MacNeil, Robert. "The Decline of Canadian Environmental Regulation: Neoliberalism and the Staples Bias." *Studies in Political Economy* 93 (2014): 81–106.

MacNeil, Robert, and Matthew Paterson. "Trudeau's Canada and the Challenge of Decarbonisation." *Environmental Politics* 27, no. 2 (2018): 379–384.

Makka, Roger, and Augie Fleras. *The Politics of Indigeneity: Challenging the State in Canada and Aotearoa New Zealand*. Dunedin, NZ: University of Otago Press, 2005.

Malm, Andreas. *How to Blow Up a Pipeline: Learning to Fight in a World on Fire*. London: Verso, 2021.

Manuel, Arthur. *Unsettling Canada: Rebuilding Indigenous Nations*. Toronto: Between the Lines, 2015.

Marsden, Susan, and Robert Galois. "The Tsimshian, the Hudson's Bay Company and the Geopolitics of the Northwest Coast Fur Trade, 1787–1840." *The Canadian Geographer* 39, no. 2 (1995): 169–183.

Marsden, William. *Stupid to the Last Drop: How Alberta Is Bringing Environmental Armageddon to Canada (And Doesn't Seem to Care)*. Toronto: Knopf Canada, 2007.

Massey, Doreen. "A Global Sense of Place." *Marxism Today,* June 1991: 24-29.

Mathias, Joe, Miles G. Richardson, Audrey Stewart, Murray Coolican, Edward John, Tony Sheridan, and L. Allan Williams. *The Report of the British Columbia Claims Task Force*. Victoria: First Nations of British Columbia, Government of British Columbia, and Government of Canada, 1991.

McConnell, William H. "The *Calder* Case in Historical Perspective." *Saskatchewan Law Review* 38, no. 1 (1974): 88-122.

McCreary, Tyler. "Between the Commodity and the Gift: The Coastal GasLink Pipeline and the Contested Temporalities of Canadian and Witsuwit'en Law." In *From Student Strikes to the Extinction Rebellion: New Protest Movements Shaping Our Future*, edited by Benjamin Richardson, 122-145. Cheltenham: Edward Elgar, 2020.

McCreary, Tyler. "Beyond Token Recognition: The Growing Movement against the Enbridge Northern Gateway Project." In Black, D'Arcy, Weis, and Russell, *A Line in the Tar Sands: Struggles for Environmental Justice*, 146-159.

McCreary, Tyler. "The Burden of Sovereignty: Court Configurations of Indigenous and State Authority in Aboriginal Title Litigation in Canada." *North American Dialogue* 17, no. 2 (2014): 64-78.

McCreary, Tyler. "Crisis in the Tar Sands: Fossil Capitalism and the Future of the Alberta Hydrocarbon Economy." *Historical Materialism* 30, no. 1 (2022): 31-65.

McCreary, Tyler. "Historicizing the Encounter between State, Corporate, and Indigenous Authorities on Gitxsan Lands." *Windsor Yearbook of Access to Justice* 33, no. 3 (2016): 163-197.

McCreary, Tyler. "Mining Aboriginal Success: The Politics of Difference in Continuing Education for Industry Needs." *The Canadian Geographer* 57, no. 3 (2013): 280-288.

McCreary, Tyler. "Plaintiff Helped Win a Major Victory for Canada's Native People." *Globe and Mail*, October 10, 2018.

McCreary, Tyler. "Settler Treaty Rights." *Briarpatch*, August 1, 2005.

McCreary, Tyler. *Shared Histories: Witsuwit'en-Settler Relations in Smithers, British Columbia, 1913-1973*. Smithers: Creekstone Press, 2018.

McCreary, Tyler. "Treaties Great Deal for Non-Natives." *Saskatoon StarPhoenix*, October 3, 2013.

McCreary, Tyler, Ranu Basu, and Anne Godlewska. "Critical Geographies of Education: Introduction to the Special Issue." In "Critical Geographies of Education," edited by Tyler McCreary, Ranu Basu, and Anne Godlewska, special issue, *The Canadian Geographer* 57, no. 3 (2013): 255-259.

McCreary, Tyler, and Rick Budhwa. "At the Core of the Wet'suwet'en Conflict: How, Ultimately, Should Resource Development Be Governed?" *The Globe and Mail*, January 9, 2019.

McCreary, Tyler, and Vanessa Lamb. "A Political Ecology of Sovereignty in Practice and on the Map: The Technicalities of Law, Participatory Mapping, and Environmental Governance." *Leiden Journal of International Law* 27, no. 3 (2014): 595–619.

McCreary, Tyler, and Richard Milligan. "The Limits of Liberal Recognition: Racial Capitalism, Settler Colonialism, and Environmental Governance in Vancouver and Atlanta." *Antipode* 53, no. 3 (2021): 724–744.

McCreary, Tyler, and Richard Milligan. "Pipelines, Permits, and Protests: Carrier Sekani Encounters with the Enbridge Northern Gateway Project." *Cultural Geographies* 21, no. 1 (2014): 115–129.

McCreary, Tyler, Suzanne Mills, and Anne St-Amand. "Lands and Resources for Jobs: How Aboriginal Peoples Strategically Use Environmental Assessments to Advance Community Employment Aims." *Canadian Public Policy* 42, no. 3 (2016): 212–223.

McCreary, Tyler, and Ann Marie F. Murnaghan. "Remixed Methodologies in Community-Based Film Research." *The Canadian Geographer* 64, no. 4 (2020): 576–589.

McCreary, Tyler, and Jerome Turner. "The Contested Scales of Indigenous and Settler Jurisdiction: Unist'ot'en Struggles with Canadian Pipeline Governance." *Studies in Political Economy* 99, no. 3 (2018): 223–245.

McCreary, Tyler, and Jerome Turner. "Did the Protests Work? The Wet'suwet'en Resistance One Year Later." *The Walrus*, February 10, 2020. https://thewalrus.ca/did-the-protests-work-the-wetsuweten-resistance-one-year-later/.

McCreary, Tyler, and Shauna Wouters. "Pandemic Pipelines: How Essential Service Declarations Enabled Extractive Infrastructure Development under the Cover of COVID-19." In *Indigenous Health and Well-Being in the COVID-19 Pandemic*, edited by Nicholas D. Spence and Fatih Sekercioglu, 239–254. London: Routledge, 2022.

McDonald, James. A. "Images of the Nineteenth-Century Economy of the Tsimshian." In *The Tsimshian: Images of the Past, Views for the Present*, edited by Margaret Seguin, 40–54. Vancouver: UBC Press, 1984.

McGregor, Deborah. "Coming Full Circle: Indigenous Knowledge, Environment, and Our Future." *American Indian Quarterly* 28, no. 3-4 (2004): 385–410.

McHarg, Sandra, and Maureen Cassidy. *Before Roads and Rails: Pack Trails and Packing in the Upper Skeena Area*. Hazelton: Northwest Community College, 1980.

McKee, Christopher. *Treaty Talks in British Columbia: Negotiating a Mutually Beneficial Future*. 2nd ed. Vancouver: UBC Press, 2000.

McMahon, Fred, and Cam Vidler. *Survey of Mining Companies 2007/2008*. Vancouver: Fraser Institute, 2008.

McNeil, Kent. *Common Law Aboriginal Title*. Oxford: Oxford University Press, 1989.

McNeil, Kent. "The Onus of Proof of Aboriginal Title." *Osgoode Hall Law Journal* 37 (1999): 775–803.

McPhie, M. "A Social Licence to Operate." *Vancouver Sun*, August 30, 2006.

Miéville, China. *Between Equal Rights: A Marxist Theory of International Law*. Chicago: Haymarket Books, 2006.

Miller, Bruce G., ed. "Anthropology and History in the Courts." Special issue, *BC Studies* 95 (Autumn 1992).

Miller, Bruce G. *Oral History on Trial: Recognizing Aboriginal Narratives in the Courts*. Vancouver: UBC Press, 2011.

Miller, Jim R. *Compact, Contract, Covenant: Aboriginal Treaty Making in Canada*. Toronto: University of Toronto Press, 2009.

Miller, Jim R. *Shingwauk's Vision: A History of Native Residential Schools*. Toronto: University of Toronto Press, 1996.

Milligan, Richard, and Tyler McCreary. "Between Kitimat LNG Terminal and *Monkey Beach*: Literary-Geographic Methods and the Politics of Recognition in Resource Governance on Haisla Territory." *GeoHumanities* 4, no. 1 (2018): 45–65.

Milligan, Richard, and Tyler McCreary. "Inscription, Innocence, and Invisibility: Early Contributions to the Discursive Formation of North in Samuel Hearne's *A Journey to the Northern Ocean*." In *Rethinking the Great White North: Race, Nature and the Historical Geographies of Whiteness in Canada*, edited by Andrew Baldwin, Laura Cameron, Audrey Kobayashi, 147–168. Vancouver: UBC Press, 2011.

Milloy, John S. *A National Crime: The Canadian Government and the Residential School System, 1879 to 1986*. Winnipeg: University of Manitoba Press, 1999.

Mills, Antonia. *Eagle Down Is Our Law: Witsuwit'en Law, Feasts, and Land Claims*. Vancouver: UBC Press, 1994.

Mills, Antonia, ed. *"Hang Onto These Words": Johnny David's* Delgamuukw *Evidence*. Toronto: University of Toronto Press, 2005.

Mills, P. Dawn. *For Future Generations: Reconciling Gitxsan and Canadian Law*. Saskatoon: Purich Publishing, 2008.

Mills, Suzanne. "The Geography of Skill: Mobility and Exclusionary Unionism in Canada's North." *Environment and Planning A: Economy and Space* 51, no. 3 (2019): 724–742.

Mills, Suzanne, and Tyler McCreary. "Negotiating Neoliberal Empowerment: Aboriginal People, Educational Restructuring, and Academic Labour in the North of British Columbia, Canada: Neoliberal Aboriginal Empowerment." *Antipode* 45, no. 5 (2013): 1298–1317.

Mills, Suzanne, and Brendan Sweeney. "Employment Relations in the Neostaples Resource Economy: Impact Benefit Agreements and Aboriginal Governance in Canada's Nickel Mining Industry." *Studies in Political Economy* 91 (2013): 7–33.

Mitchell, Audra. "Revitalizing Laws, (Re)-making Treaties, Dismantling Violence: Indigenous Resurgence against 'the Sixth Mass Extinction.'" *Social & Cultural Geography* 21, no. 7 (2020): 909–924.

Mitchell, Timothy. *Colonizing Egypt*. Cambridge: Cambridge University Press, 1989.

Mitchell, Timothy. *Carbon Democracy: Political Power in the Age of Oil*. London: Verso, 2011.

Monture-Angus, Patricia. *Journeying Forward: Dreaming First Nations' Independence*. Halifax: Fernwood, 1999.

Moore, Michal, Sam Flaim, David Hackett, Susan Grissom, Daria Crisan, and Afshin Hornavar. "Catching the Brass Ring: Oil Market Diversification Potential for Canada." *The School of Public Policy Publications* 4, no. 16 (2011).

Morgensen, Scott L. "The Biopolitics of Settler Colonialism: Right Here, Right Now." *Settler Colonial Studies* 1, no. 1 (2011): 52–76.

Morgensen, Scott L. *Spaces Between Us: Queer Settler Colonialism and Indigenous Decolonization*. Minneapolis: University of Minnesota Press, 2011.

Morice, Adrien-Gabriel. *The History of the Northern Interior of British Columbia*. Toronto: William Briggs, 1904.

Morin, Mélanie. H. *Niwhts'ide'ni Hibi'it'en: The Ways of Our Ancestors*. 2nd ed. Smithers: School District #54, 2016.

Muldoon, Paul. "The Sovereign Exceptions: Colonization and the Foundation of Society." *Social and Legal Studies* 17, no. 1 (2008): 59–74.

Mulhall, David. *Will to Power: The Missionary Career of Father Morice*. Vancouver: UBC Press, 1986.

Mullan, David. "The Supreme Court and the Duty to Consult Aboriginal Peoples: A Lifting of the Fog?" *Canadian Journal of Administrative Law and Practice* 24 (2011): 233–260.

Mullins, Doreen Katherine. "Changes in Location and Structure in the Forest Industry of North Central British Columbia: 1909–1966." Master's thesis, University of British Columbia, 1967. DSpace. http://hdl.handle.net/2429/36677.

Muszynski, Alicja. *Cheap Wage Labour: Race and Gender in the Fisheries of British Columbia*. Montréal: McGill-Queen's University Press, 1996.

Myers, Mike. "An Incredible Bid for Aluminum in Uninhabited Mountain Waste." *Harvester World* 43, no. 10 (1952): 3–12.

Mynett, Geoff. *Murders on the Skeena: True Crime in the Old Canadian West, 1884–1914*. Qualicum Beach, BC: Caitlin Press, 2022.

Mynett, Geoff. *Rivers of Mists: People of the Upper Skeena, 1821–1930*. Qualicum Beach, BC: Caitlin Press, 2022.

Nadasdy, Paul. "The Anti-politics of TEK: The Institutionalization of Co-management Discourse and Practice." *Anthropologica* 47, no. 2 (2005): 215–232.

Nadasdy, Paul. *Sovereignty's Entailments: First Nation State Formation in the Yukon*. Toronto: University of Toronto Press, 2017.

Nahwegahbow, David C. "Foreword." In *Chief Kerry's Moose: A Guidebook to Land Use and Occupancy Mapping, Research Design and Data Collection*, by Terry N. Tobias, vi–vii. Vancouver: Union of BC Indian Chiefs and Ecotrust Canada, 2000.

Napoleon, Val. "Ayook: Gitksan Legal Order, Law, and Legal Theory." PhD Dissertation, University of Victoria, 2009. DSpace. http://hdl.handle.net/1828/1392.

Napoleon, Val. "Behind the Blockades." *Indigenous Law Journal* 9 (2010): 1–51.

Napoleon, Val. *Delgamuukw*: A Legal Straightjacket for Oral Histories. *Canadian Journal of Law and Society* 20, no. 2 (2005): 123-155.

Napoleon, Val. "Thinking About Indigenous Legal Orders." In *Dialogues on Human Rights and Legal Pluralism*, edited by René Provost and Colleen Sheppard, 229–245. Dordrecht: Springer, 2013.

National Energy Board. *Filing Manual*. Calgary: National Energy Board Publications Office, 2012.

National Indian Brotherhood. *Indian Control of Indian Education*. Ottawa: National Indian Brotherhood, 1973.

Newman, Dwight G. *Revisiting the Duty to Consult*. Saskatoon: Purich Publishing, 2014.

New Relationship Trust Corporation. *Feedback Summary from Regional Engagements across B.C.: What We Heard from You*. North Vancouver: New Relationship Trust Corporation, 2007. http://www.newrelationshiptrust.ca/downloads/final-report-summary.pdf.

Nikiforuk, Andrew. *Tar Sands: Dirty Oil and the Future of a Continent*. Vancouver: Greystone Books and David Suzuki Foundation, 2008.

Noble, Bram, and Courtney. R. Fidler. "Advancing Indigenous Community—Corporate Agreements: Lessons from Practice in the Canadian Mining Sector." *Oil, Gas, and Energy Law Intelligence* 4 (2011): 3143.

Notzke, Claudia. *Aboriginal Peoples and Natural Resources in Canada*. North York, ON: Captus Press, 1994.

Notzke, Claudia. "A New Perspective in Aboriginal Natural Resource Management: Co-management." *Geoforum* 26, no. 2 (1995): 187–209.

Nowry, Laurence. *Man of Mana: Marius Barbeau*. Toronto: NC Press, 1995.

O'Faircheallaigh, Ciaran. "Aborigines, Mining Companies and the State in Contemporary Australia: A New Political Economy or 'Business as Usual'?" *Australian Journal of Political Science* 41, no. 1 (2006): 1–22.

O'Faircheallaigh, Ciaran. "Community Development Agreements in the Mining Industry: An Emerging Global Phenomenon." *Community Development* 44, no. 2 (2013): 222–238.

O'Faircheallaigh, Ciaran. "Environmental Agreements, EIA Follow-Up and Aboriginal Participation in Environmental Management: The Canadian Experience." *Environmental Impact Assessment Review* 27, no. 4 (2007): 319–342.

Office of the Wet'suwet'en. "Event Galvanizes Opposition to Enbridge Tar Sands Pipeline." News release, Wilderness Committee, July 7, 2009.

Overstall, Richard. "Encountering the Spirit in the Land: 'Property' in a Kinship-Based Legal Order." In *Despotic Dominion: Property Rights in British Settler*

Societies, edited by John P.S. McLaren, A.R. Buck, and Nancy E. Wright, 22–49. Vancouver: UBC Press, 2005.

Özden-Schilling, Tom. "Cartographies of Consignment: First Nations and Mapwork in the Neoliberal Era." *Anthropological Quarterly* 92, no. 2 (2019): 541–573.

Özden-Schilling, Tom. "Technopolitics in the Archive: Sovereignty, Research, and Everyday Life." *History and Theory* 59, no. 3 (2020): 394–402.

Pachauri, Rajendra. K., Myles R. Allen, Vicente R. Barros, John Broome, Wolfgang Cramer, Renate Christ, John A. Church, Leon Clarke, Qin Dahe, Purnamita Dasgupta, and Navroz K. Dubash. *Climate Change 2014: Synthesis Report. Contribution of Working Groups I, II and III to the Fifth Assessment Report of the Intergovernmental Panel on Climate Change*. Geneva: IPCC, 2014.

Pasternak, Shiri. "The Fiscal Body of Sovereignty: To 'Make Live' in Indian Country." *Settler Colonial Studies* 6, no.4 (2016): 317–338.

Pasternak, Shiri. *Grounded Authority: The Algonquins of Barriere Lake against the State*. Minneapolis: University of Minnesota Press, 2017.

Pasternak, Shiri. "Jurisdiction and Settler Colonialism: Where Do Laws Meet?" *Canadian Journal of Law and Society* 29, no. 2 (2014): 145–161.

Pasternak, Shiri, and Tia Dafnos. "How Does a Settler State Secure the Circuitry of Capital?" *Environment and Planning D: Society and Space* 36, no. 4 (2018): 739–757.

Paul, Daniel N. *We Were Not the Savages: A Mi'kmaq Perspective on the Collision between European and Native American Civilizations*. 2nd ed. Halifax: Fernwood, 2000.

Pearce, Margaret, and Renee. P. Louis. "Mapping Indigenous Depth of Place." *American Indian Culture and Research Journal* 32, no. 3 (2008): 107–126.

Penikett, Tony. *Reconciliation: First Nations Treaty Making in British Columbia*. Vancouver: Douglas & McIntyre, 2006.

Penner, Derrick. "Coastal GasLink in Hot Water over Pipeline Environmental Violations" *Vancouver Sun*, October 23, 2022. https://vancouversun.com/business/energy/coastal-gaslink-in-hot-water-over-pipeline-environmental-violations.

Perry, Adele. *On the Edge of Empire: Gender, Race, and the Making of British Columbia, 1849–1871*. Toronto: University of Toronto Press, 2001.

Peters, Sheila. *Canyon Creek: A Script*. Smithers: Creekstone Press, 1998.

Peterson St-Laurent, Guillaume, and Philippe Le Billon. "Staking Claims and Shaking Hands: Impact and Benefit Agreements as a Technology of Government in the Mining Sector." *The Extractive Industries and Society* 2, no. 3 (2015): 590–602.

Peyton, Jonathan, and Aaron Franks. "The New Nature of Things? Canada's Conservative Government and the Design of the New Environmental Subject." *Antipode* 48, no. 2 (2016): 453–473.

Pinder, Leslie H. *The Carriers of No: After the Land Claims Trial*. Vancouver: Lazara Press, 1991.

Popowich, Morris. "The National Energy Board as Intermediary Between the Crown, Aboriginal Peoples and Industry." *Alberta Law Review* 44, no. 4 (2007): 827–862.

Potkins, Meghan. "Coastal GasLink Price Tag Climbs to $14.5 Billion and Could Go Even Higher." *Financial Post*, February 1, 2023. https://financialpost.com/commodities/energy/oil-gas/coastal-gaslink-price-tag-climbs-go-higher.

Potkins, Meghan. "'Horrified': Trans Mountain's Latest Big Cost Increase Catches Watchers by Surprise." *Financial Post*, March 15, 2023. https://financialpost.com/commodities/energy/oil-gas/tmx-costs-skyrocket-what-need-know-trans-mountain-pipeline.

Promislow, Janna. "Irreconcilable? The Duty to Consult and Administrative Decision Makers." *Canadian Journal of Administrative Law and Practice* 26 (2013): 251–274.

Prudham, Scott. *Knock on Wood: Nature as Commodity in Douglas-Fir Country*. New York: Routledge, 2004.

Prudham, Scott. "Sustaining Sustained Yield: Class, Politics, and Post-War Forest Regulation in British Columbia." *Environment and Planning D: Society and Space* 25, no. 2 (2007): 258–283.

Radcliffe, Sarah A. "Geography and Indigeneity III: Co-articulation of Colonialism and Capitalism in Indigeneity's Economies." *Progress in Human Geography* 44, no. 2 (2020): 374–388.

Rajala, Richard A. *Clearcutting the Pacific Rain Forest: Production, Science, and Regulation*. Vancouver: UBC Press, 1998.

Raunet, Daniel. *Without Surrender Without Consent: A History of the Nisga'a Land Claims*. Vancouver: Douglas & McIntyre, 1996.

Ray, Arthur J. "Creating the Image of the Savage in Defence of the Crown: The Ethnohistorian in Court." *Native Studies Review* 6, no. 2 (1990): 13–29.

Ray, Arthur J. "Fur Trade History and the Gitksan-Wet'suwet'en Comprehensive Claim: Men of Property and the Exercise of Title." In *Aboriginal Resource Use in Canada: Historical and Legal Aspects*, edited by Kerry Abel and Jean Friesen, 301–316. Winnipeg: University of Manitoba Press, 1991.

Ray, Arthur J. *Indians in the Fur Trade: Their Role as Trappers, Hunters, and Middlemen in the Lands Southwest of Hudson Bay, 1660–1870*. Toronto: University of Toronto Press, 1998.

Ray, Arthur J. *Telling It to the Judge: Taking Native History to Court*. Montréal: McGill-Queen's University Press, 2011.

Rich, Edwin Ernest. *The Fur Trade and the Northwest to 1857*. Toronto: McClelland & Stewart, 1967.

Rifkin, Mark. *Beyond Settler Time: Temporal Sovereignty and Indigenous Self-Determination*. Durham: Duke University Press, 2017.

Rifkin, Mark. "Indigenising Agamben: Rethinking Sovereignty in Light of the 'Peculiar' Status of Native Peoples." *Cultural Critique* 73 (2009): 88–124.

Roberts, John. *The Modern Firm: Organizational Design for Performance and Growth*. Oxford: Oxford University Press, 2008.

Robinson, Ira. M. *New Industrial Towns on Canada's Resource Frontier*. Chicago: Department of Geography, University of Chicago, 1962.

Rose, Samuel W. "Two Thematic Manifestations of Neotribal Capitalism in the United States." *Anthropological Theory* 15, no. 2 (2015): 218–238.

Rossiter, David A. "Producing Provincial Space: Crown Forests, the State and Territorial Control in British Columbia." *Space and Polity* 12, no. 2 (2008): 215–230.

Roth, Christopher F. *Becoming Tsimshian: The Social Life of Names*. Seattle: University of Washington Press, 2008.

Ryan, Teresa L. "Territorial Jurisdiction: The Cultural and Economic Significance of Eulachon *Thaleichthys pacificus* in the North-Central Coast Region of British Columbia." PhD Dissertation, University of British Columbia, 2014. DSpace. http://hdl.handle.net/2429/46515.

Said, Edward W. *Culture and Imperialism*. New York: Vintage Books, 1994.

Salomons, Geoff H., and George Hoberg. "Setting Boundaries of Participation in Environmental Impact Assessment." *Environmental Impact Assessment Review* 45 (2014): 69–75.

Sam, Cecilia. "Power and Equality: 'One' Meets 'Two' on Burns Lake Indian Reserve No. 18." Master's thesis, University of British Columbia, 2000. DSpace. http://hdl.handle.net/2429/10949.

Sanders, Douglas. "The Nishga Case." *BC Studies* 19 (1973): 3–20.

Santos, Boaventura de Sousa. *Toward a New Legal Common Sense: Law, Globalization, and Emancipation*. 2nd ed. Cambridge: Cambridge University Press, 2002.

Scott, Dayna N. "Extraction Contracting: The Struggle for Control of Indigenous Lands." *South Atlantic Quarterly* 119, no. 2 (2020): 269–299.

Scott, James C. *Weapons of the Weak: Everyday Forms of Peasant Resistance*. New Haven: Yale University Press, 1985.

Scott, Tracie L. *Postcolonial Sovereignty? The Nisga'a Final Agreement*. Saskatoon: Purich Publishing, 2012.

Scottie, Joan, Warren Bernauer, and Jack Hicks. *I Will Live for Both of Us: A History of Colonialism, Uranium Mining, and Inuit Resistance*. Winnipeg: University of Manitoba Press, 2022.

Shervill, R. Lynn. *Smithers: From Swamp to Village*. Smithers: Town of Smithers, 1981.

*Smithers: Grand Trunk Pacific Freight and Passenger Division Headquarters*. Smithers: Bulkley Valley Historical and Museum Society, 1978. Facsimile of the first edition published 1914 by Aldous and Murray (Vancouver).

Simpson, Audra. *Mohawk Interruptus: Political Life Across the Borders of Settler States*. Durham: Duke University Press, 2014.

Simpson, Jeffrey, Mark Jaccard, and Nic Rivers. *Hot Air: Meeting Canada's Climate Change Challenge*. Toronto: McClelland & Stewart, 2008.

Simpson, Leanne Betasamosake. *As We Have Always Done: Indigenous Freedom through Radical Resistance*. Minneapolis: University of Minnesota Press, 2017.

Simpson, Leanne Betasamosake. *Dancing on Our Turtle's Back: Stories of Nishnaabeg Re-Creation, Resurgence, and a New Emergence*. Winnipeg: ARP Books, 2011.

Simpson, Leanne Betasamosake. *A Short History of the Blockade: Giant Beavers, Diplomacy, and Regeneration in Nishnaabewin*. Edmonton: University of Alberta Press, 2021.

Simpson, Michael, and Philippe Le Billon. "Reconciling Violence: Policing the Politics of Recognition." *Geoforum* 119 (2021): 111–121.

Sinclair, Murray, Marie Wilson, and Chief Wilton Littlechild. *Honouring the Truth, Reconciling for the Future: Summary of the Final Report of the Truth and Reconciliation Commission of Canada*. Toronto: Lorimer, 2015.

Slattery, Brian. "The Metamorphosis of Aboriginal Title." *Canadian Bar Review* 85 (2006): 255–286.

Slowey, Gabrielle A. *Navigating Neoliberalism: Self-Determination and the Mikisew Cree First Nation*. Vancouver: UBC Press, 2008.

Snelgrove, Corey, Rita K. Dhamoon, and Jeff Corntassel. "Unsettling Settler Colonialism: The Discourse and Politics of Settlers, and Solidarity with Indigenous Nations." *Decolonization: Indigeneity, Education & Society* 3, no. 2 (2014): 1–32.

Sommerville, Melanie. "Naturalising Finance, Financialising Natives: Indigeneity, Race, and 'Responsible' Agricultural Investment in Canada." *Antipode* 53, no. 3 (2021): 643–664.

Sparke, Matthew. "A Map that Roared and an Original Atlas: Canada, Cartography, and the Narration of Nation." *Annals of the Association of American Geographers* 88, no. 3 (1998): 463–495.

Stanford, Jim. "Staples, Deindustrialization, and Foreign Investment: Canada's Economic Journey Back to the Future." *Studies in Political Economy* 82 (2008): 7–34.

Stanley, Anna. "Resilient Settler Colonialism: 'Responsible Resource Development,' 'Flow-Through' Financing, and the Risk Management of Indigenous Sovereignty in Canada." *Environment and Planning A: Economy and Space* 48, no. 12 (2016): 2422–2442.

Statistics Canada. "Aboriginal Peoples in Canada: Key Results from the 2016 Census." *The Daily*, October 25, 2017. https://www150.statcan.gc.ca/n1/daily-quotidien/171025/dq171025a-eng.htm.

Stern, Philip. "'Bundles of Hyphens': Corporations as Legal Communities in the Early Modern British Empire." In *Legal Pluralism and Empires, 1500–1850*, edited by Lauren Benton and Richard J. Ross, 21–47. New York: New York University Press, 2013.

Sterritt, Neil J. *Mapping My Way Home: A Gitxsan History*. Smithers: Creekstone Press, 2016.

Sterritt, Neil J. "Unflinching Resistance to an Implacable Invader." In *Drumbeat: Anger and Renewal in Indian Country*, edited by Boyce Richardson, 267–294. Toronto: Sunhill Press, 1989.

Sterritt, Neil J., Susan Marsden, Robert Galois, Peter R. Grant, and Richard Overstall. *Tribal Boundaries in the Nass Watershed*. Vancouver: UBC Press, 1998.

Stevenson, Jane. *A Trail of Two Telegraphs: And Other Historic Tales of the Bulkley Valley and Beyond*. Halfmoon Bay: Caitlin Press, 2013.

Stevenson, Marc G. "Indigenous Knowledge in Environmental Assessment." *Arctic* 49, no. 3 (1996): 278–291.

Stoffle, Richard W., and Michael J. Evans. "Holistic Conservation and Cultural Triage: American Indian Perspectives on Cultural Resources." *Human Organization* 49, no. 2 (1990): 91–99.

Strong-Boag, Veronica. *Fostering Nation? Canada Confronts Its History of Childhood Disadvantage*. Waterloo: Wilfrid Laurier University Press, 2011.

Swart, Neil C., and Andrew J. Weaver. "The Alberta Oil Sands and Climate." *Nature Climate Change* 2, no. 3 (2012): 134–136.

Swyngedouw, Erik. "Impossible Sustainability and the Post-political Condition." In *Making Strategies in Spatial Planning: Knowledge and Values*, edited by Maria Cerreta, Grazia Concilio, and Valeria Monno, 185–205. Dordrecht, NLD: Springer, 2010.

Sze, Julie. *Environmental Justice in a Moment of Danger*. Oakland: University of California Press, 2020.

Talbot, Frederick A. *The New Garden of Canada: By Pack-Horse and Canoe through Undeveloped New British Columbia*. London: Cassell and Company, 1911.

Taylor, Alison, Tracy Friedel, and Lois Edge. *Pathways for First Nation and Métis Youth in the Oil Sands*. Ottawa: Canadian Policy Research Networks, 2009.

Temper, Leah. "Blocking Pipelines, Unsettling Environmental Justice: From Rights of Nature to Responsibility to Territory." *Local Environment* 24, no. 2 (2019): 94–112.

Tennant, Paul. *Aboriginal Peoples and Politics: The Indian Land Question in British Columbia, 1849–1989*. Vancouver: UBC Press, 1990.

Thom, Brian. "Reframing Indigenous Territories: Private Property, Human Rights and Overlapping Claims." *American Indian Culture and Research Journal* 38, no. 4 (2014): 3–28.

Thomas-Müller, Clayton. "The Rise of the Native Rights-Based Strategic Framework: Our Last Best Hope to Save our Water, Air, and Earth." In Black, D'Arcy, Weis, and Russell, *A Line in the Tar Sands: Struggles for Environmental Justice*, 240–252.

Tobias, T.N. *Chief Kerry's Moose: A Guidebook to Land Use and Occupancy Mapping, Research Design, and Data Collection*. Vancouver: Union of BC Indian Chiefs and Ecotrust Canada, 2000.

Tobias, T.N. *Living Proof: The Essential Data-Collection Guide for Indigenous Use-and-Occupancy Map Surveys*. Vancouver: Union of BC Indian Chiefs and Ecotrust Canada, 2009.

Trudeau, Justin. "Prime Minister Trudeau Announces Decisions on Major Energy Projects in Canada." Office of the Prime Minister. Recorded November 29, 2016. Video, 14:58. https://pm.gc.ca/en/videos/2016/11/29/prime-minister-trudeau-announces-decisions-major-energy-projects-canada.

Trusler, Scott. "Footsteps amongst the Berries: The Ecology and Fire History of Traditional Gitxsan and Wet'suwet'en Huckleberry Sites." Master's thesis, University of Northern British Columbia, 2002. UNBC Digital Institutional Repository. https://doi.org/10.24124/2002/bpgub222.

Trusler, Scott, and Leslie M. Johnson. "'Berry Patch' as a Kind of Place—the Ethnoecology of Black Huckleberry in Northwestern Canada." *Human Ecology* 36 no. 4 (2008): 553–568.

Tsing, Anna Lowenhaupt. *Friction: An Ethnography of Global Connection*. Princeton: Princeton University Press, 2005.

Tsiroulnitchenko, Evguenia, and Elspeth Hazell. *Economic Activity of the On-Reserve Aboriginal Identity Population in Canada: Gross Domestic Product Estimates for Indian Reserves, 2000 and 2005*. Ottawa: Centre for the Study of Living Standards, 2011.

Turkel, William J. *The Archive of Place: Unearthing the Pasts of the Chilcotin Plateau*. Vancouver: UBC Press, 2007.

Turner, Christopher, and Gail Fondahl. "'Overlapping Claims' to Territory Confronting Treaty-Making in British Columbia: Causes and Implications." *The Canadian Geographer* 59, no. 4 (2015): 474–488.

Turner, Frederick Jackson. "The West and American Ideals." In *The Frontier in American History* by Frederick Jackson Turner, 290–310. New York: Henry Holt and Company, 1921. Essay originally published October 1914 in *The Washington Historical Quarterly*.

Turner, Frederick Jackson. "The Significance of the Frontier in American History." In *The Frontier in American History* by Frederick Jackson Turner, 1–38. New York: Henry Holt and Company, 1921. Essay originally published 1893 in *The Report of the American Historical Association*.

Unist'ot'en Camp. "Message from Unist'ot'en Member Karla Tait." Posted December 31, 2018. Facebook video, 4:15. https://www.facebook.com/unistoten/videos/732136867163868/.

Unist'ot'en Healing Centre. "Unist'ot'en Camp." Posted December 6, 2018. YouTube video, 3:23. https://www.youtube.com/watch?v=MQ2fr00t6CQ.

Usher, Peter J., Frank J. Tough, and Robert M. Galois. "Reclaiming the Land: Aboriginal Title, Treaty Rights and Land Claims in Canada." *Applied Geography* 12, no. 2 (1992): 109–132.

Van Kirk, Sylvia. *Many Tender Ties: Women in Fur-Trade Society, 1670–1870*. Norman, OK: University of Oklahoma Press, 1983.

Veltmeyer, Henry, and Paul Bowles. "Extractivist Resistance: The Case of the Enbridge Oil Pipeline Project in Northern British Columbia." *Extractive Industries and Society* 1, no. 1 (2014): 59-68.

Venema, Kathleen R. "'Under the Protection of a Principal Man': A White Man, the Hero, and His Wives in Samuel Hearne's *Journey*." *Essays on Canadian Writing*, no. 70 (2000): 162-190.

Viveiros de Castro, Eduardo. "Perspectival Anthropology and the Method of Controlled Equivocation." *Tipití: Journal of the Society for the Anthropology of Lowland South America* 2, no. 1 (2004): 1.

Wainwright, Joel, and Joe Bryan. "Cartography, Territory, Property: Postcolonial Reflections on Indigenous Counter-Mapping in Nicaragua and Belize." *Cultural Geographies* 16, no. 2 (2009): 153-178.

Wale, Vera, and Gordon Jack. *Gitxsan Dictionary-Giganix version 1.3*. Accessed 26 July, 2023. https://docplayer.net/170885532-Gitxsan-dictionary-giganix-version-1-3-gitxsan-to-english.html.

Walters, Mark. "British Imperial Constitutional Law and Aboriginal Rights: A Comment on *Delgamuukw v. British Columbia*." *Queen's Law Journal* 17 (1992): 350-413.

Warkentin, Germaine. *Canadian Exploration Literature*. Don Mills: Oxford University Press, 1993.

Watts, Michael. "Economies of Violence: More Oil, More Blood." *Economic and Political Weekly* 38, no. 48 (2003): 5089-5099.

Watts, Michael. "Empire of Oil: Capitalist Dispossession and the Scramble for Africa." *Monthly Review* 58, no. 4 (2006): 1-17.

Watts, Michael. "Righteous Oil? Human Rights, the Oil Complex, and Corporate Social Responsibility." *Annual Review of Environment and Resources* 30, no. 1 (2005): 373-407.

Weaver, Sally M. *Making Canadian Indian Policy: The Hidden Agenda, 1968-70*. Toronto: University of Toronto Press, 1981.

Weber, Max. "Politics as a Vocation." In *From Max Weber: Essays in Sociology*, edited by Hans. H. Gerth and C. Wright Mills, 77-128. New York: Oxford University Press, 1946.

Weiner, Annette B. *Inalienable Possessions: The Paradox of Keeping-While-Giving*. Berkeley: University of California Press, 1992.

Weis, Tony, Toban Black, Stephen D'Arcy, and Joshua Kahn Russell. "Introduction: Drawing a Line in the Tar Sands." In Black, D'arcy, Weis, and Russel, *A Line in the Tar Sands: Struggles for Environmental Justice*, 1-20.

White, Graham. "Cultures in Collision: Traditional Knowledge and Euro-Canadian Governance Processes in Northern Land-Claim Boards." *Arctic* 5, no. 4 (December 2006): 401-414.

White, Richard. *The Middle Ground: Indians, Empires, and Republics in the Great Lakes Region, 1650-1815*. Cambridge: Cambridge University Press, 1991.

Whyte, Kyle P. "Indigenous Science (Fiction) for the Anthropocene: Ancestral Dystopias and Fantasies of Climate Change Crises." *Environment and Planning E: Nature and Space* 1, no. 1-2 (2018): 224-242.

Wickham, Molly. "Initiating the Process of Youth Decolonization: Reclaiming Our Right to Know and Act on Our Experiences." In *For Indigenous Minds Only: A Decolonization Handbook*, edited by Waziyatawin and Michael Yellow Bird, 179-203. Santa Fe: School for Advanced Research Press, 2012.

Wild, Nettie, dir. *Blockade: It's About the Land and Who Controls It*. Montréal: National Film Board, 1993.

Wilson, Shawn. *Research Is Ceremony: Indigenous Research Methods*. Halifax: Fernwood Publishing, 2008.

Windsor, J.E., and J.A. McVey. "Annihilation of Both Place and Sense of Place: The Experience of the Cheslatta T'en Canadian First Nation within the Context of Large-Scale Environmental Projects." *The Geographical Journal* 171, no. 2 (2005): 146-165.

Wolfe, Patrick. "Settler Colonialism and the Elimination of the Native." *Journal of Genocide Research* 8, no. 4 (2006): 387-409.

Wood, June. *Home to the Nechako: The River and the Land*. Victoria: Heritage House, 2013.

Wood, Patricia, and David A. Rossiter. "Unstable Properties: British Columbia, Aboriginal Title, and the 'New Relationship.'" *The Canadian Geographer* 55, no. 4 (2011): 407-425.

Wood, Patricia, and David A. Rossiter. "Fantastic Topographies: Neo-liberal Responses to Aboriginal Land Claims in British Columbia." *The Canadian Geographer* 49, no. 4 (2005): 352-366.

Woolford, Andrew. *Between Justice and Certainty: Treaty Making in British Columbia*. Vancouver: UBC Press, 2005.

Zent, Stanford. "A Genealogy of Scientific Representations of Indigenous Knowledge." In *Landscape, Process and Power: Re-evaluating Traditional Environmental Knowledge*, edited by Serena Heckler, 19-67. New York: Bergahn Books, 2009.

Žižek, Slavoj. *The Ticklish Subject: The Absent Centre of Political Ontology*. London: Verso, 1999.

# Index

*Figures and maps indicated by page numbers in italics*

Aboriginal corporate liaisons, 158
Aboriginal Post-Secondary Education Strategy and Action Plan, 150
Aboriginal rights
    BC backlash against, 138-40
    BC treaty process and, xxii-xxiii, 84
    *Delgamuukw, Gisdaywa* case (1997) and, 70-71, 75
    extinguishment of, 41-42, 67, 71, 75, 77-78, 84, 243-44
    Joint Review Panel for the Northern Gateway Project on, 189
    reassertion of, 38-39, 40-43
    settler colonialism and, 185-88, 249
Aboriginal title
    *Baker Lake* case (1979) and, 94-95
    BC treaty process and, 79-80
    *Calder* case (1973) and, 41-42, 43
    *Delgamuukw, Gisdaywa* case (1997) and, xxii, 71, 72, 73-75, 76, 81-82, 89, 95-97, 123, 222, 223
    economic component of, 141
    *Haida Nation* case (2004) and, 139
    Indigenous resurgence and, xxii
    justified infringement of, 137-38, 142
    Office of the Wet'suwet'en on, 123
    resource development and, 76
    settler sovereignty and, 185-88
    *Tsilhqot'in Nation* case (2014) and, 222-23
Aboriginal traditional knowledge (ATK). *See* traditional use and occupancy studies
accumulation, xxv, xxviii, 162, 169, 246-47
*adaawk* (oral history of a *wilp*), 52-58, 59, 60, 90, 96, 176. See also *cin k'ikh*
Agamben, Giorgio, 201-02
agriculture, 19, 23, 27-28
Alberta. *See* Athabasca tar sands
Alcan, 31-32
Alec, Bill, 27
Alec, Frank (Dunen, later Woos, Wet'suwet'en hereditary chief), 193, 194-95, 208, 235
Alfred, Dolores, 178-79
Alfred, Henry (Wah Tah K'eght, Wet'suwet'en hereditary chief), 199-201, 202
Alfred, Sue (Wilat), *178*, 178-79

315

Anaskaski (Insggisgï; Gitdumden *yikh*),
  121, 274n99
Antgulilibix (Mary Johnson, Gitxsan
  hereditary chief), 52–53, 54, 55,
  57
anthropology, 183
Athabasca tar sands, xv–xvii, xxv, xxvi,
  xxvii–xxx, 228–31. *See also*
  Enbridge Northern Gateway
  Pipeline
Austin, Antoinette (Hagwilakw,
  Wet'suwet'en hereditary chief),
  203, 204–05, 208
Austin, Ron (T'sek'ot, Wet'suwet'en
  hereditary chief), 199

Babine Indian Agency, 18
*Baker Lake (Hamlet) v. Canada (Minister
  of Indian Affairs and Northern
  Development)* (1979), 94–95
*balhats* (potlatch)
  *cis* (plume of feathers) and, 195
  Darlene Glaim (Gyolo'ght) and, 192
  at Hagwilget and Witset, 108
  kinship and territorial relations
    maintained through, 9–10, 10–
    11, 14, 29, 64, 196, 239
  in opposition to pipeline
    development, 209, 243
  reciprocal gifting and, xxiii–xxiv,
    11, 29, 238
  settler colonialism and, 18, 20
band governance, 18–19, 105–06, 244
Baptiste, Jean, 26–27
Barbeau, Marius, 92
Barman, Jean, xx
Barnes, Trevor, 140
Barricade Treaty (1906), 21
Bekkie, John, 26
Bell, Lindsay, 158–59

Berger, Thomas
  *Calder* case (1973) and, 93
  *Northern Frontier, Northern
    Homeland* (Berger Inquiry
    report), xx, xxi, 93
BHP Diamonds, 95
Bïwinï (Owen Lake), 26, 114
Bïwinï Kwah (Owen Creek), 114
Blomley, Nicholas, 47
Borrows, John, 4, 67, 74
Bowles, Samuel, 148
Brice-Bennett, Carol, 92
British Columbia
  Aboriginal Post-Secondary
    Education Strategy and Action
    Plan, 150
  on Aboriginal title and rights, 42,
    138–40
  colonial policies, 22–23, 25, 28, 32,
    35
  establishment as colony, 15–16
  New Relationship with Indigenous
    peoples, 140–41, 149–50, 169
  treaty process, xxii–xxiii, 78–80,
    83–85
  See also *Delgamuukw, Gisdaywa v.
    British Columbia* (1997);
    Enbridge Northern Gateway
    Pipeline; liquefied natural gas
British Columbia Assembly of First
  Nations, 140
British Columbia Claims Task Force,
  77–78
British Columbia Environmental
  Assessment Office, 236
British Columbia Indian Lands
  Settlement Act (1924), 25
Brody, Hugh, 4
Broman Lake (C'iggiz), 25, 30
Broman Lake Band, 79. *See also*
  Wet'suwet'en First Nation

Brown, Kevin, 203
Brown, Martha (Xhliimlaxha, Gitxsan hereditary chief), 55
Brown, William, 13–14
Bulkley River. *See* Widzin Kwah
Burns Lake (BC), 26
Burns Lake (Tselh K'iz Bin), 26, 30
Burns Lake Aboriginal Communities Working Group, 160
Burns Lake Agency, 30
Burns Lake Band. *See* Ts'il Kaz Koh
Byrd, Jodi, 118, 184, 203

Calder, Frank, 41
*Calder et al. v. Attorney-General of British Columbia* (1973), 41–42, 43, 68, 83, 89, 91–92, 93, 94
Canada (federal government)
    on Aboriginal land claims, 41–42
    resource-extractive economic agendas, xv–xvi, xxv, xxviii–xxix, 216–17, 227–31
    *See also* settler colonialism
Canadian Association of Petroleum Producers (CAPP), xv
Canadian Energy Research Institute, xxvii
Canadian Environmental Assessment Act (1992 and 2012), 97–98, 101, 189
Canadian Environmental Assessment Agency, xxix, 216
canneries, 21, 25. *See also* salmon fisheries
carbon dioxide, xxv–xxvi, 259n37
Carrier. *See* Dakelh
Carrier Sekani Tribal Council (CSTC), 42, 78–79, 103, 106, 108–09, 110, 119
Carruthers, John, 168
cartography, 58–60, 92, 99

Cas Yex (Cas Yikh; Gitdumden *yikh*), 121, 192, 234, 274n99
Chamberlin, Edward, 237
Cheslatta Carrier Nation (formerly Cheslatta Band), 31–32, 42, 78, 79, 107, 164
Chevron, 231, 236
chiefs, hereditary, 10, 121–22, 243–45
child apprehensions, 36–38, 241
Christie, Gordon, 67, 74
C'iggiz (Broman Lake), 25, 30
*cin k'ikh* (trail of song, oral history)
    introduction, 4–5, 52, 64, 122, 176
    *Delgamuukw, Gisdaywa* (1997) and, 56–57, 59, 60, 96, 183, 267n8
    older spelling as *kungax*, 260n5
    vs. traditional use and occupancy studies, 90
    *See also adaawk*
cis (plume of feathers) ceremony, 195, 206–09
Citizens Plus (Red Paper), 149
climate change, xxv–xxvi, 170–71, 245
Coastal GasLink Pipeline, 213–14, 231–36, 232, 243
Collins Overland Telegraph Line, 17
colonialism
    accumulation and, xxv, xxviii, 162, 169, 246–47
    *See* settler colonialism
community investment fund, 167–68
conservation, holistic, 99, 101, 131
Conservative Party. *See* Harper, Stephen
consult, duty to, 137–38, 139–40, 141–42, 186–88, 212
contrapuntal, 60, 176–77, 183
Cooney, Jim, 142–43
corporate social responsibility, 143, 145
Coulthard, Glen, xix, xxiv
COVID-19 pandemic, 230, 235–36

Cruikshank, Julie, 58, 180
Culhane, Dara, 58
cultural triage, 99, 101, 131

Dakelh (Carrier), 8-9, 13, 14, 31, 42, 78-79. *See also* Carrier Sekani Tribal Council; Cheslatta Carrier Nation; Lake Babine Nation; Nee-Tahi-Buhn; Skin Tyee Band; Ts'il Kaz Koh; Wet'suwet'en First Nation
Daly, Richard, 10, 11, 29, 238
Darby, Dennis, 235
David, Johnny (Maxlaxlex), 27, 55
Decker Lake (T'aco), 25, 30, 79
Delgamuukw (Ken Muldoe, Gitxsan hereditary chief), 46
*Delgamuukw, Gisdaywa v. British Columbia* (1997)
  introduction, xxii, xxxvi-xxxvii, 45-48
  on Aboriginal title, 71, 72, 73-75, 76, 81-82, 89, 95-97, 123, 222, 223
  *adaawk* and *cin k'ikh* (oral history) and, 52-58, 59, 60, 90, 96, 183, 267n8
  authority and jurisdiction in, 61-65, 67-72, 74-75
  cartographic knowledge and, 58-60
  disciplinary workings of power within, 50-52
  on duty to consult, 137-38
  effects on resource governance, 91, 169
  evidentiary complexity of, 45, 48-49, 55
  Gitxsan and Wet'suwet'en strategy, 46, 49-50, 61, 63
  hereditary chiefs (fluidity of *wilp* and *yikh*) and, 65-67
  legal citation of, 258n20, 268n26

McEachern decision, 46-47, 59-60, 66-67, 68-71, 77
New Relationship framework and, 140
opposition to pipelines and, 119-20, 122-23
Supreme Court of Canada decision, 60-61, 71-75, 81-83, 95-97
on traditional use and occupancy, 89, 91, 95-97
treaty negotiations and, 75-78, 80, 81-83, 84-85
Dennison, Jean, 134, 135, 142
Department of Fisheries and Oceans, 32
Department of Indian Affairs, 18, 30, 39, 42
Department of Transportation, 35
Derrida, Jacques, 128
Dewdney, Edgar, 17
*dïdikh* (clan), 9, 10, 12, 50, 261n44
dilbit (diluted bitumen), 126, 221
*dinï ze'* (male hereditary chiefs), 192, 280n43
dispossession, xix, 246-47
Djakanyax (Tsa Kën Yikh; Tsayu *yikh*), 121, 274n99
Doering, Ray, 156-57, 161-62
Dorsett, Shaunnagh, 5, 62
Douglas, James, 16
Duff, Wilson, 91-92
Dumont, Marjorie, 178-79
Dunen (Frank Alec, Wet'suwet'en hereditary chief), 193, 194-95, 208, 235
duty to consult, 137-38, 139-40, 141-42, 186-88, 212

Edmonds, Penelope, xx
education
  disciplinary functions, 148, 153-55

Enbridge facilitation of, 150–52
Indigenous desire for, 148, 149–50
residential schools, 23–24, 36, 37, 148–49, 241
Enbridge Northern Gateway Pipeline
introduction, xvii–xviii, xxxvii–xxxviii
Aboriginal Economic Benefits Package, 136, 155, 157, 160, 163, 165, 167–68
Aboriginal liaisons, 158
community investment fund, 167–68
court challenges by Gitxaala and Haisla, 223–24
economic incentives for Indigenous peoples, 135–37, 155, 156–63
educational opportunities for Indigenous peoples, 150–55
equity partnerships with Indigenous peoples, 133–34, 136, 163–67, 168, 170, 278n117
failure of, 215–16
feather trespass warning (Smithers), 203–06, 207–08
federal approval of, 221–22
Harper's intervention in, 216–17
Indigenous engagement, 102–03, 170–71
maps of proposed route, *xiv*, *100*
Office of the Wet'suwet'en, oppositional approach, 102, 110–11, 119–27, 130–31, 206, 219–20
Skin Tyee, collaborative research approach, 102, 110, 111–19, 120–21, 127, 206
traditional use and occupancy studies and, 101–02, 103–05, 110–11, 127, 129–31

Trudeau's rejection of, 225–27, 228
Wet'suwet'en sovereignty, enactments of, 209–10, 211–12, 224–25
*See also* Pacific Trails Pipeline
—Joint Review Panel (JRP)
introduction, xxxviii, 177–78
*cis* ceremony (Burns Lake), 206–09
colonial listening and constraints, 178–85, 188–91, 195–97
final report, 217–21
photographs, *178*, *181*, *200*
translation of Wet'suwet'en terms, 193
Wet'suwet'en sovereignty, enactments of, 178–79, 191–95, 197–201, 202
Energy East pipeline, 230
Energy Summit (2008), xvii
environmental movement, xxix–xxx, 243
equity partnership, Indigenous, 133–34, 136, 163–67, 168, 170, 278n117
Evans, Michael J., 99, 131
extinguishment, 41–42, 67, 71, 75, 77–78, 84, 243–44

feathers
*cis* (plume of feathers) ceremony, 195, 206–09
feather trespass warning, 203–06, 207–08
Felix George Reserve, 26
Fiddler, Tom, 158, 159, 160–61
financial inclusion
introduction, 163
community investment fund, 167–68
equity partnership, 133–34, 136, 163–67, 168, 170, 278n117
First Nations Summit, 140

Fisher, Robin, 9
fisheries. *See* salmon fisheries
Fiske, Jo-Anne, 195
forestry, 28, 34–35, 175
fossil fuels, xxv–xxvii, 259n37. *See also* dilbit (diluted bitumen); Enbridge Northern Gateway Pipeline; liquefied natural gas; resource development; tar sands
Foucault, Michel, 86, 153
Francois Lake (Nintah Bin), 26, 30, 79, 107
Fraser Canyon Gold Rush, 16
Freeman, Milton, 92
Freser Institute, 140
frontier, xx–xxi, 257n14
Furniss, Elizabeth, xx
fur trade, 5, 6–7, 7–9, 12, 13–14, 15, 144–45

Gagnon, Alphonse (Kloumkhun, Wet'suwet'en hereditary chief), xvii
Galois, Robert, 92
Gauvreau, N.B., 19
George, Felix, 26
George, Gloria (Smogelgem, Wet'suwet'en hereditary chief), 234
George, Herb (Satsan, Wet'suwet'en hereditary chief), 4, 5, 49, 61
George, Leonard, 234
George, Thomas, 27
gifting, reciprocal, xxiii–xxiv, 11, 12, 29, 237, 238
Gilserhyu (Gilseyhu, C'ilhts'ëkhyu; dïdikh), 10, 121, 192–93, 251, 261n44, 279n17
Gintis, Herbert, 148

Gisdaywa (Gisdewe; Wet'suwet'en hereditary chief name)
    Alfred Joseph, 46
    spelling, 258n20
Gitanmaax (Gitxsan community), 17, 18, 20, 37, 42, 76, 267n226
Gitanyow (Kitwancool; Gitxsan community), 42, 65, 267n227, 269n59
Gitdumden (Gidimt'en; dïdikh), 10, 121, 235, 236, 251, 261n44
Gitksan Wet'suwet'en Tribal Council (formerly Gitksan-Carrier Tribal Council), 42, 76, 78, 108
Gitsegukla (Kitseguecla; Gitxsan community), 42, 76, 267n226
Gitwangak (Kitwangak; Gitxsan community), 42, 76, 267n226
Gitxaala Nation, 223–24
Gitxsan, xxii, 13, 17–18, 42, 238. *See also Delgamuukw, Gisdaywa v. British Columbia* (1997)
Gitxsan Treaty Office, 80–81, 164, 166
Glaim, Darlene (formerly Gyolo'ght and Woos, Wet'suwet'en hereditary chief), 192, 234
Glen Vowell (Sikadoak, Sik-e-Dakh; community), 42, 76, 267n226
globalization, xxxiv, 142
Goldstein, Alyosha, 164
Good Medicine Group, 233
Goohlaht (Gguhlat; Wet'suwet'en hereditary chief name)
    Lucy Namox, 66
    spelling, 269n64
Gottesfeld, Allen S., 33, 124
Grand Trunk Pacific (GTP) railway, 22
Grant, Peter, 56
Green, Jeff, 161
grounded normativity, xxiv, 242

Gunanoot, David ('Niik'aap, Gitxsan hereditary chief), 55
Gyolo'ght (C'oligit; Wet'suwet'en hereditary title)
    Darlene Glaim, 192, 234
    spelling, 280n42

Haatq (Gitxsan hereditary chief), 17
Hagwilakw (Hagwil'awh; Wet'suwet'en hereditary title)
    Antoinette Austin, 203, 204–05, 208
    spelling, 281n81
Hagwilget (Tsë Kyah; community)
    introduction, 13, 106, 107–08, 254, 273n65
    Coastal GasLink and, 234
    colonial administration, 18, 20, 30
    Enbridge Northern Gateway Pipeline and, 102–03, 110
    Gitksan-Carrier Tribal Council and, 76, 108
    salmon fisheries and, 33–34
*Haida Nation v. British Columbia* (2004), 139, 186
Haisla, 13, 223–24
Hansen, James, xxvi
Hanson, Olaf, 28
Hargus, Sharon, xii, 257n7
Harley, J.B., 99
Harper, Stephen (Conservative Harper government), xv–xvi, xxv, xxix, 216–17, 225, 227, 233
Harris, Cole, 22, 35–36
Harvey, David, xxviii
Hayter, Roger, 140
Hazelton (BC), 17, 18
Hazelton Band, 20
hearings, governance, 210–11
Helin, Calvin, 144
hereditary chiefs, 10, 121–22, 243–45

Holder, Janet, 150, 159
holistic conservation, 99, 101, 131
Holland, Christine (Knedebeas, Wet'suwet'en hereditary chief), 193, 239–40
Holland, George, 56
Honcagh Bin (Uncha Lake), 25, 30, 79. *See also* Nee-Tahi-Buhn
Huber, Matthew, xxvi
huckleberries, 11
Hudson's Bay Company (HBC), 6–7, 8, 9, 13, 15, 16
Hunt, Alan, 85
Hunt, Sarah, 183
hunting, 23, 28–29, 33. *See also* fur trade
Huson, Freda, 240–41, 242, 243
hydro developments, 31–33

#IdleNoMore, 217
impact benefit agreements (IBAs), 134–35, 141–42, 159
Indian Act (1876), 18, 23, 27, 39, 43, 105
Indian Chiefs of Alberta, 149
Indigenous knowledge. *See* traditional use and occupancy studies
Indigenous peoples
    Berger Inquiry (Mackenzie River Pipeline Inquiry) and, xx–xxi
    Citizens Plus (Red Paper), 149
    development, new relationship with, xix–xxiii, 85–86, 245–46, 248–49
    duty to consult with, 137–38, 139–40, 141–42, 186–88, 212
    education and, 148, 149–50
    environmental movement and, 243
    impact benefit agreements (IBAs) and, 134–35, 141–42, 159
    languages, 12–13

mobilizations against energy
developments, xvi–xvii, xix–xx,
xxiv–xxv, xxix–xxx, xxxv–xxxvi,
214–15, 236–37
place-based mobilizations, xxiv,
xxxiv, 203
resurgence, xix, xxii, xxiii–xxiv, 43,
242
vs. settlers, 237–38
sovereignty, 71–72, 177, 211–12, 249
See also Aboriginal rights;
Aboriginal title; *Delgamuukw,
Gisdaywa v. British Columbia*
(1997); Enbridge Northern
Gateway Pipeline;
reconciliation; settler
colonialism; sovereignty;
traditional use and occupancy
studies; treaties, modern;
Wet'suwet'en; *other specific
communities and peoples*
Innis, Harold, 6
Intergovernmental Panel on Climate
Change
*Fifth Assessment Report*, xxv
International Energy Agency (IEA),
xxv–xxvi, xxvii, xxviii, xxix, 223
International Pacific Salmon Fisheries
Commission, 32
Inuit (Inuit Tapirisat of Canada), 92,
94–95
Inuvialuit Final Agreement (1984), 95

Jenness, Diamond, 27, 64
Jim, Victor (Misalos), 194
Jobs, Growth, and Long-Term
Prosperity Act (Bill C-38, 2012),
xxix, 216–17
Jobs and Growth Act (Bill C-45, 2012),
xxix, 217

Johnson, Fred (Lelt, Gitxsan hereditary
chief), 55
Johnson, Leslie Main, xxiv, 4
Johnson, Mary (Antgulilibix, Gitxsan
hereditary chief), 52–53, 54, 55,
57
Joint Review Panel (JRP). *See under*
Enbridge Northern Gateway
Pipeline
Joseph, Alfred (Gisdaywa,
Wet'suwet'en hereditary chief),
46
Joseph, Jack (Moricetown Band chief),
24, 27

Kamalmuk (Gitxsan hereditary chief),
18
Kelm, Mary-Ellen, 24
Kemano Project, 31–33
Kenney Dam, 32, 107
Keynes, John Maynard, 30
Keystone XL pipeline, 230
Kinder Morgan. *See* Trans Mountain
Pipeline
King, Thomas, 3
kinship networks, 9–10, 14, 50
Kispiox (Gitxsan community), 17, 18–19,
42, 76, 267n226
Kitseguecla (Gitsegukla; Gitxsan
community), 42, 76, 267n226
Kitwancool (Gitanyow; Gitxsan
community), 42, 65, 267n227,
269n59
Kitwangak (Gitwangak; Gitxsan
community), 42, 76, 267n226
Kiyaxwinits (Këyikh Winïts;
Gitdumden *yikh*), 121, 274n99
Kloumkhun (Lho'imggin, Wet'suwet'en
hereditary chief name)
Alphonse Gagnon, xvii
spelling, 257n7

Knedebeas (Nedïbïs; Wet'suwet'en
    hereditary chief name)
  Christine Holland, 193, 239-40
  Sarah Layton, 238-40
  spelling, 282n16
  Unist'ot'en Camp and, 242
  William Warner, 224, 233
Kovach, Margaret Elizabeth, xxxiii
KPMG, 77
Kuokkanen, Rauna, 238, 240
Kwanbeahyax (Kwin Begh Yikh;
    Laksilyu *yikh*), 121, 234, 274n99

Lake Babine Nation (Lake Babine
    Band), 31, 42, 79, 164
Lakes District Tribal Council, 42. *See
    also* Carrier Sekani Tribal
    Council
Laksamshu (Likhts'amisyu; *dïdikh*), 10,
    121, 204-06, 208, 235, 252,
    261n44
Laksilyu (Likhsilyu; *dïdikh*), 10, 121,
    252, 261n44
Lamer, Antonio, 73-74, 95-96, 123
land
  colonial policies, 16, 19-20, 25, 71
  intergenerational responsibility
    for, 238-40
  reserves, 19-20, 25
  traditional Wet'suwet'en
    management, 11, 20
  *yin tah* (territory), 10, 14, 29, 203
  *See also* Aboriginal title; traditional
    use and occupancy studies
languages, Indigenous, 12-13
Larsen, Soren, 32
Layton, Sarah (Knedebeas,
    Wet'suwet'en hereditary chief),
    238-40
Leggett, Sheila, 180, 182, 189, 195-96,
    198

Lelt (Fred Johnson, Gitxsan hereditary
    chief), 55
Levant, Ezra, xxvii
Lhe Lin Liyin, 204-05, 206, 208
liaisons, Aboriginal corporate, 158
Liberal Party. *See* Trudeau, Justin
Likhdïlye (Russell Tiljoe, Wet'suwet'en
    hereditary title), 194
Lilloos (Lïlus, Wet'suwet'en hereditary
    title)
  Emma Michell, 55, 56
  spelling, 267n21
Limerick, Patricia, xx
liquefied natural gas (LNG), 213-14,
    231-36, *232*
LNG Canada, 213, 234
Loring, R.E., 18, 20
Lutz, John, 24, 27, 36

MacDonald, Lindsey Te Ata O Tu, 211
Mackenzie, Alexander, 8
Mackenzie Valley Pipeline Inquiry
    (Berger Inquiry)
  *Northern Frontier, Northern
      Homeland* (report), xx, xxi, 93
MacNeil, Robert, 228
Mahoney, Patrick M., 94
Manuel, Arthur, 79-80, 84
map biography, 92. *See also*
    cartography
marriage, 10-11
Massey, Doreen, xxxiv
Maxan Lake (Tasdlegh), 25, 30, 79
Maxan Tom, 25
Maxlaxlex (Mikhlikhlekh;
    Wet'suwet'en hereditary title)
  Johnny David, 27, 55
  spelling, 267n21
McEachern, Allan
  on authority and sovereignty, 61,
    68-71

decision in *Delgamuukw, Gisdaywa* case, 46-47, 59-60, 66-67, 68-71, 77
dislocation of *Delgamuukw, Gisdaywa* case, 51
Gitxsan and Wet'suwet'en evidence and, 49, 52-55, 56-58, 138, 183, 267n8
on hereditary chiefs, 66-67
on territorial boundaries, 59-60
McFarlane, J.N., 35
McKee, Christopher, 77
McLachlin, Beverley, 186, 187
McNeil, Kent, 96
McPhie, Michael, 143
McVeigh, Shaun, 5, 62
Michell, Dan (Wigetimschol), 66, 242
Michell, Emma (Lilloos), 55, 56
Miéville, China, 145
Mills, Antonia, 204, 208
Mills, P. Dawn, 81
Mills, Suzanne, 159
Misalos (Victor Jim, Wet'suwet'en hereditary title), 194
Misdzï Kwah (Parrott Creek), 114, 116
Mitchell, Timothy, 51
Morice, Fr. A.G., 13
Morice Lands and Resource Management Plan, 125
Morice River. *See* Widzin Kwah
Moricetown. *See* Witset
Morice Water Management Area, 125
Morin, Mélanie, 12
Morris, Roy (Woos, Wet'suwet'en hereditary chief), 234
Muldoe, Ken (Delgamuukw, Gitxsan hereditary chief), 46
Muldoon, Paul, 211

Nadasdy, Paul, 70, 98
Nadina Lake (Natl'ënlï Bin), 114

Nahwegahbow, David C., 90
Nak'azdli (Dakelh community), 14
Na'Moks (Namox, Namoks; Wet'suwet'en hereditary chief name)
John Ridsdale, 197-99, 200, 209
spelling, 269n63
vacancy, 66
Namox, Lucy (Goohlaht, Wet'suwet'en hereditary chief), 66
National Energy Board, xxix, 98, 101, 146, 180, 188, 216, 226, 230
National Energy Board Act, 189
National Indian Brotherhood, 149
Natl'ënlï Bin (Nadina Lake), 114
natural gas. *See* liquefied natural gas
Navigable Waters Protection Act, 217
Naziel, Warner (Toghestiy, later Smogelgem, Wet'suwet'en hereditary chief), 203, 204-05, 208, 235
Nechako River, 31-33
Nedut'en, 9, 13-14, 18, 20, 21, 31, 42, 78-79
Nee-Tahi-Buhn, 79, 103, 106-07, 109, 110, 164, 233, 253
Netanlï Bin (Skins Lake), 25, 30, 114
New Relationship framework, 140, 149-50, 169
New Relationship Trust Corporation, 140-41
'Niik'aap (David Gunanoot, Gitxsan hereditary chief), 55
Nïntah Bin (Francois Lake), 26, 30, 79, 107
Nisga'a, 13, 41, 43, 91-92, 93, 266n222
Nisga'a Final Agreement (2000), 83-84, 138
Nishga Tribal Council, 41, 266n222
Northern Gateway Pipeline. *See* Enbridge Northern Gateway Pipeline

North West Company (NWC), 7-9
Northwest Territories, 92, 94, 95

occupancy. *See* traditional use and occupancy studies
O'Faircheallaigh, Ciaran, 155
Office of the Wet'suwet'en (formerly Wet'suwet'en Treaty Office)
    appropriation of settler governance discourses, 130-31
    cabin-building program along pipeline route, 224
    *cis* (plume of feathers) ceremony, 206-09
    creation of and purpose, 80-81, 109-10
    on cumulative impact assessment, 240
    Enbridge engagement with, 102, 164
    feathering by Lhe Lin Liyin and, 204
    Joint Review Panel process and, 206
    on salmon fishery, 124-26
    traditional use and occupancy study, 102, 110-11, 119-27, 130-31, 219-20
Ogden, Peter Skene, 261n39
oil. *See* Enbridge Northern Gateway Pipeline; fossil fuels; resource development; tar sands
Omineca Band, 30, 32, 42, 78-79, 253, 267n227. *See also* Nee-Tahi-Buhn; Skin Tyee Band; Wet'suwet'en First Nation
oral history. *See adaawk*; *cin k'ikh*
*Oregon Treaty* (1846), 15
O'Reilly, Peter, 20
Owen Creek (Bïwinï Kwah), 114
Owen Lake (Bïwinï), 26, 114

Özden-Schilling, Tom, 59

Pacific Trails Pipeline, 231, 236
parallax, xxx-xxxi, 211, 247
Parrott Creek (Misdzï Kwah), 114, 116
Pasternak, Shiri, 62-63, 105
Paterson, Matthew, 228
Patrick, Betty, 195
Patrick, Frank (Wah Tah Kwets, Wet'suwet'en hereditary chief), 234
Paul, Daniel, 3
Pennington, Catherine, 151-52, 154
Perret, Michelle, 203-04
Perry, Adele, xx
Pete, August, 27
Pierre, Damien, 194, 198
Pinder, Leslie Hall, 52, 56
place-time extension, 239
Plant, Geoff, 64-65, 138-39
political ontology, 176, 184
politics of refusal, 197
potlatch. *See balhats*
Poudrier, A.L., 19
Price Waterhouse, 77

Rabnett, Ken A., 33, 124
railway, 22, 25-26, 28, 106-07
Ray, Arthur, 13, 14
reciprocal gifting, xxiii-xxiv, 11, 12, 29, 237, 238
reconciliation
    BC treaty process and, 83-84
    *cis* (plume of feathers) ceremony and, 209
    compromise and, 187
    duty to consult and, 186
    economic opportunities and, 159, 163, 164
    educational initiatives and, 152, 153, 154

enduring violence of, 227-28
industry-Indigenous partnerships and, 136, 144-48, 162-63, 168-71
with resource development, xxi-xxii, xxxvii, 134-35, 140, 213, 215, 223
Red Paper (Citizens Plus), 149
refusal, politics of, 197
reserves, 19-20, 25
residential schools, 23-24, 36, 37, 148-49, 241. *See also* education
resource development
    approach to, xxiii, xxx-xxxi, 214-15, 245-46, 247-49
    Berger Inquiry (Mackenzie River Pipeline Inquiry) on, xx-xxi
    Conservative vs. Liberal approaches, 227-29
    contrapuntal approach to, 176-77
    corporate social responsibility, 143, 145
    duty to consult, 137-38, 139-40, 141-42, 186-88, 212
    impact benefit agreements (IBAs), 134-35, 141-42, 159
    Indigenous economic and financial inclusion, 155-56, 163, 164
    Indigenous mobilizations against energy developments, xvi-xvii, xix-xx, xxiv-xxv, xxix-xxx, xxxv-xxxvi, 214-15, 236-37
    industry-Indigenous partnerships, 136, 144-48, 162-63, 168-71
    New Relationship framework, 140-41
    parallax approach to, xxx-xxxi, 211, 247
    reconciliation with Indigenous peoples, xxi-xxii, xxxvii, 134-35, 140, 213, 215, 223

review process, Conservative attempts to streamline, xxix, 216-17
social licence, 142-44, 164, 169, 229
*See also* Enbridge Northern Gateway Pipeline; liquefied natural gas; tar sands
*Re Southern Rhodesia* (1919), 69
respect (*wiggus*), 182
Ridsdale, John (Na'Moks, Wet'suwet'en hereditary chief), 197-99, 200, 209
Ridsdale, Mike, 207, 208-09
Roberts, John, 6
Rose, Samuel, 162
Round Lake Tommy (Wah Tah Kwets, Wet'suwet'en hereditary chief), 26, 27
Royal Commission on Indian Affairs, 25-26
Royal Commissions on Forestry, 34
Royal Proclamation (1763), 7, 16, 68, 69-70, 73
Rush, Stuart, 62

Said, Edward, 177
salmon fisheries
    colonial policies, 21, 22, 25, 32, 33-34
    Enbridge Northern Gateway Pipeline and, 111, 126, 216-17, 221, 224
    Hagwilget and, 13
    Office of the Wet'suwet'en concerns, 124-25
    Unist'ot'en Camp and, 241
Sam, Mathew, 27
Samooh (Simuyh; Wet'suwet'en hereditary chief), 66, 269n64
Sam Willie, 25
Santos, Boaventura de Sousa, 127

Satsan (Sats'an, Wet'suwet'en
    hereditary title)
  Herb George, 4, 5, 49, 61
  spelling, 260n8
Sa'un (Sa'on; Wet'suwet'en hereditary
    title)
  George Williams, 182
  spelling, 279n17
Sayax (Sa Yikh; Laksamshu *yikh*), 121,
    274n99
Secwépemc, 230
self-determination, xxi, xxxiv, 69, 144,
    169, 219-20. See also sovereignty
self-government, 40, 43, 71, 72, 74, 78,
    81. See also sovereignty
settler colonialism
  Aboriginal rights and, 138-39, 185-
    86, 249
  band governance, 18-19, 105-06,
    244
  child apprehensions, 36-38, 241
  colonial governance, imposition of,
    14-18
  critical approach to, 3
  dispossession and, xix, 246-47
  fur trade, 5, 6-9, 12, 13-14, 15, 144-
    45
  Harper on, xvi
  Indian Act (1876), 18, 23, 27, 39, 43,
    105
  industry-Indigenous partnerships
    and, 136, 144-48, 162-63, 168-71
  intergenerational trauma, 241
  invention of, 5-6
  Keynesian colonialism, 30
  land policy and reserves, 16, 19-20,
    25, 71
  *Oregon Treaty* (1846), 15
  residential schools, 23-24, 36, 37,
    148-49, 241
  Royal Proclamation (1763), 7, 16, 68,
    69-70, 73
  on settlers vs. Indigenous peoples,
    237-38
  *terra nullius*, 99
  Treaty of Niagara (1764), 7
  weapons of the weak and, xxxiii,
    260n68
  welfare, 30, 36, 106
  White Paper (1969), 39-40, 43, 149
  *See also* reconciliation; resource
    development
Sikadoak (Sik-e-Dakh, Glen Vowell;
    community), 42, 76, 267n226
Simpson, Audra, 71-72, 177, 183, 197
Simpson, Leanne Betasamosake
  on colonial effacing of Indigenous
    sovereignty, 179
  on colonial extraction, 145
  on Indigenous mobilizations
    against resource development,
    xix, 241
  on Indigenous resurgence and
    self-recognition, xxiv, 242,
    258n32
  on Indigenous sovereignty, 71-72,
    203
  on state recognition, 249
Skins Lake (Netanlï Bin), 25, 30, 114
Skin Tyee, 25
Skin Tyee Band
  introduction, 103, 106, 107, 109, 253
  Coastal GasLink and, 233
  collaborative traditional use and
    occupancy study, 102, 110, 111-
    19, 120-21, 127, 206
  Enbridge engagement with, 164
*skiy ze'* (children of chiefs), 192, 280n43
Slattery, Brian, 82
Sloan, Gordon, 34
Slowey, Gabrielle, 144

Smithers (BC), xxxi, 22, 35
Smogelgem (Smogilhgim;
    Wet'suwet'en hereditary chief
    name)
- Gloria George, 234
- spelling, 262n54
- Warner Naziel, 235

social licence, 142-44, 164, 169, 229
Sommerville, Melanie, 164
sovereignty
- Agamben on, 201-02
- colonial listening and, 178-85, 188-91, 195-97
- enactments of Wet'suwet'en sovereignty, 178-79, 191-95, 197-201, 202, 203-06, 209-10, 211-12
- forestry conflict and, 175-76
- Indigenous sovereignty, 71-72, 177, 211-12, 249
- nested sovereignty, 61, 177
- settler vs. Indigenous sovereignties, 185-88, 197, 210-12
- Weber on, 68-69
- *See also* self-determination; self-government

Sparke, Matthew, 50-51, 52, 59
Spookwx (Gitxsan hereditary chief), 13
Stern, Philip, 6
Sterritt, Neil, 4, 59, 76
Stoffle, Richard W., 99, 131
Storms, Marc, 233
Swyngedouw, Erik, 197

T'aco (Decker Lake), 25, 30, 79
Tacot (Tyee Lake), 26-27
Tait, Karla, 241-42, 243
Tait-Day, Theresa, 234
*Taku River Tlingit First Nation v. British Columbia* (2004), 187-88

Talbot, F.A., 21-22
tar sands, Athabasca, xv-xvii, xxv, xxvi, xxvii-xxx, 228-31. *See also* Enbridge Northern Gateway Pipeline
Tasdlegh (Maxan Lake), 25, 30, 79
TC Energy (formerly TransCanada), 213, 231, 234, 235, 236. *See also* Coastal GasLink Pipeline
*terra nullius*, 99
Thomas-Müller, Clayton, 243
Tibbetts, David, 26
Tiljoe, Elsie, 192-93, 194
Tiljoe, Russell (Likhdïlye), 194
time-space compression, 237, 239
title. *See* Aboriginal title
Tobias, Terry, 90
Toghestiy (Warner Naziel, Wet'suwet'en hereditary title), 203, 204-05, 208, 235
Tough, Frank, 92
traditional use and occupancy studies
- introduction, 89-91
- *Baker Lake* case (1979), 94-95
- Berger Inquiry (Mackenzie Valley Pipeline Inquiry) on, 93
- *Calder* case (1973), 91-92, 93
- cultural triage and holistic conservation strategies, 99, 101, 131
- *Delgamuukw, Gisdaywa* case (1997), 89, 91, 95-97
- Enbridge Northern Gateway Pipeline and, 101-02, 103-05, 110-11, 127, 129-31
- history of, 91-98
- Inuit Tapirisat of Canada, 92
- map biography approach, 92
- Northwest Territories and, 95

Office of the Wet'suwet'en,
oppositional approach, 102,
110–11, 119–27, 130–31, 219–20
settler resource governance and,
91, 97–99, 127–29
Skin Tyee, collaborative approach,
102, 110, 111–19, 120–21, 127, 206
undecidability of knowledge
translations, 127–31
TransCanada (now TC Energy), 213,
231, 234, 235, 236. See also
Coastal GasLink Pipeline
translation
knowledge, 113, 123, 127–31
language, 53, 56, 193
Trans Mountain Pipeline, 215, 228–30, 236
traplines, 28–29, 59. See also fur trade
treaties, modern
backlash against, 138–39
BC process, xxii–xxiii, 78–80, 83–85
*Delgamuukw, Gisdaywa* case (1997)
and, 75–78, 80, 81–83, 84–85
Gitxsan and Wet'suwet'en treaty
offices, 80–81
Nisga'a Final Agreement (2000),
83–84, 138
overlapping claims, 78–79
Treaty of Niagara (1764), 7
Troy, Ann, 32
Trudeau, Justin (Liberal Trudeau
government), 225, 226, 227–30
Trudeau, Pierre Elliott, 39
Trusler, Scott, 11
*ts'akë ze'* (female hereditary chiefs), 192,
280n43
Tsayu (dïdikh), 10, 121, 209–10, 252,
261n44
Tsee K'al K'e Yex (Tsë Kal K'iyikh;
Laksilyu *yikh*), 281n66

T'sek'ot (Dzïggot; Wet'suwet'en
hereditary title)
Ron Austin, 199
spelling, 281n67
Tsë Kyah (community). See Hagwilget
Tselh K'iz (Tsichgass Lake), 25
Tselh K'iz Bin (Burns Lake), 26, 30
Ts'ëlkiy' Kwah (Lamprey Creek), 114
Tsichgass Lake (Tselh K'iz), 25
*Tsilhqot'in Nation v. British Columbia*
(2014), 222–23
Ts'il Kaz Koh (formerly Burns Lake
Band)
introduction, 106, 253, 267n227
Carrier Sekani Tribal Council
(CSTC) and, 42, 79, 109
Coastal GasLink and, 233
colonial governance, 30
Enbridge Northern Gateway
Pipeline and, 102–03, 110, 164
reserve land, 26, 31
Tsing, Anna Lowenhaupt, xxxiv
Tsleil-Waututh Nation, 229
Turner, Frederick Jackson, xxi, 257n14
Turner, J.W. (Happy), 26
Tyee Lake (Tacot), 26–27
Tyee Lake David, 26

Uncha Lake (Honcagh Bin), 25, 30, 79.
See also Nee-Tahi-Buhn
undecidability, 128
Union of BC Indian Chiefs, 140
Unist'ot'en (Yex T'sa Wilk'us or Yikh
Tsawilhggis; Gilserhyu *yikh*),
121, 224, 236, 274n99, 282n17
Unist'ot'en Camp, 224, 231, 233, 235,
240–43
Unist'ot'en Healing Centre, 241–42
United States National Environmental
Policy, 99
Usher, Peter, 92

Vancouver Island (colony), 15
Vowel, A.W., 21

Wah Tah K'eght (Ut'akhgit; Wet'suwet'en hereditary chief name)
    Henry Alfred, 199-201, 202
    spelling, 281n66
Wah Tah Kwets (Ut'akhkw'its; Wet'suwet'en hereditary chief name)
    Frank Patrick, 234
    Round Lake Tommy, 26, 27
    spelling, 264n138
weapons of the weak, xxxiii, 260n68
Weber, Max, 68-69
Weis, Tony, xxix-xxx
welfare, 30, 36, 106
Western Union Company, 17
Wet'suwet'en
    introduction, xvii-xix, xix-xx, xxxv-xxxviii
    adaptations to colonial impositions, 24-25, 27-28, 29
    authority, basis in land and lineage, 10-11, 63-64
    author's positionality, xxxi-xxxii
    child apprehension and welfare reliance, 36-38
    colonial governance, 16-19, 20, 30-31
    colonial land policy and reserves, 19-20, 25-27
    community-engaged methodolgy, xxxii-xxxiv
    contemporary bands and governance, 106-10
    Energy Summit (2008), xvii
    fishing and hunting restrictions, 21, 22-23, 33-34
    forestry and, 28, 34-35, 175
    fur trade and, 5, 9, 12, 13-14
    future possibilities with, 244-45
    hereditary chiefs, 10, 121-22, 243-45
    hydro developments and, 31-33
    kinship networks, 9-10, 14, 50
    land, intergenerational responsibility for, 238-40
    land, traditional management of, 11, 20
    linguistic exchange and transculturation, 12-13
    liquified natural gas (LNG) pipelines and, 231, 233-36, 243
    marriage, 10-11
    memorandum of understanding with hereditary chiefs (2020), 243-44
    political ontology, 176, 184
    reciprocal gifting, xxiii-xxiv, 11, 12, 29, 237, 238
    residential schools and, 23-24
    resource development, opposition to, 214-15
    resource exploitation and, 35-36, 38
    traplines and, 28-29
    Unist'ot'en Camp, 224, 231, 233, 235, 240-43
    yikh (house), 9, 10-11, 20, 50, 64-66, 80-81
    yin tah (territory), 10, 14, 29, 203
    See also *balhats* (potlatch); *cin k'ikh* (trail of song, oral history); *Delgamuukw, Gisdaywa v. British Columbia* (1997); Enbridge Northern Gateway Pipeline; Gitksan Wet'suwet'en Tribal Council; Indigenous peoples

Wet'suwet'en First Nation (formerly Broman Lake Band), 79, 103, 106, 109, 164, 233, 254
Wet'suwet'en Matrilineal Coalition, 234–35, 244
Wet'suwet'en Treaty Office. *See* Office of the Wet'suwet'en
White Paper (1969), 39–40, 43, 149
Whyte, Kyle, 4
Wickham, Gary, 85
Wickham, Molly, 37–38
Widzin Kwah (Morice and Bulkley rivers), 13, 17, 33–34, 114, 125, 198, 240–41. *See also* Hagwilget; Witset
Wigetimschol (Wigidimsts'ol; Wet'suwet'en hereditary title)
    Dan Michell, 66, 242
    spelling, 269n63, 284n79
*wiggus* (respect), 182
Wilat (Sue Alfred, Wet'suwet'en hereditary title), *178*, 178–79
William, Warner (Knedebeas, Wet'suwet'en hereditary chief), 224, 233
Williams, George (Sa'un), 182
*wilp* (house), 50, 52, 64–66, 80–81. See also *yikh*
Wilson, Shawn, xxxiii
Witset (Moricetown)
    introduction, xvii, 106, 107–08, 254, 273n65
    Coastal GasLink and, 233
    colonial administration, 13, 18, 19, 20, 27, 30
    day school, 24
    *Delgamuukw, Gisdaywa v. British Columbia* (1997) and, 76
    Enbridge and, 110
    Energy Summit (2008) in, xvii
    first contact with settlers, 9, 12, 261n39
    fisheries, 9, 33
    Hagwilget and, 13
    as Kyah Wiget (Këyikh Wigit), 262n64
    reserve land, 20
Woodside Petroleum, 231, 236
Woos (Wos; Wet'suwet'en hereditary chief name)
    Darlene Glaim (formerly Gyolo'ght), 192, 234
    Frank Alec, 235 (*see also* Dunen (Frank Alec))
    Roy Morris, 234
    spelling, 283n44
World Bank, 143
World War I, 27
Woyenne Reserve, 31

Xhliimlaxha (Martha Brown, Gitxsan hereditary chief), 55

Yex T'sa Wilk'us (Yikh Tsawilhggis or Unist'ot'en; Gilserhyu *yikh*), 121, 224, 236, 274n99, 282n17
*yikh* (house), 9, 10–11, 20, 50, 64–66, 80–81
*yin tah* (territory), 10, 14, 29, 203
Youmans, Amos, 17

Žižek, Slavoj, 197